Understanding International Diplomacy

This book provides a comprehensive new introduction to the study of international diplomacy, covering both theory and practice.

The text summarises and discusses the major trends in the field of diplomacy, developing an innovative analytical toolbox for understanding diplomacy not as a collection of practices or a set of historical traditions, but as a form of institutionalised communication through which authorised representatives produce, manage and distribute public goods. The book:

- traces the evolution of diplomacy from its beginnings in ancient Egypt, Greece and China to our current age of global diplomacy;
- examines theoretical explanations about how diplomats take decisions, make relations and shape the world;
- discusses normative approaches to how diplomacy ought to adapt itself to the twenty-first century, help remake states and assist the peaceful evolution of international order.

In sum, *Understanding International Diplomacy* provides an up-to-date, accessible and authoritative overview of how diplomacy works and ought to work in a globalising world.

This new textbook is essential reading for students of international diplomacy, and highly recommended for students of crisis negotiation, international organisations, foreign policy and international relations in general.

Corneliu Bjola is University Lecturer in Diplomatic Studies at the University of Oxford, UK. He is co-editor of *Arguing Global Governance: Agency, Lifeworld and Shared Reasons* (2010) and author of *Legitimating the Use of Force in International Politics: Kosovo, Iraq and the Ethics of Intervention* (2009).

Markus Kornprobst is Chair of International Relations at the Vienna School of International Studies, Austria. He is author of *Irredentism in European Politics: Argumentation, Compromise and Norms* (2008) and co-editor of *Arguing Global Governance: Agency, Lifeworld and Shared Reasons* (2010) as well as *Metaphors of Globalization: Mirrors, Magicians, and Mutinies* (2008).

Understanding International Diplomacy

Theory, practice and ethics

**Corneliu Bjola and
Markus Kornprobst**

Routledge
Taylor & Francis Group

LONDON AND NEW YORK

First published 2013
by Routledge
2 Park Square, Milton Park, Abingdon, Oxon OX14 4RN

Simultaneously published in the USA and Canada
by Routledge
711 Third Avenue, New York, NY 10017

Routledge is an imprint of the Taylor & Francis Group, an informa business

© 2013 Corneliu Bjola and Markus Kornprobst

British Library Cataloguing in Publication Data
A catalogue record for this book is available from the British Library

Library of Congress Cataloging-in-Publication Data
Bjola, Corneliu.
Understanding international diplomacy : theory, practice and ethics / Corneliu Bjola and Markus Kornprobst.
pages cm
Includes bibliographical references and index.
1. International cooperation. 2. International relations. I. Kornprobst, Markus. II. Title.
JZ1308.B58 2013
327.2–dc23
2012049164

ISBN: 978-0-415-68820-8 (hbk)
ISBN: 978-0-415-68821-5 (pbk)
ISBN: 978-0-203-77496-0 (ebk)

Typeset in Baskerville by
GreenGate Publishing Services, Tonbridge, Kent

Printed and bound in Great Britain by
TJ International Ltd, Padstow, Cornwall

To our students

Contents

Discussing normative approaches   147

10   Remaking the diplomat   149
        Introduction 149
        Diplomatic representation 150
            The raison de système *150*
            Paradiplomacy 152
        Diplomacy and power 154
        Diplomatic recruitment and training 158
        Summary 163
        Study questions 164
        Recommended further reading 164

11   Remaking states   166
        Introduction 166
        The institutionalisation of peacebuilding 168
        The fundamental question: to intervene or not to intervene? 170
        What ought to be the end of peacebuilding? 172
        What ought to be the means to this end? 174
        Summary 179
        Study questions 179
        Recommended further reading 179

12   The peaceful remaking of the world   181
        Introduction 181
        Preventive diplomacy 182
        International criminal justice 189
        Summary 195
        Study questions 196
        Recommended further reading 196

PART VI
Conclusion   199

13   Towards inclusive diplomacy   201
        Studying diplomacy as communication 201
        Adding to our understanding 203
        Anti-diplomacy 204
        A glimpse into the future: inclusive diplomacy? 206

        Glossary   208
        References   223
        Index   239

Illustrations

Figures

Tables

Boxes

Acknowledgements

We would like to thank Marijan Bilic, Cris Boonen and Sophie Rosenberg for their superb research assistance. We would also like to thank Michele Acuto, Anthony Burke, Richard Caplan, Costas M. Constantinou, Noé Cornago, James Cotton, Karin Fierke, Stacie Goddard, Gunther Hellmann, Marcus Holmes, Ron Krebs, Andrew Lawrence, Ned Lebow, Gerhard Loibl, William Maley, Jan Melissen, Gavin Mount, Werner Neudeck, Hanspeter Neuhold, Tom Row, Antje Wiener and Hans Winkler for inspiring discussions on diplomacy and very helpful comments on our attempts to make sense of the phenomenon.

Markus Kornprobst is very grateful to Genny Chiarandon and Christine Vonwiller for always having his interests in studying diplomacy in mind when expanding our collections at the libraries of the Vienna School of International Studies and the Austrian Foreign Ministry. Furthermore, he is indebted to the Vienna School for partially funding this research.

Corneliu Bjola expresses his gratitude to the Oxford Department of International Development and the John Fell Fund of Oxford University Press for partially funding this project.

We would like also to extend our thanks to Andrew Humphrys and Annabelle Harris who have been tremendously helpful in assisting us with the publication of the book as well as to the blind peer reviewers for their valuable and constructive criticism. In writing this book, we also took quite a lot of inspiration from our students. It is very much with them and their contributions to our class discussions in mind that we have written this book. We, therefore, dedicate this book to them.

Abbreviations

ANC	African National Congress
APEC	Asia-Pacific Economic Cooperation
ASEAN	Association of Southeast Asian Nations
AU	African Union
AU PSC	Peace and Security Council (Africa Union)
CCP	Common Commercial Policy
CD	Conference for Disarmament
CFSP	Common Foreign and Security Policy
CPCC	Civilian Planning and Conduct Capability
CSDP	Common Security and Defence Policy
CTBTO	Preparatory Commission for a Comprehensive Nuclear-Test-Ban Treaty Organization
DDR	Demobilization, Disarmament and Reintegration
EEAS	European External Action Service
EFSF	European Financial Stability Facility
EFSM	European Financial Stabilisation Mechanism
EPC	European Political Co-operation
EPLF	Eritrean People's Liberation Front
EUMC	European Union Military Committee
EUMS	European Union Military Staff
EU PSC	Political and Security Committee (European Union)
ExComm	Executive Committee
FAO	Food and Agriculture Organization of the United Nations
FPA	Foreign policy analysis
Frelimo	*Frente de Libertaçao de Moçambique*
GATT	General Agreement on Tariffs and Trade
GMG	Global Migration Group
HR	High Representative of the Union for Foreign Affairs and Security Policy
IAEA	International Atomic Energy Agency
ICBL	International Campaign to Ban Landmines

ICEM	Intergovernmental Committee for European Migration
IFAD	International Fund for Agricultural Development
IFP	Inkatha Freedom Party
ILC	International Law Commission
ILO	International Labour Organization
IMF	International Monetary Fund
IOM	International Organization for Migration
IPCC	Intergovernmental Panel on Climate Change
IRO	International Refugee Organization
MPLA	*Movimento Popular de Libertaçao de Angola*
NATO	North-Atlantic Treaty Organization
NGO	Non-governmental organisation
NP	National Party
NPT	Treaty on the Non-Proliferation of Nuclear Weapons
OAS	Organization of American States
OECD	Organisation for Economic Co-operation and Development
ONUC	United Nations Operation in the Congo
OPCW	Organization for the Prohibition of Chemical Weapons
OSS	Sahara and Sahel Observatory
PBSO	Peacebuilding Support Office
PFDJ	People's Front for Democracy and Justice
R2P	Responsibility to protect
Renamo	*Resisténcia Nacional Mocambicana*
SAARC	South Asian Association for Regional Cooperation
SSR	Security Sector Reform
SWAC	Sahel and West Africa Club
TEC	Treaty establishing the European Community
TPLF	Tigray People's Liberation Front
TPP	Trans-Pacific Partnership
UNAIDS	Joint United Nations Programme on HIV/AIDS
UNCCD	Permanent Secretariat of the United Nations Convention to Combat Desertification
UNCTAD	UN Conference on Trade and Development
UNDESA	UN Department of Economic and Social Affairs
UNDP	United Nations Development Programme
UNEP	United Nations Environment Program
UNESCO	United Nations Educational, Scientific and Cultural Organization
UNFCCC	United Nations Framework Convention on Climate Change
UNFPA	United Nations Population Fund

UNGA   United Nations General Assembly
UNHCR   United Nations High Commissioner for Refugees
UNICEF   United Nations Children's Fund
UNITA   *Uniao Nacional para Independência Total de Angola*
UNITAR   United Nations Institute for Training and Research
UNODC   United Nations Office on Drugs and Crime
UNPBC   United Nations Peacebuilding Commission
UNRRA   UN Relief and Rehabilitation Administration
UNSC   United Nations Security Council
UNSG   UN Secretary-General
WFP   World Food Programme
WHO   World Health Organization
WTO   World Trade Organization

Part I
Introduction

1 Why and how to study diplomacy

Why study diplomacy?

There may never have been a better time to study diplomacy! The outstanding economic progress of China in recent decades has been raising concerns among scholars and policy-makers alike about whether the potential redistribution of power from the West to the East would lead to regional and global instability. The risk of catastrophic climate change keeps up the pressure on the international community to find ways to break the current stalemate of climate negotiations. The revolutionary events following the so-called 'Arab Spring' are fundamentally changing the regional relations of the Middle East and North Africa, which have had major repercussions for global politics as well. The future of the nuclear non-proliferation regime is anything but unrelated to diplomatic efforts to dissuade states such as Iran to go nuclear and to persuade states such as North Korea to abandon its nuclear weapons programme. In the late 2000s, the global financial crisis left its mark on the global economy, with many states and regional organisations (especially the Euro zone members within the EU) struggling to cope with sovereign debt crises.

The forces of globalisation, and with it the need to steer these forces into warranted directions, underpin many of these challenges. We seem to be situated in an 'in-between era', where international politics – and with it diplomacy – needs fresh ideas and new initiatives of diplomatic engagement to interact with a changing world. The need for such a reorientation is nothing particularly new. Diplomacy has a history of adapting and reinventing itself to changing political conditions. However, the challenge for diplomats has surprisingly remained similar throughout different historical ages: how to properly recognise, interpret and project relevant forms of power by communicating with one another. In other words, what exactly is there to understand about diplomacy and how can we make sense of it? This book does not aim to provide *the* answer to this question, but to explore how this question can be addressed from a variety of perspectives: historical, legal, cognitive, social or ethical. In so doing, we hope to convince the readers that diplomacy represents a unique, multi-faceted, effective and highly relevant instrument for managing relationships of estrangement between political communities, while retaining their institutional, ideological and social differences.

As a way of unpacking these arguments, this chapter will proceed in three steps. The first section will explain the centrality of communication to the diplomatic practice. The second section will explain why and how we plan to broaden the toolbox available for studying diplomacy by drawing on insights from related disciplines. The chapter will conclude with an overview of the themes to be covered in each chapter of the book.

How to define diplomacy?

What distinct insights does diplomacy offer to us for understanding how the world 'hangs together'? What ontological boundaries (→ glossary: ontology) delineate the field of diplomatic inquiry and how helpful are they in assisting scholars theorise about conditions of conflict and cooperation in world politics or about considerations of power, authority and legitimacy as constitutive frameworks of international conduct? In short, what turns diplomacy into a core analytical and practical method of international engagement? The answer we provide in this book is that diplomacy cannot be understood without taking seriously the role of communication as an ontological anchor of diplomatic interaction.

Diplomacy is the institutionalised communication among internationally recognised representatives of internationally recognised entities through which these representatives produce, manage and distribute public goods.

This definition has three key features. First, diplomacy is, on its most fundamental level, about *communication*. More precisely, it is about a peculiar form of communication that is highly *institutionalised*. There are a plethora of rules and norms that diplomats become socialised into and these rules and norms govern the communication among diplomats. On the one hand, therefore, our definition is not far removed from Adam Watson's highly influential claim that diplomacy revolves around dialogue. He, too, wrote about diplomacy as an institution and, choosing the term 'dialogue', he also put communication centre stage in his writings on diplomacy (Watson 1982). On the other hand, we use the term communication more broadly. The literature on diplomacy exhibits a somewhat celebratory streak when it suggests that diplomacy is about peaceful communication and dialogue. Diplomacy certainly has the general tendency – and lots of potential – for peaceful solutions of conflicts. But diplomacy is not always innocent. The declaration of war, for instance, is as much a diplomatic act – very much an institutionalised communicative act – as mediation and negotiation of peaceful resolution of conflicts. So are attempts to build coalitions with other states to go to war.

Second, processes of *double recognition* make an individual an actor in the diplomatic field. These processes are very straightforward when it comes to an ambassador representing a state. States are recognised as entities on the diplomatic stage (see Box 1.1), for instance through the UN Charter and the 1961 Vienna Convention on Diplomatic Relations. The latter also codifies the accreditation process through which a host state recognises the ambassador of a sending state. Some books on diplomacy state this more simply. Watson, for instance, writes only about states. Yet this is, in our view, a bit too simple, especially in our global age. Of course, states are still key entities in the diplomatic game. To this very day, diplomacy privileges states. With few exceptions, for instance, it is states that are members of the UN. But this does not mean that we can understand today's diplomacy by looking only at states. The UN Secretariat, for example, is oftentimes recognised as a diplomatic player in its own right. Its representatives, above all the Secretary-General but also his Under-Secretary-Generals, are acknowledged to act on behalf of this recognised international entity. In similar ways, the chairpersons and other high-ranking representatives of, say, Amnesty International and Greenpeace, become diplomatic actors (although they may not necessarily self-identify as such). Diplomacy, in other words, has a lot to do with recognition. Who is recognised changes over time. Thus, our definition stays open with regard to who is recognised. This enables us to discuss changes from, say, Richelieu's times to our global age of diplomacy.

> **Box 1.1 Declaratory versus constitutive theory of statehood**
>
> According to the 1933 Montevideo Convention on the Rights and Duties of States, a political community possess sovereignty (i.e., has legal personality under international law) if it 'possess the following qualifications: (a) permanent population; (b) defined territory; (c) government; and (d) capacity to enter into relations with the other states' (International Conference of American States 1933 Article 1). The case of state-like entities such as Taiwan, Palestine or Kosovo, which meet these conditions but do not enjoy full legal personality, exposes a limitation of the declaratory theory of statehood. The constitutive theory of statehood seeks to address this inconsistency by arguing that states actually require consent 'either to the creation of the state itself, or to its being subject to international law with respect to the states affected' (Crawford 1979: 12). Therefore, collective recognition is not merely a formality but rather an 'indispensable precondition for a political community's status as a sovereign state in international relations and law' (Fabry 2010: 7). Without recognition, political communities do not enjoy the protections granted to states by the UN Charter, nor can they fully engage in economic, political or legal relations with other states. At the same time, questions persist about the threshold of collective recognition (e.g., which and how many countries need to recognise a polity as a state in order for this polity to enjoy the status of statehood), whether recognition should be withdrawn to failed states, or whether collective recognition should include provisions about the domestic character of the prospective state.

Third, diplomacy is about *producing, managing and distributing public goods*, that is, goods that are important for the well-being of a community and where the use by some members of the community does not reduce the availability of the public good to others. Traditionally, diplomacy has been primarily about engaging in communication for the purpose of achieving a particular type of public good: the protection of the state against external interventions (i.e., security). In the twentieth century, diplomatic communication expanded to address a growing number of other public goods, including economic welfare, development, environmental protection, health safety and migration control. More recently, it has become increasingly evident that many of these public goods are interrelated and hence diplomats need to be proficient in how to juggle competing priorities of public goods. Equally important, globalisation is redefining some of these public goods into global public goods, that is, goods that are important for the well-being of multiple political communities. Issues that have traditionally been merely national are now global because they are beyond the grasp of any single nation (e.g., environment, health, peace, justice). This transformation introduces a new set of challenges for how diplomats manage public goods and may even lead to the end of diplomacy as we know it today.

Broadening horizons for studying diplomacy

The purpose of this book is not to argue for one perspective or the other. It is also not to arrive at a new one. Instead, it is to *introduce the reader to different compartments of the toolbox available for making sense of diplomacy*. It is up to the reader to choose from the material we provide and make sense of diplomacy, both in terms of how diplomacy works and how it ought to work. Very much in the spirit of broadening the toolbox available for studying diplomacy, we also encourage the reader to go beyond the material we have selected for this book, for example by listing recommended further reading.

Some of these compartments are taken from the literature on diplomacy. In this way, this book bears resemblance to other textbooks on diplomacy. It summarises the state of the art. Yet most of these compartments are borrowed from literature that does not deal with diplomacy in much depth or does not explicitly address the phenomenon at all. Thus, we want to reach out further than existing books on diplomacy. Outside of the discipline of international relations (IR), we borrow insights from a number of disciplines, including economics, history, law, philosophy (especially political theory), psychology and sociology (especially social theory). Many of the authors whose works we discuss have never written anything on diplomacy. But their arguments help us understand aspects of diplomacy that remain otherwise under-appreciated. Given the multi-faceted nature of diplomacy, we seek to introduce the reader to a multi-faceted way of studying diplomacy. Crossing disciplinary and sub-disciplinary boundaries is our means for achieving this end.

Our multi-perspectival *Leitmotiv* also finds expression in how we deal with research that addresses fields of study that are often seen as competitors of research on diplomacy. We explore criss-crossings between the study of diplomacy on the one hand and literature on global governance, foreign policy analysis and international relations theory on the other. Global governance is not the same as diplomacy. The manner in which communication is institutionalised in the diplomatic field gives rise to distinct interaction patterns. The recognition of actors, for instance, is much narrower in the field of diplomacy than the literature on global governance conceives of actorness. But there is a lot to be learnt from writings on global governance. In the age of global diplomacy, diplomats have to stand their ground in processes of global governance. They have to act in multiple policy fields and with multiple actors, some inside and some outside the diplomatic realm. Thus, engaging with the literature on global governance helps us understand today's diplomacy.

To some extent we concur with the abovementioned attempts to delineate diplomacy studies from foreign policy analysis (FPA). Diplomacy and FPA are not the same. While the former focuses on the making of foreign policy in a domestic setting, the latter deals more with how political entities, once they have formulated their foreign policies, pursue these policies on the international level. Yet these foci are a matter of degree. There is no absolute boundary. Studies of diplomacy are gained from an understanding of how policies are formulated, no matter whether this formulation takes place on the domestic level only or whether there is input from the international level as well. Hedley Bull had it exactly right when he argued that the study of diplomacy has to pay attention to policy formation (Bull 1995).

Finally, we also explore overlaps between IR, and in particular international relations theory, and diplomatic studies. It is especially approaches that take agency seriously and explore the complex processes through which agents are shaped by structures and, vice versa, agents shape structures, that are of major relevance for the study of diplomacy. The latter, no question about it, is agency-focused. Studies of diplomacy foreground the work of the diplomat. But diplomats are embedded in context, some of which is very much of their own making, and this context enables and constrains their actions.

Overview

This book is organised as follows: Part II traces the evolution of diplomacy from its beginnings in ancient Egypt, Greece and China to our current age of global diplomacy. Chapter 2 traces the institutionalisation of diplomacy in the ancient world and discusses the further evolution of this institutionalisation up until WWI. Starting with Wilson's visions for a new diplomacy and leading up to twenty-first-century diplomacy, Chapter 3 addresses the addition of the multilateral layer to diplomacy. Chapter 4 deals with today's widening of the diplomatic field, i.e. the multiplication of issue areas and actors.

Part III maps the diplomatic field. It identifies two building blocks for analysing diplomacy: context and tasks. The context enables and constrains diplomacy to perform its tasks and, vice versa, the performance of these tasks shapes the context that constitutes diplomacy. Looking at diplomatic contexts in depth, Chapter 5 discusses international public law (especially the 1961 Vienna Convention on Diplomatic Relations) as well as deeper backgrounds, i.e. ideas constituting diplomacy that actors take so much for granted that they do not reflect upon them anymore. Chapter 6 details the doings of the diplomat. It distinguishes four clusters of practices: messaging, negotiation, mediation and talk.

Part IV builds on the previous part by discussing explanations of diplomatic outcomes. Chapter 7 is concerned with the making of decisions: how do diplomats make decisions? In our answer, we focus on four different logics of action: consequences, appropriateness, argumentation and practice. Chapter 8 addresses the making of relations: how do diplomats make relations among the entities they represent? We offer different sets of prescriptions of relationship-making based on three competing schools of thought, Realism, Liberalism and Constructivism. Chapter 9, focusing on the deeper background, asks an even more profound question: how do diplomats make the world that we inhabit? The answer, we argue, lies with the role that diplomats play as makers of cultures of anarchy and international deontologies.

Part V also builds on Part III but switches from explanation to a normative mode. Striking a balance between analytical and normative understandings of diplomacy is a delicate but critical endeavor (Bjola 2008). Diplomacy is full of normative problems and moral conundrums. We deal with three of them, each located at a different level of analysis. Foregrounding the individual level, Chapter 10 examines how diplomatic representation should be conducted, what forms of power are appropriate to use in diplomatic relations, and what forms of diplomatic training and expertise are more suitable for the twenty-first-century diplomat. Moving to the state level, Chapter 11 asks questions about diplomacy's recent involvements in remaking states (especially peacebuilding). Should diplomacy get involved in remaking other states; if so, how? Chapter 12 is dedicated to the key puzzle of diplomacy: how ought diplomacy to safeguard peaceful changes in world politics? We investigate the strengths and limitations of two important instruments, preventive diplomacy and international criminal justice, that may assist diplomats in their mission to generate peaceful change.

Finally, Part VI, the conclusion, summarises the main analytical and normative contributions of the book to understanding how diplomacy works or ought to work, discusses how useful the concept of anti-diplomacy is for grasping the limits of diplomatic conduct and explains why and how the concept of inclusive diplomacy may assist diplomats in coping with future challenges.

Part II
Tracing diplomacy

2   Historical evolution

Chapter objectives

- To offer readers a concise overview of the historical evolution of diplomacy to the present day.
- To highlight the key transformative moments of the diplomatic practice.
- To introduce readers to the main contributions and limitations of diplomacy in facilitating international peace and cooperation.

Introduction

The word 'diplomacy' is rooted in Greek (*diploma*: double-folded document; letter of recommendation or conveying a licence or privilege). Historically, the origins of diplomacy lay with the first decisions of human communities to reach an understanding with their neighbours about the limits of their hunting territories. But even though these early diplomatic exchanges allowed for the establishment of some basic rules of representation, communication and conflict management, they did not result in the creation of any permanent institutions. Basically, diplomatic interaction was not sufficiently frequent or important and hence it lacked the incentives required to develop complex institutional relations. Good faith and the enforcement of the safety regulations were perennial problems, especially when the sanction for the safety of the diplomatic messenger was seen as divine.

Since these first stages of interaction, however, diplomacy has changed significantly. These changes will be systematically treated in this chapter, in which developments are described in three distinct diplomatic periods, both inside and outside of the Western world: ancient, medieval and modern diplomacy (before World War I). This task will be accomplished according to three sub-themes: (1) representation procedures – in which we examine the roles, characteristics and perceptions of the diplomat; (2) communication methods – in which we trace key developments and procedures of diplomatic engagement; and (3) conflict management – in which we describe the evolution of various instruments for resolving international disputes.

Ancient diplomacy

The ancient proto-diplomatic systems involved no permanent institutions but rather *ad hoc* missions, taking place as circumstances arose. The patterns of diplomatic representation, communication and negotiation developed by ancient states were largely influenced by the perceived levels of power asymmetry. Among the small but independent Greek city-states, no single city was powerful enough to rule over the others, nor were the city-states overwhelmed from outside. The cities thus diplomatically engaged with each other as equals. By contrast, the Egyptian, Roman, Persian or Chinese diplomatic methods primarily served to assert, establish and maintain their alleged political, religious or military superiority over neighbours or any other groups with which they interacted.

Representation procedures

In the ancient Greek system, three types of diplomatic representation were recognised. First and foremost, the *angelos* or *presbys* (messenger and elder, respectively) were diplomatic envoys sent for 'brief and highly specific missions'. The second type, the *keryx* (herald), had special rights of personal safety. And the third was the *proxenos* (→ glossary), who would 'act ... for another state while remaining resident in his own state' out of a general sympathy for the political system or culture of another state (Hamilton and Langhorne 1995: 9–10). *Angelos* and *presbys* were supposed to perform well oratorically before the city-state council of the host state. This meant that they were often chosen by the assembly of the city for their 'known respectability', 'reputed wisdom' and for their maturity (Nicolson 1988 [1954]: 6). However, the suaveness or negotiation skills of the Greek ambassadors were not necessarily the crucial selection factors, as their diplomatic strategies were often publicly – and rather restrictively – determined by the people of the sending state. Indeed, instructions given to *angelos* were 'irksomely strict and elaborate' (Murray 1855: 9).

In contrast, *proxenos* played a facilitating role in the handling of inter-state negotiation. In bad times, their main duties consisted of offering hospitality and assistance to visitors from the relevant state. And at times, they would be asked to give advice on the domestic situation in the state they represented. But in good times, the *proxenos* could play a more influential role in shaping public policy, specifically in commerce, culture and politics. They were expected to protect their nationals located in the receiving-state, handle their legal administration and promote trade and commerce between the two states in general. It is important to note that many current concepts of diplomacy found no place in Greek language and practice. For example, no theory of diplomatic immunity prevailed at the time, as envoys relied on the traditional codes of religion and hospitality in their movements (Mosley 1971: 321).

The Romans inherited from the Greeks the lack of a formal structure for dealing with matters of foreign policy, but also the appreciation for the talent of speaking fluently in public and the ability to persuade by argument. The similarities between the two diplomatic methods nevertheless stop here. In view of the fact that formally the Senate had the ultimate authority on matters of foreign policy, Roman envoys – called either *nuntii* or *oratores* – were appointed from within senatorial ranks. They were provided with credentials and instructions, which were supposed to be closely followed. Their main task was to find someone worthwhile to talk to and then report back to the Senate, which would sanction or decline to accept the results of their negotiation. With the expansion of the empire, the decision-making power on diplomatic matters gradually transferred into the hands of the emperor. The emperor often relied on his governors to deal with foreign embassies and execute diplomatic decisions, but his personal involvement in diplomacy remained strong and motivated by the desire to present the public with a façade of Roman control over international negotiations.

Ancient Egyptians both sent and received diplomatic missions. The Pharaoh used to maintain close contact with the rulers of neighbouring powers via special envoys with ambassadorial functions. The common practice in the region was to appoint diplomatic messengers from among the high officers of the administration, who were supposed to be experienced in state affairs and fully cognizant of royal policy (Munn-Rankin 2004: 25). Diplomatic relations between Egypt and other powers in the region, including Babylonia, and Assyria, around mid-fourteenth century BC, are detailed in some thirty-five items of correspondence in the Amarna Letters. In principle, the rulers corresponded on a basis of equality, as 'great kings'. They referred to each other as 'my brother' as opposed to 'sons', which would have indicated the status of the vassal (Munn-Rankin 2004: 13). In practice though, the Egyptian ruler enjoyed an advantage over his Asiatic counterparts. As the leader of a hegemonic power that was more self-sufficient in prestige goods than the other powers and enjoyed a near monopoly on the production of gold, the Pharaoh was able to bargain from a position of strength thus often forcing his counterparts to make humiliating concessions.

Communication methods

The ancient Greek diplomatic system had a number of characteristics that presented a high level of sophistication. They included, for example, the constant flow of missions, the mutual respect of diplomatic immunities, the treaties and alliances that resulted from diplomatic interaction and the high standard of public debate. These features allowed diplomats to become increasingly effective in working out regulations that were widely observed, such as 'defining the position of aliens, the grant of naturalisation, the right of asylum, extradition, and maritime practices' (Nicolson 1988 [1954]: 9). On matters of treaties, Greek envoys worked under restrictive instructions. While most treaties were quite simple documents, they were nevertheless concluded after reference to, and approval of, public assemblies. The Spartans eventually introduced the institution of conference diplomacy to address the problem of how to deal with numerous dependent allies after prolonged wars.

The widespread suspicion of diplomats in ancient Greece also meant that missions were often composed of several diplomats. The number of ambassadors involved in a mission could be as many as ten (see Box 2.1). The size of these missions was also intended to increase the weight of the case brought to the other city-state and to facilitate the representation of different opinions that were held by the citizens in the sending state. However, it often had a negative effect on the overall effectiveness of the mission due to personal disagreements between individual ambassadors on the mission. At times, negotiating partners would play upon such internal animosities to divide the mission against itself.

One of the most important Roman contributions to the Greek diplomatic legacy was, for instance, the practice of declaring war. According to this practice, any declaration of war had to follow a proper procedure (i.e., the *jus fetiale* proceeding; → glossary), and had to offer a legal justification for the war. The college of *Fetiales* informed the enemy of the grievances of Rome and, if nothing happened after a fixed period, then a declaration of war would be made at the border of the enemy's

---

Box 2.1 Greek diplomatic missions

The sophistication of the Greek diplomatic system is illustrated by the fact that diplomatic negotiations were conducted orally and in accordance with some publicly controlled rules:

> The several members of an Embassy (there were often as many as ten Ambassadors in a single mission) would each deliver a set speech to a foreign monarch or Assembly, much as happens in the ordered international conferences of today. If the negotiations resulted in a treaty, the terms of that treaty were engraved in a pure attic on a tablet for all to see. Its ratification was accomplished by the public exchange of solemn oaths.
>
> (Nicolson 1988 [1954]: 7)

---

territory and a javelin (cornel wood spear) would be cast into his land (Hamilton and Langhorne 1995: 14). As legal grounds for waging war, the Romans invoked the following: violation of a treaty, truce or armistice; an offence committed against an ally; violation of neutrality; violation of sanctity of ambassadors; refusal to surrender an ambassador who had violated his neutrality; unjustifiable rejection of an embassy; violation of territorial rights; refusal of a peaceful passage of troops; and refusal to surrender an individual who committed a crime (Ballis 1973: 25).

Archival documentation of early Chinese diplomatic exchanges indicates a complex dynamic centred on ceremony, status claiming and procedure. In AD 57, for example, an emissary from the state of Wa (the ancient name of Japan) travelled to the Han capital to offer tribute, and he received a seal and a ribbon from the emperor. In these early centuries, 'a China-centered universe was assumed on both sides ... and Wa most desired to be accepted as a vassal within that orb' (Fogel 2009: 9). Some authors, in recognition of the likely influence of Sun Tzu's *Art of War*, suggest the doctrinal principle of ancient Chinese diplomacy was actually to ensure victory by subduing the enemy without fighting (Deshingkar 2004: 90). Princes made court visits that were mainly ceremonial goodwill functions and they frequently communicated by envoys, sending them on courtesy missions and for preparing interstate agreements. Exchange of valuable gifts was customary in diplomatic procedure, as was the immunity granted to diplomatic envoys.

Conflict management

Peace agreements in ancient Greece did not necessarily mean what its negotiators wanted it to mean. Often, they were formulated ambiguously in order to allow different states on different occasions to interpret them to their own advantage. Still, these peace agreements mattered, especially when they were reinforced by oaths. For pacific conflict resolution, arbitration was a quite customary device. Indeed, forty-six cases of dispute arbitration had been adjudicated between 300 and 100 BC (Nicolson 1988 [1954]: 8). The designated arbiter was either another state or an individual – often a philosopher of good reputation or even a victor at the Olympic Games. Ambassadors were often entrusted with important communication and they were even required to 'decide on the justice of a war ... and to proclaim and consecrate it according to certain established formalities' (Murray 1855: 9).

Religion often played a significant role in framing diplomatic practices of conflict resolution. The Greeks believed, for instance, that the conduct of international affairs was governed by 'certain divinely ordained principles' (Nicolson 1988 [1954]: 9). Being regarded as under the guardianship of Zeus, treaties and allies were ascribed a divine authority that made it wrong to break them without good reason. The rules of 'civilized conduct' developed by ancient Greeks included fair treatment of prisoners, non-use of poisoned weapons and treacherous stratagems, observance of truces and armistices, prohibition of warfare during religious festivals or athletic contests, as well as inviolability of important temples, sanctuaries and embassies (Phillipson 2001: 182–191). In addition, Greeks developed the first forms of international organisations. Festivals such as the Olympic Games represented 'a period of deliberately controlled international relations' (Hamilton and Langhorne 1995: 11), during which agreements on cooperation were frequently discussed.

Persian kings oftentimes resorted to preventive diplomacy in their interaction with the Greek city-states between the sixth and fourth century BC. In fact, Persians were more successful through diplomacy than they were in war against the Greeks. They aimed to maintain the balance of power between the Greek city-states by operating as 'neutral' treaty brokers in wars fought by the Greeks in the fourth century. The strategic objective was to prevent any city-state from becoming powerful enough to challenge the Persian military superiority. In short, the Persian-Greco relations were pragmatic and constantly evolving in response to political circumstances from two sides, whose capacities for direct confrontations were reduced by numerous internal problems (Rung 2008).

The Romans had a notable respect for international treaties which were used for establishing peace, building alliances and dividing spoils. By 264 BC, more than 150 separate treaties had been concluded, which greatly increased Rome's military strength, since, rather than requesting tribute, Rome demanded contingents of soldiers to supplement its armies (Campbell 2001: 4). While in the early days of the Republic, the Romans used to conclude agreements on a reciprocal basis, this practice was later drastically changed by the introduction of new forms of treaties 'under which the federated parties were constrained to recognize the *maiestas populi romani*, or, in more modern terms, to surrender to the Roman Senate the control of foreign policy and defence' (Nicolson 1988 [1954]: 16). The Romans also created the *praetor peregrinus* in 242 BC, who was expected to settle disputes of a commercial nature between foreigners or between a foreign party and a Roman citizen based on *jus gentium* (the law of nations).

Medieval diplomacy

During the early Middle Ages, diplomatic relations in both the Western and non-Western world were relatively infrequent and subject to little organic development. In the later Middle Ages, European diplomacy took an institutional leap relative to that in the non-Western world under the impact of two factors. On the one hand, the belief in the unity of Christendom that underlay political thought and activity – *republica christiana* – introduced a level of harmony among the emerging political entities. On the other hand, the legacy of the Roman law joined forces with the evolving body of canon law to establish a universalistic foundation for regulating diplomatic relations. It was at this time that European diplomacy professionalised. 'It was the

Byzantines who taught diplomacy to Venice; it was the Venetians who set the pattern for Italian cities, for France and Spain, and eventually for all Europe' (Nicolson 1988 [1954]: 24–25).

Representation procedures

The main form of diplomatic representation during the early Middle Ages in Europe was the nuncius (→ glossary), an agent whose main function was to provide a channel of communication between rulers and to explore opportunities for concluding treaties and alliances (see Box 2.2). The practical and legal identification of the nuncius with the principal also meant that the nuncius enjoyed a status of immunity from the harm that could be inflicted upon him. This security of the person – often based on religious grounds – and the special status of the ambassador were mutually understood. Indeed, harm inflicted upon the nuncius was often interpreted as harming his principal. Nuncii would usually carry 'consecrated staffs in their hands', in order to secure their inviolability (Murray 1855: 13).

In the later Middle Ages, the increased complexity of European societies and the growth of diplomatic interaction rendered the employment of nuncii insufficient because of the great delays and potential failures inflicted in their missions. As a result, a new type of official function was established, the procurator, with increased powers of representation and negotiation. Unlike nuncii, procurators were given full powers (*plena potestas*) to enter into private contracts and to negotiate agreements on behalf of their leaders. At times, principals repudiated the actions of procurators that had exceeded their mandates or they withdrew mandates altogether, after which no procurator could conclude agreements on behalf of the principal (Hamilton and Langhorne 1995: 27). The diplomatic influence of procurators is also illustrated by the fact that even the most solemn acts, such as contracting and completing, short of consummating, a marriage alliance could be carried out by a procurator by standing in for the bride or groom as it happened, for instance, in the case of the proxy engagement between the Holy Roman Emperor Frederick II and Isabella of England in 1234 (Queller 2004: 197).

In parallel with the work of nuncii and procurators, a growth in trade helped develop the consular system, with most notably French, Italian and Spanish merchants electing consuls to supervise their commerce and adjudicate disputes in the East. In 1223, Marseille established consuls in Tyre and Beirut. During the fifteenth and sixteenth centuries, the Capitulations treaties between Christians and Muslims further developed the consular functions by granting civil and criminal jurisdiction

---

Box 2.2 Medieval diplomats

The nuncius was sometimes instructed to engage in propagandising, fomenting revolts and breaking unfriendly relations. In the formation of the League of Friuli (1384), Venice sent nuncii to Friuli, towns dependent on that city, and the church of Aquileia, urging them to resist foreign encroachment. Even more, a state that felt itself injured could employ nuncii to deliver a protest, an ultimatum or even a declaration of war. They were also sent in times of war to an ally to coordinate efforts against the common enemy (Queller 2004: 195).

over nationals in the Byzantine Empire. During the fifteenth century, there were exchanges of consuls between Great Britain, Denmark, Italy, the Netherlands and Sweden. Around this time, China also posted officers in the West that were in effect consuls. The sixteenth century saw significant change: consuls were now appointed by sending states as official representatives, diplomatic functions involved protecting state interest in trade and commerce, and some privileges and immunities were attached (Chatterjee 2007: 250).

Communication methods

In the early medieval period, principals used messages to communicate with each other in order to prepare for personal meetings. In this communication process, the nuncius was often described as a 'living letter', because he was supposed to communicate the messages 'in a way that was as near a personal exchange as possible' (Hamilton and Langhorne 1995: 24). The significance of the use of a nuncius instead of a letter laid in the meanings a person can convey beyond the written word. Indeed, his attitude, his actual wording and his responses to questions were of vital importance to the communication between principals. Letters of instructions were particularly important in cases of negotiation as they provided specific guidelines and often the exact words the envoy had to use for extracting and making concessions.

In their diplomatic communications, the Byzantines frequently emphasised their political and military superiority, the longevity of the empire and the contrasting fates of its enemies. In order to impress and subdue 'barbarians', great attention was paid to diplomatic ceremony, including showing visitors around various majestic palaces and churches or dazzling them with lavish welcoming receptions in the throne room. 'The treatment of ambassadors throughout a visit was designed to impress, without allowing them to associate in any way with other than official persons or to see anything which it was not decided that they should see' (Hamilton and Langhorne 1995: 16). Diplomacy in Byzantium was thus characterised by an elaborate ceremonial and propaganda system. Furthermore, it was fairly continuous and well-developed. Bribery, flattery and marriage were used to avoid war and the Byzantines also used information about barbarian potentates and prominent persons of various ranks to build alliances and thwart military invasions (Shepard 2004).

On the other side of the globe, the Chinese diplomatic dominance of the Sino-Japanese relations started to be challenged in the seventh century. In 607, the Japanese mission to China tried to establish parity in diplomatic status by referring to the Japanese ruler as 'the son of heaven in the land of the rising sun' and to the Chinese ruler as 'the son of heaven in the land of the setting sun' (Wan 2010: 155). The Chinese emperor did not accept the letter. However, shared Confucian values enabled a high degree of mutual acceptance and a reduced sense of threat. Consequently, the Japanese did not think that they should challenge the existing Chinese world order, a fact reinforced by Japan's economic conditions in which continued commerce with other Asian states was seen as vital.

Conflict management

Religion was the most important source of inspiration for various methods of conflict management throughout the medieval period. As the Catholic Church became a major user of diplomacy during its struggle with the Roman Holy Empire during the thirteenth century, canon law and Roman law combined to form a key instrument for framing and adjudicating diplomatic disputes, up to the time of the Reformation. The canonists determined the (un)justness of war and breakers of peace and they framed rules of diplomatic conduct. The origins of the just war doctrine go back, for instance, to this period and to the writings of St. Augustine, Thomas Aquinas and Hugo Grotius. While many diplomatic relations in the Middle Ages were conducted under the form of private law whereby ratification was not obligatory or even customary, agreements made by nuncii or procurators without full powers could become binding only on formal approval by principals (Queller 2004: 211), a practice that still resonates today with the process or ratification of international treaties.

The rise of Islam in the sixth century brought about non-Christian understandings of the legal procedures and justifications for conflict management. Written in the ninth century, the Islamic Law of Nations made a clear distinction between Dar al-Islam (the territory of Islam) and Dar al-Harb (territory of war, inhabited by all those of non-Islamic faith). A state of war was assumed to exist between the two until the time when the former would conquer the latter. Many rulers in the Middle East had ideologies of kingship that asserted the legality and legitimacy of their rule over various – often overlapping – audiences. The Mamluk sultans – who ruled Egypt and Syria from 1250 to 1517 – saw themselves, for instance, as the martial guardians of Islam and Islamic society. These conflicting ideologies introduced intolerance into their – rather frequent – diplomatic exchanges, which was 'the most prominent arena both for expressing legitimacy, and for denigrating the claims of rivals' (Broadbridge 2008: 6). Still, their diplomatic interaction was based on respect for diplomatic immunity and an understanding of the importance of ceremony. Indeed, the amount of food and money spent on the guest ambassador reflected the status of the sender's embassy and the diplomats' behaviour during meetings was carefully calculated to project the status of both sides.

Competing religious conceptions of conflict management also emerged in Latin America. In the second quarter of the fifteenth century, the Aztec and Inca were able to conquer vast amounts of territory in a relatively short period of time. These conquests were successful because Aztec and Inca had manipulated traditional religious concepts and rituals in such a way that it gave them decisive advantages over their competitors. For example, Aztec elites were increasingly obsessed with legitimising their ancestry and emphasised the militaristic cult of war and human sacrifice of their culture. Also, they portrayed their migration history and current occupations in terms of the will of the Mexican patron deity (Conrad and Demarest 1984: 25–27). Similarly, the Inca used a 'psychology of submission' and propaganda to remind the subjects of the empire's power (Ogburn 2008: 225).

Modern diplomacy

At the end of the fifteenth century, a series of transformations in Europe combined to trigger a major diplomatic innovation: the establishment of the institution of the resident ambassador (→ glossary). Whereas previously, the effectiveness of drafts signed by diplomatic envoys had often been dependent on ratification by the principal, the increased pace of diplomacy improved the social status of ambassadors. Key to the success of this structural transformation was the process of religious fragmentation unleashed by the Reformation, which basically destroyed the medieval principle of religious universality thus making room for a new territorial-sovereign legitimating principle, the *raison d'état* (→ glossary), to emerge as the dominant doctrine of international conduct.

Representation procedures

The establishment of the new office of resident ambassador was based on the need of rulers to know as much as could be known about the internal affairs of the neighbouring states (see Box 2.3). The potential instability of the governments of the early sovereign states led them to frantically attempt to prevent subversion 'pursued by diplomatic agents plotting with opposition groups' (Hamilton and Langhorne 1995: 33). Resident ambassadors were expected to acclimatise themselves to local conditions in order to assess to what extent they could intervene in local political intrigues. In addition, resident ambassadors were expected to watch the safety of their fellow countrymen and to aid them in their business abroad.

The social background of the resident ambassador was not uniform, at least in the early days of the institution, but this had an uneven impact on the quality of diplomacy. England's residents were typically gentry of modest descent and generally competent, the French were nobles of lower rank with a good sense of seizing strategic opportunities, the Spanish employed high-calibre people of noble origin and were well-reputed for their diplomatic skills, the Venetians were members of leading families who dedicated themselves to voluminous and not always relevant reporting, while the Dutch residents came from all walks of life and allegedly were not excessively effective in the day-to-day management of diplomatic contacts (Carter 2004). Gradually, it became increasingly plain that the skills of the resident diplomat were a crucial asset. As one observer pointed out, 'it would be impossible indeed to estimate such qualities too highly. The fate of nations very often hangs on the judicious conduct of a diplomatist. His success depends almost entirely in the confidence and esteem which he inspires' (Murray 1855: 43).

These resident ambassadors were therefore required to meet a number of requirements (Nicolson 1988 [1954]: 35–36):

He must be a good linguist and above all a master of Latin, which was still the *lingua franca* (→ glossary) of the time. He must realize that all foreigners are regarded with suspicion and must therefore conceal his astuteness and appear as a pleasant man of the world. He must be hospitable and employ an excellent cook. He must be a man of taste and erudition and cultivate the society of writers, artists and scientists. He must be a naturally patient man, willing to spin out negotiations and to emulate the exquisite art of procrastination as perfected in the Vatican. He must be imperturbable, able to receive bad news without manifesting displeasure, or to hear himself maligned and misquoted without the slightest twinge of irritation. His private life must be so ascetic as to give his enemies no opportunity to spread scandal. He must be tolerant of the ignorance and foolishness of his home government and know how to temper the vehemence of the instructions he receives. Finally, he should remember that overt diplomatic triumphs leave feelings of humiliation behind them and a desire for revenge: no good negotiator should ever threaten, bully or chide.

Box 2.3 The rise of resident ambassadors in Italy

Italy was the model of what Europe as [a] whole was soon to become. The five large powers, Milan, Venice, Florence, the Papacy and Naples, remained in an unstable equilibrium while small states like Lucca, Mantua and Ferrara were protected against aggression only by the mutual jealousies of their powerful neighbours. Resident ambassadors thus proved their usefulness by serving as a check and as a means of raising the diplomatic alarm when any power threatened to upset the balance. Their widespread establishment helped avert crises by making possible rapid realignments in the patterns of alliances (Mattingly 2004: 222).

Failure to follow such prescriptions could lead to serious diplomatic tensions. The refusal to receive ambassadors could be prompted by varied circumstances. First, when an ambassador had any previous misunderstanding at another court, the court to which he was afterwards accredited might refuse to receive him until the matter has been satisfactorily arranged. Second, a sovereign might refuse to receive an ambassador from a desire to avoid some inconvenient ceremony which his arrival or presence would entail. Third, a sovereign may also refuse to receive an ambassador who had given cause of offence or who is personally disagreeable to him (Murray 1855: 57).

The quest for control over how diplomats exercised their missions and later the introduction of the concept of 'continuous negotiation' (→ glossary) by the Cardinal Richelieu led to the establishment of the first foreign ministry by France in 1626, *Ministère des Affaires Etrangères*, which literally meant the ministry of 'strange affairs'. Richelieu justified the centralisation of diplomacy on two grounds. On the one hand, he believed that:

> It is very important to be careful in choosing ambassadors and other representatives, and one cannot be too severe in punishing those who exceed their powers, since by such errors the reputation of rulers and the interests of states are compromised.
>
> (Richelieu 1947: 355)

On the other hand, he thought negotiations would never be effective unless they were directed by a single authority, especially since 'continuous negotiation' multiplied the possibilities of contradiction and misunderstanding.

While the institution of the resident diplomat gradually became common practice in Western Europe, the adoption of this form of diplomatic representation in the rest of the world was slow, fragmentary and varied substantially depending on the actors' willingness to accept the European diplomatic style or their capacity to carry out diplomatic relations in the first place. In the East, for instance, Suleyman the Magnificent was

> anxious to play a role in Europe, yet the [Ottomans] were so convinced of their natural superiority to the rest of the world ... that they remained for another two centuries unwilling to adopt the European notion of the resident

ambassador or venture much beyond the temporary application of military force as the basis of policy.

(Hamilton and Langhorne 1995: 37)

The interests of Russia – which emerged from the post-Mongol period – were both Asiatic and European. It lasted until 1586 for the first French ambassador to reach Moscow and Russia did not reciprocate until 1615.

In pre-colonial Africa, diplomatic relations were established for the negotiation of agreements, the delimitation of frontiers, the settlement of past disputes and the resolution of potential crises. Africa was not *terra nullius* (i.e., 'empty land' or 'land belonging to no one') before the European colonisation (Smith 1989: 141). It was characterised by coherent and rational international relations of peace and war. African rulers made use of two types of diplomats, ambassadors and messengers, who broadly resembled the roles of medieval procurators and nuncii respectively. The ambassador had the status of a plenipotentiary and could settle a dispute on his own authority. Messengers had no such power as they merely transmitted orders or information and could not engage in negotiation (Irwin 1975: 93). But with either type of diplomatic interaction, the African rulers insisted that proper respect should be paid to their representatives abroad.

Communication methods

The main duty of the resident ambassador was to gather information regarding domestic political conditions in the host state and report back relevant developments to chancelleries at home. To this end, ambassadors were required to build close relationships with the individuals with whom the power rested, form good channels of communication between the two governments and to advise the sending government on the best course of action. Resident ambassadors generally enjoyed a significant degree of discretion in pursuing their missions. They alone could decide at what moment and on what terms their instructions could be best executed and they could interpret the purposes and motives of one government to the other (Nicolson 1988 [1954]: 82–83).

The reports they sent back were 'very detailed, seemingly filled with political trivia and endless verbatim accounts of conversations that the resident had' (Hamilton and Langhorne 1995: 33). This style of reporting was maintained so that the secretaries and clerks in the chancellery could identify important connections that were neglected by the resident ambassador on the spot. However, the ever-growing volume of diplomatic exchanges between diplomatic residents and home chancelleries was not accompanied by the development of an effective and competent bureaucratic administration. This often had the effect of slowing down the pace of diplomatic relations and of even misplacing texts of treaties. The creation of the foreign affairs ministry spearheaded by Richelieu therefore represented a logical and necessary step for streamlining diplomatic activity.

Much attention was paid to the affirmation of an ambassador's *haute bourgeoisie* background by ceremonial. First, diplomatic ritual was a clear measure of the aspirations and responses to status recognition among the parties (see Box 2.4). The sending state could demonstrate its wealth and power and its rating of the importance of the recipient by the lavishness of the mission and the seniority of its head. The receiver, on

---

Box 2.4 The policy of diplomatic prestige

In the early sixteenth century, the powers in Europe were France, ruled by Francis I, and the Holy Roman Empire, led by Charles V. Henry VIII of England needed desperately to forge an alliance with one of the parties. In 1520, Henry and Francis I agreed on a meeting near Calais, France. In attempting to outshow the other, the kings spared no expense in their displays of wealth. They erected pavilions made with cloth of gold (real filaments of gold sewn with silk to make the fabric), organised jousts and other competitions of skill and strength, banqueted each other lavishly, in all ways trying to outdo and outspend one another. This ostentation earned the meeting the title 'Field of the Cloth of Gold'. The feasting ended abruptly when King Henry challenged King Francis to a wrestling match that ended in Francis throwing Henry to the ground and besting him. The meeting, which had taken place over three weeks (June 7 – June 24, 1520) nearly bankrupted the treasuries of France and England, and was useless politically. Francis and Henry signed no treaty, and a few weeks later Henry signed a treaty of alliance with the Holy Roman Emperor, Charles V. Within a month, the Emperor declared war on Francis, and England had to follow suit (Russell 1969).

---

the other hand, said something about its standing by the quality of reception offered, the grandeur of accommodation, the nature of celebrations and the value of the gifts. Indeed, 'the envoys of powerful or friendly governments enjoyed far more distinguished honors than were granted to others' (Murray 1855: 36).

Essential to communication was language. Before the fifteenth century, Latin was the prevailing mode of diplomatic communication both in terms of written treaties and oral exchanges. With the decline of the Holy Roman Empire and the deepening of religious fragmentation, the use of Latin among diplomats became rare and negotiations through interpreters became more common. While French became frequently used by the Russian nobility, by the end of the seventeenth century Russia also had an excellent service of foreign language, which included fifteen translators (*perevodčik*) and fifty interpreters (*tolmach*) of Latin, Italian, Polish, Romanian, English, German, Swedish, Dutch, Greek, Tartar, Persian, Arab, Turkish and Georgian. Most often they were foreigners in Russian service or former prisoners of war (Zonova 2007: 13). It was only in the eighteenth century that French had grown to be the dominant diplomatic language, a status it retained until the end of World War I when it gradually became replaced by English.

Ambassadors enjoyed certain advantages that facilitated their access to information and communication. Most importantly, they enjoyed diplomatic immunities. These immunities – notably the physical inviolability of ambassadors, the ambassadorial lifting of indictment for civil or criminal offences and the freedom to practise religion in private – were granted to diplomats on the basis of religious, legal and practical sources. First, religious reasons were grounded in the 'sacred' attribute of the ambassador, who was perceived to act for the general. Second, Roman law incorporated legal sanctions for diplomatic immunity, the scope of which was subsequently extended by canon law (e.g., to residences) under the threat of excommunication, and later by legal precedents under the doctrine of extraterritoriality (Hamilton and Langhorne 1995: 41, 45).

Third, practical considerations led states to reciprocally respect the safety of envoys. Indeed, the rulers were generally convinced that diplomatic immunity, granted on a reciprocal basis, was a precondition to overcome the hazards of length and physical dangers that plagued diplomatic missions in the Middle Ages. Mattingly (1955: 48) explains this as follows:

> The law was intended to give the ambassador every privilege and immunity necessary for the performance of his office. It was not intended to protect him in the abuse of those privileges and immunities for other ends, any more than it protected the tax collector who practices blackmail.

Another important development was the standardisation of matters of payment and accommodation of ambassadors. For a long time, resident ambassadors were provided free accommodation and an allowance by the host government. This practice frequently caused difficulties to diplomats securing necessary funds for obtaining access to information and keeping up 'the scale of entertainment which the standing ... of its principal would suggest' (Mattingly 1955: 166). From the fifteenth century onwards, the practice of paying resident diplomats by the sending authorities became gradually widespread, rendering them independent of the host with regard to allowances or accommodation (Hamilton and Langhorne 1995: 57). However, the standardisation of payment by the sending state did not mean the end of complaints about financial resources and quite often potential ambassadors refused to serve on the grounds that they might stand to lose financially by taking up the mission (Roosen 1973: 136).

Conflict management

The establishment of the Westphalian conception of territorial sovereignty as a constitutive principle of international order helped create a new configuration of hierarchical relations in Europe between great and smaller powers. This order often led to an excessive preoccupation with status recognition and diplomatic precedence (see Box 2.5). Symbolic ceremonial was understood to send precise messages about the relationship between the parties involved and to indicate the significance of the matters discussed. Also, relationships between the several permanent embassies were established through ceremonial, meaning that 'each ambassador would struggle for the highest position relative to others on all occasions, but never more so than at formal court functions' (Hamilton and Langhorne 1995: 64).

This element of diplomacy was taken very seriously. The Pope tried to settle the issue of diplomatic precedence by producing a memorandum in 1504 in which he placed himself first, followed by the kings of France, Spain, Aragon and Portugal. The memorandum failed to allay diplomatic tensions and continued to be a major source of political irritation and occasionally military brinkmanship for almost two centuries. The Congress of Vienna finally settled the issue in 1815 by establishing precedence among diplomatic envoys according to the date they presented their credentials. The Congress of Aix-la-Chapelle in 1818 further clarified that representatives at conferences must sign treaties in alphabetical order.

Marriages played an important role in managing diplomatic relations by bolstering the legitimacy of new sovereigns, creating durable political alliances and managing crises. Marriage negotiations between Elisabeth I and the Duke of Anjou were framed by both domestic considerations regarding the settlement of the question

---

Box 2.5 Diplomatic ranking

A dramatic diplomatic incident caused by precedence rivalry happened in London on September 30, 1661, on the occasion of the state entry of the Swedish ambassador. The Spanish ambassador de Watteville sent his coach with a train of about forty armed servants. The coach of the French ambassador, Comte d'Estrades was also on the spot, escorted by 150 men, of whom forty carried firearms. After the Swedish ambassador had landed and taken his place in the royal coach, the French coach tried to go next, and on the Spaniards offering resistance, the Frenchmen fell upon them with drawn swords and poured in shot upon them. On learning of this incident, King Louis XIV sent instructions to his own representative at Madrid to demand redress. In case of a refusal a declaration of war was to be notified. The King of Spain, anxious to avoid a rupture, recalled de Watteville from London and announced that he had prohibited all his ambassadors from engaging in rivalry in the matter of precedence with those of the Most Christian King. The question was finally disposed of by the 'Pacte de Famille' of August 15, 1761. Article XVII stipulated that at Naples and Parma, where the sovereigns belonged to the Bourbon family, the French ambassador was always to have precedence, but at other courts the relative rank was to be determined by the date of arrival. If both arrived on the same day, then the French ambassador was to have precedence (Satow 1979: 17).

---

of the dynastic succession and larger European issues involving England's relationship with Spain (Mears 2001: 458–459). The Habsburg Empire staked out its claims to European hegemony by actively pursuing a diplomatic strategy of embedding dynastic unions into a web of political alliances, peace treaties and cordial diplomatic relations (Fichtner 1976: 247). The British attempt in the 1840s to coax the French and Spanish governments into settling the marriage question of Queen Isabella of Spain and her younger sister, the Infanta Luisa Fernanda, in a way that suited London, Paris, Madrid and Vienna, was part of the strategy to maintain the precarious diplomatic equilibrium among the main European powers (Guymer 2010).

The conclusion of secret treaties was the preferred method of protecting or advancing state interests in line with the doctrine of *raison d'état*, but was also a major source of diplomatic tensions. In 1516, Henry VIII of England entered into negotiations with Charles V of Spain directed against Francis I of France, whereupon Charles made a secret treaty with Francis. In 1668, England and the Netherlands made a secret treaty to force Louis XIV of France to make peace with Spain, but that made no impression on him. Louis had already made a secret treaty with the Emperor of Austria by which they were to divide the Spanish dominions on the death of the then king. In 1815, after Napoleon had been banished to Elba, the Allies met in Congress at Vienna to readjust the map. During the Congress, England, France and Austria entered into a secret treaty directed against Russia and Prussia, their putative allies. The secret was so little a secret that the Czar knew of it immediately after the treaty was signed. Napoleon III secretly proposed to Bismarck that France should be given Belgium and Luxemburg as the price of his friendship to the new German Confederation (Low 1918: 211–212).

In time, the Great Powers (Great Britain, Austria, Prussia, Russia and France) increasingly recognised the need for direct meetings to prevent dangerous escalation of diplomatic tensions. Conference diplomacy had its modern origins in the congresses of Osnabrück and Münster that restored peace in Europe through the

1648 Peace of Westphalia after thirty years of religious conflict (see also Chapter 4). This was followed by the congress of Utrecht in 1712–1713 that brought together 83 plenipotentiaries to resolve the issue of European hegemony brought about by the question of the Spanish succession (Meerts and Beeuwkes 2008). Most importantly, the Concert of Europe (→ glossary) established in the aftermath of the 1814 Vienna settlement of the Napoleonic Wars introduced the practice of regular face-to-face consultation among the leaders of the Great Powers. The five powers met on forty-one occasions to address a number of thorny diplomatic issues concerning matters in Spain, Greece and Belgium. In so doing, the congress system helped prevent a direct conflict between the Great Powers until the Crimean War in 1856 (see Box 2.6).

An interesting consequence of the nineteenth-century conference diplomacy was the articulation of a rudimentary doctrine of the *raison de système* (→ glossary), that is, the acceptance by states with enough power of the moral obligation to pursue their interests with prudence and restraint so that serious damage to the functioning of the international society could be avoided. A disgraceful application of this principle was reflected in the diplomatic support lent by European leaders to the idea of not allowing colonial disputes to unsettle the balance of power (→ glossary) on the continent (see Box 2.7). They implemented this doctrine by refraining from providing support

---

Box 2.6 The Concert of Europe in action

The London Conference on Grecian Affairs (1827–1832), an ongoing conference at the ambassadorial level and the first of its kind, was set up to solve the Greek Question (preventing the Greek rebellion against the Ottoman rulers from descending into a great power war) once and for all. The ambassadors negotiated a French occupation of the Greek mainland, and the constitution, frontiers, population and even king of the new state. Such a thing – jointly midwifing the birth of a nation-state – had never been done before. On top of that, here it was done deliberatively: proposals were put forward and debated out of the heat and light of high politics. Because the negotiators did not constantly have to keep their eye on Russia they could freely discuss the problem. Moreover, the minutes and final protocols were made public, and were referred to by the Great Powers in the war diplomacy (Mitzen 2005: 13–14).

Box 2.7 Colonial partition of Africa

The Berlin West Africa Conference involved a series of negotiations between 15 November 1884 and 26 February 1885, in which the major European nations met to decide all questions connected with the Congo River basin in Central Africa. The conference, proposed by Portugal in pursuance of its special claim to control of the Congo estuary, was necessitated by the jealousy and suspicion with which the great European powers viewed one another's attempts at colonial expansion in Africa. The general act of the Conference of Berlin declared the Congo River basin to be neutral (a fact that in no way deterred the Allies from extending the war into that area in World War I); guaranteed freedom for trade and shipping for all states in the basin; forbade slave trading; and rejected Portugal's claims to the Congo River estuary – thereby making possible the founding of the independent Congo Free State, to which Great Britain, France and Germany had already agreed in principle (Encyclopædia Britannica 2011).

to colonial resistance movements and by occasionally engaging in partition by agreement of colonial spoils (Darwin 2001: 9).

Summary

- Ancient diplomatic interactions were conducted on an *ad hoc* basis. The patterns of diplomatic representation, communication and negotiation were largely influenced by the perceived levels of power asymmetry among the various political entities. Imperial powers primarily used diplomacy to establish and maintain their political, religious or military superiority over neighbours or any other groups with which they interacted.
- Religious unity served to establish a universalistic foundation for regulating diplomatic relations in the early Middle Ages. In Europe, most diplomatic exchanges during this period were conducted by nuncii and procurators. However, unlike nuncii, procurators were given full powers (*plena potestas*) to enter into private contracts and to negotiate agreements on behalf of their leaders.
- The establishment of the modern institution of the resident ambassador was the result of the rise of the secular sovereign state after the 1648 Peace of Westphalia and the growing need for 'continuous and confidential' negotiation as a means of preventing dangerous diplomatic escalations among the Great Powers. The broader discretion that resident ambassadors enjoyed in pursuing their missions was accompanied by a gradual consolidation of their diplomatic immunities first on a religious, then on a legal and practical basis.
- After the Congress of Vienna, conference diplomacy emerged as an effective method of conflict management in the nineteenth century. By making visible the balance of power to those who constituted it, the Concert of Europe encouraged self-restraint among its members.

Study questions

- How do ancient Greek, Roman and Egyptian methods of diplomatic representation differ from each other? What factors may explain these differences?
- How did religion shape diplomatic methods of conflict management in the ancient versus medieval times? What diplomatic contribution did the Concert of Europe make to conflict management in the nineteenth century?
- Diplomacy established permanent institutions of representation only at the end of the fifteenth century. What explains this slow development?
- What factors enabled the rise of diplomatic immunity in the modern period? How was the issue addressed in the ancient and medieval periods?
- How important was the issue of diplomatic prestige during the Middle Ages?
- What challenges did diplomatic communication face in the medieval versus the modern period?

Recommended further reading

Berridge, Geoff, H. M. A. Keens-Soper and Thomas G. Otte. 2001. *Diplomatic theory from Machiavelli to Kissinger: Studies in diplomacy*. Houndsmill, Basingstoke, Hampshire and New York: Palgrave.
This book offers an introductory guide for students to four centuries of diplomatic thought through the writings of major scholars, statesmen, international lawyers and historians.

Hamilton, Keith and Richard Langhorne. 1995. *The practice of diplomacy: Its evolution, theory, and administration*. London and New York: Routledge.
This volume tracks the historical development of diplomatic relations and methods from the earliest period up to their current transformations in the late twentieth century, showing how they have changed to encompass new technological advances and the needs of modern international environments.

Kissinger, Henry. 1994. *Diplomacy*. New York: Simon & Schuster.
This is an seminal book that describes how the art of diplomacy has created the world in which we live, and how the United States' approach to foreign affairs has always differed vastly from that of other nations.

Nicolson, Harold. 1988. *The evolution of diplomatic method: Cassell history*. London: Cassell.
Written by a well-reputed British diplomat, this classic text offers an insightful historical overview of diplomacy in Ancient Greece and Rome, Renaissance Italy, seventeenth-century France, and the twentieth century.

Satow, Ernest Mason. 1979. *Satow's guide to diplomatic practice*. 5th edn. London and New York: Longman.
An international classic, this volume provides a comprehensive survey of the rules, laws and conventions covering the conduct of diplomacy, not only between individual nations, but also through international organisations.

3 The new diplomacy after World War I

Chapter objectives

- To familiarise readers with the historical justifications for the new diplomacy in the post-World-War-I period.
- To understand the institutional legacy and limitations of the new diplomatic principles on current methods of international engagement.

Introduction

The patterns of diplomatic engagement among European powers during the eighteenth and nineteenth centuries were described by Harold Nicolson as the 'old diplomacy' (→ glossary) on the basis of five characteristics. In the first place, Europe was regarded as the most important of all continents. Indeed, it was generally understood that no war could become a major war if none of the five major European powers was involved. Second, the Great Powers were greater than the Small Powers, since they 'possessed a more extended range of interests, wider responsibilities, and, above all, more money and more guns' (Nicolson 1988 [1954]: 74). This global hierarchy did, however, imply a third principle, namely that the Great Powers had a common responsibility for the conduct of the smaller powers and the maintenance of peace. A joint intervention by the Great Powers in a small-state conflict was generally accepted to prevent the conflict from developing in a Great-Power crisis (for more details on the European balance-of-power system, see Chapter 8).

Fourth, the preservation of peace in the Westphalian international order required a professional diplomatic service of high standards of education and experience. The composition of diplomatic corps during this period was predominantly of aristocratic origin, a fact that allowed diplomats to develop a corporate identity independent of their national identity. Fifth, 'continuous and confidential' negotiation was essential for successfully managing relations between the main powers. This was made possible by the fact that the parties generally remained rational and courteous, since public expectations and time pressure had little influence on negotiations. In turn, this resulted in agreements that were 'no hasty improvisations or empty formulas, but documents considered and drafted with care' (Nicolson 1988 [1954]: 77).

The methods of the 'old diplomacy' were gradually exported by European powers all over the world. Throughout the nineteenth century, the network of international diplomatic relations continued to expand to the extent that by 1914 there were forty-one British missions abroad, nineteen of which were outside of Europe (Hamilton and Langhorne 1995: 110). However, the expansion of diplomatic relations was often complicated by local or regional political situations. In Asia, and to some extent in Africa, local rulers were often reluctant to open their countries to alien influences and political structures were sometimes irreconcilable with the Westphalian principle of territorial sovereignty. In the Far East, on the other hand, European powers needed, at times, to employ their superior military capabilities to secure permanent representation.

The World War I (WWI) significantly altered modern diplomacy. Against the backdrop of its alleged role in precipitating the immense devastation brought about by the war, the 'old diplomacy' suffered a huge reputational blow. Critics claimed the root of the problem lay with 'the commercial and imperial rivalries of the recent past, the concomitant arms races, the pursuit of balance-of-power policies, [and especially] the secret treaties and conventions which has underpinned and buttressed the pre-war alliances and ententes' (Hamilton and Langhorne 1995: 136). In short, the entire diplomatic profession was blamed for being unable to halt the drift towards war and strong calls to action were heard for a fundamental revision of diplomatic practices and institutions.

The transition from the old to 'new diplomacy' (→ glossary) was prepared by three other factors. First, there was a widespread desire for colonial expansion among the Great Powers, especially Germany, which significantly affected foreign policy. However, the balance of power limited this desire – there was a general recognition that acquiring too much would be imprudent and harmful for the diplomatic relations between the Great Powers. Territorial expansion and colonial wars put significant strains on diplomatic relations from two different angles: it both intensified rivalry among the Great Powers for colonial acquisitions and boosted claims to self-determination among the colonies.

Second, the rapid increase in the speed of communication exerted a considerable influence on the old methods of diplomatic interaction and negotiation. Before the development of new communication technologies (e.g., the telegraph, telephone), it took many months for messages to be sent, received and answered and it was common for ambassadors to receive detailed instructions for their missions. Often, this meant that diplomats 'missed opportunity after opportunity' because they 'spent their time writing brilliant reports on situations that had entirely altered by the time their dispatches arrived' (Nicolson 1988: 82). The number, urgency and complexity of issues to be discussed between governments thus demanded more frequent and direct contact between foreign secretaries, hence the growing importance of bilateral or multilateral conferences as a new form of conduct of diplomatic relations.

Third, the rising influence of the United State in global affairs also meant that the rules of diplomatic conduct had to adjust accordingly, especially since Americans were deeply distrustful of the European diplomatic methods. The concept of 'new diplomacy' actually gained historical importance once introduced by the US President Woodrow Wilson towards the end of WWI. In essence, the American diplomatic creed rested on 'the belief that it was possible to apply to the conduct of *external* affairs, the ideas and practices which, in the conduct of *internal* affairs, had for generations been regarded as the essentials of liberal democracy' (Nicolson 1988: 84).

Against the backdrop of WWI, these factors came together to facilitate new think-ing about the goals and methods of diplomatic interaction. The proponents of 'new diplomacy' argued that foreign policy could not rely upon secrecy and balance of power. They advocated, instead, three new guiding principles of diplomatic conduct that have remained valid to the present day: public accountability as a means of ensur-ing that foreign policy stays anchored in popular consent (especially in the context of democratic states); self-determination as an extension at the level of states of the liberal principle of individual rights; and collective security as a mechanism for eliminating the arbitrary use of force. This chapter will review the evolution of these three critical features of the new diplomacy, examine their impact on the role of modern diplomats and assess the extent to which the three initial promises have been delivered.

Open covenants of peace: accountable diplomacy

The case for accountability

Wilson placed on top of his famous Fourteen Points (→ glossary) the demand for 'open covenants of peace, openly arrived at, after which there shall be no private international understandings of any kind but diplomacy shall proceed always frankly and in the public view' (Wilson 22 January 1918). The emphasis put on transparency and accountability was not accidental as it revealed a deep clash between two impor-tant schools of thought, which WWI brought fully to light.

On the European side, transparency was seen as deeply problematic on two accounts. On the one hand, diplomacy traditionally constituted a royal prerogative, one of the last remaining divine attributes of monarchs and hence, the argument went, it could not be subject to public scrutiny, even within constitutional monar-chies. On the other hand, the history of war and conflict in Europe shaped among policy-makers an understanding of foreign affairs as a self-contained field, largely immune to methods of domestic policy. For this reason, diplomacy, it was argued, required sophisticated management strategies to be effective, which went beyond the comprehension of the common citizen. On this basis, excessive transparency and accountability was perceived to run the risk of crippling diplomatic decision-making and of unnecessarily fuelling international tensions.

On the American side, neither argument made much sense, partly because of the more democratic character of the US political system at that time, and partly because of the country's unique geographical position. In his farewell address, George Washington clearly warned his fellow country people of the dangers of imitating the European diplomatic ambitions and methods:

> Why, by interweaving our destiny with that of any part of Europe, entangle our peace and prosperity in the toils of European ambition, rivalship [sic], interest, humor or caprice? ... I hold the maxim no less applicable to public than to pri-vate affairs, that honesty is always the best policy.
>
> (Washington 1924)

These principles did not stop Americans from engaging in their own version of expan-sionist diplomacy in the Western Hemisphere under the authority of the Monroe doctrine (→ glossary), but congressional oversight of US foreign policy helped con-solidate the belief in the validity of democratic constraints on diplomacy.

Deeply rooted in the liberal tradition, the idea that all international treaties should be transparently negotiated and ratified by parliaments like all other domestic laws came thus to be seen as the best protection against war, especially given the context of the breakout of WWI. To what extent would Germany have been willing to support Austria in its dispute with Serbia if the treaty between them had been properly subjected to public and parliamentary scrutiny? Similarly, to what extent would Austria and Germany have stayed determined to go to war had they known about Italy's secret treaty with France, under which Italy agreed to remain neutral should Germany attack France? In the words of a close observer at the time, accountability 'would not bring Utopia, but it would make diplomacy honest, straightforward, clean; it would make almost impossible the chicanery, fraud, intrigue that for centuries have deluged Europe in blood and brought misery' (Low 1918: 220).

By insisting that state actors engage each other in conditions of transparency and accountability, Wilson's call has had an enduring impact on diplomacy and has remained manifest to the present day. At the same time, the original promise that 'diplomacy shall proceed always frankly and in the public view' has arguably remained unfulfilled (Wilson 22 January 1918). It is not that diplomatic institutions lack parliamentary oversight – most democratic countries are well advanced in this regard – but rather that diplomatic decision-making and scrutiny still takes place mainly behind closed doors, with little or only formal input from the public. This invites the question of whether a certain degree of 'democratic deficit' is not actually necessary for diplomacy to be effective as public disclosure of all reports involving diplomatic negotiations and relations may actually undermine their effectiveness.

Wilson himself had to confront this dilemma. Faced with the prospect of a protracted and fruitless peace conference (Kissinger 1994: 232), Wilson had to backtrack on his promise to have an 'open conference' in Paris and allowed the Great Powers to take control of the conference proceedings and conduct all negotiations in closed meetings. The situation aggravated to the point that it prompted a French commentator to lament that 'everything took place in darkness ... The Congress of Vienna was less secret than that in Paris' (Marquardt 2011: 86). Since Wilson's time, the principle of diplomatic accountability has become firmly institutionalised in many countries, but the fundamental question still persists: where should the line be drawn between diplomatic accountability and effectiveness? This trade-off has been addressed by the US, the EU and Iran in different ways, to be discussed further below.

Parliamentary oversight

The US has one of the strongest systems of parliamentary oversight of the executive branch in foreign policy-making. Indeed, the US Congress can control foreign policy through two specialised committees: the Senate Committee on Foreign Relations and the House Committee on Foreign Affairs. These committees oversee the foreign policy decisions of the US President and they authorise the US Department of State's budget. The Senate Committee on Foreign Relations is responsible, for instance, for overseeing the foreign policy agencies of the US government, including the Department of State, the US Agency for International Development, the Millennium Challenge Corporation and the Peace Corps. The Committee also reviews and considers all diplomatic nominations and international treaties, as well as any piece of legislation relating to US foreign policy. For this purpose, it organises regular hearings and publishes reports on special issues (US Senate Committee on Foreign Relations 2011).

In addition to these two specialised committees, the Congress exercises oversight over foreign policy through a few other bodies. The Select Intelligence Committee monitors the activities of the CIA and other Intelligence agencies, the House National Security Committee and the Senate Armed Services Committees deal with defense matters, the House Ways and Means Committee and the Senate Finance Committee give advice on matters related to international trade, while the Appropriation Committees of the House and Senate frequently have legislation reviewed pertaining to foreign aid. The requirement for the executive branch to report all its commitments abroad, the sixty-day time limit on how long the US President may deploy military forces abroad without congressional authorisation, the budgetary restrictions on foreign policy funding and the committee oversight system are powerful instruments of congressional control of the US diplomatic agenda, but their relevance must not be overstated. Congressional authority in foreign affairs is often weakened by the use of legislative 'escape clauses' by the President in the name of national security, the ideological divisions between the two main parties and the advantage the executive branch enjoys in taking the initiative in foreign policy (McCormick 2005: 330–331).

Under the direction of the High Representative of the Union for Foreign Affairs and Security Police (HR), the European External Action Service (EEAS) acts as a body functionally autonomous from the Commission and the Council that is nevertheless accountable, through various forms, to the European Parliament and the European Commission, as well as to member states through the Foreign Affairs Council. The latter operates autonomously in day-to-day management of foreign affairs but, from a legal perspective, prepares and implements decisions that are taken by the institutions in accordance with the rules governing the policy field concerned. For example, when Common Security and Defence Policy (CSDP) is concerned, the Council retains decision-making authority. The policies enacted by the EEAS are formulated in part by the Foreign Affairs Council which, while chaired by the HR, provides the mandate for his/her work. Despite her chairmanship role, she must, as a matter of legal principle, remain silent. There is, however, much leeway as to how silent the HR must in fact remain in the decision-making.

Though the European Parliament only held a formally consultative role in the drafting of the EEAS establishing mandate, the EP exerts influence over the EEAS through budgetary control, access to confidential information and high-level personnel vetting – an institutional architecture that suggests a gradual empowerment of the Parliament in determining the EU's external relations. First, Parliament and Commission maintain full budgetary control of the EEAS, over operational and administrative budgets, established through the newly created role of a Chief Operating Officer for administrative and budgetary questions who internally oversees the expenses, costs and organisation of the EEAS. The European Commission is in charge of the operational expenditures of the budget and these remain within the Commission section of the budget. Indeed, as declared in the Council Decision 2010/427/EU, the Foreign Affairs Committee and the Budgets Committee bureaus have stronger scrutiny rights over Common Foreign and Security Policy (CFSP) missions financed out of the EU budget (Council of the EU 26 July 2010).

Second, the Parliament is involved in evaluating, falling short of formally approving, high-ranking diplomatic personnel in EU delegations around the world. The auditions of diplomatic personnel by the EP are only allowed after their appointment and before their deployment (EU High Representative 8 July 2010: para 5). The European Commission President has acquired a new prerogative, through the Lisbon Treaty changes, of dismissal of members of the Commission, which includes the HR. This prerogative endows some basic influence to the executive body of the EU and by extension to the European Parliament. Third, Parliament has the right to be informed on CFSP and CSDP developments. Indeed, written into the High Representative's mandate, and in accordance with Article 36 of the Treaty on EU (TEU), is 'to regularly consult the European Parliament on the main aspects and basic choices of the CFSP' and to 'ensure that the views of the European Parliament are duly taken into consideration' (Council of the EU 2010: Preamble para 6).

In sum, parliamentary oversight remains strongest at the budgetary level and rather weak at the substantive policy-making level. As noted, Parliament does not hold strong sway over high-level appointments, Parliament's requests for briefings by appointed representatives must not necessarily be granted, the HR maintains control over the sharing of confidential information with MEPs and many substantive policy directives come from other bodies.

In the Iranian theocratic system, the Supreme Leader of the Islamic Revolution retains the final word on foreign policy, but several major officers are responsible for foreign policy drafting: the Supreme Leader, the President as chair of the High Council for National Security (HCNS), the Head of the Expediency Council and the Foreign Minister. With the HCNS serving as 'the nerve centre of policymaking in Iran and the key body in which foreign policy is debated', the President has 'undoubted primacy' for the direction of foreign policy (Jones 2009: 99). Parliamentary oversight on foreign policy-making remains rather weak, with most policy being formulated in these bodies of the executive branch and ultimately decided upon by the Supreme Leader. One mechanism of parliamentary involvement is the participation of the Speaker of Parliament in the High Council for National Security, which formulates the foreign, military and security policies of Iran.

More substantially, the Parliament, known as the Majlis, serves as a forum for the discussion of foreign policy issues and seeks to indirectly affect the executive policy, especially through committees such as the Foreign Affairs Committee. For example, the Majlis can formally request clarification relating to the executive diplomatic actions and, according to a constitutional clause, has the authority to approve or reject international treaties, memoranda of understanding and contracts entered into by the executive. Parliament does retain the authority to summon the President or the Foreign Minister, though this power is rarely used and its ramifications limited. In an unprecedented request since the establishment of the Islamic republic in 1979, the Iranian President Ahmadinejad was questioned in March 2012 by Parliament on his foreign and domestic policies, facing accusations of challenging the authority of the Supreme Leader.

In June 2011, in response to the Foreign Minister Ali Akbar Salehi's making a controversial nomination as his deputy, thirty-three Iranian legislators petitioned the speaker of the Majlis for the Minister's impeachment. The parliamentary impeachment process was cancelled only when Salehi's nominee submitted his resignation

(Bozorgmehr 21 June 2011). Finally, the Council of Guardians, which consists of six theologians appointed by the Supreme Leader and six jurists nominated by the judiciary and approved by parliament, remains the most influential decision-making body on domestic matters but plays only an indirect, supporting role in the shaping of foreign policy. Its role is limited to formally ensuring that the President's diplomatic initiatives do not contradict the constitution and the laws of Islam. In practice, the Council powers are 'usually of a technical nature and largely deal with Iran's bilateral agreements with other countries' (Jones 2009: 100).

Self-determination: equality and democracy

The case for self-determination

Woodrow Wilson's vision of the post-war order outlined in a series of addresses to the US Congress drew on two related principles, both deeply rooted in the American liberal tradition of political egalitarianism and democratic rights: the first stated that all sovereign entities, small nations and the Great Powers alike, should be entitled to the same treatment and rights in their relations with each other, while the second contended that political institutions, whether national or international, should be based on the 'consent of the governed' (see Box 3.1).

Wilson's call was nothing less than revolutionary for diplomacy. On the one hand, he drew a clear line against colonial and imperial forms of government by insisting that no state could claim sovereign authority over any other state. On the other hand, he implied that foreign policy should concern itself not only with traditional matters of inter-state negotiation, but it should also aim to reach deeper and foster 'regime change' (a term which he, of course, did not use at the time) when the rights of the people are abused. To be sure, neither the equality nor the democratic version of the self-determination principle was thoroughly pursued at the end of the war. Not only did the US decline to stay engaged in European affairs through the newly established League of Nations, but the inherent tensions and contradictions of the principle also proved difficult to handle. The principle of sovereign equality risked, for instance, putting the US on a diplomatic collision course with its European allies, especially Britain and France, who were predictably very protective of their colonial empires.

Box 3.1 The Wilsonian concept of self-determination

The equality of nations upon which peace must be founded if it is to last must be an equality of rights; the guarantees exchanged must neither recognize nor imply a difference between big nations and small, between those that are powerful and those that are weak. Right must be based upon the common strength, not upon the individual strength, of the nations upon whose concert peace will depend ... And there is a deeper thing involved than even equality of right among organized nations. No peace can last, or ought to last, which does not recognize and accept the principle that governments derive all their just powers from the consent of the governed, and that no right anywhere exists to hand peoples about from sovereignty to sovereignty as if they were property.

(Wilson 1917)

The diplomatic compromise was to restrict the application of the principle to Europe, especially to the territories of the Austro-Hungarian Empire. The latter's disintegration led to the rise of four new states in Central Europe (Austria, Hungary, Czechoslovakia and Yugoslavia) in addition to the five already established following the withdrawal of Russia from the war (Estonia, Latvia, Lithuania, Finland and Poland). Self-determination for non-European peoples was temporarily 'entrusted to nations who by reason of their resources, their experience or their geographical position [could] best undertake this responsibility', that is, to prepare the former colonies for self-government (League of Nations 1924: Article 22). After World War II (WWII), the UN modelled its trusteeship system after the League's mandate framework and officially completed its mission with the termination of the Palau's trusteeship status in 1994.

The translation of the principle of self-determination from a theoretical construct into a diplomatic strategy revealed three major limitations. First, if strictly applied, self-determination could lead to endless political fragmentation as no partition formula would likely be able to accommodate the variety of claims to be potentially raised in territories with entrenched ethnic or religious divisions. Second, self-determination might also prove a recipe for regional instability by fuelling irredentist claims, stirring regional rivalries and offering the Great Powers cheap diplomatic opportunities to exploit internal divisions as it happened with Nazi Germany in the late 1930s (see the case study in Chapter 9). Third, if the 'consent of the governed' is a principle of great relevance not only for domestic but also international politics, does the international community have a responsibility to implement it in countries where the principle is lacking or it is deficient?

Legal formulations

In an attempt to address these tensions, the international community has since adopted a set of legal measures that aim to clarify the scope of the right to self-determination and to limit possible abuses. Article 2.1 and Article 55 of the UN Charter gives, for instance, full recognition to 'the principle of equal rights and self-determination of peoples' (UN 1945). The 1970 Declaration of Principles of International Law Concerning Friendly Relations is generally viewed as the most authoritative document on the matter as it not only recognises self-determination as a basic principle of international law, but it also specifies acceptable methods for its achievement such as 'the establishment of a sovereign and independent State, the free association or integration with an independent State or the emergence into any other political status freely determined by a people' (UN General Assembly 24 October 1970). The self-determination principle now informs or complements other principles of international law and hence it has to be read in conjunction with the principle of non-intervention, prohibition of the use of force, equality of states and equality of peoples within a state (Brownlie 2003: 555).

The diplomatic response to the question of secession has embraced three different forms. The potential risks of border revisions for regional stability prompted, for instance, the Organization of African Unity to adopt a pragmatic resolution in 1964, which urged the protection of the integrity of colonial borders, regardless of ethnic divisions, based on the *uti possidetis* principle (→ glossary). For others, secession without constitutional authorisation is only a remedial right, a last resort measure against large-scale and persistent violations of basic human rights, hence the humanitarian intervention in Kosovo. Finally, 'de facto' independence is not the same as 'de facto' sovereign statehood, as the latter implies 'a legal status attaching to a certain state of affairs by virtue of certain rules' (Crawford 2006: 5). In other words, the right to self-determination by secession is insolubly linked to conditions of collective recognition of statehood.

The latter point brings back Wilson's indirect reference to the necessity of promoting democracy as a long-term solution to achieving international peace. Wilson recognised the potential risks of this approach by making plain that, whereas self-determination was a universal principle, the same did not necessarily apply to democracy: 'I am not fighting for democracy except for the peoples that want democracy ... If they don't want it, that is none of my business' (quoted in Thompson 2010: 35). The notion of 'regime change' stayed relatively dormant until the end of the Cold War, but it has since strongly resurfaced through the US' commitment to spreading democracy worldwide either by peaceful or military means. The test for diplomats and policy-makers alike remains nevertheless the same as in the time of Wilson: how to avoid the notion of democratic peace turning into a 'democratic war' (→ glossary) under the ideological guise of liberal-expansionist policies.

Conference diplomacy

Another important consequence of the self-determination principle has been the rise of conference diplomacy. To be sure, these forms of diplomatic engagement had been around long before WWI (see the case of the Concert of Europe on page 25). However, transportation, financial and security issues limited the use of conference diplomacy in the ancient and medieval period primarily to issues of post-conflict settlement. The number of international conferences steadily increased in the nineteenth century, but they really exploded after WWI (see Table 3.1). This was partially

Table 3.1 Number of international conferences by decade, 1840–1939

	Number of conferences
1840–1849	5
1950–1859	22
1860–1869	75
1870–1879	149
1880–1889	284
1890–1899	469
1900–1909	1,082
1910–1919 (WWI)	974
1920–1929	2,913
1930–1939	3,655

Source: (Leguey-Feilleux 2009: 275)

the result of the growing number of actors and issues that required diplomatic resolution ranging from the territorial delimitation of the new states to the mitigation of concerns regarding post-war reparations or to the negotiation of issues of naval disarmament.

In addition, many leaders held the belief that international conflict was essentially the result of communication failure, which could be avoided if those ultimately responsible for making foreign policy decisions would tackle the issues in face-to-face meetings rather than indirectly through diplomats. This attitude reinforced confidence in the value of conference diplomacy as an instrument of crisis management, especially since a number of Great Powers such as the US, the Soviet Union and later Germany did not take part, at the time, in multilateral institutional frameworks such as the League of Nations (→ glossary).

Aside from crisis management, which has distinctly remained its core function – as illustrated, for instance, by the multitude of summits held by EU leaders during the eurozone crisis in 2010–2013 – conference diplomacy has evolved to cover other important aspects of diplomatic activity. From a *consultative* perspective, conference diplomacy often serves as a forum for exchange of information and general discussion of issues of common interest. For example, the Nuclear Security Summits held in Washington in 2010 brought together fifty global leaders to discuss a working plan for improving global nuclear security (US State Department 2010). From a *negotiating* perspective, conference diplomacy allows parties to review progress under an agreement concluded earlier or to prepare a new draft treaty. The annual Conference of the Parties (COP) to the UN Framework Convention on Climate Change (UNFCCC) provides, for instance, a forum of discussion to about 1,000 delegates from over eighty countries to review progress in implementing the provisions of the 1997 Kyoto Protocol and to negotiate a successor treaty.

The benefit of multilateral inclusiveness of conference diplomacy comes though at a price. Keeping large numbers of delegations together is expensive and may lead to serious logistical complications. This is why multilateral conferences are by necessity short-term events and this often results in the issue under discussion being left undecided. The Law of the Sea Conference took, for instance, nine years to complete its work, while the World Trade Organization (WTO) Doha negotiation round failed to make progress more than a decade after its launch. In addition, in the age of media saturation, multilateral conferences are prone to politicisation. They may increase expectations for leaders to achieve spectacular results, oftentimes in blatant disregard of the advice of professional diplomats. At the same time, the publicity generated by these conferences may invite attempts by various groups to hijack the conference by bringing up highly divisive and ideological issues that are mostly irrelevant for the topic of the conference.

What are the factors that make conference diplomacy a success or a failure? First of all, preparation is essential, especially for world conferences that generally require three or four years of preparatory work. The parties convening a conference usually establish a preparatory committee which is supposed to write and negotiate a preliminary draft, put together a detailed conference agenda and make sure all relevant stakeholders, including non-governmental organisations (NGOs) or international organisations, are duly consulted (Leguey-Feilleux 2009: 281). Cultural and ideological compatibility may also play an important role, especially during top-level summits between heads of state and government, by potentially reinforcing misperceptions and raising unwarranted expectations. The failure of President Kennedy's encounter with the Soviet leader Nikita Khrushchev in Vienna in June 1961 has been, for instance, largely credited to the inability of the two leaders to overcome their ideological differences.

The effectiveness of conference diplomacy also lies with the degree to which the parties involved possess the critical capacity necessary to translate the conference decisions into concrete policies. The G20 has recently emerged, for instance, as a key diplomatic forum of global negotiations largely because its flexible institutional structure and strong joint economic capacity allows it to deliver good results, currently on financial matters and perhaps on environmental issues as well in the future. Despite lacking a permanent institutional structure and formal competences, the G8 is nevertheless able to exercise strong leadership in global governance by often delegating the implementation of its decisions to a network of key international institutions (the IMF, the World Bank, the Organisation for Economic Co-operation and Development (OECD), etc.) that are controlled by the G8 members (Gstöhl 2007). Finally, while broader participation in conference diplomacy may amplify coordination problems and reduce consensus opportunities, heterogeneous and autonomous representation of the main stakeholders may nevertheless prove essential in overcoming resistance in the implementation phase (Carr and Norman 2008).

Collective security: the power of law and deliberation

The case for collective security

Wilson's last of his Fourteen Points called for the establishment of a 'general association of nations … for the purpose of affording mutual guarantees of political independence and territorial integrity to great and small states alike' (Wilson 1918). This was supposed to build on and reinforce the other two diplomatic components of the new diplomacy. At the individual level, public scrutiny of diplomacy served to restrain risky behaviour of diplomatic elites by making foreign policy decision-making more transparent and accountable. At the domestic level, self-determination took aim at removing sources of political oppression, which were seen as a major cause of war. Finally, at the systemic level, collective security pledged to prevent military competition between states by facilitating mutual trust, international cooperation and peaceful settlements of international disputes. While the first two components have since taken solid roots in diplomatic practice, collective security still remains work in progress despite two bold attempts to institutionalise it, first through the League of Nations and after WWII through the UN.

Ironically, the idea of a collective security organisation emerged in Britain, the long-standing defender of balance-of-power politics, mainly because the British government wanted to secure the US' entry into WWI. In America's view it was not the absence of a balance of power that undermined international order but the pursuit of it. For Wilson, the security of the world called not for the defence of national interest or Realpolitik but rather of peace as a legal concept (Kissinger 1994: 222–223). Although the idea evoked little enthusiasm from professional diplomats, Wilson's determination to have his way, the desire of the British to retain American goodwill, and the hopes of the French that such an organisation would prove effective in policing Germany and maintaining the security of France, ensured the triumph of the league idea (Hamilton and Langhorne 1995: 158). The League of Nations was created to facilitate the peaceful resolution of disputes by disallowing member states to go to war with each other until they had exhausted the League's procedures for arbitration and conciliation.

The Covenant of the League of Nations established a number of procedures by which disputes 'likely to lead to a rupture' would be submitted by the signatories 'either to arbitration or judicial settlement or to enquiry by the [League] Council' (League of Nations 1924). The members agreed 'not to go to war with any party to the dispute which complies with the recommendations of the [Council] report' (Article 15) and 'to respect and preserve as against external aggression the territorial integrity and existing political independence of all Members of the League' (Article 10). The Covenant also introduced a major qualification to the customary right to war: the right of conquest no longer existed! The use of force was considered legitimate only for self-defence and, even then, only under limited conditions. Recourse to war was left open in two circumstances: if the Council of the League failed to reach a unanimous decision concerning the matter under dispute or if one of the parties failed to comply with the decision taken by the Council (Article 15). Member states that ignored those rules were deemed to be subject to economic sanctions and threats by the military might of the remainder of the membership.

The League's gradual inability to enforce its rules led eventually to its demise (see Box 3.2), but its key provisions were revived after WWII by the UN Charter. Article 2(4) of the Charter establishes, for instance, a general prohibition not only on the use of force, but also on the threat to use force. The Charter makes reference to only two exceptions to Article 2(4): individual or collective self-defence (Article 51), and collective security (Chapter VII). In both cases, the use of force is considered legitimate as long as the objective of the intervention is 'to conserve and defend values already enjoyed' not 'to attack and acquire values held by another' (McDougal and Feliciano 1994: 18–19).

In other words, the Charter puts emphasis on the *preservation* not on the *transformation* of the existing territorial and political arrangements (e.g., the upholding of the Westphalian principle of sovereignty). Article 51 thus acknowledges the right of states to defend themselves against an armed attack, individually or collectively, but this recognition is not absolute. In fact, the right of self-defence has a residual character since all UN member states are supposed to be protected by the shield of

---

Box 3.2 The Abyssinia crisis

The Italian invasion of Abyssinia (Ethiopia) in 1935, in open defiance of the League of Nations' covenant, forced a difficult choice upon France and Britain between supporting the League and alienating Italy; or allowing the League to be flouted and depriving it of any future role in international politics in order to maintain Italian friendship. The attempt of the French and British diplomatic services to compromise in order to preserve both the League of Nations as a body potentially capable of imposing collective punishment, and Italy as a significant opponent of Nazi expansionist plans over Austria and the Balkans, ended in the worst of all possible outcomes: the League destroyed and Italy on Germany's side. The League did impose arms and trade sanctions against Italy, but they only lasted seven months and did not include severe restrictions on materials required for the military campaign (Ristuccia 2000).

collective security. Under Article 51, the occurrence of an 'armed attack' is a manda-
tory requirement for the legitimate exercise of the right of self-defence. According to
this logic, no pre-emptive action against a potential threat can be considered lawful
under the UN Charter. Nevertheless, customary international law appears to be more
generous on this issue: anticipatory self-defence (→ glossary) could be legitimately
invoked as long as it meets two conditions, of necessity and proportionality. In other
words, a state contemplating a pre-emptive action will need to demonstrate that the
threat of an armed attack by another state is imminent, and that the response will be
proportional to the threat.

Diplomatic challenges

The interpretation and enforcement of the Charter's provisions has been entrusted
to the Security Council, the main UN executive organ. The structure of the Council
reflects the international distribution of power at the end of World War II, a situation that is being increasingly resented by a number of established or emerging
powers including India, Brazil or Japan (for more on this issue, see Chapter 12). Five
permanent seats of the Security Council belong to the winning powers (US, Britain,
France, Soviet Union/Russia and China), while the remaining ten seats are assigned
by rotation to other members of the UN. The five permanent members also granted
themselves the right to veto decisions considered by the Council as per Article 27
of the Charter (UN 1945). These two features of the Security Council were meant
to address one of the major weaknesses of the League of Nations: the alienation or
exclusion of a major power from the decision-making body responsible for setting
and implementing rules of international conduct.

From a diplomatic perspective, collective security raises two important challenges:
first, how to convince the Great Powers to go along with it and, second, what to do in
case they refuse? Formal equality and participation in the debates of the League of
Nations did not render the power factor irrelevant. In fact, the League's procedure
for settling disputes was rather a 'system of detours, all of which led to one or other
of the following two issues: agreement or disagreement between Great Britain, Italy,
France and Germany' (Carr 2001: 98). The UN veto system (→ glossary) introduced
by the UN Charter addressed this limitation by offering major powers strong incentives to stay engaged in the system. On the negative side, it allows them to block any
resolution perceived as detrimental to their interests, or to their allies. This is one of
the main reasons why the list of violations of the UN Charter framework by the permanent members and their allies used to be so extensive during the Cold War.

Current debates concerning the extension of the concept of collective security
to matters involving pre-emptive action and humanitarian intervention (→ glossary)
reinforce the point that power cannot be easily tamed by institutional frameworks.
Ultimately, it may matter less whether the Security Council will have the legal power
to authorise pre-emptive or humanitarian interventions in accordance with Articles
41 and 42 (see Box 3.3), but rather whether the decision will satisfy the interests of
the permanent five members of the Security Council. In all fairness, diplomats at the
UN should act cautiously in asking the Great Powers to take on responsibilities for
which they do not seem themselves prepared. The real test of diplomatic skill is not to
achieve laborious but inapplicable legal frameworks, but to diligently build coalitions
inside and outside the Security Council that can deliver results.

Box 3.3 Recommendations of the UN High Level Panel on Threats, Challenges, and Change for authorising the use of force

- *Seriousness of threat:* is the threatened harm to state or human security of a kind, and sufficiently clear and serious, to justify prima facie the use of military force? In the case of internal threats, does it involve genocide and other large-scale killing, ethnic cleansing or serious violations of international humanitarian law, actual or imminently apprehended?
- *Proper purpose:* is it clear that the primary purpose of the proposed military action is to halt or avert the threat in question, whatever other purposes or motives may be involved?
- *Last resort:* has every non-military option for meeting the threat in question been explored, with reasonable grounds for believing that other measures will not succeed?
- *Proportional means*: are the scale, duration and intensity of the proposed military action the minimum necessary to meet the threat in question?
- *Balance of consequences:* is there a reasonable chance of the military action being successful in meeting the threat in question, with the consequences of action not likely to be worse than the consequences of inaction?

(UN 2004: para 207)

The solution to the conundrum therefore rests with diplomats building the strongest case possible in favour or against the legitimacy of the collective security action. This would involve three steps. First, the decision has to be anchored on firm legal foundations drawing on the most relevant legal standards in the UN Charter and customary international law. Second, the justification for or against the intervention has to meet the highest moral standards of the international community with respect to the use of force, such as the guidelines defined by the UN High Level Panel on Threats, Challenges, and Change. Third and most critically, diplomats have to make sure their arguments are thoroughly persuasive by meeting conditions of deliberative legitimacy (→ glossary) (Bjola 2005: 279–280). This implies the facts supporting their case are truthful and complete, as informed by the best evidence available; all affected parties are allowed to participate in the debate with equal rights to present an argument or to challenge a validity claim; and finally, participating actors show genuine interest in using argumentative reasoning for reaching an understanding on the decision to use force (Bjola 2009: 76). This diplomatic approach may not be able to override the interests of the Great Powers all the time, but it could make it much more difficult for them to justify their actions purely in terms of national interest.

Summary

- The new diplomacy emerged from the ashes of WWI and drew inspiration from three principles: *public accountability* as a means of ensuring that foreign policy stays anchored in popular consent; *self-determination* as the extension at the level of states of the liberal principle of individual rights; and *collective security* as a mechanism for restricting the arbitrary use of force.
- The demand for public accountability has translated into the requirement for governments to make frequent statements on foreign policy, submit all treaties

and diplomatic engagements to the Parliament, accept rigorous oversight of foreign affairs by specialised parliamentary committees and promote competitive recruitment for the selection of diplomatic personnel.

- Self-determination introduced the principle of sovereign equality according to which no state could claim sovereign authority over any other state. At the same time, it planted the idea that foreign policy should concern itself not only with traditional matters of inter-state negotiation, but it should also aim to reach deeper and foster 'regime change' when the rights of the people are abused.
- Designed as a diplomatic alternative to balance-of-power politics, collective security serves to prevent military competition between states by facilitating mutual trust, international cooperation and peaceful settlements of international disputes. Originally designed to deal with violations of state sovereignty, the concept of collective security is currently under pressure to accommodate concerns of pre-emptive action and humanitarian intervention.

Study questions

- What factors facilitated the transition from the old to the new diplomacy?
- What trade-offs take place between democratic accountability and effectiveness and how have the US, the EU and Iran addressed the issue?
- What are the two components of the Wilsonian principle of self-determination and what challenges have both raised for diplomatic practice?
- How does conference diplomacy in the twentieth century differ from that of the Concert of Europe?
- What is collective security supposed to achieve, what diplomatic limitations does the principle face and what can be done to make it more effective?

Recommended further reading

Bjola, Corneliu. 2009. *Legitimising the use of force in international politics: Kosovo, Iraq and the ethics of intervention.* London and New York: Routledge.
This book examines the conditions under which the decision to use force can be reckoned as legitimate in international relations. Drawing on communicative action theory, it provides a provocative answer to the hotly contested question of how to understand the legitimacy of the use of force in international politics.

Carr, Edward Hallett. 2001. *The twenty years' crisis, 1919–1939: An introduction to the study of international relations.* Houndmills, Basingstoke, Hampshire and New York: Palgrave.
This is a classic work in international relations, which provides a powerful critique of the application of the new diplomacy to European affairs before WWII.

Crawford, James. 2006. *The creation of states in international law.* 2nd edn. Oxford: Oxford University Press.
Addressing such questions as the unification of Germany, the status of Israel and Palestine, and the continuing pressure from non-State groups to attain statehood, even, in cases like Chechnya or Tibet, against the presumptive rights of existing states, this book discusses the relation between statehood and diplomatic recognition as it has developed since the eighteenth century.

Housden, Martyn. 2011. *The League of Nations and the organization of peace.* Harlow: Pearson.
This book illustrates how an understanding of the League of Nations, its achievements and its ultimate failure to stop World War II, is central to our understanding of diplomacy and international relations in the inter-war period.

Ikenberry, G. John (ed.). 2009. *The crisis of American foreign policy: Wilsonianism in the twenty-first century.* Princeton: Princeton University Press.
This text traces the influence of the liberal internationalist tradition on the US foreign policy since the end of World War II.

4　Multiplicities of global diplomacy

Chapter objectives

- To discuss key features of global diplomacy: multiplication of issue areas and actors.
- To provide an overview of the issue areas in which diplomacy gets involved.
- To identify traditional and non-traditional diplomatic actors.
- To describe how diplomatic interaction in these issue areas contributes to the making of system-defining principles.

Introduction

This chapter continues to trace diplomacy from its beginnings to the global age. The last chapter already started dealing with an important post-WWII development, i.e. the increasing number of actors (→ glossary) and issues they get involved in. This chapter will elaborate on these observations. The multiplication of actors and the multiplication of issue areas amount to the key features of today's global diplomacy.

Whereas diplomacy traditionally dealt primarily with matters of war and peace, as well as, to a considerable extent, with economics, it now deals with *many issue areas that were previously considered domestic policy fields* only (e.g., health), or were not even regarded as policy fields of much significance at all (e.g., environment). The proliferation of issue areas goes hand in hand with the *proliferation of actors on the diplomatic stage*. Diplomacy is no longer reserved for the foreign services of states. The latter get competition from within the state, such as ministries of finance, economics or environment ministries, who tend to have easier access to specialised knowledge. In a similar vein, international civil servants – working, for instance, for a specialised UN agency or the World Bank – sometimes have a grasp of the details of an issue area that is difficult to match for foreign services, especially the ones of smaller states. The proliferation of issue areas also provides opportunities for NGOs and activists to leave a mark. They can do so, for instance, by providing detailed knowledge to a broader public. Amnesty International's and Human Rights Watch's reports on human rights abuses are a good example of this mechanism.

This chapter discusses the six major issue areas of global diplomacy: war and peace, economics, development, environment, health and migration. The discussion of each issue area follows the same pattern: we identify key actors, instruments and challenges in these fields.

War and peace

The UN Charter endorses what amounts to the paramount norm in international affairs and provides mechanisms to safeguard it. The norm is state sovereignty. The principal instruments to safeguard it are measures for the pacific settlement of disputes (Chapter 6) and enforcement measures (Chapter 7). The latter is supposed to contain the 'teeth' of the UN system, i.e. a system of collective security. The Security Council (→ glossary) is the primary organ on matters of security. It is only the Security Council that has the authority to decide upon enforcement measures. There are five permanent members, who have a veto power: China, France, Russia, the United Kingdom and the US. There are also ten non-permanent members each of whom is elected for two years.

The diplomatic resolve at the Dumberton Oaks and San Francisco Conferences, which agreed upon the UN system in the 1940s to defend state sovereignty, has to be understood in the context of its times. World politics had just experienced two world wars. Making the repetition of such a tragedy impossible in the future was taken to be the primary objective of the UN.

In the post-WWII era, inter-state conflicts are much less likely to escalate into war than in previous eras. Take the management of border conflicts, for example. There are many reasons why states quarrel with one another but a particularly explosive one, which has pre-occupied diplomacy ever since, revolves around clashing claims to territory (Vasquez 2009). Territorial conflicts underpin most of today's most troubling inter-state disputes: China claims the whole of Taiwan, the demarcation line between North Korea and South Korea has been unstable ever since partition in the aftermath of WWII, Pakistan and India are locked into a dangerous dispute over Kashmir, and Armenia and Azerbaijan quarrel over Nagorno-Karabakh. These problematic cases notwithstanding, however, post-WWII diplomacy has been, all in all, rather successful with managing and even resolving territorial disputes.

The 1975 Helsinki Final Act codified a territorial status quo norm in Europe, which greatly facilitated the resolution of long-standing territorial disputes, such as between Germany and Poland as well as Germany and the Soviet Union/Russia. In other regions, too, there is a notable agreement on the territorial status quo, at least among governments. Considering the arbitrariness of its state borders, Africa has been successful in keeping border disputes at bay. There is even the encouraging development that states sometimes submit their quarrels to the International Court of Justice for arbitration. The long-standing dispute between Cameroon and Nigeria over the Barkassi Peninsula was resolved in this way in 2008.

While the UN was founded to do something about inter-state disputes, *there have been many more intra-state disputes since the end of WWII* and these have been much more destructive than inter-state disputes. To list only the most deadly ones between 1945 and 2000, the civil war in Bangladesh in 1971 cost 1.5 million people their lives (of which a million were civilians). Just the first three years (1998–2000) of the war in the Democratic Republic of the Congo alone left 1.5 million people dead. The war that Cambodia's Pol Pot regime waged against its own people killed 1.8 million civilians. Intra-state fighting in the Sudan killed 2 million people between 1983 and 2000 alone. The staggering number of casualties during the Chinese civil war – only for the years of 1946 to 1950 – stands at 6.2 million (5 million civilians). Several internal conflicts killed a million people, again mostly civilians: Ethiopia (1962–1989), Nigeria (1967–1970), Angola (1980–1995) and Afghanistan (1990 and 2000) (Leitenberg

2006). The move away from an absolute interpretation of sovereignty and towards the responsibility to protect (R2P) (→ glossary) has to be understood with these shocking facts in mind.

The UN has struggled to find responses to these problems ever since. Legally speaking, the challenge for the UN is to find ways of managing intra-state conflicts without damaging the sovereignty pillar on which the UN is built. The latest attempt at doing so has been the endorsement of the responsibility to protect. This principle qualifies the sovereignty principle.

In 2005, the World Summit Outcome (see Box 4.1), which was adopted by the General Assembly (→ glossary), attempted to formalise humanitarian reasons for intervention when it defines the principle of responsibility to protect. In the context of this principle, sovereignty is not an absolute privilege, but its exercise is linked to a state's responsibility to protect its own population. If a state is not able to protect its population, it is the responsibility of the international community to help this

---

Box 4.1 2005 World Summit Outcome: responsibility to protect

The World Summit postulates the responsibility to protect in two paragraphs. Paragraph 138:

> Each individual State has the responsibility to protect its populations from genocide, war crimes, ethnic cleansing and crimes against humanity. This responsibility entails the prevention of such crimes, including their incitement, through appropriate and necessary means. We accept that responsibility and will act in accordance with it. The international community should, as appropriate, encourage and help States to exercise this responsibility and support the UN in establishing an early warning capability.

Paragraph 139:

> The international community, through the UN, also has the responsibility to use appropriate diplomatic, humanitarian and other peaceful means, in accordance with Chapters VI and VIII of the Charter, to help protect populations from genocide, war crimes, ethnic cleansing and crimes against humanity. In this context, we are prepared to take collective action, in a timely and decisive manner, through the Security Council, in accordance with the Charter, including Chapter VII, on a case-by-case basis and in cooperation with relevant regional organizations as appropriate, should peaceful means be inadequate and national authorities manifestly fail to protect their populations from genocide, war crimes, ethnic cleansing and crimes against humanity. We stress the need for the General Assembly to continue consideration of the responsibility to protect populations from genocide, war crimes, ethnic cleansing and crimes against humanity and its implications, bearing in mind the principles of the Charter and international law. We also intend to commit ourselves, as necessary and appropriate, to helping States build capacity to protect their populations from genocide, war crimes, ethnic cleansing and crimes against humanity and to assisting those which are under stress before crises and conflicts break out.
>
> (UN General Assembly 24 October 2005)

state. If the state is itself the perpetrator of crimes such as genocide, war crimes, ethnic cleansing and crimes against humanity, the international community has the responsibility to intervene, if necessary with measures listed in Chapter VII of the UN Charter. This sounds very far-reaching. But Chapter VII measures are to be authorised by the Security Council. In this way, it's still very much a (powerful) states' and not a populations' world. It is also telling that the Canadian government recently instructed its diplomatic service to use the R2P principle much less frequently and much more cautiously. This has happened even though Canada had been the champion of the principle in the first place and even though unfolding humanitarian catastrophes such as in Syria provide lots of reasons for taking R2P seriously.

Perhaps the most well-known piece of art in front of the UN Headquarters in New York is the sculpture entitled Non-Violence by Fredrik Reuterswärd. It depicts a giant gun with an equally giant knot in the barrel. The sculpture serves as a reminder that diplomacy ought to be about preventing violence and armed conflict. Indeed, *arms control* has been an important field of diplomacy, inside and outside the UN, since the end of WWII. Weapons of mass destruction are a particular focus of attempts to reduce and even eliminate entire categories of weapons. In current parlance, weapons of mass destruction are often referred to as CBRN: chemical, biological, radiological ('dirty bomb') and nuclear. With the exception of radiological weapons, there is a fairly dense institutional framework helping diplomacy to govern these categories of weapons. Just to highlight some of these institutions, there is the Convention on the Prohibition of the Development, Production and Stockpiling of Bacteriological and Toxin Weapons and on their Destruction (or just Biological Weapons Convention), which was signed in April 1972. There is the Convention on the Prohibition of the Development, Production, Stockpiling and Use of Chemical Weapons and on their Destruction (Chemical Weapons Convention) and the Organization for the Prohibition of Chemical Weapons (OPCW) based in The Hague. And there is the Treaty on the Non-Proliferation of Nuclear Weapons (Nuclear Non-Proliferation Treaty; NPT), whose implementation is linked to the International Atomic Energy Agency (IAEA) and the Preparatory Commission for a Comprehensive Nuclear-Test-Ban Treaty Organization (CTBTO) in Vienna. Additionally, all of these arms control regimes are connected to the Conference for Disarmament (CD) in Geneva. As far as radiological weapons ('dirty' bombs) are concerned, institutionalisation is still at a nascent state. The 2010 Nuclear Security Summit in Washington was Barack Obama's attempt to foster such an institutionalisation amid fears that terrorist networks could acquire and use radiological weapons.

This leads us to *international terrorism*. This issue has been around for quite some time. In 1994, the UN General Assembly passed a resolution that called for the elimination of international terrorism (UN General Assembly 9 December 1994). Yet since the September 11 attacks on the World Trade Center and the Pentagon, international terrorism has been pushed up the diplomatic agenda, in particular by the US and its allies. To this date, there are no instruments comparable to, say, the institutions on arms control listed above. But there have been important developments. These include the mark that counterterrorism has left on foreign services. As Kleiner observes correctly, counterterrorism

has also brought along additional tasks for diplomacy. Foreign ministries have established counter-terrorism units. They cooperate with international partners.

The State Department's counter-terrorism office, for example, tries to enhance the capacities of partner countries to resist the terrorist threat. Therefore, it developed anti-terrorism assistance, counter-terrorism finance and terrorist interdiction programs with other countries.

(Kleiner 2010: 20)

The last sentence alludes to a theme that will recur in this section again and again. Different issue areas become more and more intertwined. Counterterrorism, for example, may appear to be a narrowly confined security issue. But it is an issue that has important economic dimensions as well. The next section deals with economics in more depth.

Economics

Economics is another diplomatic issue area that has been around for a very long time. While it was usually relegated to a clear-cut second place behind war and peace in the past, economic issues have become as important, in routine diplomatic interactions even more important, than matters of war and peace.

Some of the architecture of our current economic system goes back to US-led efforts to reorganise the international economic system in the 1940s. The 1944 Bretton Woods Conference created the International Bank for Reconstruction and Development (usually simply referred to as the World Bank) and the International Monetary Fund (IMF). It was also agreed to set up an international trade organisation. With the US Congress not ratifying the agreement, the General Agreement on Tariffs and Trade (GATT) came into being as a substitute. Yet the global economic architecture evolved considerably over time. International organisations (→ glossary) such as the World Bank became important actors on the diplomatic scene as opposed to mere arenas in which state diplomacy takes place (St Clair 2006). Diplomacy negotiated new international organisations into being, such as the World Trade Organization. It also institutionalised less formalised forums designed to discuss and decide about how to develop international economic institutions further. Most importantly, what started as an informal G5 meeting at the library of the White House with delegations from the US, Germany, the United Kingdom, France and Japan, has moved via the G6 (+Italy), G7 (+Canada) and G8 (+Russia) to today's G20 (+South Africa, Mexico, Argentina, Brazil, China, South Korea, India, Indonesia, Saudi Arabia, Turkey, the EU and Australia). Arguably, even the term G20 is no longer fully adequate because there are a number of top international civil servants, mostly from the IMF and the World Bank, who participate in the meetings. Furthermore, host states of the annual summits are entitled to invite a limited number of non-member states.

The evolution of the G20 shows very well that the diplomatic architecture in the field of economics is *more flexible* than in the field of war and peace. It is not that it is much more egalitarian. The G20 still amounts to an exclusive club and, within it, some members have much more clout than others. But still, more easily amendable rules of membership and decision-making make for a steering mechanism that is more easily adaptable than, say, the Security Council where the permanent seats and the veto powers are carved into stone. In this context, it is also noteworthy that traditional state diplomacy has reached out to international business. The Global Compact, for instance, introduced at the 1999 World Economic Forum in Davos, is an attempt to link the UN and international business. It is guided by principles for business activities that are derived from broad UN goals, such as human rights and development. The World Social Forum, the annual counter-event to the World Economic Forum sessions in January each year, has also assumed an important place in the international political economy, although it understands itself very much as a counter-movement to what is going on in established forums and organisations. It is an important opportunity for NGOs to debate with one another and to infuse their ideas to a global audience. These ideas, if NGOs are successful in mobilising public opinion, do not stop at the gates of 'official' international political economy. If NGOs, for example, would not have been as adamant about the eradication of poverty as they have been, a firmly established international organisation such as the World Bank may not have moved its practices in this direction the way it has done in the last decade.

This overview of actors already shows that sovereignty, while still being a foundational principle, does not shape the international political economy the way it puts its stamp on matters of war and peace. The reason for this is fairly straightforward. Economic issues such as international trade and finance do not at all stop at the gates of the nation-state. Indeed, globalisation (→ glossary) has put the nation-state increasingly on the defensive with economic flows transcending borders and pressuring state capitals to react rather than act. Note, for instance, that more than half of the 100 biggest economies in the world are firms and not states, and this economic power leaves its mark on the international system (Kaplan 2000; Dicken 2007: 38).

Let us have a look at global trade and finance in a bit more depth. International trade has always been an important sub-field of economics and, historically, it *generated a number of innovations in diplomacy.* Perhaps most notably, diplomatic attempts to facilitate trade led to the creation of what is now often seen as the first international organisation, i.e. the Central Commission for Navigation of the Rhine. The organisation was created by the Congress of Vienna in 1815 (and is still in operation). Another important development growing out of trade has been the establishment of free trade zones and regional organisations. The European unification effort has been at the forefront of this development for some time, but regional cooperation and integration schemes are found virtually everywhere in the world by now. In some world regions, there is considerable competition among regional groupings. Take Asia, for example. There is the Association of Southeast Asian Nations (ASEAN), but there is also the South Asian Association for Regional Cooperation (SAARC) and the Asia-Pacific Economic Cooperation (APEC). To some extent, these organisations can simply be seen as sub-regional groupings. But the boundaries between these groupings are very much a political issue. Especially India and China carry out diplomatic skirmishes about who participates in what organisation. Extra-regional powers are of importance, too. The 2011 initiative for a Trans-Pacific Partnership (TPP) is a cornerstone in Washington's attempts to reach out across the Pacific and strengthen economic ties with Australia, Brunei Darussalam, Chile, Malaysia, New Zealand, Peru, Singapore and Vietnam.

Trade is a *major regionalising force.* Almost three-quarters of the merchandise exports of European states is bound for another European state. In Asia, more than half of merchandise exports are intra-regional. North America comes close to this number as well. Yet trade is also a globalising force. When it comes to Europe, Asia and North America, the reminder of these exports goes to other regions. The share of inter-regional trade in other regions, especially Africa and the Middle East, is much higher (World Trade Organization 2011). This, too, led to important diplomatic innovations. The WTO's 1994 Understanding on Rules and Procedures Governing the Settlement of Disputes is a case in point. By international standards, this arrangement makes for a very effective tool of conflict resolution. At the request of a complaining party, the Dispute Settlement Body, composed of representatives of all WTO members, establishes a panel to deal with the matter in dispute unless there is unanimity for refraining from doing so. The panel, to be composed by impartial experts, is to be accepted by the parties to the dispute unless there are 'compelling reasons' to the contrary (Article 8). The panel's report is accepted unless the Dispute Settlement Body decides against it with unanimity or one of the parties to the dispute appeals against it. In the case of an appeal, the Appellate Body, which represents WTO membership, revisits the legal interpretations by the panel. There is no possibility to appeal against the decision by the Appellate Body and there are several provisions that facilitate implementation, such as the possibility to appoint an arbitrator.

While the post-WWII increase of global commercial trade and services is remarkable, it pales compared to the finance sector. There is an obvious reason for this. In the digital age, financial transactions travel fast and effortlessly. From April 2007 to April 2010, for example, the *trend of higher and higher turnovers at global foreign exchange markets* continued unabated. It grew from a daily average of US$3.3 trillion to a staggering US$4 trillion (Bank for International Settlements 2010). Major players in this game tend to be concentrated in a handful of global cities, such as London, New York, Tokyo, Singapore and Hong Kong. Given these tremendous flows, scholars ask the question whether diplomacy is still able to control them in a meaningful way. Those who answer this question in the positive allude to the instruments available for diplomacy to influence financial markets. Many of these instruments are located at the Bank for International Settlements, including the Basel Committee on Banking Supervision, the Committee on the Global Financial System and the Financial Stability Forum. The IMF and the World Bank, of course, are important organisations as well (Porter 2009).

Yet a quick glance over the last years shows very clearly how volatile the market is and how difficult diplomacy finds it to assume a steering function. The so-called 'credit crunch' started in the US when the major lenders Fannie Mae and Freddie Mac could no longer continue business without state intervention on 7 September 2008, and was then rapidly felt all over the world. State-funded rescue packages followed, for instance, for the Hypo Real Estate in Germany by 6 October, and a week later for the British banks Royal Bank of Scotland and Lloyds TSB. Since then, global diplomacy has been struggling to domesticate the forces of global financial flows in order to prevent a global downturn of the economy.

On the regional level, too, diplomats attempt to infuse a measure of stability into markets that does not come naturally to these markets. This is anything but an easy task. The EU and current attempts to get the debt crises in a number of Euro states under control (especially in Greece) are quite a dramatic illustration of these problems. While intra-EU diplomacy – featuring not only national foreign services but also other important players such as national ministries of finance and economics and EMU institutions such as the European Central Bank – designs one emergency measure after the other, markets in general, and the rating agencies Standard & Poor's, Moody's and Fitch in particular, have not reacted too kindly to the

European Financial Stability Facility (EFSF) and the European Financial Stabilisation Mechanism (EFSM).

Development

Another key issue area of global diplomacy is the field of international development. It is closely interwoven with the field of economics in general and global trade and finance in particular. As this section shows, understandings of development, too, have not stayed the same. Global diplomacy in general and Western donors in particular have looked at the issue of development through different dominant prisms over the years. These prisms have evolved from a narrow economic focus to a broader political approach. The latest one, focusing on good governance, has a strong human security dimension as well. Thus, the broadening of the prisms has led to criss-crossings across different diplomatic fields. Most notably, it connected development with the field of war and peace.

Early on, global diplomacy privileged an understanding of development as a *national economic issue*. When decolonisation occurred in the late 1950s and early 1960s, there was plenty of optimism about the economic trajectories of the newly independent states of the global south. In a highly influential article, Walt Rostow likened this trajectory to a plane taking off from the ground (Rostow 1960). Rapid industrialisation was considered to be the fuel powering this take-off. The World Bank and the IMF, although originally created for the reconstruction of war-torn Europe, were supposed to be major facilitators of this endeavour. They funded, for instance, major infrastructural projects that were considered to provide the necessary prerequisites for such industrialisation, such as major damns and highways. The take-off, however, did not happen, especially not in the poorest areas of the global south that required development the most.

In the face of these failures, global diplomacy struggled to adopt a new lens through which to look at development. By the 1980s, a network of economic experts, Western donors and international institutions (the World Bank and the IMF) had replaced the focus on the national economy with an emphasis on *integrating developing economies into the world economy*. Structural adjustment programmes were supposed to be the principal means for achieving this goal. On the conditionality of reducing government expenditure, opening up domestic markets for imports and taking measures to build more export-oriented economies, developing states received loans from the World Bank as well as other bilateral and multilateral creditors. Sometimes referred to as Washington Consensus, this seeming paradigm (→ glossary) shift, however, did not change the record of international developmental policies around. Those states and people who were in need the most profited the least from the opening of markets in the aftermath of the Cold War (→ glossary). They were simply not ready to compete on an equal footing in the global economy from one moment to the next.

In the late 1980s, a new prism arrived. It revolves around the concept of *good governance*. This prism is considerably different from the above approaches. It is a broader lens through which to look at development. There is not just a rather technocratic and narrow understanding of a global free market economy, but there is an emphasis on the political dimensions of development. Albeit defined somewhat differently in various documents and contexts, there are certain key features that are common to most, if not all, interpretations of good governance. These include the rule of law and democracy (at times only implicit), a transparent and efficient state bureaucracy, human rights and sustainability, and justice and the absence of corruption.

Three concepts closely associated with good governance are *human development, sustainable development* and *human security.* These concepts illustrate how different the current understanding of development is from the Washington consensus and the early dream of rapid modernisation. Human development puts the human being at the centre. Conceptually speaking, development is no longer simply considered a macro-economic exercise whose successes and failures can be seen in macro-economic data such as GDP and exports. But measures of successes and failures are, ultimately, about how close human beings come to developing their potentials. The emphasis on sustainable development also marks an important conceptual departure. Successes and failures of development are not only to be measured in the here and now, but also in the future. This has important repercussions for how to deal with environmental resources. The concept of human security provides a bridge between the diplomatic fields of peace and war on the one hand and development on the other. As defined in the influential UN Development Programme's (UNDP) 1994 Human Development Report, human security is about freedom from want and freedom from fear. The report underlines that development is inescapably intertwined with these two basic freedoms.

This shift from narrow economic to broader economic-political understandings of development was facilitated by the increasing recognition of NGOs by nation-states as actors on the diplomatic scene. Recognition comes in various shapes and forms. There is the issue-based stamp of approval, for instance when the UN accredits an NGO for a particular endeavour such as the High-Level Dialogue on Financing for Development. But there is also the more general stamp of approval that applies to major NGOs. Development NGOs such as Oxfam, CARE International and Save the Children International have a global distribution of offices. While most offices are geared towards helping at the locales where help is needed, there are also offices in major decision-making centres such as New York that are reminiscent of an embassy or a permanent mission of a state. Similarly to the latter, the head of such an office is usually titled 'representative'. Representatives of states and influential NGOs tend to follow similar rules and routines in their interactions as representatives of states.

As Chapter 5 will show in detail, NGOs are often quite successful in performing agenda-setting functions. In the case of the development field, they contributed to broadening the prism through which global diplomacy looks at the issue of development. Development NGOs tend to take a more holistic approach, often very much informed by what happens at the local (or micro) level. In the 1980s, this approach very much clashed with the structural adjustment directives of traditional donors, and NGOs were very vocal about it. The move to the global governance perspective takes some of the long-time criticisms raised by NGOs into account. Other criticisms remain unaddressed, which makes for a continuation of the notable tensions between development NGOs on the one hand and governmental and intergovernmental donors on the other.

By the mid-1990s, the concept of good governance had become more and more influential in diplomatic discourse. The UN General Assembly endorsed the concept in 1996 (UN General Assembly 1 May 1996). By 2000, when the EU and developing states from the African, Caribbean and Pacific regions signed the Cotonou Agreement, good governance already made a self-evident early entry into the document. The

African Union (AU) even established a peer review mechanism, which is meant as an intra-African check on African governments and their performance with regard to good governance. The omnipresence of talk on good governance notwithstanding though, it is disputed to what extent good governance really is a concept driving development policies and to what extent it is only empty rhetoric. The World Bank, in particular, is often singled out for criticism by scholars and activists alike. For them, good governance is mere window-dressing. In their view, the same old failing recipes of development have been tried over and over again ever since decolonisation occurred.

Even the most hard-nosed defender of the World Bank would admit that there are many persisting and severe problems of international development. In 2000, the General Assembly adopted the UN Millennium Declaration. The Declaration features a substantial section on development and – in contrast to many other comparable documents – sets clearly defined targets of development and a timeline when these targets ought to be met. These include goals to halve the proportion of people in the world whose income is less than 1$ a day, of people suffering from hunger and of people with no access to safe drinking water by 2015 (UN General Assembly 2000: Article 19). The results reached so far are encouraging and discouraging at the same time. They are encouraging because some regions of the world – most notably South-Eastern Asia and Eastern Asia – are well on target. But they are also discouraging because progress in other regions, especially Sub-Saharan Africa, Southern Asia and the Caribbean but also the Caucasus and Central Asia is still far removed from meeting the Millennium targets.

Environment

Although a fairly new arrival on the diplomatic scene, environmental diplomacy has burgeoned since the 1970s. Arguably, the 1949 Scientific Conference on Conservation and Utilization of Resources was the first international forum for discussing environmental issues. On a general level, the 1972 UN Conference on the Human Environment (Stockholm Conference) and, on a more specific level, the Third UN Convention on the Law of the Sea (UNCLOS) in 1974 were important steps towards institutionalising global environmental governance. By the late 1990s, there had already been more than 200 international environmental treaties in place. Many more have been added since, and many more are to be expected in the future.

There are a *host of different actors* in this field. NGOs, ranging from general environmental NGOs such as Greenpeace to more specialised ones such as the Rainforest Action Network, play an important role by providing information and putting pressure on state actors by raising awareness as well as mobilising publics. In order to exchange information and engage in dialogue with one another, but also in order to make their voices heard, environmental NGOs exhibit a strong tendency towards coalition-building. The Climate Action Network (CAN), for instance, is a network consisting of over 700 international and national NGOs. This tendency of coalition-building and networking is found in issue areas other than the environment as well.

States are represented not only by foreign service diplomats but increasingly by 'new' diplomats from environmental ministries and agencies too. The reason for this is obvious. Environmental issues often require highly specialised expertise, and this requirement is not always easily met by foreign services, whose personnel is primarily trained in general terms. For the same reason, scientists are also very important actors on the environmental stage. In this field, politics ultimately has to rely on cutting-edge research that identifies environmental problems as well as their causes, and proposes steps to overcome these problems.

There is an *array of global environmental problems.* Some are more regionally confined while others are truly global in nature. Some are more at the forefront of our minds while others get all too easily forgotten. The victims of nuclear testing belong to the latter category. During the Cold War's nuclear arms race, more than 2,000 nuclear tests were conducted, mainly by the US and the Soviet Union. The repercussions of these tests, especially the surface tests, are still very much felt among communities settling around former test sites. Around Semipalatinsk, a former Soviet test site located in Kazakhstan, the cancer rate is almost three times higher than in the rest of the country and there is also a much higher likelihood of mental deficiencies in children (Greenpeace 2006). The peaceful use of nuclear energy, too, has its pitfalls. The nuclear meltdown in Chernobyl in 1986 is estimated to have caused 25,000 cancer deaths among the population living around the site (Union of Concerned Scientists 22 April 2011). Problems caused by chemical toxins such as mercury may be less spectacular but they can also have disastrous consequences (Esty 2008).

Deforestation and, often linked to it, desertification are issues that are frequently discussed on the diplomatic stage. While almost a third of the world's land area is still covered by forests, vast areas of forests, equivalent to the size of Panama, are lost every year. If deforestation continues at the current rate, the world's rainforests will disappear entirely within the next 100 years (National Geographic n.d.). Desertification adversely affects the lives of 250 million people, oftentimes threatening their already fragile livelihoods. As many as one billion people are at risk if desertification continues at the current pace.

Deforestation and desertification accelerate climate change. It is widely believed in the scientific and diplomatic communities that so-called greenhouse gas emissions (especially carbon dioxide, but also methane, nitrous oxide and sulphur hexafluoride) are major culprits of climate change. Yet global trends of worldwide emissions do not justify too much optimism. Since the end of WWII, greenhouse gas emissions have increased steeply with the sharpest increase in carbon dioxide emissions happening in 2004. The trend is likely to continue. By 2025, greenhouse gas emissions are estimated to increase by another 50 per cent compared to today's levels. This sharp increase is mainly due to the rapidly growing emissions in developing countries. Yet blaming developing countries for these discouraging figures would be misplaced. A small number of states from the global south and north are responsible for the lion's share of emissions. China, the US and the EU (in this order) together account for almost half of global emissions; adding Russia, India and Japan the combined total is close to two-thirds; and finally adding Brazil, Canada, Mexico, Indonesia, Iran, South Korea, Australia, Ukraine and South Africa, we get close to the 80 per cent mark (World Resources Institute 17 February 2009).

There are many instruments, organisations and diplomatic forums that are dedicated to dealing with environmental issues. When it comes to desertification, for example, there are at least eight international organisations and UN agencies addressing the issue: the Food and Agriculture Organization of the UN (FAO), the International Fund for Agricultural Development (IFAD), the Sahel and West Africa Club (SWAC), the Sahara and Sahel Observatory (OSS), the UN Environment

Program (UNEP, especially the Drylands and Development Center), the UN Institute for Training and Research (UNITAR), the Permanent Secretariat of the UN Convention to Combat Desertification (UNCCD) and the World Bank. This institutional thickening in the field is, in principle, to be welcomed. Yet it also causes some *problems of coordination and even competition.*

No environmental issue receives as much public and diplomatic attention as climate change. While the Stockholm Conference in 1972 may be seen as an important early encounter with this issue, the creation of the Intergovernmental Panel on Climate Change (IPCC) in 1988 marks the starting point for a more sustained diplomatic engagement with this field. The IPCC is an expert body, composed of world-renowned climatologists who are appointed by their respective governments. On 21 December 1990, the General Assembly adopted Resolution 45/212, which set up a negotiation committee on climate change. Two years later, all of these efforts yielded an important outcome. The 1992 UNFCCC (or Rio Declaration) was signed, in which the state parties agreed to monitor their carbon dioxide emissions. In 1997, the parties reached consensus on legally binding targets for the reduction of greenhouse gases. Since then, there have hardly been any major diplomatic successes in this issue area. More recent climate summits, such as Copenhagen in 2009 and Durban in 2011, have averted the collapse of the global environmental regime but have not developed the regime any further. The numbers, outlined above, speak for themselves. Despite the institutionalisation of an international regime on climate change, greenhouse gas emissions have not been cut. On the contrary, they have further increased and have done so significantly. The facts that the US has not ratified the Kyoto Protocol and that Canada exercised its right to withdraw from the Protocol in December 2011 do not add to the strength of the climate regime.

Health

The beginnings of a sustained diplomatic effort to create an international framework for governing global health issues can be traced back to the creation of the World Health Organization (WHO), which is affiliated with the UN, in 1948. In the 1970s, issues of global health were pushed up the agenda in several UN agencies. This led to the 1978 Alma Ata Declaration, which 'enshrined health as a fundamental human right' (Thomas and Weber 2004). Three years later, the WHO followed up on the Declaration and formulated the ambitious goal to make equal access to healthcare a reality by the year 2000. It formulated a strategy entitled 'Health For All'. The above-mentioned Millennium Development Goals also formulate a number of important goals relating to global health governance.

As global health statistics show, however, *a lot remains to be done* if we want to be able to at least somehow approximate the Health-For-All postulate. Around 115 million children worldwide under the age of five are underweight. Millennium Development Goals notwithstanding, the figures of underweight African children have significantly increased from 24 million in 1990 to 30 million in 2010. In Asia, the absolute number is much higher: 71 million children are estimated to be underweight. While there are fewer deaths of children under the age of five worldwide, the figures are still shockingly high. In 1990, there were 12.4 million. By 2000, the number was at 8.1 million. Pneumonia and diarrhoeal diseases are the main causes of these deaths. While the worldwide numbers of women dying during pregnancy and childbirth have decreased significantly (from 546,000 in 1990 to 358,000 in 2008), maternal deaths show very clearly how unequally distributed access to basic healthcare is; 99 per cent of all maternal deaths occur in developing countries. Africa accounts for almost 40 per cent of maternal deaths worldwide (World Health Organization 2011: 12–16).

HIV/AIDS remains a global epidemic. Over 33 million people are estimated to be infected with HIV worldwide. Access to antiretroviral therapy remains highly unequal in the world, with people living in low-income and middle-income countries experiencing much more difficulties to get access than people living in the global north. The problem of access to essential medicines is not confined to HIV/AIDS but applies more generally. Between 50 and 90 per cent of all drugs purchased in low-income and middle-income countries are paid out of pocket. This makes it impossible for many people to get essential medicines; the more expensive they are, the more impossible it becomes to buy them (Thomas and Weber 2004).

With health issues oftentimes still sidelined by national foreign services, national ministries of development and developmental agencies, international organisations and agencies, and locally, nationally and transnationally operating NGOs are important players in this field. Given the many different actors in this issue area, coordination is an important challenge. Take, for instance, just the number of international organisations and agencies dealing with the problem of HIV/AIDS: the UN Children's Fund (UNICEF), the World Food Programme (WFP), the UNDP, the UN Population Fund (UNFPA), UN Educational, Scientific and Cultural Organization (UNESCO), the WHO, the World Bank, the UN Office on Drugs and Crime (UNODC) and the International Labour Organization (ILO). In order to coordinate at least the work of the UN agencies and their affiliates in this field, the UN created the Joint UN Programme on HIV/AIDS (UNAIDS) (Seckinelgin 2005).

Global health problems are related to a host of other issues and issue areas. Development has been mentioned above already. Disaster relief, addressed in Box 4.2 is another one of them.

Migration

The globalisation of world politics goes hand in hand with major increases of migration flows. From 1970 to 2000, the number of international migrants worldwide rose from 82 million to 175 million. The 1990s account for most of this marked increase. The principal direction of flow has been from developing to developed countries, especially the US, the EU countries and Australia. One out of five international migrants lives in the US (International Organization for Migration 2005: 394). Migrants are mixed in terms of their skill levels. In 2010, the OECD classified 43 per cent of them as low skill, 35 per cent as intermediate skill and 22 per cent as high skill. Migration of the latter category of migrants leads to the so-called 'brain drain', which amounts to a serious impediment for developing economies. There are numerous countries where at least one-third of people with a tertiary education live outside the country in which they were born: Belize, Barbados, Congo (Brazzaville), Ghana, Guyana, Jamaica, Cambodia, Mozambique, Mauritius, the Seychelles, Tonga, Trinidad and Tobago, Saint Vincent and Grenadines, the US Virgin Islands, Samoa and Zimbabwe (Dumont *et al.* 2010).

Box 4.2 Disaster relief

Natural disasters such as earthquakes, floods and famine are, of course, nothing new. In the early thirteenth century, for instance, an earthquake in the Middle East may have killed as many as a million people in present-day Egypt and Syria. What is new though is that the number of reported disasters has grown steadily since the 1970s and that detailed coverage of these disasters is brought home to us via television and the internet. This puts more and more pressure on state leaders, national foreign services and national development agencies to provide help in these situations. It seems that during these relief operations the seemingly self-evident maxim that state diplomacy is all about the selfish pursuit of the national interest is suspended. A well-documented case that points in these directions is George W. Bush's response to the 2004 Asian tsunami, which killed almost a quarter of a million people and left many survivors without shelter, sufficient food and safe drinking water. Bush initially pledged US$7 million to efforts of disaster relief. When the severe humanitarian consequences of the tsunami became increasingly obvious, he doubled the amount to US$15 million. There is strong evidence that the UN, coupled with media coverage, made a major difference for what was to follow then. At a press conference, Jan Egeland, the UN Under-Secretary-General for Humanitarian Affairs, accused rich countries of being 'stingy' despite the ongoing large-scale suffering. Egeland had not singled out the US. But the US media interpreted this differently (and certainly not in line with Egeland's original intentions). *The Washington Post*, usually not among the most Bush-critical newspapers, ran the story 'UN official slams US as "stingy" over aid'. Four days after this remark, and faced with a media coverage that called for more help, Bush increased the emergency aid to US$350 million (Steele 2007).

Focusing on the drivers of international migration, international law distinguishes the special category of refugee from other forms of migration. In the 1951 Convention Relating to the Status of Refugees (Refugee Convention), a refugee is defined as someone who is persecuted, for instance based on race, religion, nationality or political opinion, as the distinctive driver forcing a refugee out of his or her country. The number of refugees has increased significantly from 1970 to 1990. In 1970, there were 5.3 million refugees worldwide. By 1980, the figure had risen to 9.6 million and, by 1990, to 12.3 million. After this peak, the number decreased to 9.5 million in 2000 (International Organization for Migration 2005: 309).

The diplomatic institutionalisation of this issue area *has not kept up with these flows of migration.* During WWII, the UN Relief and Rehabilitation Administration (UNRRA) was set up, replaced by the International Refugee Organization (IRO) in the aftermath of WWII, which in turn was soon replaced by two institutions: the UN High Commissioner for Refugees (UNHCR) and the Intergovernmental Committee for European Migration (ICEM). Their names give away the original primary purpose of these institutions, i.e. the management of the large numbers of displaced people in war-torn Europe. The ICEM was reformed in 1989 and renamed the International Organization for Migration (IOM). The 1951 Convention Relating to the Status of Refugees (Refugee Convention) remains the key international accord on the rights of refugees and, thus, marks the perimeter within which the UNHCR's activities ought to take place.

It is widely acknowledged, however, that the current level of international institutionalisation is out of sync with the need for a stronger steering mechanism in this issue area. There are at least two major problems. First, thus far diplomacy has generated little to protect the rights of migrants who are not refugees. There is the 1990 UN International Convention on the Protection of the Rights of All Migrant Workers and Members of Their Families, but the agreement remains poorly ratified (Koser 2010). There are many international organisations that are active in the issue area of migration but it is a major challenge to coordinate their work. Agencies such as the ILO, the UN Conference on Trade and Development (UNCTAD), the UNDP, the UN Department of Economic and Social Affairs (UNDESA), UNESCO, the UNFPA, UNICEF, UNITAR, the UNODC – Box 4.3 explains why it is part of this list – and the World Bank touch upon the issue of migration and attempt to coordinate themselves through the Global Migration Group (GMG). Yet in the absence of a strong institutional body on migration (for instance, a UN agency), this coordination remains a constant struggle, and more holistic perspectives on migration are not easily designed by these institutions.

Second, today's diplomatic thought on migration remains deeply permeated by a clear-cut dichotomy between economic migrants on the one hand and refugees on the other. Being classified in the latter category provides a migrant with a number of rights; being classified in the former category leaves him or her with a much weaker status. Yet many people leaving countries such as Somalia or the Congo do not necessarily fit into the refugee category. They are 'survival migrants' as Betts puts it, i.e. they leave their country of origin because of an existential threat they face but this threat may not necessarily be constituted by persecution as codified in the 1951 Geneva Convention (Betts 2010). In other words, there may be a need to either broaden the definition of refugee or create a new category of migrants that deserves special protection. This debate notwithstanding, there is little question that migrants in general, even the most clear-cut economic migrants, deserve more protection than they get at the moment. There are figures suggesting that as many as 2,000 migrants die each year when they attempt to cross the Mediterranean from Africa to Europe; 600 are estimated to die when they try crossing into the US from Mexico (Koser 2010).

Box 4.3 Human trafficking

The International Labour Organization (ILO) estimates that there are close to 2.5 million trafficked persons at any given point in time. Human trafficking is a business that generates annual profits of about US$32 billion (ILO 2008). The UN Office on Drugs and Crime (UNODC) summarises the chilling facts: 'Every year, thousands of men, women and children fall victim to traffickers … Through coercion, deceit or force, they are exploited for their labour, sex or even their organs' (UNODC 2011: 22). Among the reported abuses, sexual exploitation ranks first with almost 80 per cent. Most trafficked people are women (over 80 per cent) (UNODC 2011: 23). Combating human trafficking is a very difficult task. There are international organisations that address the problem, most notably the ILO, the UNODC and UNICEF. The 1998 Rome Statute constituting the International Criminal Court lists the forms of abuses associated with human trafficking as crimes against humanity. But with many states not enacting law required for curbing trafficking and not dedicating sufficient resources to the cause, it is unlikely that these international efforts will eradicate human trafficking any time soon.

Summary

- There is a *multiplication of issue areas*. Traditionally, matters of peace and war were at the forefront of diplomacy. In our days, economics features as prominently as peace and war. In the daily routines of diplomacy, involvement with economic issues has even surpassed dealings with war and peace. Moreover, more and more issue areas have been added. In this chapter, we discussed development, environment, health and migration.
- There is also a *multiplication of actors*. New issue areas – but also the deepening of established ones – requires expertise that often challenges national foreign services, whose diplomats are trained on more general terms. Specialised ministries and agencies, for example environment, economics and finance, step in. International organisations, NGOs and highly trained experts also become part of the diplomatic game.
- The *issue areas become more and more interwoven*. The concept of human security, for example, provides clear linkages between development on the one hand and peace and war on the other. Yet the linkages even go further and encompass every issue area we have discussed in this chapter. Individual security and the potential to develop has a lot to do with health and the state of the environment. There are linkages to migration and refugees as well, although they feature less frequently in diplomatic discourse.

Study questions

- In the age of global diplomacy, which issue areas move into the foreground and which ones into the background?
- What is the role of the general diplomat in a diplomatic system that deals more and more with specialised policy fields and issues?
- Is the age of global diplomacy to be equated with a multilateral turn of diplomacy?
- Has global diplomacy kept pace with globalisation flows?
- What are, from an ethical point of view, the most urgent world problems to be dealt with by the diplomatic community?

Recommended further reading

Buzan, Barry and Richard Little. 2000. *International systems in world history: Remaking the study of international relations*. Oxford: Oxford University Press.
The move towards global diplomacy that this chapter sketched takes place within a broader evolution of the international system. Buzan and Little's book provides a very good overview of this evolution.

Kleiner, Jürgen. 2010. *Diplomatic practice: Between tradition and innovation*. Singapore and Hackensack, NJ: World Scientific.
Kleiner vividly describes the everyday practices of what we refer to as global diplomacy. This practitioner's account is very readable.

Pigman, Geoffrey A. 2010. *Contemporary diplomacy: Representation and communication in a globalized world*. Cambridge: Polity.

This is a detailed and convincing scholarly account of how diplomacy has changed since the end of the Cold War. Similar to Chapter 5, Pigman puts communication centre stage in his book.

Ruggie, John G. 1986. Continuity and transformation in the world polity: Toward a neorealist synthesis. In *Neorealism and its critics*, edited by Robert O. Keohane. New York: Columbia University Press.

Although written before the end of the Cold War, this chapter provides a very good analytical scheme for thinking about changes of diplomacy and the international system in which it operates.

Part III
Mapping the diplomatic field

5   Contexts of diplomacy

Chapter objectives

- To identify the contexts that constrain as well as enable diplomats to perform their tasks, and make diplomacy in the first place.
- To discuss diplomatic law and introduce readers to the 1961 Vienna Convention on Diplomatic Relations.
- To address less easily visible, widely taken for granted layers of contexts (deeper backgrounds).

Introduction

Traditionally, diplomacy has been the realm of lawyers trained in international law. The reason for this is obvious. They are experts on the context (→ glossary) in which diplomacy takes place. To this very day, law – especially international public law – is an important component of this context. It shapes what counts as appropriate standards in diplomacy and what does not. Yet law is not the only component of the context that guides diplomats for how to interact with other diplomats. Diplomats are also situated in deeper contexts that shape their interaction. These deeper layers of context provide clues for which kinds of solutions to which kinds of problems are conceivable and which ones are not, play a crucial role in processes through which actors become recognised as players on the diplomatic scene and provide repertoires of taken for granted ideas for making arguments and justifications in diplomatic encounters.

To be sure, this chapter writes about *contexts* and not just a single context. Meaning – no matter whether it finds its expression in a legal document or not – is contested. In a global political system, this is very much to be expected. Some actors place more emphasis on some norms than others, for example. Or they interpret the same norm rather differently. Or they invoke different norms when addressing the same problem. Or, drawing from different contexts, they do not even come to agree on a phenomenon as constituting a problem to be addressed by the diplomatic community. Nevertheless, there is an ideational backbone that holds global diplomacy together. It is these convergences around some influential ideas that we address in this chapter.

In what follows, we first focus on the 1961 Vienna Convention on Diplomatic Relations: we briefly trace its making, provide an overview of its key stipulations and discuss the issue of updating the 1961 Convention. Then, we switch to deeper backgrounds: we deal with overlaps between deeper backgrounds and international law, put under scrutiny how contending scholarly approaches (English School, Liberalism, Constructivism) make sense of deeper backgrounds and, finally, address the evolution of deeper backgrounds in the age of global diplomacy.

The making of the Vienna Convention

Today's diplomatic law provides the procedural guidance for ensuring the functionality of diplomatic institutions, especially the resident embassy. How ought the host state to treat the embassy of a foreign state within its borders, and how ought it to treat the diplomats working in the embassy? Vice versa, what ought to be the dos and don'ts of resident diplomats? There are many codified and non-codified provisions. Headquarter agreements of international organisations such as the 1947 agreement between the UN and the US, establishing the inviolability of UN premises, for instance, are among these. Yet the 1961 Vienna Convention on Diplomatic Relations remains the cornerstone of diplomatic law. Hence, this section focuses on this Convention.

In the seventeenth century, the Dutch legal scholar and philosopher Hugo Grotius already postulated two important principles: 'Now there are two rights of ambassadors which we see are everywhere referred to the law of nations. The first is that they be admitted, the second, that they be free from violence' (Grotius, on the Right of Legation, in Berridge 2004: 101). But it was only in the early nineteenth century, when the Concert of Europe put pressure on states to put their communication channels on more solid legal ground, that attempts to codify the evolving customary diplomatic law found their first more influential codified expressions. In 1815, the Vienna Regulation was an important move towards codification of existing practices. Resolutions adopted by the Institute of International Law in 1895 and 1929, the Havana Convention regarding Diplomatic Officers in 1928 and the Harvard Draft Convention on Diplomatic Privileges and Immunities of 1932 followed (Denza 2008: 1–12).

In its very first session in 1949, the International Law Commission (ILC) included the codification of diplomatic law on its list of codifying tasks. The ILC is an important institution. Many international conventions have been drafted by it. Composed of legal experts with various backgrounds – academic, diplomatic corps, international organisations, etc. – its members are elected by the General Assembly for the duration of five years. In the early 1950s, Yugoslavia took the initiative in the UN General Assembly and advocated for prioritising the codification of diplomatic law. With this initiative finding a friendly response from other member states, the General Assembly requested the ILC to work on a draft convention. The Commission drafted articles for such a convention and, by 1958, redrafted them, taking into account comments by the General Assembly and twenty-one member states. This prepared the ground for a conference in Vienna, where negotiations among the 81 participating states were concluded successfully between 2 March and 14 April 1961. The Vienna Convention was signed on 18 April. It is to date by far the most comprehensive attempt to codify diplomatic law. It has been ratified by almost 190 states. To the few states who have not ratified it, the Convention applies as customary law.

The Vienna Convention is very much a product of its time. In the 1950s and 1960s, world politics was still understood – almost exclusively – as *inter-state politics*. Thus, the

Vienna Convention is all state embassies and diplomats authorised to speak on behalf of sovereign states (→ glossary: sovereignty). Denza puts it very well, when she writes that the Convention is all about codifying 'the rules for the exchange of embassies among sovereign States' (Denza 2008: 1). To what extent the Convention contains novel elements and to what extent it merely codifies customary law is not entirely undisputed among legal scholars. While Denza writes about a 'progressive codification' (Denza 2008: 5) of customary law, Brown downplays the 'progressive' and puts more emphasis on the codification (Brown 1988). But these differences in scholarly opinion are anything but large. It is clear that exercises in codification of already existing customary law played a major role in writing the Convention.

Four major provisions

There are four major provisions: first, mission premises (and the private residences of heads of missions) are *inviolable*. According to Article 22 of the Convention, this inviolability does not only mean that the mission (such as an embassy) ought not to be entered without the consent of the head of the mission (such as an ambassador). It also means that the host country has the obligation to protect the 'premises of the mission against any intrusion or damage and to prevent any disturbance of the peace of the mission or impairment of its dignity'. Second, there is the often-quoted *diplomatic immunity*. The overarching goal of the Convention is to ensure the functionality of the embassy. This cannot be achieved just by protecting the premises of the embassy. But protection has to be extended to the diplomats working in the embassy as well. The Convention does this in a fairly strong fashion. Again, not only is the host state obligated not to violate the diplomat's rights. According to Article 31, the diplomat ought to enjoy immunity from criminal jurisdiction and, with some exceptions, also civil and administrative jurisdiction. According to Article 29, the host state is also obligated to protect the diplomat against attacks from non-state actors within its territory; it has to 'prevent any attack on his person, freedom or dignity'. Third, the host state has the duty to *protect the communication lines* between the embassy and its sending state. Some of the stipulations of Article 27 sound rather antiquated. There is talk about the 'diplomatic bag', how it is to be transported on an airplane, how it is to be off-loaded and so on. But the gist of Article 27 is as important as ever. With diplomacy being all about communication, the functionality of an embassy cannot be guaranteed without the protection of this communication. Yet note that Article 27 is about the communication between embassy and sending state. There is no right of embassies to communicate at free will in the host country. Fourth, embassies *ought not to interfere* in the domestic affairs of their host country. The Convention does not bestow rights only to embassies and obligations only to host states. There are also stipulations where this balance reads the other way round. Non-interference belongs to this category. Diplomatic missions, as envisaged by the Convention, are vehicles for facilitating state-to-state communication with 'state' standing for the upper echelons of the executive (especially foreign ministries and the chief executive). They are not vehicles that entitle a mission to try to influence the broader public in the host country.

When Brown (1988) writes about the Vienna Convention as 'one of the surest ... multilateral regimes in the field of international relations', he has the Convention's compliance record in mind. All in all, this compliance record has been – despite some ambiguous formulations and the continuing relevance of customary law to interpret the Convention – very solid. This does not mean, however, that the regime is free of contestation. This contestation is often partly due to the evolving nature of law and partly due to states as well as individual actors trying to get the justice that suits them best.

An important contested case pertaining to diplomatic immunity was General Augusto Pinochet's arrest in London in October 1998. That month, the Spanish judge Baltasar Garzón set a chain of events in motion that indicates a major shift in international law. He issued an international arrest warrant against Pinochet for crimes committed during the General's seventeen-year reign of terror in his native Chile. Garzón justified this warrant with crimes (ninety-four counts of torture featured prominently) committed against Spanish citizens. Although this cast aside – for legal reasons – compelling evidence for thousands of cases of murder and torture during Pinochet's reign in Chile for the time being, the consequences were soon felt. UK magistrates, applying the European Convention on Extradition, arrested Pinochet. The General tried to make a case before the High Court that the arrest warrants against him were null and void, most importantly because of Article 39(2) of the Vienna Convention, which guarantees former heads of state remain immune from the criminal jurisdiction of foreign states (Bianchi 1999: 255). It was only in March 1999 that the Lords came to a decision. They ruled that Pinochet could be extradited but only be prosecuted for crimes that he committed after 1988. This is when the UK had incorporated legislature for the UN Convention against Torture in the Criminal Justice Act. On the one hand, this qualification amounted to a major drawback. It threw out much of what Pinochet was supposed to stand trial for. This drawback became even bigger when the Lords ruled a year later that Pinochet had to be set free due to medical reasons. On the other hand, however, the decision signals a move towards *universal jurisdiction*. Some crimes are just so horrendous that they warrant jurisdiction by domestic courts over individuals even if their alleged crimes were committed outside of the boundaries of the state within which this court is located and the individuals are not otherwise associated with this state (e.g., by citizenship or permanent residency).

Contestation about alleged cases of diplomatic interference into domestic affairs abound but tend to be less spectacular than the above case on diplomatic immunity. Democratisation efforts by Western countries in the global south are sometimes met with staunch rejection. In extreme cases, these accusations are accompanied by declaring a diplomat who allegedly interfered with domestic affairs *persona non grata*. Box 5.1 elaborates on this diplomatic institution. In 2008, for example, Hugo Chavez – in his very own determined rhetorical fashion – declared US ambassador Patrick Duddy *persona non grata* and expelled him from Venezuela. Thereafter, the US Chargé d'Affaires John Caulfield became the target of Chavez's ire for allegedly meeting with exiled Venezuelan oppositional groups in Puerto Rico. While Chavez's reaction may be extreme and, of course, fuelled by a principled stance against the US, there really is a tension between democratisation efforts and the diplomatic non-interference norm. Western states often try to bypass this tension by delegating democratisation tasks to agencies not officially or only indirectly linked to government. The German political foundations, especially the Konrad-Adenauer-Stiftung, Hanns-Seidel-Stiftung, Friedrich-Ebert-Stiftung and Friedrich-Naumann-Stiftung, are such entities. The National Endowment of Democracy in the US and the British Westminster Foundation for Democracy serve similar purposes (Kleiner 2010: 82).

Box 5.1 *Persona non grata*

Given the immunity granted to diplomats in the Vienna Convention, there is only so much host countries can do to diplomats they accuse of misdoings. Yet Article 9 of the Convention codifies one of the sharpest weapons available in such cases: to declare a diplomat *persona non grata*. The sending state then ought to recall such a diplomat to his or her capital. If this does not happen, the Convention reserves the right to 'refuse to recognize the person concerned as a member of the mission'. Yet this last sanction is rarely applied. In diplomatic practice, declaring a diplomat *persona non grata* amounts to expelling this diplomat from the host country. Reasons why a host state declares a diplomat *persona non grata* vary widely. In 1996, for example, Canada threw out a Ukrainian vice-consul for alleged drunk driving and similar offenses. In 2004, Mexico declared a Cuban diplomat *persona non grata* after Castro had declared that Mexico's prestige had 'turned into ashes'. In 2005, a Czech diplomat had to leave Belarus due to alleged sexual misconduct. In a case that was in the newspaper headlines for quite some time, the UK declared four Russian diplomats *personae non gratae* in 2006, when Moscow refused to extradite Andrej Lugovoy. The latter was suspected of having killed Alexander Litvinenko with the radioactive isotope polonium-210 in London. The victim and alleged perpetrator had formerly been associated with the Soviet and Russian intelligence services. The Russian government responded by making four British diplomats pack their suitcases. During the Cold War, allegations of spying were the main reason for declaring a diplomat *persona non grata*. The numbers of expelled diplomats could be quite considerable. In 1971, Britain sent 105 Soviet citizens home, many of them diplomats.

Aside from these cases of contestation, there are also a few clear-cut and widely recognised problems of compliance with the Vienna Convention. Again, it is important to emphasise that the compliance record, all in all, is strong. But there are at least three exceptions that are worth mentioning. First, while states, all in all, comply with the stipulation that mission premises are inviolable, there are cases where this inviolability is violated. The most headline-producing event in this regard was, without much doubt, the Iran Hostage Crisis. In the wake of the Iranian Revolution, a crowd of about 5,000, most of them reportedly Islamist students, marched onto the US embassy on 1 November 1979. That day, the crowd eventually dispersed peacefully. Three days later, it was an altogether different matter. About 3,000 protestors gathered, including a large group of armed individuals, self-identifying as 'Muslim Student Followers of the Imam's Party'. They stormed the embassy and took fifty-two American citizens hostage. Negotiation, mediation and even the condemnation of the act by the International Court of Justice (→ glossary) did little to resolve the crisis quickly. It took 444 days for the hostages to be finally released (Barker 2006: 9). In 2011, there was suddenly again a lot of mentioning of the Iran Hostage Crisis, when Iranian protestors, shouting 'Death to England!', forced their way into the British Embassy in Teheran. Again, many of them were students. Yet this time, there was merely damage to the building and the British diplomats were detained only very briefly. Note that what was at issue in both cases was not so much that the Iranian state directly attacked the mission premises. But the Iranian state – in the 1979 case much more so than in the 2011 case – failed to protect the mission premises. This, too, constitutes a violation of the Vienna Convention.

Second, despite diplomatic immunity, there are cases in which diplomats become targets. In 1979, the Iranian government failed not only to protect the US mission premises but, of course, also US diplomatic personnel. But there is a long list of worse treatment of diplomats (and innocent bystanders). US diplomats have been especially frequently targeted. On 18 April 1983, a suicide bombing against the US embassy in Beirut left more than sixty people dead, including seventeen American citizens. Fifteen years later, an even more destructive attack hit the US embassy in Nairobi. On 7 August 1998, a terrorist truck bomb killed almost 300 people and wounded as many as 5,000. Al-Qaeda claimed responsibility for the attack (US State Department n.d.). Twelve of them were American citizens. These cases are not violations of the Vienna Convention unless one would want to make the unrealistic claim that the Lebanese and Kenyan governments could have prevented such an attack. In 2012, there was a series of attacks on US embassies. Box 5.2 discusses these at greater length.

Yet, to be sure, it is not only US diplomats that are subjected to ill-treatment. In 2002, for instance, African ambassadors requested better protection from the Russian authorities for their personnel in Moscow. They were concerned about racist attacks. This concern was substantiated when Ghana's ambassador, Francis Y. Mahama, was beaten up when he went for a walk in a park in Moscow (Kleiner 2010: 130). During the 2012 attacks on US diplomats, embassies and diplomats of allied nations (for example France, Germany and the United Kingdom) were under siege, too.

Third, while the above two exceptions to the strong compliance record of the Vienna Convention rarely occur, the tempering with communication lines occurs much more frequently. How much of this happens in our days is difficult to tell but, judging by the past record, host states are often rather eager to find out what messages embassies send back and receive from their capitals. During the Cold War, the FBI went as far as to build a tunnel underneath the Soviet embassy in order to tap communication lines (Denza 2008: 11). The US diplomatic offensive prior to the 2003 Second

---

Box 5.2 2012 attacks on US diplomats

In June 2012, a small cinema screened the movie *The Innocence of Bin Laden* in Los Angeles. The anti-Islamic film depicts the Prophet Muhammad, among other things, as a coward and child molester. In July, a user with the pseudonym 'sam bacile' uploaded some clips taken from the film on the online portal YouTube under the titles *The Real Life of Muhammad* and *Muhammad Movie Trailer*. Yet the radical group hiding behind the pseudonym left a mark with its amateurish film only in early September when the Egypt-based salafist television channel *Al-Nas* broadcasted Arab translations of the YouTube clips, vilified them and turned its rage against the West in general and the US in particular. From then, protests spread across the Islamic world. In the early evening of 11 September, protesters stormed the yard of the US embassy in Cairo, tearing down the US flag. Egyptian riot police prevented a further escalation. Later this evening, gunmen – heavily armed with rocket-propelled grenades and anti-aircraft guns – started firing on the US consulate in Benghazi (Libya) out of a group of protestors. For about an hour, they succeeded in taking the main consulate building, killing four Americans, including the US Ambassador to Libya, Christopher Stevens. Elsewhere in the region (Tunisia, Sudan, Lebanon, Iraq and Yemen) and beyond it (Afghanistan, Pakistan and Indonesia) angry protests took place but did not escalate to the extent they did in Benghazi.

Gulf War strongly suggests that this kind of spying is anything but past practice. On 2 March 2003, *The Observer* published an article based on a leaked memo written by a top official of the US National Security Agency, which orders to intensify surveillance operations 'particularly directed at … UN Security Council Members (minus US and GBR, of course)' (Beaumont *et al.* 2003). It seems that the operations were primarily directed against Angola, Cameroon, Chile, Mexico, Guinea and Pakistan (then non-permanent members of the Security Council). But the above quote leaves China, and Russia, and even the long-standing US allies France and Germany (then also a non-permanent member) also in the equation.

Updating the Vienna Convention?

We have seen from the above that the Vienna Convention is at the core of codi-fied diplomatic law. Following a *functional approach* – postulating a set of norms that guarantees the functioning of resident embassies – it is a pillar on which modern diplomacy is built. Although there are some notable problems with implementation, all in all the compliance record is strong. This has probably quite a bit to do with the fact that the drafters of the Vienna Convention did not pluck its stipulations out of thin air. For the most part, they codified what had been customary law and what had been taken for granted by the diplomatic community for a long time.

It clearly shows, however, that the Vienna Convention was written before the age of global diplomacy. The multiplication of actors and issue areas was still very much in its infancy. *Today's diplomacy cannot be reduced to the functionality of the resident embassy.* Customary diplomatic law and a host of other norms that do not qualify as law but, nevertheless, have important effects (see below) have developed since the drafting of the Vienna Convention. New actors and new processes, often underpinned by globalisation and global governance ($\rightarrow$ glossary: governance), have taken shape over time.

It is, therefore, no coincidence that there are calls for a thorough overhaul of the Vienna Convention or a new convention altogether. Siracusa, for example, cau-tions that international organisations and even transnational corporations – as well as their role in global diplomacy – should be included in such a convention (Siracusa 2010: 1). The role of NGOs would warrant some written specification as well as, for example, the 2012 diplomatic asylum case of WikiLeaks founder Julian Assange suggests. Box 5.3 discusses this case. Yet, for the time being, the codification of diplo-matic law seems to proceed as slowly as ever. It took hundreds of years for the Vienna Convention to be written, signed and ratified. It may take at least a few more dec-ades for a new convention to be adopted that takes into account the move to global diplomacy.

Deeper backgrounds

Let us take a step back. According to an influential definition by the American Law Institute, international law 'consists of rules and principles of general application dealing with the conduct of states and of international organizations and with their relations *inter se*, as well as with some of their relations with persons, whether natural or juridical' (The American Law Institute 1987).

Box 5.3 Diplomatic asylum and Julian Assange

In 2012, the case of Julian Assange produced a series of newspaper headlines. Assange is the founder of WikiLeaks, which is a very well-known, non-for-profit online publishing platform dedicated to global transparency. Its radical pursuit of transparency brought it into conflict with nation-states, in particular the US. WikiLeaks leaked classified information on US interventions and their aftermath in Iraq and Afghanistan, publishing shocking *ius in bello* and *ius post bellum* violations. WikiLeaks also leaked classified material about Guantanamo Bay. In 2010, the organisation released a host of US State department diplomatic cables. This suddenly made diplomacy much more transparent than Wilson had postulated (see Chapter 3). The cables were at times not very generous about the host countries and their decision-makers from where US diplomats sent these cables. The US found itself compelled to apologise in a number of cases. In 2010, the Swedish Chief Prosecutor Marianne Ny issued an arrest warrant on allegations about rape against Assange. Assange, expecting to be extradited from Sweden to the US and charged for espionage there, looked for ways out. In 2012, he applied for asylum at the Ecuadorian embassy in London. A diplomatic stand-off between the UK and Ecuador followed. Ecuador granted Assange diplomatic asylum. It is very much disputed in international law, however, whether the institution of diplomatic asylum exists, with European diplomats tending to deny and Latin American ones tending to postulate it. In terms of the 1961 Vienna Convention, this is a very tricky case. The Ecuadorian embassy is inviolable. Thus, the UK cannot simply storm the embassy, as some media reported it would. In the context of the Vienna Convention, the UK would have a very strong means at its disposal though. It could cease diplomatic relations with Ecuador. From this moment on, the embassy building is no longer inviolable. Indeed, it is no longer an embassy.

This definition makes a lot of sense to an international lawyer. It also makes a lot of sense to a more sociologically inclined social scientist. But the latter interprets the sentence much more broadly than the former. Whereas the former has in mind legal rules and principles, the latter thinks of the plethora of oughts and ought nots – legal or non-legal – that constitute 'standards of behavior' (Florini 1996: 364). Some of these reach so deeply that they constitute the very institution of diplomacy and the diplomat. There is an important insight here. Just because norms (→ glossary) do not qualify as legal norms does not mean that these norms are inconsequential. On the contrary, many non-legal norms are *so deeply seated in the background of diplomats that they assume a taken for granted quality*. These norms are so powerful that diplomats, for the most part, are no longer aware of them; they rarely, if ever, reflect upon them. Geoffrey Wiseman refers to them as diplomatic culture (Wiseman 2005: 409).

This view of norms may appear to some like a fairly recent intellectual development (or even fad). It is in line with Peter Berger and Thomas Luckmann's path-breaking *The Social Construction of Reality*. Founding texts of this theory of being – in short, ontology (→ glossary) – on diplomacy and international relations include Nicolas Onuf's *World of our Making* (Onuf 1989) and Friedrich Kratochwil's *Rules, Norms, and Decisions* (Kratochwil 1989). But literature on diplomacy has always heavily focused on these background norms, although they featured under different labels. Indeed, early literature on diplomacy is all about procedural background norms. It was aimed at teaching the diplomat the procedural dos and don'ts of the diplomatic world. Even more so, it aimed at turning these norms into the second nature of the diplomat, i.e. something that comes naturally and does not always have to be thought about.

The most frequently quoted diplomacy book of the seventeenth century, Abraham de Wiquefort's *L'Ambassadeur et ses Fonctions* (*The Ambassador and his Functions*), focuses heavily on manners and tact of the diplomat. The book does not try to teach legal rules but standards of behaviour that are supposed to sink into the background of the diplomat. This is, in principle, not all that different from trying to teach a young child to brush her teeth every day in the morning. The expected result of such an exercise is to make this norm a self-evident and unquestioned standard of behaviour. Arguably, François de Callière's *De la Manière de Négocier avec les Souverains* (*On the Art of Diplomacy*), published in 1716, focuses even more heavily on manners and tact. The discipline and rules that the author advocates are all about behavioural markers that make a good diplomat. This pattern of writing about diplomacy continued well into the twentieth century (Satow 1917).

Books on diplomacy may not be that heavily centred on manners and tact any more. But the latter are still recognised as highly important by diplomatic practitioners. Diplomatic academies all over the world tell their students and trainees a lot about protocol. Take, for instance, the Foreign Service Institute of the US Department of State. It teaches how to address others, how to introduce oneself and others, what titles one is supposed to use while addressing others, how to behave as a guest, whom to invite, informal entertaining, formal entertaining, how to dress and so on (US Department of State 2005). Just the first issue alone – addressing others – may very well turn out to be a minefield of misunderstandings, especially for a novice. At the beginning of a speech, for instance, the formula for addressing the audience has to be correct. In our days, the 'Dear Excellencies, Ladies and Gentlemen' is often used as a short-hand. But, in addition to this, high-ranking people in the audience may very well expect to be greeted and thanked for their coming individually. Niceties are important in diplomatic talk. They are also important when it comes to presenting an argument. There is a time for being antagonistic. Yet usually diplomatic talk filters out a lot of anger, frustration and antagonism or hides it in subtle formulations, which are more or less standardised in the diplomatic world. Subtle hints are usually understood by a diplomatic audience.

For the general public, standing outside of these discursive norms, this nice talk can be shocking, especially when it takes place in the midst of disaster. To refer to a highly misplaced case of soft talk – which many diplomats, especially in hindsight, find shocking, too – the first Security Council Resolution on the Rwandan Genocide did not use the word genocide at all, and employed merely the word 'condemn' to describe the Security Council's stance towards the unfolding events. It used the expression 'strongly condemn' only once; this was to condemn attacks on UN personnel. The Security Council passed this Resolution, S/RES/912 (1994), on 21 April 1994 (UN Security Council 1994). This is more than two weeks after the fastest genocide in human history, which cost at least half a million people their lives, had begun.

Three schools of thought on deeper backgrounds

Literature on diplomacy deals with procedural and substantive norms – and taken for granted ideas in general – in depth. There is the central claim by the English School that diplomacy constitutes an *international society*. Hedley Bull addresses diplomatic culture in considerable depth. At the core of this culture, according to Bull, is a particular way of reasoning and communication based on shared norms:

> He [the diplomat] seeks always to reason or persuade rather than to bully or threaten. He tries to show that the objective for which he is seeking is consistent with the other party's interests, as well as with his own. He prefers to speak of 'rights' rather than of 'demands', and to show that these rights flow from rules or principles which both states hold in common, and which the other state has already conceded.
>
> (Bull 1995 (1977): 165)

In a similar vein, Watson understands diplomacy as a civilising process. Diplomatic norms channel interaction towards continuous dialogue (Watson 1982). In a recent re-formulation of English School thought on diplomacy, Sharp echoes this argument. Norms constituting diplomacy, he contends, privilege the maintenance of peaceful relations (Sharp and British International Studies Association 2009).

   Liberal international thought, too, helps to understand diplomatic backgrounds, although it may not always address diplomacy explicitly. The index of the influential *International Regimes*, edited by Stephen Krasner, does not even feature an entry for diplomacy. But Krasner's famous definition of international regime has a lot to say about substantive norms structuring diplomacy in a given policy field. He defines a *regime* as 'implicit or explicit principles, norms, rules, and decision-making procedures around which actors' expectations converge in a given area of international relations' (Krasner 1983: 2). Diplomats, as some of the chapters in Krasner's edited book highlight, feature prominently among these actors. They are key actors in, say, the international trade, environmental and nuclear non-proliferation regimes. The definition highlights that there are dense constellations of cooperation, in which established ideas about how things are and how things are to be done guide the actors involved. Some of these ideas are implicit; in our language, they are in the background. Krasner has a hierarchy in mind when it comes to these established implicit and explicit ideas. Principles are 'beliefs of fact, causation, and rectitude' (Krasner 1983: 2). What we refer to as norms in this book is differentiated into a much narrower understanding of norms as well as rules and decision-making procedures. In Krasner's terminology, norms broadly delimit rights and obligations. Rules and, even more so, decision-making procedures are more specific.

   The English School and also Liberalism (→ glossary) go beyond norms when it comes to making sense of diplomatic backgrounds. Bull's rich notion of *culture*, for example, cannot be reduced to norms. Watson alludes to *practices* and Sharp elaborates on what these practices are. Krasner's concept of principles is interesting, too. They are, among other things, about what the world is like and what causes what. This amounts to much more than the oughts and ought nots of norms. Constructivism (→ glossary) – oftentimes equally hesitant to address diplomacy explicity as Liberalism – frequently refers to *norms*. The path-breaking studies of Kratochwil and Onuf have been mentioned above already. But Constructivist scholars use a number of different concepts to capture different dimensions of the background as well. To mention only the most frequently discussed ones among these, there is *identity* (→ glossary), which is often conceptualised as the narrative (Somers 1994) through which internationally salient entities such as nation-states define themselves. There is the *episteme* (→ glossary), which Ruggie, borrowing from Foucault (1970 [1966]), defines as a lens through which international actors look at the world. The lens that he writes about is the territorially demarcated world of the sovereign nation-state. This is a highly interesting point. This world, albeit somewhat beleaguered due to the pressures of globalisation, is so deeply ingrained in our thinking about global politics that we hardly ever come up with the idea of reflecting upon it. But this imagination has to be explained, too – precisely because it is so much taken for granted. The concept of *episteme* is helpful in this regard. Finally, there is the concept of the *habitus* (→ glossary). Scholars on world politics, drawing either from Norbert Elias (Elias *et al.* 2000; Bjola and Kornprobst 2007) or Pierre Bourdieu (Bourdieu 1998; Hopf 2002) use this term to describe the socially acquired predispositions through which actors orient themselves. These predispositions are akin to the operational system of a computer. Socially acquired means that they are learnt through social interaction.

Illustrations of deeper backgrounds

To a surprising degree, we are back at the classics of the diplomacy literature. De Wiquefort and de Callière, for instance, understood manners and tact very much along lines comparable to scholarship on the *habitus*. When we follow Elias' route of conceptualising the *habitus*, we are also back at Watson's argument that diplomacy is a civilising process. Precisely this process is at the core of Elias' theorising. He holds that, over time, humankind will acquire a non-violent *habitus*. If this really is possible, diplomacy – as Watson points out correctly – would be very important for advancing this civilising process in world politics. Diplomacy, as often emphasised, has an important role to play in such a civilising process because it offers chances to prevent war by communicating with one another.

Getting at these deep backgrounds is not easy on a methodological level because they are so much taken for granted. Poststructuralist research provides some important insights about how to uncover what usually passes as self-evident. In his writings on diplomacy, James Der Derian makes diplomacy strange by inquiring into how it came into being (deconstruction). By uncovering the many contingencies of its evolution, he clarifies that diplomacy is a human construct – not more but also not less (Der Derian 1987). Poststructuralists, being adamant that this human construct is full of inequalities and injustices, seek a distance from it. Costa Constantinou proposes a seemingly unlikely but rather powerful means for doing so: make strange and laugh about diplomacy (Constantinou 1996).

We will revisit these different conceptualisations of deeper backgrounds in the explanatory and normative Parts IV and V of this book, respectively. Yet what is really important for the purpose of this part is that there are these deeper backgrounds. There is not just international law. International law itself is embedded in these deeper backgrounds. Furthermore, the deeper backgrounds sometimes provide guidance where international law provides no guidance yet. The deeper backgrounds do so on two levels. They matter procedurally and substantively. Take, for example, Marshall's juxtaposition of old and new diplomacy as an illustration for procedural norms. He contends that the former was secretive and the latter is much more open (Marshall 1997). Although the evolution of the former to the latter is anything but complete, there is something to this differentiation.

Major multilateral conferences on various issues, ranging from the environment to women, from poverty to land mines and so on, along with the involvement of NGOs and extensive media coverage, are a far cry removed from the secret pacts and alliance automatisms leading up to WWI. Customary diplomatic law, not even to speak about codified law, has been slow to catch up with these developments. A major stumbling block is that the move beyond sovereign states as subjects of international law (along with a few exceptions that have been around for a while, such as the International Committee of the Red Cross) is still very much incomplete. Hence, a number of non-traditional diplomatic actors such as NGOs are not easily fitted into diplomatic law. Yet there is the deeper background that has proven more flexible in accommodating these changes. At major multilateral conferences, for example, a general NGO participation norm applies. In principle, any NGO involved in an issue area at stake is eligible for accreditation (→ glossary). Box 5.4 provides an example for such an accreditation process.

Deeper backgrounds also matter on a substantive level. A good illustration for a deeply taken for granted idea underpinning law and its interpretation is the Idea of Europe. The Idea may be summarised in the formula that the standing apart of nations breeds war, whereas their cooperation and integration breed peace. Box 5.5 discusses this *episteme* in more depth. The Idea is not a legal norm. It is not even a norm. It was the lens of looking at the past, present and future of Europe that drove visionary diplomats – among them the statesmen Konrad Adenauer, Jean Monnet, Robert Schumann, Paul-Henri Spaak – in their European unification efforts. Without this shared background idea, perhaps it could be most fruitfully conceptualised as *episteme* (Kornprobst 2008: 22–26), there would have been no Treaty of Paris establishing the European Coal and Steel Community, no Treaties of Rome developing this Coal and Steel Community into the European Communities and no Maastricht Treaty establishing the EU (TEC).

Box 5.4 Applying for NGO accreditation

Applying for accreditation at major multilateral conferences is a fairly straightforward process. For example, negotiations of the International Negotiating Committee for a legally binding instrument on mercury, which started in 2009, require the following files:

- 'A copy of your organization's constitution, charter, statutes or by-laws, including any amendments to these documents, and a list of affiliates (if any);
- A statement of the organization's mission and scope of work, including detailed accounts of the extent of outreach, indications of interactions within the community or other activities. Supporting documentation could include a published mission statement (available on a website or in brochures);
- A proof of interest in the environment or health sector, including description of activities you have undertaken over the last two years or more demonstrating an interest in the environment, health, or related sectors. Such proof could include annual reports, conference or seminar reports, press releases and copies of media statements, newsletters or other periodicals.'

(UNEP 2011)

Box 5.5 The Idea of Europe

The Idea of Europe accepts that Europe consists of distinct nation-states but postulates that these are not autonomous from one another. Their fate is understood as being inescapably intertwined. In the past, Europe had failed to understand this shared fate, causing a series of disasters. Only overcoming the divisiveness of Europe's nation-state borders through cooperation and integration makes it possible for Europe to prevent these tragedies from reoccurring. Historically, the Idea of Europe tended to gain influence among intellectual elites all over Europe after major catastrophes. They used the Idea of Europe to make sense of what happened and to find ways to prevent disasters from reoccurring. Early accounts of the Idea were about state interactions, for instance by Maximilian de Béthune, duc de Sully who wrote shortly after the Thirty Years War, and the Abbé de Saint-Pierre (1986 [1712]) and Jeremy Bentham (1974 [1789]) who were influenced by the Enlightenment's belief in progress. A seminal statement of the Idea (applied not only to Europe but the world) is David Mitrany's essay *A Working Peace System*, written in the middle of World War II. It is only after World War II that the Idea starts to leave its mark on European diplomacy. Arguably, the Idea is weakening because the generation that experienced the cruelties of WWII has left the diplomatic stage and is replaced by actors to whom a recurring of Europe's past catastrophes seems entirely impossible.

Summary

- Diplomats are embedded in *contexts*. These contexts constitute the diplomat and diplomacy in the first place. Without these contexts, there would be no diplomacy!
- International public law, especially diplomatic law, makes for an important dimension of these contexts. It stipulates the dos and don'ts of diplomats and host state institutions. To date, the 1961 Vienna Convention on Diplomatic Relations is still at the core of diplomatic law. Reflecting a different diplomatic age, however, it is highly state-centric and offers only little guidance on how to deal with the multiplications of global diplomacy (especially the advent of non-traditional diplomatic actors).
- Diplomats are trained to reflect on international public law and justify their stances in terms of this law. Yet there is a host of ideas they use to orient themselves in the diplomatic world that they do not reflect upon. They are so powerful and deeply ingrained that diplomats, in their everyday practices of doing diplomacy, simply take them for granted. We refer to the repertoires of these deeply ingrained ideas as *deeper backgrounds*.
- There are *three schools of thought* that help the scholar to think about how to conceptualise deeper backgrounds: Liberalism, English School and Constructivism. Liberalism postulates a much thinner concept of background than Constructivism does. The English School is located somewhere in the middle but closer to Constructivism.

Study questions

- What are the strengths and weaknesses of diplomatic law in ensuring the functionality of global diplomacy?
- In what ways do legal and sociological scholars converge and diverge in defining rules and principles? What repercussions does this have for the study of diplomacy?
- Is diplomacy a civilising institution?
- Do *epistemes* drive regional integration efforts?
- What methodological challenges are there for research on deeper backgrounds and how are they to be met?

Recommended further reading

Constantinou, Costa M. 1996. *On the way to diplomacy*. Minneapolis: University of Minnesota Press.
This book deals with evolving diplomatic backgrounds in depth. Putting poststructuralist insights to use, Constantinou makes strange what usually passes as diplomatic orthodoxies.

Denza, Eileen. 2008. *Diplomatic law: Commentary on the Vienna Convention on Diplomatic Relations*. 3rd edn. Oxford: Oxford University Press.
Frequently cited by scholars and routinely used by practitioners, this is an authoritative commentary on the 1961 Vienna Convention.

Neumann, Iver. 2007. 'A speech that the entire ministry may stand for, or: Why diplomats never produce anything new'. *International Political Sociology* no. 1 (2): 183–200.
Putting the Norwegian case under scrutiny, Neumann deals with the deeper background that shapes work at a foreign service and its resulting practices. Neumann is quite critical. The deeper background has a tendency to perpetuate itself. It does not foster innovation.

Wiseman, Geoffrey R. 2005. 'Pax Americana: Bumping into diplomatic culture'. *International Studies Perspectives* no. 6 (4): 409–430.
This is a case study on the 2003 US-led intervention against Saddam Hussein's Iraq. The author identifies key diplomatic norms in the field of war and peace. Then, he discusses how the US transgressed them and with what consequences.

6 Tasks of global diplomacy

Chapter objectives

- To identify the main tasks of diplomacy.
- To discuss different ways of performing these tasks.
- To provide an overview of how literature on diplomacy conceptualises these tasks.
- To relate the tasks to diplomatic contexts.

Introduction

No matter what kind of diplomatic actor and no matter what kind of issue area this actor addresses, it is possible to identify key tasks of diplomacy. This chapter refers to these as *messaging, negotiation, mediation* and *talk.* Not every kind of diplomat engages in these tasks in the same way. At the risk of oversimplification, traditional diplomats representing states tend to perform all four tasks whereas non-traditional diplomats representing international governmental or NGOs oftentimes do more messaging and talking than negotiation and mediation. The category of talk may come as a surprise to the reader. Yet, in our view, this is a key category in the age of global diplomacy. Persuasion, for instance, which is a distinct form of talk, is omnipresent in diplomacy. The power of the word is not to be underestimated. Without it, non-traditional diplomats would have precious little means of influencing.

The tasks we discuss may best be summarised under the heading of communication. Diplomacy is about communication. Messaging, negotiation, mediation and talk – along with the sub-categories we identify – are different modes of communication. Above everything else, the diplomat is a communicator.

Inventing messages to communicate as well as understanding these messages and generating convergences around some of them across different diplomatic actors are made possible by the contexts in which these actors are embedded. To put this differently, the contexts make it possible for actors to come to imagine a message they seek to send in the first place. It also makes it possible for them to make sense of the messages sent by others. Furthermore, it delineates the possibilities for different actors to converge on an agreement – however tentative this convergence may be in many cases.

Being a diplomat, therefore, has a lot to do with *putting contexts to use in order to perform communicative tasks.* This putting backgrounds to use, in turn, produces and

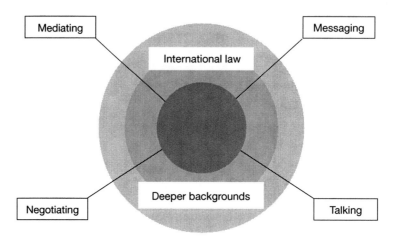

Figure 6.1 Interplay of diplomatic contexts and diplomatic tasks

reproduces the contexts. Figure 6.1 summarises the interplay of backgrounds and tasks. The grey area in between law and deeper backgrounds indicates the overlap between them, as discussed in Chapter 5.

This chapter is organised into four parts. We start with the task of messaging, which may very well be the oldest function of the diplomat. We continue with discussing negotiation and then mediation, including track-two and back-channel diplomacy, in some depth. Finally, we focus on the category of talk, emphasising that we consider it much more consequential than the everyday usage of the term may suggest.

Messaging

Diplomats are *messengers*. When it comes to traditional state diplomacy, the messages that diplomats convey tend to run in two directions. On the one hand, diplomats convey messages from their capital to the capital of the host state. In its purest form, the diplomat is confined to conveying this message in every detail. There is no room to manoeuvre. Declarations of war very much belong to this category. Take, for instance, the German declaration of war on the Soviet Union. On 21 June 1941, Friedrich-Werner von der Schulenburg, the German ambassador to Moscow, was radioed a telegram from Berlin, which was classified as 'state secret' and 'very urgent'. The telegram contained a fateful message to the Soviet government, culminating in the following summary:

> To sum up, the Government of the Reich declares, therefore, that the Soviet Government, contrary to the obligations it assumed,
> 1 has not only continued, but even intensified its attempts to undermine Germany and Europe;
> 2 has adopted a more and more anti-German foreign policy;

3   has concentrated all its forces in readiness at the German border. Thereby
the Soviet Government has broken its treaties with Germany and is about to
attack Germany from the rear, in its struggle for life. The Führer has therefore ordered the German Armed Forces to oppose this threat with all the
means at their disposal.

(Public Broadcasting Service (PBS) 2009)

Predictably, the declaration of war blamed the victim to be the perpetrator. The
last sentence is the actual declaration of war. Schulenburg really was just its messenger; he was not its author. He had joined the Nazi Party shortly after Hitler came
to power. In 1934, he had become Hitler's ambassador to Moscow. In 1939, he had
pushed for the Hitler–Stalin Pact, in which the two sides agreed not to attack one
another and delineated their spheres of influence at the expense of a number of
Eastern European states. In the morning of 22 June 1941, Schulenburg went to the
Kremlin and conveyed his fateful message to Vyacheslav Molotov, the Soviet foreign
minister. Molotov asked Schulenburg why Berlin was breaking the Hitler–Stalin Pact.
Both Schulenburg and Molotov had been architects of this Pact. Ignoring the order
not to 'enter any discussion of this communication', also contained in the telegram,
Schulenburg reputedly replied: 'For the last six years I've personally tried to do everything I could to encourage friendship between the Soviet Union and Germany. But
you can't stand in the way of destiny' (Public Broadcasting Service (PBS) n.d.). Three
years later, the *Volksgerichtshof* (People's Court) found him guilty for conspiring to
assassinate Hitler near Rastenburg, close to the Eastern front. He was hung in Berlin-
Plötzensee. Diplomats do not always agree with the messages that they have to convey.

On the other hand, diplomats convey messages from the host state back to the
capital. They tell their capital what is happening in the host state. This very much
includes what happens underneath the surface. In his *Advice to Raffaeloo Girolami*,
Machiavelli writes about how to penetrate the secrecy of courts:

[T]o find out all the intrigues, and to conjecture the issue correctly, that is
indeed difficult, for you have nothing to depend upon except surmises aided by
your own judgment. But as the courts are generally filled with busybodies, who
are always on the watch to find out what is going on around them, it is very desirable to be on friendly terms with them all, so as to be able to learn something
from each one of them.

(Machiavelli, Advice to Raffaeloo Girolami, on his departure,
23 October 1522, as ambassador to the emperor Charles V,
in Spain: Machiavelli in Berridge 2004: 42)

This information-retrieving function is usually confined to details about planned policies. Some of it takes place in the grey area of what the Vienna Convention allows and
does not allow, or even beyond. Chapter 5 on contexts and diplomatic law alluded
to this. In rare occasions, the messaging from the host state back to the capital is
more conceptual in nature. Among these, Kennan's *Long Telegram* has been one of
the most influential messages ever sent by a diplomat. It is well worth looking at this
document in some depth, too.

In early 1946, the US Treasury was puzzled by Moscow's lack of support of the
World Bank and the IMF, which had just been created. The Treasury, as much of

the US bureaucracy, still thought of the Soviet Union as an ally. The Soviet scepticism against these new international institutions, therefore, came as a surprise. The Treasury sent a request to the US embassy in Moscow to explain this behaviour. This request found its way onto the desk of George F. Kennan, then Deputy Chief of Mission of the US to the Soviet Union. Kennan started his telegram with apologising for the unusual format and length of the telegram.

He provided a detailed five-step analysis about the general trajectory of foreign policy. First, he claimed that the beliefs in a 'capitalist encirclement' as well as the impossibility of peaceful co-existence between capitalism and socialism, inevitable infighting within the capitalist camp and the necessity to prevent such infighting in the socialist camp formed the key premises of Moscow's understanding of world politics. Second, he contended that Moscow inferred from this that 'everything must be done to advance relative strength of USSR as factor in international society', to deepen and exploit differences among capitalist states and to stamp out deviant tendencies in the socialist world (such as social democracy). Third, he predicted that Moscow's overt policies would revolve around advancing Soviet power and prestige, for instance in the Third World and in international organisations. Fourth, he forecast that the Soviet Union's covert policies would pay special attention to 'rank and file of Communist Parties', instalment of puppet regimes (for example Turkey) and 'everything possible will be done to set major Western Powers against each other'. These four points taken together, according to Kennan (1946), amounted to a huge challenge:

> In summary, we have here a political force committed fanatically to the belief that with US there can be no permanent modus vivendei that it is desirable and necessary that the internal harmony of our society be disrupted, our traditional way of life be destroyed, the international authority of our state be broken, if Soviet power is to be secure.

Fifth, Kennan elaborated on how the US should respond to this challenge. At the core of these elaborations is a juxtaposition. The Soviet leadership, Kennan held, was '[i]mpervious to the logic of reason'. But 'it is highly sensitive to the logic of force'. In Kennan's view, therefore, the challenge could be met if the West – and especially the US – stood firm. This standing firm would have a military component but it would also encompass putting forward 'a constructive picture of sort of world we would like to see'. The strength to stand firm could only come out of US society: 'Much depends on health and vigor of our own society. World communism is like malignant parasite which feeds only on diseased tissue.'

Kennan's message was not without consequences. It is a landmark document whose key arguments found their way into the minds of American elites and the public. Some of the channels through which this occurred are quite clear by now. In summer 1946, President Truman asked one of his closest advisors, Clark Clifford, to write a report on US foreign policy. Clifford used the *Long Telegram* as the foundation for his report, which Truman considered very important and helpful. Half a year later, Kennan published an article entitled 'The sources of Soviet conduct' under the pseudonym 'X' in *Foreign Affairs*, thus diffusing it to a wider audience. The article bears a strong resemblance to the Long Telegram. We will come back to the Long Telegram at the end of this chapter because it is not only a good illustration for messaging but also how innovation and messaging are intertwined.

But let us conclude this section on another note. *Non-traditional diplomatic actors are important messengers as well.* Take NGOs, for example. For them, the target audience is not an administration back home but a public (national, regional or global). NGOs such as Amnesty International and Human Rights Watch issue regular reports on human rights abuses worldwide. These reports make a difference. In the worst case scenario, they merely raise awareness but the problem persists. Yet there are even cases in which states, put under pressure by public opinion, rethink their practices. When the George W. Bush Administration, starting with the intervention in Afghanistan, transferred al-Qaeda and Taliban suspects to Guantanamo Bay in Cuba in 2002, it did so not only because it was deemed as being located outside of US legal jurisdiction by the US Department of Justice but also because the distant outpost in the Carribean was considered far removed from scrutiny by journalists and activists. The former allowed for detention conditions and interrogation techniques way below those permissive in the US while the latter was supposed to shield against criticism of these conditions and techniques. Not even the distant outpost, however, could provide such a shield. Human rights NGOs did in-depth research on how the officially labelled 'unlawful combatants' were brought to Cuba and how they were treated there. These reports led to a public outcry against the detention facility. George W. Bush and his defence secretary, Donald Rumsfeld, withstood this pressure. Yet Bush's successor, Barack Obama, ordered the suspension of proceedings at Guantanomo Bay and the closure of the facility within a year soon after he assumed office.

International organisations, too, are important messengers. Through annual reports, say on economic growth and financial transactions, development and good governance, international migration and transmittances and so on, as well as through more *ad hoc* fact-finding endeavours, for instance the IAEA inspectors in Iraq in 2002 or CTBTO observations on nuclear testing during North Korea's 2009 test contribute to making global reality. International organisations, as Barnett and Finnemore point out, have a particular kind of authority that predisposes many other actors to listen to them. They are seen as non-political entities serving not themselves but the global community. This makes their word count (Barnett and Finnemore 1999).

Negotiation

Negotiations come in different shapes and forms. On the one hand, consider the simple convergence on a fundamental and highly consequential decision in a meeting between Churchill and Stalin. On 9 October 1944, the two leaders discussed future spheres of influence in Moscow. Late in the evening, Churchill put an important item on the agenda: 'Let us settle about our affairs in the Balkans.' He continued: 'We have interests, missions, and agents there. Don't let us get at cross-purpose in small ways. So far as Britain and Russia are concerned, how would it do for you to have ninety per cent dominance in Rumania, for us to have ninety per cent of the say in Greece, and go fifty-fifty about Yugoslavia?' Churchill wrote these figures on a piece of paper. Stalin looked at the list, listened to the translation, paused quickly, 'took his blue pencil and made large tick upon it, and passed it back to us'. Churchill was rather satisfied with the meeting: 'It was all settled in no more time than it takes to sit down.' Ultimately, this account, taken from Siracusa (Siracusa 2010: 55–56), originates with Churchill. Stalin may not have been that passive an actor and other things may have happened a bit differently as well. But the gist of it matches more elaborate studies by historians. It is rather remarkable how easily the two leaders reached a decision that would crucially shape the fate of Europe for decades to come.

On the other hand, there are issues where even more or less constant negotiation and re-negotiation does not yield any breakthroughs. Climate change negotiations belong to this category. On 21 December 1990, the General Assembly adopted Resolution 45/212, which set up a negotiation committee on climate change. Two years later, the UNFCCC (or Rio Declaration) was signed. This document, as its name suggests, was anything but a detailed agreement; it was very much a framework. In particular, the commitments in Article 4 remain broad and vague. Negotiations among the great number of parties – with some NGO involvement – continued in order to arrive at more tangible outcomes. The 1997 Kyoto Protocol was a step forward in this regard but still remained rather general in nature. In Article 17, it explicitly called for elaboration of 'relevant principles, modalities, rules and guidelines'. Despite regular climate summits, such an elaboration has not taken place. The 2005 Montreal climate summit, which finally adopted the 2001 Marrakesh Accords formally, provided a small step into this direction. More recent summits, however, such as Copenhagen in 2009 and Durban in 2011, were more dedicated to prevent the entire climate change regime from collapsing than to institutionalise it more firmly.

Since negotiations come in so many different shapes or forms, it is best to define them broadly. Thompson's definition is helpful in this regard: 'Negotiation is an interpersonal decision making process necessary whenever we cannot achieve our objectives single-handedly' (Thompson 2009: 2). The multi-faceted nature of negotiations notwithstanding, is it possible to generalise what makes for successful negotiations?

Game theory has established itself as an influential angle from which to approach this question. Game theory asks the question of *how players, locked into a single game, can reach optimal results for these players.* Using chess as a metaphor provides an entry into the basic conceptual toolkit of game theory. There are two players (actors) sitting on a board (context). They pursue strategies (e.g., a particular opening) in order to win the game (→ glossary). Here, the metaphor reaches its limits. A game such as the often employed prisoners' dilemma is not about winning all the way down. It is about finding a set of strategies and counter-strategies that are configured in a way that no unilateral deviation from it by either one of the players improves a player's pay-off. This set is called a Nash equilibrium. In studies on diplomacy, game theory finds wide application in particular policy fields such as peace and war (Touval and Zartman 1985) as well as in more general attempts to capture the dynamics of diplomatic negotiations (Putnam 1988).

There are plenty of other scholarly angles from which to make sense of negotiation. Political psychology cautions that negotiators are not always the computational machines that game theory makes them out to be. *Emotions* (→ glossary), in particular, matter. They constitute the affective dynamics between players, which, in turn, has repercussions for the selection of their strategies and even their interest formation. *Perceptions* (→ glossary) are important, too. They affect how player A sees player B, including the power that B has in the eyes of A (Goldman *et al.* 2003: 77). More sociologically inclined approaches elaborate on the intangible aspects of power, for example by studying the repercussions of *status and prestige* on negotiations (Cohen 2001). *Occupational culture* is another important concept. Diplomats, no matter where they come from, converge around some taken for granted ideas about what diplomacy is and how to do it, including how to negotiate. This facilitates their negotiations (Salacuse 1998). In the language of Chapter 5, there are convergences around background ideas that constitute diplomacy in general and diplomatic negotiations in particular in the first place.

There are also rather unscholarly angles from which to make sense of negotiations. Box 6.1 discusses some of them.

At this point, the reader may object that this overview of negotiation has been rather state-centric so far. Indeed, there are many actors outside of the foreign services of nation-states who leave their mark on negotiations in world politics. Yet in order to see what they do, we have to go beyond the scholarly accounts of negotiation listed above. *Informal networks*, for example, are of key importance for negotiations. They crucially shape negotiations and their outcomes before the negotiations even take place. Usually, it is not just traditional diplomats who make up these networks but there are actors representing NGOs, transnational corporations, international organisations etc. as well. It is through the interaction in these informal networks that actors make up their minds about interests and how to act accordingly (Jönsson and Strömvik 2005). Even more so, actors arrive at interpretations about the world and the seemingly self-evident oughts and ought nots for how to act through interaction in these networks. Some actors occupy nodes in this network that enable them to diffuse their understandings of the world and these actors are not necessarily traditional diplomats.

Actors representing international organisations, for example, have *social construction power*. Barnett and Finnemore correctly point out that they 'define shared international tasks (like 'development'), create and define new categories of actors (like 'refugee'), create new interests for actors (like 'promoting human rights') and transfer models of political organisation around the world (like markets and

---

Box 6.1 Limitations of scholarly perspectives on negotiation

For all the scholarly angles there are, they cannot capture every nuance of negotiations. François de Callières, for instance, recommended to the negotiator to 'drink in such a manner as not to lose control of his own faculties while endeavouring to loosen the self-control of others' (de Callières in Freeman 1997). This may not be the most scholarly of all perspectives but one should not forget that diplomacy is not just about giving prepared grand speeches in great halls but that the moments that move negotiations along are often informal in nature. Depending on setting and cultural differences, this may sometimes include a drink or two. When Konrad Adenauer, West Germany's chancellor, travelled to Moscow in 1955 to negotiate about the return of German prisoners of war, he did have this aspect in mind. He ordered his delegation to take plenty of rollmops (pickled herring fillets) with them, and eat them before informal negotiation rounds. He expected these rounds to involve more than a glass of vodka, and hoped for the alcohol-absorbing quality of the fatty fish. What role the fatty fish exactly played is rather unclear but the negotiations were successfully concluded. The Soviet Union agreed to release the last 10,000 German prisoners of war. In return, West Germany agreed to open diplomatic relations with the Soviet Union. The highly sensitive issue of West German recognition of East Germany did not feature in the agreement.

democracy)'. These categories, in turn, form the building blocks of many negotiations (although these negotiations may not always leave their definitions untouched). Note how foundational, and thus consequential, this knowledge is. Whether someone enjoys protection as a refugee or is classified as an 'illegal alien', to use a US phrase, makes a huge difference for this person. When it comes to defining these categories, international bureaucracies play an important role (Barnett and Finnemore 1999: 699).

NGOs, too, are often excluded from the actual negotiation processes leading to international agreements, or they are relegated to mere observer status. But *raising awareness* about a problem, at times even putting an issue on the bargaining table in the first place, and *framing* such a problem in a way that it gives the message a punch into the right direction has a lot to do with the communicative work of NGOs prior to inter-state negotiations. In 1997, 133 states signed the Anti-Personnel Mine Ban Convention in Ottawa. What looks, at first glance, like a typical inter-state agreement has the authorship of NGOs written all over it. In the 1990s, 'some one thousand NGOs from over sixty countries' started their vigorous campaign to ban landmines. Jody Williams emerged as their coordinator and the resulting International Campaign to Ban Landmines (ICBL) gained more and more momentum (Price 1998). At the beginning of the momentum was an information campaign. The ICBL brought shocking statistics to world opinion. About 500 people – mostly civilians – were killed or maimed by land mines each week. This information campaign was linked to international law and deeper backgrounds. Randomly striking against civilians is incompatible with established *ius in bello*. The campaign gained more and more legitimacy. The ICBL became an authority to be listened to, especially after being awarded the Nobel Peace Prize in 1997. By the mid-1990s, the Campaign had found strong resonance among traditional diplomatic circles. States such as Belgium, Canada and Germany became outspoken proponents of a ban on landmines. Lloyd Axworthy, Canadian foreign minister, seized the right moment and hosted a meeting in Ottawa in December 1997, where the negotiations were concluded successfully.

The Anti-Personnel Mine Ban Convention should be seen as a qualified success. Some major powers, including China, Russia and the US, have neither signed nor ratified the Convention. Yet 159 states have done so, and this makes for a significant step forward. Yet determining negotiation success or failure – or degrees thereof – is not always easily done. This applies especially to negotiations about peace. Under what conditions does a ceasefire agreement qualify as a successful bargain? Take, for example, the civil war in Bosnia-Herzegovina. Numerous ceasefires were negotiated and breaking them, often within hours of their conclusion, became a routine, especially for the Bosnian Serb side. Under what conditions does a peace agreement qualify as a success? This question is even more tricky. Encounters between Israel and Palestine illustrate this all too well. There were seemingly major breakthroughs, especially the Oslo Accords, signed by Yitzak Rabin and Yasser Arafat. But these seeming breakthroughs always had the drawback that some of the potentially explosive issues pertaining to land (borders between Israel and a newly established Palestinian state) and people (return of Palestinian refugees, Jewish settlements) were shelved in the hope that once the peace process had come into full swing, even these issues could be resolved. To this date, they remain unresolved. We will return to this case in our next section, which deals with mediation.

Mediation

Leading negotiations to the conclusion of an agreement is often a rather complicated task for the parties on the bargaining table. This is why they sometimes accept the involvement of third parties, who are not directly involved in the conflict and try to facilitate the negotiations. Such involvement is called mediation. Christopher Mitchell provides a useful and broad definition of this diplomatic task: it is an 'intermediary activity ... undertaken by a third party with the primary intention of achieving some compromise settlement of issues at stake between parties, or at least ending disruptive conflict behaviour' (Mitchell 1981: 287). In principle, any conflict may be mediated in the diplomatic realm. The conflict may be about an economic, environmental, health issue and so on as long as this issue is deemed to have an international dimension. In practice, mediation efforts about security issues are the most visible. Thus, most of our empirical illustrations in this section are taken from this issue area.

Focusing on states, the literature on mediation lists several reasons why mediators offer their facilitating role to conflicting parties. One of them is *standing* in the international community. De Callières contends that mediation raises a state's prestige. 'Nothing is more proper to raise the reputation of his power, and to make it respected by all nations' (de Callières 2004). The current, more empirically inclined literature on mediation also looks at prestige and mediation but draws the causal arrow in the opposite direction. Great powers – i.e. states with a lot of prestige in the sense de Callières was writing about it – get more frequently involved in mediation than small and middle powers. Taken together, these arguments may suggest a more complex hypothesis in which the link between prestige and mediation runs both ways. Great powers, *qua* their great power status, feel the need to get involved as mediators much more often than smaller powers do, and this, in turn, may contribute to them reproducing this great power status.

Aside from prestige, states may also mediate because they are *concerned about the destabilising repercussions* of continuing conflict for the international system. Washington's long-standing mediation efforts in the Middle East, especially between Israel and Palestine, fall under this rubric. Former US President Bill Clinton, for instance, was adamant about his opinion that resolving this conflict would have important positive consequences not only for the whole of the Middle East but also for world politics. Among other things, he expected such a resolution to siphon off fuel for the agitation and terrorist campaigns by Islamic fundamentalists.

Yet it is not only states who engage in mediation. International organisations – on the global and regional levels – often have mediation tasks *enshrined in their charters and other key constitutive documents*. Chapter VI of the UN Charter, dealing with the pacific settlement of disputes, puts emphasis on mediation in Article 36, i.e. the first article of this chapter. In his Agenda for Peace, Boutros Boutros-Ghali also stresses the importance of mediation and underlines approvingly that, in UN practice, '[f]requently it is the Secretary-General himself who undertakes the task' (Boutros-Ghali and UN 1992). Regional organisations such as the AU, Arab League and the EU prescribe to their members to seek mediation if disputes in the region arise. At times, the interpretation of this mandate to mediate is so strong that it violates what is sometimes seen as a key characteristic of mediation, i.e. that the parties to a conflict agree to the mediation effort. The Arab League's move to dispatch an observer mission to Syria in late 2011 and especially its January 2012 recommendation to replace Bashar al-Assad's regime with an inclusive power-sharing agreement occurred despite al-Assad's constant attempts to deny the Arab League a meaningful role in the conflict.

NGOs and NGO-like entities engage in mediation, too. They can do so with major success. The Community of Sant-Egidio helped to bring the decades-old Mozambican civil war to an end. In the early 1990s, the Community mediated between the *Frente de Libertaçao de Moçambique* (Frelimo) and the *Resistência Nacional Mocambicana* (Renamo). In 2002, the parties signed a peace agreement at the seat of the Community in Rome.

There are different types of mediation. Some of these types qualify even if we would use a more narrow textbook definition of mediation that puts heavy emphasis on voluntary agreement by the conflicting parties. But not all of them would do. Bercovitch and Kadayifci-Orellana (2009), looking at the strategies employed by the mediators, distinguish three types. First, there are *communication-facilitating strategies*. Mediators confine themselves to passing on messages from one conflict party to the other. They may also add credible information of which the conflict parties had previously been unaware. Second, there are *procedural strategies*. Assuming less of a passive role, mediators attempt to create an environment in which negotiations can be led to a successful conclusion. This ranges from suggesting places and times for negotiations to an agenda-setting function. Even something as seemingly mundane as the right place for negotiations may play a major facilitating role. Third, there are *directive strategies*. Assuming a distinctly active role, mediators strongly intervene in the negotiation process, for example by providing incentives and issuing ultimatums.

Any of these types, but in particular the first one, may be closely associated with a peculiar kind of negotiation. While back-channel (→ glossary) negotiations are not necessarily associated with mediation, they often are. Facilitating communication frequently has something to do with opening up communication channels between conflict parties that are shielded from the public limelight and interference from possible spoilers within the conflict parties. This shield has a number of advantages. It makes it possible for leaders – usually via their closest advisors – to explore a range of options that would otherwise be unthinkable.

Take the Oslo Agreement, for example. The main goal of the Norwegian mediators, especially Terje Rød-Larsen and Mona Juul, was to establish an informal back-channel through which Yitzak Rabin and Yasser Arafat could freely talk about possible avenues for peace. Rabin and Arafat chose Simon Peres and Mahmoud Abbas, respectively, as chief negotiators. During twelve rounds of negotiations Peres and Abbas not only realised that the other side was prepared to make concessions that had previously been deemed unthinkable but also that they developed an interpersonal relationship that would prove crucial for moving the negotiations along. All of this happened at a time when even talking to who was widely taken to be the enemy still risked a major backlash at home. The shield also has disadvantages though. Not trying to include possible spoilers early on can upset the negotiation process at a later stage or make the implementation impossible. Related to this, the back-channel may lead to groupthink. Leaders and especially their close aides involved in the back-channel negotiations may overestimate what is possible; they may engage in groupthink (Putnam and Carcasson 1997). The Oslo Accords bear some of these scars. The negotiations were completed in August 1993 and then signed in Washington on 13 September 1993. But implementation collapsed amidst strong and determined domestic opposition in Israel and Palestine. This opposition cost Rabin his life, when he was killed by the right-wing extremist Yigal Amir.

Most of the literature on mediation attempts to identify the causes of success and failure of mediation. Notwithstanding the problems of defining what success in negotiations actually is (see previous section), many different explanations are provided. Table 6.1 outlines the most frequently discussed ones among these. Some of them are in notable tension to one another, while others are complementary.

The literature puts a strong emphasis on *impartiality*. If there was a top-ten of causes for success to which analysts subscribe, this would be it and always has been. Berridge, in his overview of classical writings on diplomacy, comments on an important agreement among the authors: 'They are unanimous that a mediator is, *by definition*, impartial' (Berridge 2004: 4). Vattel is also adamant about impartiality. A 'mediator should observe an exact impartiality' (Vattel 2004: 189). Wicquefort, writing about an instruction manual for a diplomat engaging in mediation, formulates the same postulate in even more absolute terms. This manual has to

> recommend to him first, and above all things, indifference, without which all his offices would be useless; in which the legate ought to be so exact that not only no partiality should be discovered in his conduct, but also that none should be observable in the actions or words of his domestics.
>
> (Wicquefort 2004: 133)

Impartiality, in short, tends to be seen as a *sine qua non* for successful mediation. Other explanations focusing on the mediator are also influential, although none as influential as impartiality. There is the argument that the mediator's experience makes a major difference (Kleiboer 2002). There is also the contention that the mediator has to *represent a powerful entity* with plenty of resources at its hands. Strong states are expected to be more successful mediators than weak ones (Greig 2001). Other hypotheses focus on the types of mediation as outlined above. On the one hand, there is the opinion that mediation strategies have to be *more robust* than merely facilitating information. When it comes to robustness, the authors have directive mediation in mind (Beardsley 2008). On the other hand, there is also the opinion that the provision of *credible information* facilitates mediation (Kydd 2006). Trying to

Table 6.1 Explaining success and failure of mediation

Explanatory focus	Key explanans
Mediator	Impartiality
	Experience
	Power
Mediation	Robustness
	Information
Conflict	Ripeness
	Regime type
Mediator and parties	Positive identification
	Legitimacy

reduce the tension between these two hypotheses, there is also a middle-ground argument proposing that only high-quality information facilitates mediation; otherwise information-facilitating mediation is less likely to be successful than more robust strategies (Savun 2008).

Some hypotheses suggest that it is actually not the mediation but *the conflict itself* that is the main determinant of the outcome of mediation efforts. There is again the argument that conflicts have to be ripe for resolution. Greig and Diehl, for example, make an intriguing point about enduring rivalries. They suggest that mediation has little chance early and late in the rivalry. The most promising window is in the middle, ca. twenty-five years into the rivalry (Greig and Diehl 2006). Furthermore, some authors submit that regime type matters. Democracies are considered more amenable to conflict resolution by mediation than authoritarian regimes (Bercovitch and Kadayifci-Orellana 2002).

Finally, there are also arguments focusing on the *relationship between the mediator and the conflict parties*. Positive identification between conflict parties on the one hand and the mediator on the other, it is argued, generate trust and, thus, facilitate mediation. This positive identification can be rooted in religion (Bercovitch and Kadayifci-Orellana 2009) or other, more malleable cultural bonds (Carnevale and Choi 2000). Another approach stresses the salience of the legitimacy of the mediator. Legitimacy, as other intangible resources to make mediation work, is generated through the interaction between mediators and conflict parties (Jabri 1996).

Talk

This heading may seem to capture something utterly inconsequential and, indeed, most books on diplomacy omit or at least downplay what we are discussing in this section. In our view, however, this section is as important for capturing what diplomats do and what repercussions this has for world politics as messaging, negotiation and mediation. We discuss four dimensions of diplomatic talk that go much beyond inconsequential chit-chatting.

First, there is *cheap talk*. While formal approaches such as game theory usually focus on what happens on the bargaining table (i.e., the actual haggling going on between the parties), some authors writing in this vein also look at what happens prior to the bargaining situation. Pre-bargaining is considered highly important because it allows the parties to exchange crucial information that was not available to them beforehand. There is an overlap between this insight and research on communication-facilitating mediation, where the mediator provides this information. The first rounds of negotiation in Oslo had the character of pre-bargaining, facilitated by Norwegian mediators.

Second, *rhetorical strategies* make a difference. These are the communicative moves and counter-moves through which diplomats convey their substantive orientations and, thus, take a stance on behalf of the entity they represent. In other words, the political stances that diplomats take do not come unfiltered. They are packaged in a certain way in order to make them leave a mark in diplomatic encounters. This packaging matters. The Non-aligned Movement, for example, has been very critical of nuclear suppliers and nuclear weapon states since the NPT went into force in 1970. But the diplomats of the Movement, for the most part, have packaged the criticism against nuclear weapon states and nuclear suppliers in a way that softened the criticism considerably. They have tended to stay away from delegitimating strategies (Chowdhury and Krebs 2010) such as vilifying other parties and accusing them that no deal is possible with them whatsoever. Instead, they relied heavily on less antagonistic strategies such as shaming. Far from undermining the 1970 non-proliferation deal, these strategies have contributed to reproducing it. They have played their part in emphasising norms on disarmament, peaceful use and nuclear free zones, and make them sink into the taken for granted foundation on which the nuclear non-proliferation regime is built.

Third, attempts of *persuasion* can make a major difference in world politics. Contrary to what game theory and rational choice assume, preferences are not always immutable. Communication among diplomats can change preferences. The one can persuade the other. The above illustrative case of the Anti-Personnel Mine Ban Convention hinted at this already. Activists framed this issue in terms of the Geneva Conventions and human rights provisions. In the parlance of classical argumentation theory, they took commonplaces – taken for granted ideas – and advocated a link between these commonplaces and the new norms to be invented. This mechanism is an important pathway of influence for NGOs. They have to rely on the power of the word (and occasional stunts) in order to make a difference.

Persuasion comes in various shapes and forms. *Public diplomacy* (→ glossary) has become firmly entrenched in post-WWII diplomatic practice. The term was coined by Edmund Gullion, former dean of the Fletcher School of Law and Diplomacy at Tufts University. The main goal of this kind of diplomacy is to influence the politics of the host state indirectly, i.e. via the diffusion of messages to the host state's public (see also Chapter 10). This diffusion of messages may also be accompanied by support for certain civil society actors in the host state. While the overall purpose of public diplomacy is usually to influence the foreign policy of the host state vis-à-vis the sending state, it may also be aimed at influencing foreign policy more generally or even domestic policies. Note that this takes us back into a grey area of diplomatic law, discussed above. Diplomatic law is quite clear that diplomats are not supposed to interfere in the domestic affairs of the host state. Despite these legal constraints, public diplomacy is a firmly established form of diplomacy.

In some communicative encounters, the authority of the speaker and the manner in which the message is conveyed may be as important, or even more important, than the message itself. *Celebrity diplomacy* illustrates this very well. Usually, individual members of our nascent global civil society find it extraordinarily difficult to make themselves heard. Due to their celebrity status, famous actors and musicians are exceptions in this regard. *Qua* their status, they have the authority to speak. Their talk is often accompanied by powerful images, for example Angelina Jolie or Princess Diana holding a little child suffering from malnutrition. Celebrities use various avenues to exert influence. Analysts understand Bono as a celebrity diplomat. Bono does not shy away from intermingling with state leaders. On the contrary, he looks for contacts with them, knowing very well that his 'power of attraction' can make things happen. He does 'bilateral' diplomacy, say with George W. Bush, and 'multilateral' diplomacy at international forums debating development and poverty issues. Bob Geldof, by contrast, is aptly described as 'antidiplomat' (Cooper 2008: 55). There is usually very little softening diplomatic talk, for example, when Geldof scolds officials from the World Bank, the IMF and Western state development agencies over the provision of humanitarian aid to Africa.

Fourth, there is *dialogue*. There are very few terms where diplomatic and scholarly usages are further apart. This word is omnipresent in diplomatic language. All too often it amounts to little more than a nice way of effectively ending a conversation amid disagreement, especially in multilateral settings. Alternatively, it is also used as a synonym of 'okay, we disagree but let's keep on talking' with the 'keep on talking' being a euphemism for 'I'll try to teach you!' The so-called critical dialogue of the EU with Iran in the 1990s illustrates this well. The EU embarked on this policy hoping to be able to teach Iran something about human rights. The policy may be understood as an exercise in norm diffusion.

In scholarly usage, by contrast, dialogue is the most demanding form of talk. Theorists such as Gadamer, Bakhtin, Bernstein and Ricoeur contend that dialogue is about approaching communicative encounters with an open mind. The point about dialogue is not to win one's argument and it is certainly not to dismiss other perspectives prematurely. On the contrary, dialogues require their participants to be prepared to revisit their cherished beliefs and the way they employ these to make sense of a given situation. They need to be eager to learn from different points of view. Put differently, engaging with the views of the other is a chance to get rid of, or at least revisit, one's own prejudgements and prejudices. A thought-provoking study on the end of the Cold War suggests that even high-level, inter-state diplomacy sometimes generates persuasion, and thus a fundamental re-definition of preferences. Risse argues that Soviet leaders were persuaded in top-level talks, especially by the US and West German sides, that German reunification and incorporation in the North-Atlantic Treaty Organization (NATO) would not pose a threat to the Soviet Union (and certainly a lesser one than a neutral one, Washington contended). Not having fixed preferences itself, the Soviet leadership was open to listen to good arguments (Risse 2000).

Dialogue understood in this scholarly way is an ideal that is very difficult to reach in a diplomat's everyday work. But there are some kinds of diplomacy that have the potential to come closer to this ideal than others. In a very interesting contribution, Chataway conducted interviews of traditional diplomats working for the US Department of State. One of the diplomats he quotes alludes to the importance of non-traditional channels of diplomacy:

> I worked with authoritarian regimes in South America where no dialogue is possible, but these private groups, human rights, NGOs, did the undiplomatic work I couldn't do. In authoritarian regimes, diplomats have to watch it. [A diplomat] can be an angel and condemn them, but then you won't get anything done. [NGOs and human rights groups] took the burden off my back.
>
> (Chataway 1998)

This non-traditional channel is often labelled *track-two diplomacy* (→ glossary). The concept is Joseph Montville's, a career diplomat in the American Foreign Service. Reflecting upon the troubled communication between the US and the Soviet Union during the Cold War, he postulated that there should not be only one track of diplomacy, i.e. from government to government, but also a second unofficial one that involves parliamentarians, private citizens, activists, scholars, religious communities and so on. Since there is a plethora of different types of untraditional diplomats involved in track-two diplomacy, Diamond and McDonald write about multi-track diplomacy. In their terminology, the first track is the official government-to-government route whereas the other tracks are distinguished by the type of non-traditional diplomats dominating the track. Track-three, for example, is about the business community, track-nine about the media (Diamond and McDonald 1996).

For Montville, the key advantage of track-two diplomacy is that it does not require the posturing that is needed in track-one diplomacy. The latter, in his opinion, is about standing firm and not showing weakness. The former, by contrast, can experiment and explore, and is much more open-minded. To put this differently, there is much more room for dialogue in track-two than in track-one diplomacy. Take the South African case, for example. From 1980 to 1985, moderate white South Africans and members of the African National Congress (ANC) explored ways of how to put an end to apartheid. This put together people from various walks of life, ranging from business executives to freedom fighters, from parliamentarians to activists, and from scholars to ANC officials. These rather unstructured explorations were crucial. They reduced the threat levels on both sides. Even the normative contours of a new and inclusive South African identity were taking shape during these talks, many of which took place outside of South Africa (for example in Zambia). This case illustrates well how successful track-two diplomacy can be, especially if the actors involved seize the opportunity to step into the shoes of the other, question dominant orthodoxies and dare of talking novelty into being. Changing a racially defined definition of being a South African into the rainbow nation is no small feat. These talks, which at times came to approximate the ideal of a dialogue to a considerable extent, were an important contribution to rethinking South African identity.

There are many other non-traditional channels of diplomacy. Box 6.2 deals with two of them: sports and music diplomacy.

Box 6.2 Sports and music diplomacy

There are many different routes for track-two diplomacy. Some of these even encompass what may be labelled sports diplomacy. In the early 1970s, President Nixon and his advisor Henry Kissinger sought a rapprochement with China in order to contribute to China's moving away from the Soviet Union. Given the ideological differences and the recent history of these two states – the Korean War in which Americans and Chinese soldiers fought one another had happened about two decades before – this rapprochement was anything but an easy diplomatic task. Track-two initiatives proved important to break the old mould. The so-called Ping-Pong Diplomacy was part of these initiatives. From 11 to 17 April 1971, the American ping-pong team played fun matches against the Chinese team and visited various tourist sites in China. Reflecting on this ice-breaking event, the Chinese leader Choi En-Lai said: 'Never before in history has a sport been used so effectively as a tool of international diplomacy' (Graham and Kelley 2009). In the 1990s, a case of music diplomacy caught major attention. Washington's attempts to dissuade North Korea from acquiring nuclear weapons in the Six-Party Talks (China, Japan, North Korea, Russia, South Korea, US) were accompanied by an internationally broadcast visit of the New York Philharmonic Orchestra in Pyongyang in February 2008. In this case, however, track-two initiatives could not prevent the collapse of track-one negotiations. On 14 April 2009, North Korea announced never ever to participate in such Six-Party Talks. On 25 May, North Korea conducted what was in all likelihood a successful underground nuclear test.

Summary

- *Diplomats are messengers,* for instance between sending and hosting state. The extent to which they have room to include their own interpretations and ideas in the messages varies considerably.
- *Diplomats are negotiators.* The sizeable literature on negotiations debates under what conditions negotiations are successful. There are game theoretical explanations, psychological approaches and cultural angles from which to shed light on this question.
- *Mediation* comes in where negotiating parties fail to reach an agreement by themselves. There are also several contending explanations but they converge on the importance of impartiality, which is considered something akin to a *sine qua non* for successful mediation.
- There are many *different kinds of talk, including cheap talk, rhetorical strategies, attempts of persuasion and dialogue.* Public diplomacy, which has become something like a catchphrase in diplomatic discourse, belongs to the persuasion sub-category. Persuasion is also a highly important sub-category for NGOs, who have to rely on the power of the word in order to get their message across.
- *The performance of diplomatic tasks shapes and reshapes the backgrounds that make it possible in the first place.* Traditional and non-traditional diplomats make and remake the backgrounds, which, in turn, shape the ways in which they perform their tasks.

Study questions

- Is messaging describing the world or making it?
- How does game theory help us understand the dynamics of negotiations?
- What are the advantages and disadvantages of back-channel diplomacy?
- What are the dos and don'ts of mediation?
- How do NGOs make a difference on the diplomatic scene?

Recommended further reading

Cooper, Andrew Fenton. 2008. *Celebrity diplomacy.* Boulder, CO: Paradigm Publishers.
Celebrity diplomacy is a highly interesting feature of global diplomacy. Discussing various cases and types of celebrity diplomacy, Cooper provides a very useful introduction to this phenomenon.

Jönsson, Christer. 2002. 'Diplomacy, bargaining and negotiation'. In *Handbook of international relations,* edited by Walter Carlsnaeas, Thomas Risse and Beth Simmons. London: Sage.
This is a broad overview of analytical perspectives on core diplomatic tasks, focusing on negotiation. In contrast to Starkey *et al.* (below), the author has notable leanings towards Constructivism.

Merrills, J.G. 2011. *International dispute settlement*. Cambridge: Cambridge University Press.
Merrills provides a comprehensive account of mechanisms available for international dispute settlement. The author deals in depth with mechanisms we have dealt with here as key diplomatic tasks such as negotiation and mediation. In addition to this, Merrills also addresses legal mechanisms such as arbitration.

Mitzen, Jennifer. 2011. 'Governing together: Global governance as collective intention'. In *Arguing global governance*, edited by Corneliu Bjola and Markus Kornprobst. London and New York: Routledge.
This is a thought-provoking piece on collective intentionality in what we refer to as the global age of diplomacy. The author discusses talk, and the repercussions of talk, in depth.

Starkey, Brigid, Mark A. Boyer and Jonathan Wilkenfeld. 2010. *International negotiation in a complex world*. Lanham, MD: Rowman & Littlefield.
This is a very readable introduction to the study of negotiation from a game theoretical perspective. Using the analogy of a board game throughout the book, the authors discuss context, players, stakes, moves and outcomes.

Part IV
Explaining diplomacy

7 The making of decisions

Chapter objectives

- To introduce the reader to different scholarly logics of action (→ glossary).
- To differentiate different approaches to conceptualise these logics.
- To discuss strengths and weaknesses of these approaches in explaining diplomatic decisions and decision-making.

Introduction

With the exception of the extreme form of messaging in which the diplomat is reduced to delivering a message from one capital to the next, every diplomatic task listed in Chapter 6 requires from the diplomat to make up his or her mind about what to do. How do diplomats come to compose a message? How do they arrive at a stance to defend at a negotiation table? How do they make up their minds about how to mediate in a conflict? How do they figure out how to frame their talk? This chapter, taking a broad view of decisions and decision-making, casts its net widely. It draws from the social sciences to introduce the reader to different perspectives on explaining the making of decisions.

This requires us to switch gears. While the previous chapters were first aimed at describing the evolution of diplomacy (Part II) and then outlining an analytical frame for analysing diplomatic processes (Part III), this chapter begins to explain the work of the diplomat in greater detail. In doing so, we introduce the reader to a broad analytical toolbox, highlighting strengths and weaknesses of different approaches. We take the tools of this toolbox from various disciplines, including political science, economics, psychology and sociology. Since the tools we discuss are at times rather abstract, we frequently refer to important twentieth- and twenty-first-century events and the diplomatic decisions made in order to deal with them as illustrative cases. These events share in common that they pushed decision-makers into addressing the balance between diplomatic and military responses, which helps us to highlight the strengths and weaknesses of the approaches we discuss.

This chapter is organised into five sections. First, we deal with rational choice and discuss its strengths and weaknesses by taking a look at the Cold War logic of deterrence. Second, we provide an overview of contending approaches in political psychology. Here, our illustrative case is the diplomatic run-up to the Second Gulf

War in 2003. Third, we address the logic of appropriateness and employ it to ana-
lyse continuities and discontinuities of German foreign policy since re-unification.
Fourth, we direct our attention to the logic of argumentation and evaluate its explanatory power by putting the driving forces of the end of the Cold War under scrutiny.
Fifth, we outline the logic of practice and probe its explanatory strengths and weaknesses by applying it to France's foreign policy vis-à-vis Africa.

Rational choice

Rational choice remains the dominant perspective for how to study the making of
decisions in the social sciences. On the purely individual level – how actors arrive at a
decision without taking the actions of others into consideration – the key term of this
perspective is *expected utility*. Let us look at this concept, and how it is linked to other
concepts, in a bit more depth by scrutinising the key assumptions on which theorising on expected utility is based. First, the starting assumption is that actors have *desires*
that they want to attain. Second, some of these desires are more important for the
individual than others. In technical language, the individual *rank-orders preferences* by
attributing different degrees of utility to them. It is assumed that the individual does
this consistently during a decision-making situation, i.e. it does not change the rank-
ordering. Third, the individual calculates which action *maximises* its utility.

This is a fairly straightforward mechanism of choice. It becomes more complicated
though when we factor in a common feature of decision-making situations, i.e. uncertainty. Uncertainty means that an actor's calculations cannot generate certainty about
which maximum utility can be attained. Here we have to add a fourth assumption.
An individual can only calculate which maximum utility is to be *expected*. Thus, the
individual does not calculate its utility but merely its expected utility. Calculations of
expected utility include the factor of likelihood and how to deal with it, i.e. whether
to be more risk-prone or more risk-averse.

On the interactive level, the key concept that the rational choice perspective
adds to the above is *strategy* (→ glossary). It is rare that individuals can get what
they want without taking into consideration what others may do. Individuals have
to think of the moves that others may make and choose their moves accordingly
because the interplay of moves and counter-moves crucially affects the pay-offs in
a given decision-making situation. Similar to a chess player choosing a particular
opening to a game, individuals are assumed to plan their moves. Such a plan is
called a strategy. Game theory, already alluded to in the previous chapter, is an
especially rigorous and formal device to understand how the interplay of such strategies can lead to an agreement between actors.

Rational choice is the dominant perspective in diplomatic studies. Authors use it
more or less rigorously. At one end of the spectrum, game theory makes for a very rigorous analytical tool. At other end of the spectrum, scholars make rational choice not
explicit but rely on it in order to explain empirical decision-making. The next section
discusses strengths and weaknesses of rational choice by discussing the 1962 Cuban
Missile Crisis. During the crisis, John F. Kennedy, then US President, estimated the
odds of a nuclear exchange as 'between 1 out of 3 and even' (Allison 1969). What
explains why he, ultimately, let diplomacy rather than a military solution of the crisis
prevail?

Cuba, 1962

On 14 October 1962, US air reconnaissance showed very clearly that a build-up of Soviet missiles was happening in Cuba. Khrushchev had decided not only to secure Cuba with defensive missiles (surface-to-air) but also with offensive ones (ground-to-ground). This triggered an intense crisis in which diplomacy ultimately won out against military options. Starting on 24 October and facilitated by UN Secretary-General U Thant, the leaders of the superpowers, Nikita Khrushchev and John F. Kennedy, exchanged signals for how to de-escalate the crisis. Most importantly, Robert Kennedy, the President's brother and close advisor, and Anatoly Dobrynin, the Soviet Ambassador in Washington, reached an informal agreement that the Soviet Union would ship all its missiles back from Cuba in exchange for the US withdrawing its missiles from Turkey. By the end of the year, this agreement had been implemented.

How come that diplomacy prevailed in the end? Graham Allison, in his seminal article 'Conceptual models and the Cuban missile crisis', starts off with applying a rational choice framework to the Cuban Missile Crisis. The first step in this application is to conceive the state as a unitary decision-maker. The state is anthropomorphised and treated as if it was behaving as a rational individual actor with 'rational' standing for the conformity with the key assumptions of rational choice outlined above. The second step concerns the identification of preferences. Allison, as many authors writing on diplomacy and international relations, does so 'in an intuitive fashion' (Allison 1969: 694). He observes that national security was the overriding interest for the US. He specifies that, in the context of deterrence, Mutually Assured Destruction (MAD) ($\rightarrow$ glossary) and the Cold War, this meant that the military balance must not shift in favour of the Soviet Union.

President John F. Kennedy, helped by his advisors in the Executive Committee (ExComm), discussed six strategies for how to respond to the Soviet challenge. The first strategy that was scrutinised was to do nothing. Starting from the premise that the Soviet build-up of missiles in Cuba does not change the military balance between the US and the Soviet Union, this strategy aims at downplaying the issue and not providing Khrushchev with a 'public relations' victory. Second, Washington could exert diplomatic pressure on Khrushchev in order to persuade him to remove the missiles from Cuba. Various diplomatic routes would be possible for such an endeavour, including a direct (bilateral) approach or an indirect one via the UN or the Organization of American States (OAS). Third, the US could secretly approach Fidel Castro. The goal of such an approach would have to be to lure him away from the Soviet orbit. The fourth strategy that was debated was the most militarily determined one. The US would invade Cuba, remove the missiles itself and bring the island back into its sphere of influence. Fifth, the US air force would take out the missiles through a surgical airstrike. Sixth, the US navy would conduct a naval blockade of Cuba, making it impossible for Soviet ships to deliver more missiles and other necessary hardware.

Next, the analyst dissects these strategies, determining which one provides for the maximum pay-off, given what the other side is likely to do. As Allison puts it, this is not all that complicated in this case. On the one hand, some strategies are too limited and cautious for one to expect them to make a difference. 'Do nothing' only helps if one really does not infer the necessity of the withdrawal of the missiles from the primacy of national security. Given the geographical proximity of missiles in Cuba, however, their withdrawal should be strongly preferred. Exclusively relying on 'diplomatic pressures' is a set of moves that is not very promising either. Absent any military posturing, it is unclear how the US would be able to project the necessary pressure on the Soviet Union to withdraw its missiles from Cuba. The 'secret approach to Castro' is also a set of moves that is likely to fail. Independent of whether Castro could be convinced to leave the Soviet sphere of influence (which is highly unlikely), the missiles were guarded by Soviet soldiers. Thus, the key for removing them lay in Moscow and not in Havana. On the other hand, some strategies were too risky; they could have pushed the world over the brink into nuclear disaster. This applies most clearly to the 'invasion' option. Invading Cuba could have prompted the Soviet Union to retaliate in a like-minded fashion, for instance a move against West Berlin or Turkey. From there, things could have spilled easily out of control. The 'surgical airstrike' was somewhat less risky. But it would still have involved killing Soviet soldiers guarding the missiles, with all the potential of further escalation of the crisis. It was also not entirely clear whether such a surgical airstrike would really be able to destroy all the Cuban missiles. The sixth strategy, i.e. the naval blockade, was situated in the middle of the spectrum of too little and too much resolve. It shows US determination for the Soviet Union to remove the missiles but, at the same time, gives the Soviet Union time to react and keep face. In other words, the blockade option provides an opportunity for diplomacy to diffuse the dangerous situation.

Allison aptly summarises the explanation for the choice of the blockade from the perspective of the rational actor model with the sentence: 'The blockade was the United States' only real option' (Allison 1969: 698). Indeed, he has a point. From a rational choice point of view, we should not be too surprised that John F. Kennedy opted for the naval blockade (or quarantine, as it was labelled for legal reasons) and, ultimately, for a diplomatic resolution of the crisis. Actually, from a rational choice point of view, the Cuban Missile Crisis was not that dangerous after all. It would have been irrational for either party – US and Soviet Union – to escalate the crisis further. Given the pervasive effects of MAD on the preferences and strategies of the two parties, an escalation was very unlikely to occur.

Yet we detect reasons to doubt this firm conclusion as soon as we open up the black-box called state and look into the decision-making mechanisms that happen within the state. Allison, for instance, shows that organisational routines (as opposed to reflective decision-making) deeply influenced decision-making. Perhaps most importantly, the air force, relying on its manuals and unquestioned routines, presumed that an airstrike would be much more extensive than what the ExComm had in mind. With 'surgical' not being in the manuals for how to conduct an airstrike, the airforce sketched a scenario in which airstrikes came to appear too risky to most members of the ExComm. The ExComm was bewildered about the number of sorties required, likely casualties and likely collateral damage. In the ExComm, this cast serious doubt on this option from the very beginning.

The dynamics among the ExComm members, not explicitly addressed by Allison, also allude to weaknesses of rational choice. Collective deliberations and the social relations that shape these deliberations are outside of the analytical scope of rational choice. Ultimately, it was John F. Kennedy's decision what to do. But the President, far from making the decision by himself, heavily relied on the advice of the ExComm members he trusted the most. It is no coincidence that he went with the naval blockade, to be followed by the diplomatic solution of the crisis. This was the course of events advocated by his brother Robert Kennedy and his security advisor Robert McNamara. These two ExComm members he trusted the most. Seen in this light, it is also no coincidence that Robert Kennedy took care of leading the crisis to its diplomatic conclusion by reaching agreement on what to do with the Soviets.

Lord Salisbury once flatly remarked: 'Logic is no use in diplomacy' (quoted in Freeman 1997: 161). Otto von Bismarck predicted the outbreak of WWI with anything but a Rationalist argument. He feared that 'some damned foolish' thing in the Balkans would at some stage lead to a major European war (Siracusa 2010: 32–33). Let us, however, not lose sight of the strengths of rational choice amidst all these *caveats* against all too stringent assumptions of rationality. The rational choice perspective provides for a parsimonious explanatory framework. Rational choice scholars are very much aware of the fact that they simplify the world in order to be able to explain it. In other words, these scholars do not believe that their assumptions are true. They merely defend them as being useful for conducting research.

It is up to the reader to judge under what circumstances rational choice provides for a fruitful perspective to explain diplomatic decisions. The following sections introduce the reader to major alternative perspectives. We start with psychological approaches and then move to different logics of action: appropriateness, argumentation and practice.

Psychological approaches

Since there is a plethora of angles for studying the psychology of leading diplomats and decision-makers, it is much more difficult to summarise the key unifying assumptions of political psychology than it is with rational choice. Yet whatever political psychologists may disagree about, they share the *rejection of computational goal-seeking*. They criticise rational choice assumptions for what is to them pretending that 'the mind has essentially unlimited demonic or supernatural reasoning power' (Gigerenzer and Todd 1999: 6). Psychological explanations often use the term 'judgement' to distance their conceptualisations of agency from rational choice's core assumptions.

Their starting assumption is that actors arrive at a decision-making situation with a lot of *baggage* (conceptualised, for instance, as schema or operational code). Over time, individuals acquire a background knowledge that helps them orientate themselves amidst uncertainty and complexity. Some authors hold that the baggage decision-makers acquire is so deeply seated that it moves into the sub-conscious layers of the ideational fabric. Thus, the baggage becomes a case for psycho-analysis. The baggage is held to be highly consequential. Actors are not assumed to compute endlessly until they have found the optimal outcome for themselves. Instead, they rely on heuristic devices – especially the baggage just mentioned – to tell them when to *stop searching* for alternative options. Herbert Simon's seminal contributions revolve around these stopping rules. His notion of bounded rationality holds that actors do not compute endlessly to maximise but stop to satisfy their expected utility (Simon 1957, 1982). Several approaches build on Simon's work. Prospect theory, for instance, argues that actors are risk-prone in their decision-making when they perceive loss and risk-averse when they perceive gain (Kahnemann and Tversky 1979; Levy 2000). Fast and frugal heuristics contends that actors rely on simple heuristics drawn from an adaptive toolbox to make sense of the world; ultimately, a single clue can suffice for an actor to make up his or her mind (Gigerenzer *et al.* 1999). There are also authors who highlight the emotional dimension of all of this. For some authors emotions are so inescapably intertwined with reason that they simply cannot be kept apart at all. Emotions and reason always go together; or, to put this differently, no reason without emotions (Mercer 2010).

Iraq, 2003

Let us look at another case where key diplomatic actors situated themselves at the thinning line between diplomacy and war. Yet this time, unlike with the Cuban Missile Crisis, the line was actually crossed. In 2003, the US and the United Kingdom, along with a group of other states dubbed the 'coalition of the willing', terminated diplomatic efforts to convince Saddam Hussein to disclose and dismantle his alleged weapons of mass destruction, invaded Iraq, occupied it and installed a different regime. How did they come to do so? What are the strengths and weaknesses of psychological approaches for helping us answer this question?

Judging by the sources available to us, Bush and Blair approached the Iraq question with the baggage of historical analogies and metaphors in mind. Taken together, this baggage helped them make sense of Saddam Hussein, Iraq and what to do. Historical analogies featured very prominently (see Box 7.1). None of them featured as prominently as appeasement. Bush and Blair invoked again and again the Munich analogy. The lesson of Munich 1938 ought to be that dictators have to be confronted before it is too late. In 2003, Saddam Hussein, for Blair and Bush, belonged exactly in this category.

Other historical analogies seem to have been important anchors for reasoning as well. Blair, for example, repeatedly referred to the NATO intervention against Serbia during the 1999 Kosovo conflict. In his opinion, the lesson to be learnt from Kosovo was that intervention works. Not only can it effectively counter threats against peace

---

Box 7.1 Appeasement

Early morning hours on 30 September 1938, Führerbau (Leader's Building) in Munich. Adolf Hitler, Neville Chamberlain, Benito Mussolini and Edouard Daladier sign the Munich Agreement on behalf of Germany, the United Kingdom, Italy and France, respectively. Mussolini had officially proposed territorial revisions in favour of Nazi Germany and at the expense of Czechoslovakia, which had been put together by Hitler's foreign service. Chamberlain and Daladier agree to the territorial revisions and convey to the Czechoslovak government, which was not invited to attend the conference, that it would have to fight Nazi Germany on its own if it was not to hand over the Sudetenland peacefully. A year later, Hitler showed that the kind of territorial aggrandisement he had in mind much surpassed the Sudetenland. World War II began with Germany attacking Poland. Since then, appeasement has become an important diplomatic lesson and, at times, also a powerful rhetorical weapon. Appeasing a tyrant does not work. Not confronting a dangerous dictator early enough makes things even worse; it becomes more and more difficult to defeat the tyrant. This really is an important lesson. But it is also a lesson that is prone to be instrumentalised for those trying to mobilise nations to go to war. Portraying someone as Hitler or Hitler-like (e.g., Saddam Hussein) does mobilise people. But whether the portrayal is appropriate or not is an altogether different matter.

and security but it can also be the first step towards the democratisation of a country. Metaphors with religious connotations were of significance for Bush and Blair as well. The binary opposition of 'good' and 'evil' is a *Leitmotiv* in their speeches and statements. Some authors analysing their decision-making refer to this as their Manichean worldview (Dyson 2007).

The baggage affected Bush's and Blair's interpretation of Saddam Hussein's moves, and their decisions about how to counter his expected moves. Both leaders made up their minds very early that Hussein possessed and had further developed weapons of mass destruction, especially biological and chemical ones. In 1997 already, Blair is on record for saying that 'I have now seen some of the stuff on this. It really is pretty scary. He (Saddam) is very close to some appalling weapons of mass destruction. I don't understand why the French and others don't understand this' (Dyson 2006). This assessment sounds remarkably similar to Blair's understanding of the situation six years later. By 'stuff', Blair referred to intelligence. The overestimation of threat, based on a highly selective reading of available intelligence persisted. In 2002, the Bush Administration sent Colin Powell to the UN Security Council (UNSC) in order to present evidence to the world that Iraq was a major threat to international peace and security. Among other things, Powell alleged that Iraq was developing unmanned aerial vehicles that were capable of delivering chemical and biological weapons to the US. As the UN Monitoring, Verification and Inspection Commission (UNMOVIC) later confirmed, these allegations were unfounded (Kerr 2004).

There is evidence that Bush's and Blair's emotions played their role in all of this. Indeed, no American President could possibly have reacted to 9/11 in an entirely detached manner. For Bush, given his patriotism and deep attachment to the American nation, such an emotionless response was especially unlikely to happen. When Bush declared the end of the war in May 2003, he stressed that the Iraq war had been an important success in the war against terror; with the end of Saddam's regime, an ally of al-Qaeda – ready to provide international terrorists with weapons of mass destruction – had been removed. These allegations of a link between al-Qaeda and Saddam Hussein never withstood the test of any serious scrutiny. But in the wake of 11 September 2001, they seemed fully reasonable for Bush and his advisors. The emotional dimension may very well explain at least part of this subjective reasonableness. The language used to describe Saddam Hussein also alludes to this emotional dimension. The term 'evil' has been alluded to above already; it was very frequently used to portray Saddam. The term, of course, has a very clear emotional dimension to it. The same applies to other terms used as well. Blair, for instance, referred to Saddam as a 'monster' – again this signals anything but detachment (Kennedy-Pipe and Vickers 2007).

Psychological approaches provide for important insights into decision-making in general, and Bush's and Blair's misinterpretations and miscalculations in the Iraq case in particular. We know now that Saddam Hussein, after his defeat against the US-led coalition in 1991, did not re-start Iraq's nuclear, chemical and biological weapons programmes. But psychological approaches, too, have their limits. Two of them are especially worth mentioning. First, doing empirical research and generating the kind of evidence that applying these approaches requires is sometimes a major challenge. David Owen, for instance, contends in an article in the reputable *Journal of the Royal Society of Medicine* that Blair suffers from a psychological state that the author refers to as hubris (Owen 2006). But how is this to be shown empirically?

After all, Blair may not agree to sit down on Owen's couch and provide him with the kind of in-depth information about his decision-making that would provide compelling empirical support for such a claim.

Second, many psychological approaches focus on top decision-makers at the expense of looking at the broader picture of how these decision-makers interact with advisors, organisations, bureaucracies and the broader public. Leaders, however, consult with others, for instance trusted career diplomats, and this does not always leave their views unchanged. Furthermore, some leaders are more sensitive to public opinion than others. Among psychological approaches, Janis' concept of 'groupthink' (1972) is an important exception to the tendency to neglect processes of consultation. Some decision-makers keep critical voices out of the inner circles of advisors. Thus, the group finds it quite easy to agree on interpretations of the world and how to act in it. But their perspective is a narrow one, leading to serious misinterpretations.

The remainder of this chapter deals with more sociologically inclined perspectives. Being more socially inclined, they take the social embeddedness of decision-makers more seriously. Far from being assumed as standing apart, decision-makers are presumed to be rather deeply embedded in social context. A disclaimer is necessary though. In contrast to rational choice and most psychological approaches, these perspectives do not seek to explain the exact decisions that individuals make. Instead, they attempt to understand what decisions are conceivable for actors and what decisions are inconceivable.

Logic of appropriateness

The logic of appropriateness proceeds from a different ontology (theory of being). Consequentialism, and here especially rational choice, de-emphasises the social context in which individuals are embedded. The starting point of analysis is the individual and not the collectivities and their practices that may be meaningful for the individual. The logic of appropriateness proceeds very differently. Assuming human beings are *deeply embedded in social context*, its starting point of analysis is the ideational background in which individuals are located. More so, this background is presumed to constitute these individuals as political actors; they cannot be thought of as political actors without this background. March and Olsen hold that this background is made up of rules. The repertoire of *rules*, in turn, has cognitive and normative dimensions (March and Olsen 2004: 3).

We have come across the *cognitive* dimension already, although with somewhat different connotations. When psychologists write about heuristic devices such as analogies that make it possible for actors to reason, then they, too, write about this dimension. Yet the logic of appropriateness puts a different twist on them. These cognitive rules are identity-constituting. The Munich analogy, for example, is not just a heuristic clue that an individual has come across at some stage and holds onto because it is considered useful knowledge, but it has sunk in and became part of the identity narrative of the socially embedded individual and the community (or communities) to which this individual belongs. From this scholarly point of view, it is not a coincidence that Munich 1938 featured prominently on the minds of George W. Bush and Tony Blair. This historical lesson is a key ingredient of the dominant American and British identity narratives; they are deeply ingrained in the nation, including its representatives on the diplomatic stage.

For March and Olsen, the *normative* dimension of rules is at least as important as the cognitive one. Ultimately, it is the normative dimension that drives action. Norms tell the socially embedded individual the oughts and ought nots of political conduct. The logic of appropriateness proposes that actors abide by these oughts and ought nots because they constitute their identity. Violating them would amount to violating their very Self (March and Olsen 1989). Looking through this scholarly lens, Bush and Blair were adamant about putting an end to diplomacy and resorting to war among other things because the supposed appeasement of Saddam Hussein would have meant violating a lesson of history that ought to be at the forefront of every American and British leader, respectively: Chamberlain's monumental error ought never to be repeated again.

Box 7.2 discusses how a focus on norms can help the analyst to discern the defining features of global diplomacy. The empirical illustration thereafter deals with the nexus of German diplomacy and intervention.

Germany, diplomacy and intervention, 1949–

It is easy to summarise the story of the weighing of diplomacy and military intervention in German politics before 1993. It tilted very heavily towards the former. Germany, for instance, confined itself to the so-called *Scheckbuch-Diplomatie* (chequebook diplomacy) during the First Gulf War in 1990. It endorsed the US-led intervention against Iraq aimed at liberating Kuwait but did not participate in it, except for providing funds for the war effort. This decision for *Scheckbuch-Diplomatie* and against participation in the intervention is anything but self-explanatory. The First Gulf War was a collective security effort; a member of the UN had been attacked and annexed. The UN decided to come to the rescue of this member. Yet, at the same time, deploying German soldiers abroad in order to participate at an enforcement measure was still virtually unthinkable, especially to the key protagonists, i.e. Chancellor Helmut Kohl and his Foreign Minister Hans-Dietrich Genscher.

Box 7.2 Key norms of global diplomacy

Global diplomacy is, *inter alia*, constituted by the weakening of some norms and the strengthening of others. The privileged role of national foreign services, for instance, was an unquestioned norm that fundamentally shaped international diplomacy for centuries (at least since Richelieu; see Chapter 2). Diplomacy stayed, so to say, a closed shop. With the forces of globalisation gaining in strength, and more and more attempts being made to steer these forces into warranted directions, this norm has weakened. As Chapter 4 showed, a multiplication of actors has occurred. This is underpinned by the strengthening of other norms and even the rise of new ones. On the domestic level, a norm that may be labelled multi-bureaucracy governance (e.g., ministries of foreign affairs, economics and finance in the economic issue area) has taken root. On the international level, there is – with the possible exception of the peace and war issue area – a move towards a multilateralism norm. Woven into this multilateralism norm is the recognition of some actors on the diplomatic stage that do not represent states but NGOs, multinational corporations or international organisations.

In the midst of the Yugoslav War, however, things were no longer the same. Germany had hoped that an early recognition of the break-up republics would put an end to the bloodshed. Pressuring other EU members to recognise and doing so unilaterally rather than within the framework of the EU did not stop the worst killing Europe had experienced since the end of WWII. On the contrary, fighting became fiercer, especially in Bosnia. The international community increasingly resorted to military means to put an end to the war. A no-fly zone over Bosnia was one of the means used. This no-fly zone had to be monitored. NATO conducted surveillance flights for doing so; one-third of the personnel in charge of the mission was German. Since the First Gulf War, there had been considerable diplomatic pressure by Germany's allies to make Berlin contribute to military operations. The Kohl government eventually succumbed to the diplomatic pressure, especially by the US.

It seemed that this signalled the 'normalisation' of German foreign policy; a move towards participation in military intervention as a last resort when diplomacy fails to resolve a threat against international peace. In 1999, it appeared that the normalisation hypothesis had passed a very demanding test. Joschka Fischer, the long-time pacifist (➔ glossary) of the long-time pacifistic Green Party, decided in his function as Foreign Minister and together with the social democratic Chancellor Gerhard Schröder to join the NATO intervention against Yugoslavia. Normalisation seemed to continue in 2001, when the Schröder government succeeded to get the Bundestag to join the US-led coalition in its attempt to remove the Taliban regime in Afghanistan.

From 2003 onwards, however, Germany appears to have reverted back to its more traditional hesitation to forgo diplomatic efforts and join military campaigns. Not only did Schröder and Fischer refuse to join George W. Bush's 'coalition of the willing' in 2003, but they were also openly critical of Bush's campaign in a manner German diplomacy had not dared to do since the end of WWII. In 2011, the centrist coalition government under Chancellor Angela Merkel and Foreign Minister Guido Westerwelle decided against the humanitarian intervention in Libya. Germany, then with a non-permanent seat at the UN Security Council, was the only Western country not to agree to Resolution 1973 (it abstained), which, in the American, French and British interpretation, provided the legal basis for the intervention against Muammar Qaddafi. It did not participate in the military intervention, which was spearheaded by France, the United Kingdom and the US.

How well suited is the logic of appropriateness to explain these decisions about diplomatic and military options? On the one hand, the logic provides explanatory power. Not to repeat the catastrophic wrongs of the past, in particular causing WWII and the Holocaust, is deeply ingrained in the dominant identity narrative of Germany. On the other hand, however, the logic has difficulties accounting for the participation of Germany in joint military efforts in the former Yugoslavia and Afghanistan. Here, the 1999 participation stands out even more because there was no UN mandate for the bombing campaign against Serbia.

Logic of argumentation

Thomas Risse contends that there is a third logic of action, which he labelled the logic of argumentation (Risse 2000). Risse borrows heavily from the social thought of Jürgen Habermas and, more precisely, his theory of communicative action. At first glance, Habermas' framework does not look all that different from the logic of appropriateness. Writing about the significance of a *shared lifeworld* (→ glossary: lifeworld) he places a lot of emphasis on social context. This emphasis is reminiscent of March and Olsen. At second glance, however, there is a notable difference between the two logics. In Habermas' view, analysing the shared lifeworld alone does not tell us all that much. It merely sketches the repertoire of ideas available to actors to make sense of the world. What is really important for Habermas is how actors, communicating with one another, select certain ideas rather than others from this large repertoire, how they link these ideas together to create arguments and how they come to consent that a particular argument is the most convincing one.

Habermas is a normative scholar. He uses a counterfactual as a benchmark to critique political communication in Western democracies. The counterfactual is the ideal speech situation. Ideally, there should be open access to discourse and those participating in discourse ought not to aim at making their arguments win but to figure out together which argument is *the most convincing* one, no matter who the authors of this argument are. As Habermas puts it, the aim is to let the 'force of the better argument' (Habermas 1984: 161) come to the fore.

Risse's move makes an analytical-empirical logic of action out of this normative framework. Risse contends that world politics, far from always being about the might of the strong dictating to the weak what they must – or must not – do, sometimes allows for the force of the better argument to prevail. In some cases, actors on the diplomatic scene can convince one another of the better argument. Note how this hypothesis contrasts with rational choice. As discussed above, rational choice assumes stable preferences. During a decision-making situation, preferences do not change; they are fixed. Risse suggests that these preferences are not immutable. Communicative interaction among actors can *change their preferences*; during a communicative encounter, actors can be convinced to want something that is different from what they wanted prior to this encounter. Box 7.3 elaborates on how to apply this approach to the study of diplomacy in more detail.

Soviet Union, 1990

The end of the Cold War posed a major puzzle for scholars of world politics. Established theories, emphasising continuity (i.e., stable preferences) rather than change, experienced major shortcomings in explaining what happened. Risse's development of the logic of argumentation has to be seen in this context. He provides a number of empirical illustrations for his contention that there are incidences of arguing and preference change in world politics. Mikhail Gorbachev's decision to agree to a unified Germany within NATO is one of them.

Risse submits that Gorbachev and Eduard Shevardnadze, his Foreign Minister, had been engaged in a dialogue about a new global and European security architecture with Western powers since the mid-1980s. In the course of this dialogue, the parties created a shared lifeworld; the diplomatic encounters made them increasingly share understandings about the shortcomings of the current order and the parameters of a new one.

Gorbachev, Risse continues, approached the German question without a fixed set of preferences. Thus, he was susceptible to US Foreign Minister James Baker's argument that it would be better to have a reunified Germany embedded in Western

---

Box 7.3 Diplomacy and communicative action

According to a Habermasian framework, the goal of the diplomats engaged in communicative action is to seek a communicative consensus about their understanding of the situation and the preferred course of action. The way in which diplomats engage in communicative action is by constructively challenging the validity claims inherent in the interests, preferences and norms driving each other's actions. According to Habermas, any interaction orientated to reaching understanding is defined by three validity claims (Habermas 1984: 99). The first refers to the truth of assertions made, or the conformity with interpreted facts in the world: the statements made are intersubjectively true. For instance, is Iran close to becoming a nuclear power? If so, how close? The second focuses on the moral rightness of the norms underlying arguments: the speech is right with respect to the existing normative context. Is it right for a diplomat to condemn other countries' violations of human rights while his own government suppresses human rights at home? The third validity claim concerns the truthfulness and authenticity of the speaker: the manifest intention of the speaker is meant as it is expressed. Is the diplomat willing to change her mind and adopt a new position if the arguments presented by the other side are more convincing? The logic of communicative action has been applied to various processes of international cooperation, dealing with questions such as why the internalisation of human rights norms occurs (Risse 1999), how intercivilisational dialogue can take place (Lynch 2000), how effective is decision-making in the UN Security Council (Johnstone 2003), why international negotiations are successful despite the opposition of important powers (Deitelhoff 2009) or how the use of force can be justified in international politics (Bjola 2005).

---

structures than a neutral Germany that may eventually revert back to pre-1945 policies. He was also susceptible to normative arguments, most importantly the application of the 1975 Helsinki Final Act on the issue of Germany and alliances. According to the Final Act, states ought to choose their alliances freely. In May 1990, when Gorbachev declared his principal agreement with NATO membership of a reunified Germany for the first time, he did so in response to President George Herbert Bush's framing of the issue in Helsinki terms. In short, the story Risse tells about Gorbachev is one about an uncommitted thinker who was persuaded to fundamentally break with Soviet orthodoxies of foreign policy by what were to him convincing arguments emanating from his Western counterparts.

Risse does not deny that there are other angles from which to look at this empirical issue as well. He does not pretend to be able to explain everything but merely an important aspect. Yet note that the Habermasian conceptualisation of persuasion as letting the better argument come to the fore is, nevertheless, a highly demanding conceptualisation of persuasion. After all, Habermas' point is to critique what he often referred to as modern mass democracies and their lack of communicative encounters apt for a democracy. Risse's claim that these encounters exist empirically in international affairs is not implausible. But, as he points out himself, we should expect them to be very rare occasions.

Various alternatives to this narrow conceptualisation of argumentation and persuasion exist (Crawford 2002). The advocacy literature, for example, looks at how norm entrepreneurs – oftentimes NGOs – frame their messages strategically in order to make them resonate with an audience (Finnemore and Sikkink 1998). Research on rhetorical strategies argues in a similar vein but focuses on traditional inter-state diplomacy rather than non-governmental actors (Kornprobst 2012). There is also a broader view of argumentation that tries to encompass these different perspectives on argumentation (Bjola and Kornprobst 2011: 4–10).

Logic of practice

What Habermas is to many students of argumentation, Pierre Bourdieu is to many scholars of practice. Authors on world politics interested in the logic of practice draw heavily from the French social theorist. Bourdieu gained the principal insights into his thought on practice from anthropological research on the Kabyle people in Algeria (Bourdieu 1977). He amended his framework while researching the French education system (Bourdieu 1988) and then making a more general social theory out of it (Bourdieu 1990). But his key concepts, i.e. *habitus* and field, have remained the key ingredients of his theorising.

The *habitus* is about the 'generative principles of … practices' (Bourdieu 1998: 8) or, more concretely, the 'matrix of perceptions, appreciations and actions' (Bourdieu 1977: 83) into which the individual has been socialised. This matrix *predisposes* actors to pursue certain practices rather than others. The *field* is about the organising principles of social encounters among individuals: actors participating in these encounters are not equal (power), they agree on what is at stake in these encounters (stakes) and there is a tacit consensus on the basic rules of the encounters (doxa). These organising principles put actors into (unequal) *relationships* with one another. The interplay of *habitus* and field generates *tacit common sense*. This tacit common sense amounts to reasons upon which to act. But, as the 'tacit' already indicates, these reasons are of a peculiar nature. Agents take their reasons for action for granted; they do not reflect upon these reasons and do not debate about them with others.

To put this differently, no other logic of action puts as much emphasis on what happens *underneath* the radar screen of explicit communicative exchanges as the logic of practice (Pouliot 2008). Consequentialism, especially rational choice, is all about the individual's processes of reflection. Utility maximisation, or even satisficing, is something about which actors ponder. They reflect and weigh different alternatives. The logic of appropriateness is rule-following but, at least, as it is conceptualised by students of international politics, the actors following these rules tend to be aware of them. Scholarship looks for utterances of these rules by the actors who abide by them in order to generate empirical evidence that these rules matter. The logic of argumentation, too, is very much about reflection. Actors put the social background (lifeworld) to use and debate with others what to do. The Bourdieuan view of practice, by contrast, is rather different in this regard. Actors improvise what to do and this improvisation is, ultimately, what comes naturally to them. They do not reflect on it.

France and Africa, 1960s–

For decades, France's Africa diplomacy has been rather puzzling to many analysts. They consider the institutional apparatus in charge of Paris' relations with the African continent inadequate and wonder why no more rational design has been implemented. A plethora of institutions, including the Ministry of Foreign Affairs, Ministry of Co-operation, Ministry of Defence, Ministry of Finance, the French Development Agency and the Africa section at the Presidency deal with Africa. The President plays a paramount role but, additionally, some Prime Ministers have featured prominently as well. With co-ordination among these institutions and actors being a major challenge, informal networks have been created to govern Paris' policy towards Africa. The President and his close advisors locate themselves at key nodes in these networks (*réseaux*).

The networks, however, have created their own governance problems. On a normative level, there is the problem of transparency and accountability. The networks operate far removed from the public eye. Parliament, for a long time, has been reluctant to engage in reflection about African diplomacy. As far as considerations of effectiveness are concerned, the *réseaux* do not fare all too well either. At times, national interests take a backseat to private and business interests. Furthermore, the *réseaux* intertwined national interests. Some African heads of state, especially Felix Houphouët-Boigny, the first President of Côte d'Ivoire, featured very prominently in the networks. In an institutional set-up like this, diplomacy and domestic politics go hand in hand. Houphouët-Boigny nicknamed it *Françafrique*.

Despite several upheavals and generational changes, however, there has been no paradigm change in France's Africa diplomacy. As a commentator puts it, '50 years later, *Françafrique* is still alive and well' (Boisbouvier 16 February 2010). What explains this persistence? Schlichte contends that the logic of practice explains the persistence of the parameters of French diplomacy vis-à-vis Africa. He argues that the colonial imperial idea, friendship with African states and dispersion of French culture are important ideas making up the *habitus*. Given this *habitus*, France practises the entrenched ways of conducting African diplomacy without reflecting on the 'chaotisation of institutions'.

On the one hand, this explanation has a number of strengths. The institutions underpinning France's African diplomacy are not rationally designed as a rational choice scholar would predict it. The logic of practice's insight that practice is simply doing things, acting upon common sense, provides a different angle on human rationality (→ glossary), and this angle is sometimes useful. Other logics of action, focusing on reflection rather than habit, have difficulties getting at this aspect of rationality.

On the other hand, the explanation also has its weaknesses. Not every important decision can be explained by established practices without linking them to reflective decision-making processes. Decisions to switch from diplomacy to military intervention are among these. Sure, France has a long-standing record of intervention in Africa. But this does not mean that there is no consequential reflection going on that shapes decisions of whether and how to intervene. It is this reflection that helps account for major differences across French decisions to intervene. Take, for example, the 2011 Libyan intervention. In contrast to the bulk of French interventions in Africa, the intervention in the Libyan war was not done on behalf of a long-standing allied government that was firmly established in the *Françafrique*, but sided with the newly created National Transition Council that fought the government. It was not a unilateral but very much a multilateral endeavour, principally sanctioned by the UNSC (see Box 7.4) and carried out with other NATO states, especially the United Kingdom and the US, playing a crucial role, too.

Box 7.4 Security Council Resolution 1973

In mid-February 2011, protests in Libya's coastal city of Benghazi escalated when security forces loyal to Muammar Qaddafi fired into the crowd. The escalation led to a civil war, which spread more and more across the country. Qaddafi's targeting of civilians prompted strong responses from the international community. On 26 February, the Security Council adopted S/RES/1970 (2011) in which it strongly condemned the 'widespread and systematic attacks ... against the civilian population', warned that they 'may amount to crimes against humanity', and clarified that it was acting under Chapter VII (enforcement measures) of the UN Charter. The operative clauses refer the situation in Libya to the International Criminal Court, and impose an arms embargo and travel bans against leading figures of Qaddafi's government. With the situation further deteriorating, the Security Council adopted S/RES/1973 in which it reiterated its grave concerns and decided to resort to more robust measures, above all the establishment of a no-fly zone and the authorisation for UN member states to 'take all necessary measures ... to protect civilians and civilian-populated areas under threat of attack in the Libyan Arab Jamahiriya'. Among the Security Council members, France, the United Kingdom and the US (permanent members) as well as Bosnia and Herzegovina, Colombia, Gabon, Lebanon, Nigeria, Portugal, South Africa (non-permanent) voted for the resolution. China and Russia (permanent) as well as Brazil, Germany and India (non-permanent) abstained from the vote. While the ensuing NATO intervention in Libya did protect civilians and reiterated this again and again as the purpose of the mission, the intervention also played a crucial role in shifting the military balance in favour of the National Transition Council and against Qaddafi's regime. China, India, South Africa, and especially Russia, therefore, vocally criticised Resolution 1973 and its implementation. Vladimir Putin put this into the following accusatory language: 'It [Resolution 1973] is reminiscent of medieval calls for a crusade. It allows for the invasion of a sovereign state' (RIA Novosti 21 March 2011).

Summary

- When it comes to studying diplomacy, most authors draw from rational choice assumptions. They conceptualise diplomats as *expected utility maximisers*. Diplomats, therefore, are assumed to calculate how to get what is the optimal outcome that they, locked into a decision-making situation with other players on the diplomatic stage, can achieve.

- Psychological approaches provide an alternative. Being less optimistic about the computational powers of human beings, they allude to *heuristic shortc uts* that actors use in order to make up their minds. The short cuts provide actors with clues when to stop searching for alternatives and settle for a particular course of action.

- The logic of appropriateness focuses on the *rules* that make up the social context in which agents are embedded. These rules are assumed to be cognitive and normative in nature. Taken together, they make the world intelligible for them. Actors are assumed to act appropriately, given a set of norms. They do what appears to them as *the right thing to do*.

- The logic of argumentation deals with how agents come to *assemble arguments* from a social background, and how the exchange of arguments with others *affects* these agents. It is presumed that these exchanges can leave a major mark on agents. They can change their preferences around. The potential repercussions of communicative encounters can cut even deeper; they can change identities.

- The key contribution of the logic of practice is that is looks at what happens underneath the radar screen of discourse. As far as the logics of consequences, appropriateness and argumentation are concerned, scholars take for granted that making up one's mind has something to do with reflection. Scholars of practice, by contrast, hold that many things we do, we simply do. We act upon *dispositions* without pondering about what to do.

Study questions

- How confident are rational choice and psychological approaches in diplomacy's abilities to make deterrence effective?
- How convincing is the logic of appropriateness in explaining Germany's attempts to look for a diplomatic solution to the 2003 Iraq crisis and the United Kingdom's resolve to use force?
- Is there room for a logic of argumentation in explaining epochal change in world politics?
- How much of diplomacy is acting upon common sense?

Recommended further reading

Bátora, Jozef. 2005. 'Does the European Union transform the institution of diplomacy?' *Journal of European Public Policy* no. 12 (1): 44–66.
This is an inquiry into how a logic of appropriateness has emerged in EU diplomacy, and how this may affect diplomacy more generally.

Bjola, Corneliu and Markus Kornprobst. 2011. 'Introduction: the argumentative deontology of global governance'. In *Arguing global governance*, edited by Corneliu Bjola and Markus Kornprobst, pp. 1–16. London and New York: Routledge.
This framing chapter takes stock of different conceptualisations of argumentation in different academic disciplines and proposes an inclusive and multi-perspectival research agenda.

Hopf, Ted. 2010. 'The logic of habit in international relations'. *European Journal of International Relations* no. 16 (4): 539–561.
In this article, Hopf explores habitual approaches, discusses strengths and weaknesses of Bourdieuan applications to international relations theory and advocates for a logic of habit.

Putnam, Robert D. 1988. 'Diplomacy and domestic politics: The logic of two-level games'. *International Organization* no. 42 (2): 427–460.
This continues to be a highly influential article that uses a parsimonious game theoretical model to link the domestic and international decision-making of leaders.

Stein, Janice G. 2002. 'Psychological explanations and international conflict'. In *Handbook of international relations*, edited by Walter Carlsnaes, Thomas Risse and Beth Simmons. London: Sage.
This article provides a thorough overview of psychological approaches to decision-making. The author covers approaches to individual as well as collective choice.

8   The making of relations

Chapter objectives

- To conceptualise the spectrum of diplomatic relations.
- To discuss how relations are made.
- To highlight how diplomatic relations can change fundamentally.

Introduction

Diplomacy makes relations. Whenever we hear that relations among states are deteriorating, stabilising or improving and so on, diplomacy has something to do with it. This chapter provides an overview of what kinds of relations diplomacy makes and unmakes, and, equally important, how it does so. This chapter's organisation follows Chapter 7. We provide an overview of scholarly approaches, and discuss their strengths and weaknesses by putting empirical cases under scrutiny.

Scholarship on international relations is frequently divided up into three major paradigms, i.e. Realism, Liberalism and Constructivism. Dividing up the field in this way has its pitfalls; there are plausible alternative organisational devices that stress more what contending schools of thought have in common than what keeps them apart (Kornprobst 2009). Nonetheless, dividing scholarship up into these three paradigms provides for a good overview of similarities and differences of international relations thought on the making and unmaking of relations.

First, we deal with Realist approaches that link security imperatives to balancing behaviour, and balancing behaviour to the making of relations. Our illustrative case revolves around Washington's diplomatic efforts to dissuade North Korea from becoming and consolidating itself as a nuclear power. Second, we investigate into Liberal approaches that put more emphasis on economic motives, connect these to the creation of cooperation-facilitating institutions and from there to the making of relations. We discuss the strengths and weaknesses of this lens by examining EU foreign policy. Third, we take a look at Constructivist scholarship that addresses the generative mechanisms through which relations are produced and reproduced. As an empirical illustration, we discuss Eritrean–Ethiopian (friendship to enmity) relations.

Balancing: from outlaw to ally (and vice versa)

The classic Realist statement on diplomacy and the making of relations is found in Hans Morgenthau's highly influential *Politics Among Nations*. His starting assumption is that there is *anarchy* in international politics; i.e. there is no common power (such as a world government). Thus, states have to be on guard in order to secure their *survival*. Being on guard, for Morgenthau, has a lot to do with balancing power. Only if power (→ glossary) is balanced among the major powers, they are unlikely to fight one another. Thus, the key task of diplomacy for him is to *balance*. A *diplomacy of balancing* makes possible what Morgenthau refers to as 'peace through accommodation' (Morgenthau and Thompson 1985: 562), i.e. the only kind of tenuous peace for which the anarchical international order allows.

Morgenthau's account of a diplomacy of balancing is distinctly normative. He does not believe that this is how the Great Powers always conduct their foreign affairs. But he argues that they ought to. Making this normative argument, he contrasts it with unwarranted alternatives: there ought to be no fixation on enmity and there ought to be no fanaticism. Fixation on enmity and fanaticism impede balancing. Balancing requires being *pragmatic*; it necessitates staying apart until a pragmatic move for correcting an upset balance of power is required. The Cold War, to Morgenthau, was far from being a paradigmatic case of a balance of power. The superpowers were too fixated on their mutual enmity and their ideological contestation for such a case to develop.

Henry Kissinger argues in a very similar vein. His first book *A World Restored* is an in-depth account of the Concert of Europe in the nineteenth century. The Concert, in Kissinger's view, attained a balance of power because diplomats – most of all Klemens von Metternich, the long-time Austrian Foreign Minister and also Chancellor who is considered the architect of the Concert system – avoided fixation and fanaticism. The Great Powers acted pragmatically. When one of them threatened to become preponderant, it was balanced against. Kissinger practised US diplomacy very much along these lines when he was National Security Advisor under President Nixon (see Box 8.1). Balancing arguments feature prominently among some contemporary Realist scholars as well. They tend to use the concept of 'off-shore balancing' to describe this postulate (Layne 2009).

In his highly influential *Theory of International Politics*, Kenneth Waltz converted the normativity of all of this into a theoretical framework that aimed at explaining how things really are and not just how they ought to be. His Neorealism holds that the anarchical international system leaves states with no other option but to balance. In this view, the balance of power, far from being a contingent outcome of skilful diplomatic interaction, is the natural distribution of power in the global system (Waltz 1979). More recently, Neo-classical Realism concurs with Morgenthau and Kissinger that the balance of power is not something that is to be taken for granted. Neo-classical Realists seek to explain under what conditions states balance and under what conditions they do not. In order to answer this question, they look into domestic politics. Yet they do not put an emphasis on diplomacy that is comparable to Morgenthau's and Kissinger's (Schweller 2006).

The different Realisms do not elaborate much on the spectrum of relations among states. This is due to the focus on the balance of power. If the prescription is that states ought to balance, and, therefore, stay away from 'thick' relations, or there is even a prediction that they always do so, then there is not much need to theorise on

---

Box 8.1 Kissinger, China and the US

Kissinger not only argued for balancing as an act of diplomatic prudence. He also practised it. Before the early 1970s, the US recognised the Republic of China (Taiwan) as
the official government of China. Washington did not have formal relations with the
People's Republic of China (PRC). The latter, however, was an important player. Having
emerged victoriously from the Chinese Civil War in 1949, Mao Zedong – the PRC's
founder and leader – made the seemingly natural alliance choice in favour of the Soviet
Union. After all, the two major powers shared a Marxist–Leninist ideology. From a balancing perspective, the PRC's taking sides with the Soviet Union in the Cold War was a
blow to the US. Two powerful states stood together against Washington. Thus, Kissinger,
while in office as National Security Advisor to President Nixon, tried to move China away
from the Soviet Union and further towards the US. There was an opportunity because
Mao Zedong and Nikita Khrushchev, Stalin's successor in the Soviet Union, had major
disagreements on how to advance Marxist-Leninism in world politics. Kissinger made
the most of this opportunity. He opened up back-channels for diplomacy, secretly travelled to Beijing in 1971 and thus prepared President Nixon's visit to the PRC in February
1972. It would be certainly overstating the issue that China became an ally of the US.
But, there was certainly a rapprochement. Given that there was a written communiqué
with quite far-reaching agreements for future interaction, it may be even understood
as an entente. Note that this move away from antagonism happened despite the fundamental ideological disagreements between the communist PRC and the capitalist US.
Ideology, at least in this case, did not matter for Kissinger. What mattered to him was the
global distribution of capabilities.

---

the spectrum of relations found among actors on the diplomatic stage. Yet from the
rich empirical discussions of diplomacy, especially in Morgenthau's and Kissinger's
research, it is possible to extrapolate on such a spectrum of relations. It points towards
what two authors, situated in the vicinity of Realist approaches and also studying the
Concert of Europe in depth, conceptualise as a range of relations from outlaw to ally.
Craig and George identify the *outlaw* state on the one end of the spectrum. Through
diplomatic interaction, relations with the outlaw may improve towards *detente*, from
there to *rapprochement, entente, appeasement* and, finally, even to *alliance*. The authors
provide the example of Turkey, which made a belated entry into the European society of states under Kemal Atatürk, after having been traditionally cast as an outlaw
state (Craig and George 1983: 157).

The following section discusses the strengths and weaknesses of Realist conceptualisations of relations and relationship-making by applying Realist approaches to the
case of North Korean–US relations.

Relations between North Korea and the US, 1993–2012[1]

From 1993 onwards, a pattern of interaction between the US and North Korea has
evolved that centres around Washington's attempts to curb Pyongyang's nuclear
ambitions. The recurring themes in this pattern are Washington's treatment of North

---

1 This section draws on (Kornprobst and Soreanu 3–6 September 2009).

Korea as an outlaw, to be followed by attempts of rapprochement and then again by a relapse into an outlaw relationship. Promises of positive sanctions (US to North Korea) and promises of concessions on nuclear matters (North Korea to US) amount to the key vehicles for moves towards rapprochement; mutual allegations of broken promises then undo the diplomatic successes during the implementation stage.

Despite being hampered by the absence of formal diplomatic relations – the US does not recognise the North Korean regime – negotiations made remarkable progress in 1993 and 1994. Facilitated by former US President Jimmy Carter (see Box 8.2), and concluded by high-ranking officials from the foreign ministries of both countries, Robert Gallucci and Kang Sok Ju, the Agreed Framework in October 1994 was heralded as a landmark agreement between the parties. North Korea agreed to freeze its plutonium enrichment programme and allow for IAEA inspections to verify it. The US provided a number of incentives, most importantly the promise to build light water reactor power plants (these make diversion of civilian to military uses of nuclear power much more difficult compared to the existing reactors in North Korea). Both parties also agreed to normalise their relations, seek more cooperation and work towards the goals of the NPT.

The agreement, however, unravelled in the following years amidst mutual allegations. Progress with building the light water nuclear reactors proved to be very slow. Since it took a long time for an international consortium to be founded and then to secure the funding for it, not much progress happened before 2001. In the meantime, Republicans gained control over the US Senate and voiced their dissatisfaction with the Framework Agreement. Deeply mistrusting the North Korean regime of Kim Jong-il, they considered any kind of attempt of a rapprochement utopian. The US General Accounting Office (1 October 1996) maintained that the Agreed Framework is a 'nonbinding political agreement' or

---

Box 8.2 Former heads of state as mediators

Former heads of state can fulfil important mediation functions. As discussed in Chapter 6, impartiality is usually a prerequisite for successful mediation. Once heads of state leave office, their efforts are no longer as closely tied to the national interest as before. Thus, they really can make a difference, especially if they have acquired an authority as successful mediators while being in office. Scandinavian former heads of state have a great tradition in doing so. Among these, Martti Oiva Kalevi Ahtisaari, former President of Finland, probably stands out the most. He mediated in conflicts as different as Indonesia, Iraq, Kosovo and Namibia. In 2008, he received the Nobel Peace Prize for his efforts. In Africa, Nelson Mandela used his authority very skilfully after having stepped down as South African President. In the early 2000s, for example, he mediated in Burundi. Mandela, too, is a Peace Nobel Prize laureate. He received many other awards and honours. Among these is the UN General Assembly's (UNGA) 2009 move to declare 18 July Mandela Day (this is his birthday). Former US President Jimmy Carter's mediation efforts are very noteworthy, too. For the most part, they concentrated on the Middle East. But he also mediated in other regions, for instance between Colombia and Ecuador in 2008. To a considerable extent, Carter institutionalised a mediation capacity by founding his own NGO. The Carter Center is dedicated to promoting human rights and democracy as well as to preventing and resolving conflicts around the world.

'nonbinding international agreement' rather than an international treaty or legal document. George W. Bush accused North Korea of being part of an 'axis of evil' in his 2002 State of the Union Address. North Korea responded in no uncertain terms. It ended the freeze on plutonium processing, striving with ever more vigour to acquire nuclear weapons.

A new round of talks started in 2003. The Six Party Talks brought together the six key players in Northeast Asia: Japan, North Korea, South Korea as well as the Great Powers of China, Russia and the US. During the talks, North Korea oscillated between cooperative and defiant stances. On the one hand, Pyongyang conducted nuclear tests in 2006 and 2009, and also several missile tests. On the other hand, North Korea seemed again to be susceptible to positive sanctions such as fuel aid and food aid. At various points in time, the state temporarily agreed to nuclear inspections and shut down its Yongbyon nuclear facility. Kim Yong-il died in December 2011, giving hope that the pattern may change under his successor Kim Jong-un. To date, however, there are various indications that the relational pattern between the US and North Korea may continue for some time to come. In April 2012, the new leader tried to launch a satellite (an opportunity to test missile technology) and recent intelligence suggests that North Korea may prepare for another underground nuclear test.

What are the strengths and weaknesses of Realist approaches to explain this relational pattern since 1993? There are at least three strengths. First, US responses to North Korea's nuclear ambitions, to some extent, can be explained as balancing attempts. Washington seeks to prevent the existing balance of power in the region from shifting to the disadvantage of its long-time allies South Korea and Japan. Second, Realist approaches also provide clues for explaining North Korea's ambitions. In an anarchical system, states always have incentives to become stronger than others and circumvent arms control agreements. Being stronger is the only way they can be secure from other states. Third, Realist insights into how material power is exercised help us understand some of the variations in US–North Korean relations. Positive sanctions ranging from promises to deliver light water nuclear reactors to food aid made a difference. With North Korea being susceptible to these incentives, they made moves towards *rapprochement* and success at the bargaining table possible.

There is, however, also something that the Realist focus on material power misses. Why is it so difficult to move the interaction between North Korea and the US away from outlaw relations? Why has there been again and again a relapse into the old antagonistic patterns? The insight on the difficulties of arms control in an anarchical environment notwithstanding, there are also ideational layers that underpin diplomatic relations. Realism is reluctant to address these. Mutual enmity is deeply engraved into the identity narratives of the two states. North Korea's ideology of *Juche* – being a 'do it alone' state – and its sharp demarcation from US 'imperialism' go hand in hand. On the US side, the story of US–North Korean relations focuses heavily on the Korean War, i.e. the unexpected aggression by an erratic hermit regime. Lessons (mis-)learnt from this episode have shaped Washington's politics towards North Korea and much beyond.

Hence, when it comes to conceptualising relations, there is a case to be made to go beyond the material side of things, and look into how self and other relations, ranging from enmities to friendships (and at times even further, see below), are made. Such an inquiry into how friendships are made may actually point away from an understanding of the balance of power as the only kind of tenuous peace possible. The next section on interests, cooperation and relations starts to deal with these issues; the one thereafter, focusing on identity and relations, examines them in even greater depth.

Interests: cooperative relations beyond alliance

Liberal thought focuses on the question of why international actors cooperate. This widens the spectrum of relations discussed above. While, for a Realist, the spectrum ends at ally, for a Liberal it moves further to enduring partnerships and even, through processes of *integration*, to the creation of *supranational polities* that take away autonomy and sovereignty from nation-states. The motive for building such strong ties – far removed from Morgenthau's prescription to stand apart and balance – is *interest*, especially economic interest. Simply put, states are assumed to engage in integrative schemes if this helps them pursue their interests.

The starting point of most Liberal approaches is agency as opposed to structure (e.g., the Realist concept of anarchy). Diplomacy is rarely mentioned explicitly. Yet with these accounts putting choices, negotiations and institutions at the centre of their investigations, there is plenty of room for traditional state-to-state diplomacy. Investigating on the global level, Neoliberal Institutionalism claims that states create institutions in order to maximise their expected utility. Institutions are held to *solve collective action problems*. Most importantly, they reduce transaction costs in general and make it less likely that other parties cheat in particular. Whether institutions are created or not, and, if so, how they are designed, is up to the choices and moves of the parties at the negotiation table (Martin and Simmons 1998).

The European integration process has sparked a huge literature. This literature features a number of Liberal approaches. On the one hand, there are approaches that borrow heavily from economics. Liberal Intergovernmentalism (Moravcsik 1999) echoes Neoliberal Institutionalism to a considerable extent. Actors – state governments, influenced by powerful constituents – are assumed to act *selfishly*. Integration is understood as something that does not happen in one sweep but is an evolving *process*. National governments are seen as the drivers of integration. Whether steps of integration are taken or not – say the Single European Act, the Maastricht Treaty or the Treaty of Lisbon – is up to national governments. This reserves room for diplomacy. Ultimately, it is up to diplomacy to negotiate these steps.

On the other hand, some Liberal approaches to European integration are influenced by sociological approaches as well. Written during WWII, David Mitrany's *A Working Peace System* may very well be the most influential essay ever published on integration studies. Identifying the nation-state as the root cause of war, his thought revolved around peace through integration. Deeply mistrusting politics, his work relies on *experts* as agents of integration. They are to carry out integration in narrowly confined areas when the functional need arises. Through this integration in a narrowly confined issue area, new functional needs for integration may arise (*spill-over*), and so on. Over time, there would be more and more functional integration in – and across – more and more issue areas. Mitrany even predicted that, over time, *people's loyalty would shift* from the nation-state to the functionally integrating polity. In other words, even the attachment to the nation-state would wither away. Mitrany's work not only influenced generations of scholars but also practitioners, perhaps most importantly Jean Monnet (see Box 8.3).

Box 8.3 Jean Monnet

Jean Monnet was never a traditional diplomat who moved through the ranks at the French foreign office. Nevertheless, he was a highly influential player on the diplomatic field for many decades. At the Versailles Conference, he was a close advisor to Etienne Clémentel, who was the French Minister of Commerce and Industry. Monnet advocated a much more conciliatory and cooperative peace in Europe but failed with his advocacy. The same year, he became Deputy Secretary-General of the newly founded League of Nations. During World War II, Monnet was a member of France's National Liberation Council in Algiers. Even here, he advocated for a new Europe. The fact that WWII was raging was not a reason for him to forgo his conviction that Europe could only be at peace if its nations would integrate; on the contrary, it made him hold on to this belief even more. In the aftermath of WWII, Monnet worked for the like-minded Foreign Minister Robert Schuman, and authored the Schuman Declaration in 1950. The Declaration emphasises that 'Europe will not be made all at once, or according to a single plan. It will be built through concrete achievements which first create a de facto solidarity.' The 'concrete achievements' refer to successful functional integration. The force ascribed to it is formidable; formidable enough for the 'elimination of the age-old opposition of France and Germany', which the Declaration considers the *sine qua non* for peace in Europe (EU 9 May 1950). The functional decision-making organ of the Coal and Steel Community was the High Authority. Monnet became its first President. He also played an important role in the creation of the European Economic Community, mainly through the Action Committee for the US of Europe, which he founded.

Ernst Haas' *The Uniting of Europe* is the foundational text of Neofunctionalism (Haas 1958). By now, Schmitter writes about a Neo-neofunctionalism (Schmitter 2004). Haas' work can be read as an attempt to introduce politics into functionalist thought. Based on his observations about European integration efforts in the 1950s, he argues that experts and functional integration play an important role. But politics remains in charge of letting functional integration happen. Neo-neofunctionalism, too, is not just about functional pressures but also about 'opinions and actions of national governments, associations and individuals'. For our purposes at hand, this is an important departure from Mitrany. It leaves more room for diplomacy, for example to deal with a crisis such as the sovereign debt crisis. Yet the thrust of functionalist thought stays in place. Functionalist pressures are the key force making nations move closer and closer together; political agents are deeply constrained by these pressures; they 'overshadow' them (Schmitter 2004: 61).

Mitrany did not conceive of functionalism as applicable to Europe only. It is a normative theory of international politics. Integration on a global scale, of course, is much more elusive than on the regional level. Today's authors, therefore, are much more modest when it comes to theorising on the kind of closeness of relations that can be forged on the global level. Peter Haas' conceptualisation of epistemic communities, for example, provides some interesting insights into the global age of diplomacy. He contends that *epistemic communities* – made-up of staff from national ministries, international organisations, NGOs, scientists and other experts – share a perspective about how to approach a given political issue, such as a dominant scientific paradigm for describing and explaining the depletion of the ozone layer. Given the expertise that these communities have *qua* their expert knowledge, they have a certain communicative authority, which in turn helps them to play an important role in governing this issue area (Adler and Haas 1992). In his more general theoretical account, James Rosenau distinguishes six types of governance. Four of these six types involve encounters of traditional diplomats and new diplomats, for example in *network governance* (representatives of governments meeting their counterparts from international organisations, NGOs) and *market governance* (representatives of governments, international organisations, economic elites, markets, mass publics, transnational corporations) (Rosenau 2002: 81).

Authors such as Haas and Rosenau do not claim that the whole world has become integrated, comparable to the EU. But they do claim that multiple actors perform global governance functions. None of these actors have the final authority to have their way; none of them amounts to something like a government in a traditional nation-state. Instead, governance is 'the sum of the many ways individuals and institutions, public and private, manage their common affairs. It is a continuing process through which conflicting or diverse interests may be accommodated and cooperative action may be taken' (Commission on Global Governance 1995).

EU foreign policy, 1957–

Using a tough case, this section discusses how compelling the abovementioned approaches are in explaining the evolution of the European unification process. The EU has been trying for quite some time to assert itself as a diplomatic actor in its own right; it seeks to assume a diplomatic personality in world politics. How successful has it been in doing so? How do the approaches discussed above help us in answering this question? Our discussion distinguishes three interrelated foreign policy fields of EU external relations: economics, neighbourhood and security.

Conducting foreign policy in the economic realm is anything but new for the EU. It dates back to the early years of the European unification process. What has since Maastricht become known as the TEC, one of the 1957 Rome Treaties, already contains some important provisions that mark the beginnings of the Common Commercial Policy (CCP). The common market that the Rome Treaties created almost implied these steps towards becoming an international actor. In order for a common market to function properly, member states have to agree on the tariffs to be levied at the borders of the common market area. Otherwise the common market would have been more fiction than reality. Thus, there is some evidence here for a functionalist thesis. Agreeing on a common market created the functional need for venturing into external relations – but only with regard to a small issue area.

From this small issue area, the EU's external economic policies have spread into a number of adjacent issue areas. Seen through a functionalist lens, some of this spreading can be interpreted as spill-overs. With integration deepening over time, there was more and more need to become a more complete economic actor on the diplomatic stage. Thus, it may come as little surprise that the EU has become an assertive player when it comes to multilateral trade negotiations within the framework of GATT and the WTO. The EU's embracing of other issue areas further removed from commerce and trade, by contrast, are more difficult to explain from a functionalist point of view. Early on, for example, Brussels has established itself as an actor in the area of international development. Yet it is hardly due to functional pressures that the EU signed the Yaoundé Convention (1963), Lomé Convention (1973) and the Treaty of Cotonou (2000). The salience of political decisions, originating in member states, played a key role and point more towards intergovernmental perspectives. France, mindful of its former colonial empire, was the key driving force in initiating Brussels' developmental cooperation. This network approach to governance – EU bureaucracy (mainly Commission) plus member state input from various ministries – has become more and more entrenched. Negotiating international environmental treaties, for instance, is a competence that is shared between the Commission and member states.

In the field of neighbourhood relations, the EU has been similarly successful in conducting a genuine EU foreign policy. This issue, too, has been there almost from the very beginning. Soon after the Rome Treaties had been ratified, the issue of additional members entered the debate. Denmark, Ireland and the United Kingdom applied for membership. Negotiations for accession dragged on throughout the 1960s until the three states finally became members in 1973. With accession staying very much on the agenda since then, years and years of accession practice gelled into a routine process of enlargement. The 1993 European Council in Copenhagen formulated the often-cited Copenhagen criteria for accession, above all democracy, rule of law, human rights, minority rights and market economy.

There is more to EU neighbourhood relations than accession. The Lisbon Treaty puts strong emphasis on regional politics. It stipulates that the EU seeks a 'special relationship [with its neighbours], characterized by close and peaceful relations based on cooperation'. The Union of the Mediterranean, for instance, was designed as a mechanism promoting such close relations. Even without the carrot of EU membership, the EU tries to 'EUise' its neighbourhood. The literature oftentimes refers to this as 'Europeanisation'. In North Africa and the Middle East, for example, the EU tried to play the role of human rights and democracy socialiser (Sedelmeier 2006: 118–135) and of a 'norm exporter' in general (Panebianco 2006: 136). These policies – it is all too obvious now – have not been very successful thus far. The so-called Arab Spring rebelled against and toppled dictators whom the EU had considered receptive to its teachings for a long time.

Functionalist arguments have difficulties accounting for enlargement and neighbourhood policies. They are designed to explain the deepening of integration and not the extensions of the geographical boundaries of integrating polities. Intergovernmentalist arguments rightly point out that the input of member states matters. Yet it would be too simple to explain successive rounds of enlargement merely in terms of conference diplomacy among member states. Examining the interplay of supranationalism and intergovernmentalism seems more promising. This points again to governance and network perspectives. Take, for instance, the fundamental decision in favour of enlargement at the 1993 Copenhagen summit, along with the Copenhagen criteria as a compass for this enlargement. As soon as the Cold War ended, the Commission put itself into the driving seat for moving Eastern Europe closer to the West. Numerous Commission proposals were accepted by European Councils, for example association agreements and Europe Agreements. The Directorate-General External Relations proved to be particularly determined to push forward.

By 1992, the Commission already formulated very clearly what would later become the Copenhagen criteria (EU Commission 1992: 52–60). The 1992 Lisbon European Council was still rather sceptical of enlargement (European Council 1992). Yet the advocacy gained momentum from early 1993 onwards, when Leon Brittan and Hans van den Broek assumed office as Commissioners for External Economic Relations and External Political Relations, respectively. Building a coalition with the British and Danish Council presidencies and the German government, the enlargement strategy passed a critical threshold of support. By the time of the Copenhagen European Council, many member states remained sceptical of this proposal but could be won over to compromise. The advocates conceded, for example, that enlargement must not happen at the expense of deepening European integration.

With states holding on to their sovereignty in security affairs much more tightly than in economics, the first institutionalisation of diplomatic encounters on matters of international security came somewhat belated and was distinctly inter-governmental in nature. The European Political Co-operation (EPC), created in 1969, attempted to make the foreign policies of member states converge through regular meetings and debates at the levels of heads of government and foreign ministers. The EPC was always at pains to keep the linkages between its foreign policy debates and the European Community – between intergovernmentalism and supranationalism – at a minimum. The EPC and the European Community (EC) existed parallel to one another. This changed with the 1992 Maastricht Treaty. Establishing what is now known as Common Foreign and Security Policy (CFSP), it prescribes to member states to ensure that the EU speaks with one voice in international affairs.

In order for states to accomplish this ambitious goal, the CFSP became an integral part of the EU. The 1997 Treaty of Amsterdam moved forward what is now known as the Common Security and Defence Policy (CSDP). Since 2003, the CSDP has deployed twenty field missions. The 2007 Lisbon Treaty, which entered into force only in 2009, tried to strengthen the CFSP and the CSDP further. Perhaps particularly noteworthy, the Treaty sought to cut the distance between the CFSP and the CSDP on the one hand and more integrated policy areas on the other. It created the new position of HR by merging the previous posts of High Representative for the CFSP and the European Commissioner for External Relations and European Neighbourhood Policy. The new High Representative, currently Catherine Ashton, is therefore, among other things, Vice President of the Commission. This is an important development, especially if one keeps the previously strict separation of the EPC from Community institutions in mind.

This slow but notable trend towards criss-crossings between intergovernmentality and supranationality in Brussels' foreign policy-making continues. The creation of the EEAS is a case in point. With staff drawn from the Commission, Council and the foreign services of member states, the EEAS deals with economic and financial issues, neighbourhood policy and security matters. Headed by the HR, the EEAS is an attempt by the EU to put its foreign policies under a single roof. This is meant to facilitate decision-making internally and to make it clear to the outside world who represents the EU on the diplomatic stage.

Among the three major areas of European foreign policy, integration theories encounter the most explanatory challenges when it comes to security. Functionalism offers a plausible explanation as to why there has been no integration of policies in this field yet. With functional needs spreading from adjacent fields being virtually absent, member states have to resort to the kind of grand design diplomacy in setting up new institutions against which Functionalists caution. Liberal intergovernmentalism emphasises economic motives of domestic actors as driving forces in intergovernmental bargains about integration. Again, this helps to explain why integration in the security realm has been rather elusive so far. Integration in this realm does not provide much straightforward economic advantage. What these approaches have difficulties with, however, are the successes that have been achieved. After all, there has been considerable institutional growth over the last decades.

Some of this can be explained through a governance perspective. Kirchner, for instance, writes about the EU's 'security governance' (Kirchner and Sperling 2007). But there is still considerable work to be done to specify the dynamics of security governance. Who are the actors? What are their channels of communication? How do they use these channels of communication and with what effects? How do revolutionary events or series of such events such as the violent breakdown of Yugoslavia, impact on re-fashioning governance?

Identities: from enmity to friendship and beyond

Identity is at the core of Constructivist approaches to global politics. Identity is often conceptualised as a *narrative that Self tells of itself.* This story has a strong relational component. The definition of Self requires situating oneself vis-à-vis others. Self positively identifies with some significant Others while it negatively identifies with others (and does so to different degrees).

The spectrum of relations is very broad. Alexander Wendt writes about three types of relationships: *enmity, rivalry and friendship* (see also Chapter 11). Enmity is constituted by a sharp demarcation of Self versus Other. Friendship is about a strong positive identification of Self with Other. Rivalry is located in between. Being concerned with writing a systemic theory of international politics, Wendt does not pay much attention to diplomacy. But these three types of relationships are a useful heuristic device for the study of diplomatic relations among states. US–North Korean relations, discussed above, are characterised by enmity. This relationship has proven to be enduring despite some attempts to move towards a less confrontational relationship. Great power relations, in Thompson's view, are often characterised by rivalry. Such rivalries can be rather stable and do not necessarily erupt into war, such as Franco-British relations in the nineteenth century (Thompson 1999). The Anglosphere is based on enduring friendship relations among Australia, Britain, Canada, New Zealand and the US (Vucetic 2011).

The spectrum can be further refined and extended. The most extreme form of enmity is *dehumanisation.* Being no longer recognised as a human being, the enemy is vilified as someone who is not worth living. Joachim von Rippentrop, first Hitler's ambassador in London and then foreign minister, turned Germany's diplomacy into a facilitator of war and genocide. The foreign office was in charge of diffusing propaganda to obfuscate the Holocaust and justify the war. It was also in charge of providing administrative support for the SS and the deportation of Jews in occupied territories, such as France. The Nuremberg Trials (→ glossary) found him guilty of crimes against peace, waging a war of aggression, war crimes and crimes against humanity. He was hung on 16 October 1946 (Seabury 1954). Von Rippentrop's crimes serve as a chilling reminder that diplomacy is not always the opposite of violence; it can also be a willing instrument supporting violence.

On the other end of the spectrum, some friendly relations proceed towards something that may be called *Amalgamated Self*, i.e. a process through which Self and Other cease to exist and form a new Self. The EU's attempt to forge an EU diplomatic persona in the shape of the EEAS may be interpreted as a step (although a hesitant one) towards establishing such an Amalgamated Self in the EU's relations with the outside world. This example also nicely illustrates that identities are usually contested. In the EEAS, some diplomats see themselves as more European than others. At the risk of oversimplification, those officials who are sent by the Council and the Commission tend to embrace more of a European identity than those sent by traditionally Euro-sceptical nations such as the United Kingdom. Box 8.4 draws parallels to this phenomenon on the global level.

Relational spectrums help to describe what relations are like at a particular moment in time and to what extent they have varied over time. Yet they do not explain how diplomats help produce and reproduce such relations. Explanatory approaches to this question may be grouped into two major clusters. Metaphorically speaking, the first cluster argues that identities are taught by someone akin to a *teacher*. The 'teacher' tries to socialise the 'student' into new understandings of the world and norms for how to act in it. Doing so, the former either relies on social influence or persuasion, or a mixture of the two. Exerting social influence is about distributing social rewards and punishments, for example providing the reward of a sense of belonging (indication that the 'student' belongs to a community that the 'student' seeks to belong to) or the punishment of a sense of not-belonging (an indication that the 'student' remains excluded from this community). Persuasion is about the 'teacher' assembling a message that convinces the 'student' of changing his or her identity, making it conform more closely to the 'teacher's' one (Johnston 2001). This move towards more conformity often involves adopting a new norm.

In order for social influence and persuasion to work, the 'teacher' needs to have a certain standing. At times, this standing may appear to the actors as if it was just there, without the 'teacher' having much to do for it. Yet, at other times, the socialiser has to actively work for his or her standing. Literature on diplomacy sometimes

---

Box 8.4 Dag Hammarskjöld on the international civil servant

In his much debated 1961 Oxford lecture, UN Secretary-General Dag Hammarskjöld cautioned against an intergovernmental UN Secretariat and pleaded for a truly international one. The difference, to Hammarskjöld, was straightforward. An intergovernmental Secretariat would be staffed by nation-states. This would amount to the 'acceptance of a nationalism rendering it necessary to abandon present efforts in the direction of internationalism symbolized by the international civil service' (Hammarskjöld 1961). The latter, by contrast, would be staffed by international civil servants who put UN principles, most importantly the Charter, ahead of national positions. Translating this statement into current parlance about identity, Hammarskjöld postulated an international identity – more precisely a UN identity – for the civil service he led. Fostering such an identity was a priority of his work while being in charge of the Secretariat.

conceptualises this need to actively do something for one's standing as public diplomacy. In this reading, public diplomacy is in charge of producing an image that endows the socialiser with the subtle power needed to influence a socialisee (Zhang 2006). This understanding of moulding relations through social influence and persuasion is very prevalent in EU literature. Many EU scholars hold that EU diplomacy towards its neighbourhood is deeply shaped by such attempts of socialisation. The EU is seen as the 'teacher' while prospective candidate states and other states in the neighbourhood feature as more or less willing 'students' (Schimmelfennig 2003).

The second cluster of explanatory approaches on the evolution of relations contends that actors, interacting on a somewhat more equal footing, make their relations together. They take this insight from George Herbert Mead (Mead and Morris 1962). The abovementioned Wendt, for instance, is adamant that relations evolve while actors *reciprocate*. International relations' scholars stipulate that thin modes of communication may be sufficient to forge relations among actors that are close enough to embark on common endeavours (but are still far removed from close relations of friendship). Jennifer Mitzen argues that states, by regularly communicating with one another, form a collective intentionality, which, in turn, makes sustainable cooperation such as the Concert of Europe possible (Mitzen 2011). Some studies on rhetorical strategies argue in a somewhat similar vein (Kornprobst 2012). They hold that, depending on the selection of offensive and defensive strategies by diplomats, communication may foster or undermine international regimes. In this view, diplomatic talk, therefore, is very important. Diplomats oftentimes soften their contestations while interacting with one another. They filter the explosive potentials out of their talk when addressing fellow diplomats. Box 8.5 illustrates this civilising effect.

Another conception of making relations through interaction revolves around *dialogue*. We discussed the practical and scholarly usages of the term already in Chapter 6. Among diplomatic practitioners, the usage of the term tends to be synonymous with the scholarly 'teacher–student' view on socialisation. It is employed as describing attempts to improve relations with someone by making Other at least a bit more like Self. The EU's critical dialogue with Iran is a case in point. In the scholarly use, by contrast, the term dialogue is diametrically opposed to the 'teacher–student' view. The participants of the dialogue are equal, and they aim for a deeper understanding of one another's views instead of one persuading the other. Currently, scholars often use this terminology when they talk about the dialogue of civilisations. Likely communication failures notwithstanding, dialogue sometimes leads to a better understanding of the other side and sometimes even to a convergence of views. Both are seen as contributing to improving relations. They may not necessarily reach shared identifications. Yet relations are already expected to improve if the parties no longer see each other as aliens but come to understand each other and each other's doings in more detail (Homeira 2011).

Practices are another avenue through which actors come to learn together. Practices, as Adler and Pouliot define the term, are 'socially meaningful patterns of action, which, in being performed more or less competently, simultaneously embody, act out, and possibly reify background knowledge and discourse in and on the material world' (Adler and Pouliot 2011: 4). The definition already gives away an explanatory logic. Agents come to learn background knowledge through practices of interaction. By doing something over and over again, knowledge sinks in and assumes a taken for granted quality. Practices and rhetorical strategies, mentioned above, can

Box 8.5 Rhetorical strategies and the nuclear non-proliferation regime

The nuclear non-proliferation regime, revolving around the 1970 NPT, is based on a grand compromise. Nuclear weapons states (NWS) promise to disarm; in return non-nuclear weapons states (NNWS) promise not to acquire nuclear weapons. Furthermore, NWS promise to help NNWS to reap the benefits of the peaceful use of nuclear energy; in return NNWS promise to subject themselves to regular inspections verifying that they do not divert nuclear technology for military uses. The implementation of this compromise has been highly contested ever since. Yet the rhetorical strategies used at the quinquennial Review Conferences of the NPT softened this contestation considerably. Instead of resorting to heavy rhetorical artillery such as the threat to abandon the regime altogether, the parties tend to rely on less robust strategies. Interplays of elaboration and placation strategies occur frequently. Dissatisfaction with the implementation record is channelled into constructive directions by calling for new norms and rules built on already existing ones (elaboration strategies, e.g. detailed steps for disarmament) and responses assuring that parties will move towards this direction (placation strategies, e.g. concessions on proposed steps towards disarmament). Placation is not accommodation. It simply takes the wind out of the critic's sails. The most important demand, for instance a timeline for disarmament, is not met. This leads to new demands at following Review Conferences and so on. But, judging by the ups and downs of the regime in the last two decades, this kind of softening talk does not damage the nuclear non-proliferation regime as such. In other words, it matters *how* diplomats quarrel. Some exchanges of rhetorical strategies are more conducive to the reproduction of compromises than others.

be understood as complementary approaches. The 'softening talk' that prevails in the nuclear non-proliferation regime may very well be understood as evolving from practice and being reproduced through practice. This close linkage between rhetoric and practice is also something that is found in social theory. De Certeau puts strong emphasis on it (De Certeau 1988).

Let us stay with this theorist a bit longer because he also introduced the interesting concept of *metis* to social theory. Although Iver Neumann tried to familiarise scholars of diplomacy with this concept already over a decade ago (Neumann 2002), it still remains widely neglected. *Metis* is the agential power to change relations. Someone who has *metis* knows how to make use of a favourable situation. *Metis* is the acquired experience to help create and seize opportunities for change. Crises of everyday routines are possible when actors are confronted with social constellations in which the usual indeterminacies of interpreting the world are especially pronounced. In these moments of openness actors can change structures. For the most part, these opportunities themselves are none of their doing. The indeterminacies appear mainly because of external circumstances, for example an exogenous shock. Yet actors have some room to enlarge these windows of opportunity. They can spell out the crisis of pre-established meaning that actors are confronted with in a particular situation. Most importantly, *metis* enables actors to seize these windows of opportunity. Actors who have *metis* do not lose orientation when a community experiences situational difficulties in interpreting the world. On the contrary, they understand these indeterminacies as chances for changing the world (Detienne and Vernant 1974: 295–296; De Certeau 1984).

Thinking about illustrative examples, the authors of the European unification process, especially Schuman and Monnet as well as Adenauer and Hallstein, come immediately to mind. They were determined to break with centuries of enmity between France and Germany. In the late 1940s and early 1950s, the shocks of WWII and the Holocaust constituted an opportunity for these actors to start authoring a new chapter of European history. In doing so, Europe's past disasters became an important Other from which Europeans ought to demarcate themselves as strongly as possible (Wæver 1996).[2]

In the following section, we briefly discuss Eritrean–Ethiopian relations, which moved from the friendship of two liberation movements to the enmity of two governments. The case highlights the strengths and weaknesses of Constructivist thought on relations.

From friendship to enmity: Eritrea and Ethiopia

Eritreans fought for their independence for three decades. From 1961 to 1974, several independence movements opposed Ethiopia's Emperor Haile Selassie I. After the Ethiopian revolution in 1974, Eritrean liberation movements fought the Derg, the military junta that followed the Emperor. Throughout the 1980s, the Eritrean People's Liberation Front (EPLF) and the Tigray People's Liberation Front (TPLF) fought side by side against the Derg. Facilitated by the cordial relations that had developed between the two movements, they reached an agreement in 1988 according to which the TPLF, if coming to power in Ethiopia, would support a referendum about Eritrean independence.

The EPLF and the TPLF defeated the Derg in 1991. The TPLF stood by its word. A UN supervised referendum about independence was held in 1993 and Eritrea became independent. Ostensibly trying to transform itself into a political party, the EPLF changed its name to the People's Front for Democracy and Justice (PFDJ), and moved towards forging a stronger Eritrean national identity. The need for this was all too clear to President Isaias Afewerki. During the independence struggle, he had experienced the splintering of independence movements along ethnic, religious and linguistic lines. Forging a stronger identity – not atypical for a newly independent state at all – was, therefore, important to him. The liberation struggle served as a major source of inventing an identity narrative that was meant to rally Eritreans around the flag. Ethiopia featured prominently in this narrative. Ethiopia is portrayed as an imperialist and expansionist state (Gilkes *et al.* 1999).

Forging a stronger identity went hand in hand with becoming more assertive on the international stage. Initially, this was done in tandem with the new Ethiopian government. For example, both governments responded to Sudanese attempts to destabilise Ethiopia and Eritrea by supporting rebel movements in these two countries in the same fashion. Addis Ababa and Asmara started to sponsor rebel movements in the Sudan. Yet triggered by the ambiguities of a not yet demarcated border, Eritrea responded with determined force to what Isaias perceived as Ethiopian infringements on Eritrean territory in the border area around Badme.

2 We would like to thank Raluca Soreanu for drawing our attention to the concept of *metis*.

Friendship had turned into enmity. This enmity was fuelled by a dominant identity narrative that interpreted the present almost exclusively in terms of a selective reading of the past. Eritrean observers of the border dispute believed that 'things have not changed since the time of Menelik II. Ethiopians have always been obsessed with the sea' (Dahli 2000: 1). Eritrean diplomats echoed this in unequivocal terms, alleging that the 'old Ethiopian foreign policy tactic is repeating itself' (Tekle 2000: 1), and even that 'their insane dream is to enslave the Eritrean people as well as plunder the country' (Asghedom 1999: 1). In short, history came to haunt Eritrean–Ethiopian relations once more. Eritrea interpreted the actions of Ethiopia through the prism of a formerly colonised and subjugated people that had the resolve to fight for its sovereign statehood in its historic boundaries (Kornprobst 2002).

The Eritrean–Ethiopian War, fought from 1998 to 2000, may have cost as many as 100,000 people their lives. About one-third of the Eritrean population was displaced. Without determined outside diplomatic interventions, mainly by the US but also by the OAU and the EU, it is unlikely that the fighting would have come to an end in 2000 (Prendergast 7 September 2001). Since then, Eritrea has strengthened its self-definition as a 'do it alone' country. It is telling that the Eritrean President, while probed by a journalist about his country's antagonistic relations with its neighbours in a 2010 interview on Al Jazeera, repeatedly accused the US, Ethiopia, the AU, the UN and journalists of seriously distorting history. Angry rebuttals such as 'mocking of justice and history' and 'distortion of history' abound (Al Jazeera 19 February 2010). This is not surprising. Isaias sees his own twists on history as natural and undeniable foundations of the Eritrean Self. Given this understanding of Self, it is unlikely that the enmity between Eritrea and Ethiopia will be coming to an end soon (and Ethiopia does not do much its end either). The best one can hope for is that its manifestations remain controlled – especially along the shared border.

What does this case tell us about the theoretical frameworks discussed above? To some extent, social influence and persuasion mattered to turn behaviour around. Mediators used these as vehicles to manufacture consent with the peace agreement that Eritrea's Isaias and Ethiopia's Meles signed in 2000 and that put an end to the war. Intertwined with this, simply talking to one another, as facilitated by the mediators, may have had some of the positive forum effects that Mitzen writes about. But the behavioural change – from war to an uneasy peace – hardly amounted to a relational paradigm shift. Eritrean–Ethiopian relations remain locked into an enemy relationship. When it comes to explaining the Eritrean contributions to reproducing these relations, the most promising explanatory route probably revolves around a combination of rhetoric and practice. Forging a new identity has a lot to do with political rhetoric. Isaias tries to win over fellow Eritreans about what ought to be Eritrean. In doing so, he falls back to practices he – and many other Eritreans of his generation – have deeply internalised during a decades-long war for independence from Ethiopia.

Summary

- Scholars of diplomacy and world politics differ widely on a number of key questions pertaining to relations and the making of relations. Three of these are especially important: (a) what kinds of relations are warranted (*normative* question)?; (b) how is the spectrum of relations to be conceptualised (*descriptive* question)?; and (c) how does diplomacy shape relations (*explanatory* question)?
- Among Realist perspectives, it is only Classical Realism that deals with the normative question of what kinds of relations are warranted in depth. The answer provided by scholars such as Morgenthau and Kissinger is *standing apart*. For Realists, the spectrum of relations tends to be delimited by outlaw on the one hand and ally on the other. How relations evolve has a lot to do with structural pressures to guard the security of a state in an anarchical environment.
- Liberal scholarship, partly implicitly and partly explicitly, postulates *closer* relations among states in order to safeguard peace and welfare. Functionalism, for example, argues forcefully for the formula of *peace through integration*. In line with these normative convictions, Liberals extend the relational spectrum. It does not end with alliance but moves, at least in some accounts, to the creation of a shared polity. Liberal approaches do not agree on explaining how cooperation and integration come about, tending to favour intergovernmental (e.g., Neoliberal Institutionalism and Liberal Intergovernmentalism) or functionalist approaches.
- Constructivist scholars are not always very explicit about what kind of relations they endorse but it can be easily extrapolated from their research that they consider *communities* transcending nation-state borders anchors of international stability and facilitators of global governance. The relational spectrum that Constructivists explore is very broad, ranging from enmity to friendship, and even beyond. As far as explanations for the making of relations are concerned, there is the '*teacher–student*' view and a more *interactionist* perspective.

Study questions

- On a spectrum from outlaw to ally, where are relations between the US, Russia and China located? What elements of balancing do the diplomacies of these powers exhibit?
- In the last decades, regional integration schemes have developed all over the globe.
- To what extent does the diplomatic pursuit of interests explain this development? To what extent does it explain the different degrees of integration that actors have accomplished and seek to accomplish?
- What does it take for enmity to be transformed into friendship?
- What are the intentional and what are the unintentional contributions of diplomacy to the making of relations?

Recommended further reading

Adler-Nissen, Rebecca. 2009. 'Late sovereign diplomacy'. *The Hague Journal of Diplomacy* no. 4 (2): 121–141.
Focusing on the EU, the author shows how diplomatic interaction can move relations among states closer and closer together. The author even presents evidence that this moving closer together includes a merger of national and EU interests. This is a Constructivist contribution to the literature.

Doyle, Michael. 1986. 'Liberalism and world politics'. *American Political Science Review* no. 80 (4): 1151–1169.
In this article, Doyle reminds us that Immanuel Kant has a lot to say about international politics. An important aspect of Doyle's application of Kant to contemporary world politics is the postulate that democracies move closer together through diplomatic interaction. This is a liberal contribution to the literature.

Morgenthau, Hans. J. and Kenneth W. Thompson. 1985. *Politics among nations: The struggle for power and peace*. New York: Knopf.
In this classical Realist statement on diplomacy, Morgenthau advocates a pragmatic approach to world politics. He postulates a diplomacy that stays away from thick (all too friendly or all too hostile) relations in order to have the necessary room to manoeuvre to balance.

9 The making of the world

Chapter objectives

- To help readers understand why the international order is shaped by different cultures of anarchy which diplomats actively constitute and reproduce.
- To provide an analytical framework for understanding the day-to-day construction of diplomatic relations through the collective assignment of functions to objects and beings.

Introduction

On 1 November 1814, the Great Powers of Europe met in Vienna to decide the new rules of international order in the aftermath of the Napoleonic wars. On 18 January 1919, diplomats from over thirty countries arrived at the Paris Peace Conference for the negotiation of the peace treaties ending World War I. On 25 April 1945, diplomats from fifty countries convened in San Francisco to draw up the UN Charter. In all three circumstances, diplomats negotiated a number of fundamental principles about who has the right to create international order, by what means and how responsibilities for upholding international order should be distributed among the stakeholders. In other words, they were involved in making the world! But what exactly do we mean when we say that diplomats make the world? One interpretation is that the making of the world involves the condition of arranging human relations and activities into a stable and regular pattern. This is what is usually referred to as 'order as fact', which is the opposite of disorder, chaos, instability and lack of predictability (Hurrell 2007: 2).

'Order as fact' (→ glossary) is primarily achieved by establishing effective conflict-preventing rules and institutions. Martin Wight, for instance, thought the main task of diplomats was to 'circumvent the occasions of war, and to extend the series of circumvented occasions; to drive the automobile of state along a oneway track, against head-on traffic, past infinitely recurring precipices' (Wight *et al.* 1978: 137). The drafters of the UN Charter were determined, for instance, to create a system of collective security capable of successfully withstanding the type of diplomatic and military aggressions unleashed by Germany, Italy and Japan during the 1930s. Nevertheless, the heroic image of Wight's diplomat as a protector of world peace is not always easy to reconcile with the practice. Diplomacy also has a long 'dark' history of being used for drumming up support for war (e.g., Napoleon's expansionist diplomacy), undermining norms and institutions of international cooperation (e.g., German and Italian diplomatic contempt of the League of Nations in the 1930s) and for maintaining nations under imperial control (e.g., British diplomacy in the nineteenth century).

This is why the making of the world also has a norm-oriented dimension that is, 'order as value' (→ glossary). One could think of 'order as fact' versus 'order as value' as two distinct levels of world-making. At the deeper level, one finds the norms, principles and shared understandings that frame diplomatic action (see also the section on deeper backgrounds in Chapter 5). At the policy level, one finds the pattern of diplomatic activities and institutions emerges from the application of these values in practice (see also the section on diplomatic tasks in Chapter 6). An imperialist world order is shaped and sustained, for instance, by the belief in certain hierarchical values regarding the political and normative worthiness of certain types of political communities. A world order governed by international institutions is underpinned by the belief in the primacy of international law in regulating states' behaviour. In other words, 'order as value' creates the conditions of possibility for 'order as fact', that is, for the type of international society to live in.

The questions to concern us then are how do diplomats shape 'order as value', how do they render it into 'order as fact' and what challenges do they face while making the world? The following two sections address these questions from two different perspectives. The first one draws on Alexander Wendt's work to explain the making of the world via diplomatic interactions. The key argument is that 'order as value' is largely shaped by how diplomats treat each other. By developing relationships of friendship, rivalry and enmity among states, diplomats help establish 'order as fact' via competing logics of anarchy. The case of the diplomacy of the Third Reich is then discussed to illustrate the conditions under which a culture of anarchy (→ glossary) could diplomatically degrade. The second approach draws on John R. Searle's deontological theory to explain the diplomatic construction of the world via the assignment of functions to objects and beings. The deontological perspective emphasises the role of collective intentionality in creating 'order as value' and the importance of international treaties, diplomatic precedents and soft law in establishing 'order as fact'. The case of climate change negotiations provides the background for understanding empirically how this process takes place.

Diplomats as makers of anarchic cultures

Drawing on the work of Martin Wight and the English school, Alexander Wendt disputes, in his groundbreaking book on the *Social Theory of International Politics*, the single logic of anarchy postulated by Neorealists like Kenneth Waltz (1979). He instead argues that anarchy can rest on at least three kinds of macro-level structures – Hobbesian, Lockean and Kantian (see description below) – depending on the type of roles that dominate the international system at a particular moment in time: enemy, rival and friend respectively (Wendt 1999: 247). The key point Wendt is making is that 'brute' material factors (e.g., tanks, planes, missiles) do not speak for themselves and hence there is little to learn from uncritically examining the distribution of material capabilities in the system. What actually matters are the broader social structures (e.g., norms, rules, conventions) within which material capabilities are embedded and from which they derive the meaning that gives them causal powers. In other words, it is the distribution of ideas, not of material factors, that primarily determines actors' interactions in world politics. This insight provides crucial clues about the role of diplomacy in making the world: it shapes relationships of friendship, rivalry and enmity among states. These relationships drive, in turn, competing logics of anarchy in the system, that is different strategies and modes of action to cope with the constraints of the lack of centralised authority in international politics.

While in Chapter 8 we discussed how diplomats make relations among the political entities they represent, in this chapter we go deeper and examine how the making of relations is involved in the diplomatic making of the world. Relations of enmity, for instance, are constituted by representations of the Other as an actor who denies the right to exist of the Self and refuses to limit its violence towards the Self. This generates a Hobbesian logic of anarchy of unlimited warfare, zero-sum game and empire-building tendencies. Security dilemmas (i.e., the attempts of a state to increase its security decreases the security of others) are particularly severe not because of the nature of weapons, but because of the negative intentions attributed to others. By contrast, friendship is a role structure within which states agree to settle their disputes without war or threat of war and to defend each other against attacks from third parties. This allows for the logic of anarchy to evolve into a Kantian direction characterised by the formation of security communities and collective security arrangements. Conflicts between states may still arise, but they are handled through negotiation and court arbitration even when the cost of waging war or of threatening to use force might be low. Rivalry falls somewhere in between these two role structures. Unlike enemies, rivals accept the right to existence of each other as sovereign entities. Unlike friends, however, the recognition among rivals does not extend to parties' refraining from using force for settling disputes among themselves. This gives rise to a Lockean logic of anarchy whereby war is accepted as normal and legitimate, but only in a limited manner. Weak states are not subjected to the rule of the survival of the fittest. They are protected by the restraint of strong states against violating others' territorial sovereignty.

Wendt's model of the logics of anarchy offers a powerful tool for understanding structural conditions of cooperation and conflict in world politics. What is less clear though is how exactly diplomats shape the three cultures of anarchy. This is where the concept of symbolic interactionism developed by G.H. Mead demonstrates its analytical value (see Box 9.1). Basically, relationship of friendship, rivalry and enmity are the result of the way in which diplomats treat each other. This is known as the principle of 'reflected appraisals' or 'mirroring' because actors come to see themselves as a reflection of how they think others 'appraise' them in the 'mirror' of the Other's representation of the Self (Wendt 1999: 327). When a diplomat starts treating, for instance, another diplomat as a potential enemy, then the latter may internalise this appraisal and generate reactions in line with these expectations, which, in turn, may reinforce and stabilise a structure of antagonistic identities and interests.

However, is it sufficient for diplomats to treat each other as friends in order to become friends? The answer is clearly no, as power is a crucial factor in determining the direction of the relationship. In order for diplomats to reset their relationship from one of enmity into one of rivalry or friendship, both sides need to develop shared understandings of the nature of the problems they face and of the solutions to address them. Power provides the basis for developing such shared understandings by

---

Box 9.1 Symbolic interactionism

According to Mead, individuals develop norm-regulated behaviour by taking the attitude of the 'generalized other', that is, by learning to see their actions from the perspective of the social group they belong to. However, this 'social self' encompassing the norms, roles and expectations of the others towards us represents only one component of our personality ('Me'). The other component is the individualised self ('I'). The latter represents our reflective response to the attitudes of the others. 'Me' is therefore important because it constitutes the mechanism of social control of a community over its members. 'I' is our conscious reaction of compliance or defiance of others' expectations vis-à-vis us (Mead 1934). A diplomat, for instance, is expected not to interfere in the domestic affairs of the host country ('Me') but, under certain conditions, she may find this role unacceptable ('I').

---

rewarding behaviours that support them and punishing those that do not. However, power as coercion can have only short-term effects. Deeper degrees of internalisation of the shared understandings require actors to see the new relationship as advantageous to their self-interest – as when they share mutually beneficial trade arrangements – or as normatively legitimate and constitutive of their identity – as when they share similar cultural and political values. Relationship-building is therefore the process by which diplomats make the world. Positive and good relationships increase the chance of developing Lockean or Kantian cultures of anarchy, while bad relationships may push the world into a Hobbesian direction.

The problem with this argument is that the power required by diplomats for shaping cultures of anarchy is asymmetrical. The lack of a central authority in the international system and the atmosphere of distrust induced by the security dilemma make it much easier for state representatives to turn the culture of anarchy into a self-help rather than a collaborative direction (see case study below). In other words, diplomats adapt more quickly and enduringly to negative rather than positive dynamics of international conduct. The more intensely a group of diplomats, especially of the Great Powers, behave antagonistically to each other, the more likely their behaviour would be imitated by other diplomats and by implication, the more likely the prevalent culture of anarchy within the system would become less cooperative and more hostile. Under these conditions, the direction of the Hobbesian/Lockean/ Kantian progression discussed above may appear excessively optimistic: why would cultures of anarchy move from an aggressive to a cooperative pattern of diplomatic conduct, as modern history seems to suggest, despite occasional setbacks, and not the other way around?

According to Wendt, individuals' desire for recognition provides the answer to this puzzle. Unlike Neorealist accounts that see the logic of anarchy to be primarily driven by *states'* desire for security, Wendt argues that *individuals'* desire for recognition, that is to accept the Other to have legitimate rights and social standing in relation to the Self, is the key driving force in world politics. This is so because individuals that are not recognised do not count and hence they may be killed or violated as one sees fit. Physical security is one important form by which the desire for recognition can be satisfied, but it cannot be reduced to it. Agency is not simply determined by material factors such as security or wealth, but also by the social matrix within which one constitutes itself as a moral subject. In other words, while physical security provides the minimum condition for individuals to exist, it is the broader aspect of recognition, of being treated as an equal and with respect, which drives political entities to establish international orders that progressively satisfy individuals' desire for recognition (Wendt 2003: 517).

Diplomats are the key players in the struggle for recognition (→ glossary) not least because it is through their symbolic presence that state sovereignty is being acknowledged by the other states in the system. More importantly, diplomats bear the main responsibility for the definition, negotiation and application of the foundational principles on the basis of which recognition is granted in international politics. In the classical European system, status recognition was construed as a symbolic manifestation of power by means of diplomatic ranking and precedence-setting (see also Chapter 2). The 1555 Peace of Augsburg established the principle '*cuius regio, eius religio*' ('whose realm, his religion') as the basis for recognition among dynastic-sovereign entities. The 1648 Peace of Westphalia introduced a secular-territorial conception of recognition as the legitimating principle for sovereign equality among states and princes (Hall 1999). National self-determination became the essential component of the legal recognition of statehood in the aftermath of WWII and decolonialisation. More recently, diplomats working on the Responsibility to Protect doctrine have been instrumental in associating international recognition with respect for human rights, domestic justice and minimal conditions of democracy.

The theory of the struggle for recognition does not only provide a powerful explanation of why diplomats are the key actors involved in making the world. It also points out the direction in which they are likely to take the world. As Wendt provocatively argues, only a world-state can provide the type of constraints necessary for individuals to reciprocally satisfy their desire for recognition by means short of violence. If Wendt is right, then diplomacy may involve the negotiation of four grand bargains of international order (Wendt 2003: 517–528). The first one already took place and concluded with the Peace of Westphalia in 1648. By grounding international recognition in the principle of territorial sovereignty, the Treaty of Westphalia put an end to a Hobbesian stage 'war of all against all' and provided individuals with a minimal protection against physical and ideological domination. The Lockean 'society of states' we currently live in allows states to recognise each other's legal sovereignty as independent subjects, but not that of each other's citizens. This creates a source of instability in the system, on the one hand because war between states still remains a possibility and, on the other hand, because individuals are not properly protected against abuses of their own states.

The second grand diplomatic bargain would involve the creation of a world society or a universal pluralistic security community (→ glossary). Similar to the case of the North Atlantic community today, this system would restrict the right of its members to settle disputes by violence and would extend legal protections not only to states but also to individuals. The system would nevertheless remain unstable in the absence of collective protection against aggression from 'rogue' states emerging through domestic revolution and rejecting non-violence as a rule of conduct. Therefore, it would be necessary to negotiate a third diplomatic that would allow the members of the system to defend themselves against threats under the principle of collective security ('all for one and one for all'). This Kantian model of 'pacific federation' offers an enduring resolution to the struggle for recognition, but it may be eventually forced to accept a fourth diplomatic bargain due to the asymmetrical enforcement of the norms of mutual recognition between the Great Powers and small states. To address this limitation a world-state might finally emerge as an alternative and more stable institutional arrangement.

While Wendt's theory of the struggle for recognition assumes a progressive direction of systemic evolution from a Hobbesian to a Lockean and then to a Kantian culture of anarchy, the logic of action he proposes is not deterministic. Domestic revolutions, institutional breakdowns or natural catastrophes may always derail diplomatic efforts to build a more stable and peaceful international society. The important conclusion of this argument, though, is that despite occasional setbacks, the struggle for recognition places a practical and moral obligation upon diplomats to stay the course.

Case study: the 'bad apple' diplomacy of the Third Reich

The diplomacy of the Third Reich offers an instructive case for understanding the conditions under which a not fully consolidated Lockean culture of anarchy could be diplomatically pushed back into a Hobbesian direction. The collapse of imperial Germany at the end of WWI left German diplomats with tremendous challenges to overcome. Under the terms of the 1919 Versailles Treaty, Germany was forced to pay massive reparations for the war (132 billion gold marks), accept moral responsibility for starting the war (e.g., the famous 'guilt' clause of Article 231) and to severely reduce its military strength (armed forces limited to 100,000 troops, air force banned, naval forces significantly downsized). As justifiable these conditions might have been in the eyes of the Allied Powers given the immense destruction brought about by the war, the Versailles Treaty was strongly opposed domestically in Germany. As a result, the revision of the Versailles Treaty became the paramount objective of German diplomacy, first pursued by peaceful negotiations during the Weimar Republic (1919–1933) and later by increasingly aggressive actions taken by the Nazi regime.

In the first stage, Anglo-German rapprochement was perceived by German diplomats as the most effective strategy for accomplishing this goal and to a certain extent this assumption proved right. Keen to defuse further escalations of diplomatic tensions among Western European powers, Britain supported Germany's aspiration to regain some control over its diplomatic affairs through the 1925 Locarno Treaty, which guaranteed the post-war Western borders of Germany while leaving the Eastern borders free for revisions. Together with the US, Britain also helped Germany negotiate better terms of repayment of the war reparations.

The rise of the National Socialist party to power in January 1933 changed completely the diplomatic dynamic. While many professional diplomats believed the Nazis would not be able to conduct foreign policy without their guidance, this expectation was short-lived. Soon after taking office, the new Chancellor, Adolf Hitler, directed the German Foreign Office to denounce the terms of the Versailles Treaty, withdraw the country from the League of Nations and provide diplomatic cover for a series of aggressive moves involving territorial acquisition and regime subversion in various European countries. Some of the career diplomats advised restraint or even opposition to Hitler's foreign policies, but their resistance was gradually overcome through sustained policies of nazification of the German diplomatic corps and the appointment of a stalwart Nazi, Joachim von Ribbentrop, as Minister of Foreign Affairs in 1938 (Craig 1994).

The turning point for German diplomacy came in 1938. Before 1938, one could argue that German diplomatic relations with other countries took place reasonably within the bounds prescribed by a Lockean culture of anarchy. While expressing increasingly strong dissatisfaction with its status relative to that of other European powers, Germany nevertheless accepted and recognised the territorial sovereignty of other states. However, after 1938, the German diplomacy turned anti-systemic. It was no longer interested in merely redressing the perceived injustices of the Versailles Treaty, but it aggressively sought to change the very principles on the basis of which the modern international system had been organised since the Peace of Westphalia in 1648. Its ambition switched from seeking a better position within a system of states founded on the principle of national sovereignty to establishing an international system dominated by a few empires and ruled by force. In other words, the post-1938 German diplomacy was directed at forging a Hobbesian culture of anarchy infused by empire-building ambitions, unlimited warfare and self-help imperatives.

The emblematic case to mark the transition of the German diplomacy from a Lockean to a Hobbesian outlook was the Sudetenland crisis in the summer of 1938. The end of WWI left many ethnic Germans living outside the territorial borders of Germany. In the newly created state of Czechoslovakia, about 23 per cent of the whole population was ethnically German, most of them living in a region close to the German border, the Sudenteland. In August 1938, Hitler ordered its military to make plans for the forceful annexation of this border region. In an attempt to buy more time to build up strength for confronting Germany (Ripsman and Levy 2008), the leaders of Britain and France convened with those of Italy and Germany in Munich on 29–30 September 1938 and agreed to the German annexation of the Sudetenland in exchange for a pledge of peace from Hitler. With Germany's diplomatic support, other neighbours began making demands on Czechoslovakia's territory. In the autumn of 1938, Hungary annexed territory in Southern Slovakia and Poland annexed the Tešin district of Czech Silesia. Finally, on 15 March 1939, Nazi Germany invaded and annexed the remaining Czech provinces of Bohemia and Moravia, in flagrant violation of the Munich Pact (United States Holocaust Memorial Museum 2012).

The German diplomatic onslaught unleashed on a smaller scale in Munich (see also discussion on appeasement in Box 7.1) was supposed to be replicated on a grander scale via the Tripartite Pact that was concluded on 27 September 1940 between Germany, Italy and Japan. The practical purpose of the treaty was to permit the three powers 'to assist one another with all political, economic and military means' when any one of them was attacked by 'a Power at present not involved in the European War or in the Chinese-Japanese Conflict' – by which it was meant the US and the Soviet Union (Yale Law School 27 September 1940). However, the more general objective of the diplomatic cooperation between the three powers was actually the creation of a New World Order under their imperial control and military domination. The Japanese Ambassador to Berlin, Hiroshi Ōshima, could not have been more categorical about this when he asserted that 'the policies of the tripartite powers were well-founded because nothing was a more natural development than to unite under one order all people with historical, economic, and cultural ties' (cited in Boyd 1980: 130). The only reason these plans failed and the Lockean culture of anarchy survived at the end of WWII was because the three powers suffered military defeat.

The relative easiness and swiftness with which the German diplomacy during the Nazi regime proved able to threaten the foundations of the modern international system offers some important lessons for diplomatic scholars and practitioners alike. First, the way in which a major war is being diplomatically concluded is of crucial importance for the future stability of the international system. While the punishment of the leaders responsible for starting the war and violating international law must remain an unwavering guiding principle for conflict termination settlements, policies of post-war retribution must nevertheless allow room for societal healing and for the diplomatic re-engagement of the defeated parties in the society of states. Second, when fundamental principles of international conduct are being systemically violated, especially by the Great Powers, the international community has a prime responsibility to diplomatically engage the recalcitrant elites, as early as possible, and to strongly defend these principles as opposed to compromise them. Third, the Great Powers might occasionally turn into 'bad apples' and inflict serious damage on the fabric of the international system. Short of military action, the only way in which other actors can mitigate the negative impact of 'bad apple' diplomacy is through diplomatic containment at two levels: strategically, by preventing other states from joining their ranks (hence the importance of counter-alliances) and normatively, by undercutting the authoritative appeal of the shared understandings underpinning antagonistic cultures of anarchy (hence the importance of international law).

Diplomats as makers of international deontologies

In his seminal work on the 'Construction of Social Reality', John R. Searle advances a startling thesis: he argues that we all live in an invisible sea of social facts (norms, rules, codes of conducts), which we largely take for granted and rarely question. Most importantly, these institutional facts, which he calls deontologies (see Box 9.2), only exist because we think they exist! The moment we stop attributing meaning to them, they lose the capacity to represent the world for us and by extension they cease to regulate human behaviour (Searle 1998: 105–106). In other words, what Searle tells us is that the social world does not exist out there independently of us. Wendt's cultures of anarchy happen only insofar as human beings experience them. If diplomats stop practising them then there would be no cultures of anarchy. This is an important claim that deserves close attention since it has major implications for diplomatic relations.

Box 9.2　Deontology

In the literature, there are two different understandings of deontology. On the one hand, the term is frequently associated with Immanuel Kant's work on moral duties, especially with his principle of the categorical imperative: 'act only in accordance with that maxim through which you can at the same time will that it become a universal law' (Kant 2004). John Searle's understanding of deontology, on the other hand, is much broader in scope and covers the rights, duties, obligations, authorisations, permissions, empowerments, requirements and certifications associated with a particular institution (Searle 2005: 10). A diplomat, for instance, has the deontological obligation to represent her government, the right to negotiate on its behalf and enjoys the privilege of legal immunity from the local jurisdiction.

Consider, for instance, the debate about the deterioration of diplomatic relations within the transatlantic security community in the aftermath of the US intervention in Iraq in 2003. For some, the damage was rather profound, another telling symptom of the growingly political divide between the US and its allies (Kagan 2003). More optimistic voices insisted that calls for the demise of the transatlantic community were definitely premature since the threat of jihadi terrorism would likely push the West closer together, and that a new transatlantic bargain based on the complementarity between American military might and European civilian power would not only save the transatlantic relationship but would even transform it for the better (Moravcsik 2004). Searle would instead argue the source and solution to the diplomatic crisis had little to do with Iraq or external threats but rather with whether the leaders and diplomats of the countries involved were prepared or not to continue to act as members of a security community, that is to observe their deontological responsibilities of treating each other respectfully, truthfully and with confidence in their future relationship (Bjola 2010: 202–206).

Searle defends his deontological account of the construction of social reality by means of three important concepts: collective intentionality (→ glossary), functional assignment and deontic powers. Collective intentionality refers to the beliefs, desires and intentions shared by different people as part of them doing something together. An orchestra performing a concert, an army fighting the enemy, a soccer team applying a common strategy to win the game or a group of diplomats working together to defuse an international crisis – are all cases of collective not individual intentionality. As Searle points out, 'the crucial element in collective intentionality is a sense of doing [wanting, believing, etc.] something together and the individual intentionality that each person has is derived *from* the collective intentionality that they share' (Searle 1995: 25). The diplomat in the example above might have, for instance, the individual intention to amend her negotiation preferences, but the intention is only part of the collective intentionality to avoid a dangerous diplomatic escalation leading to military conflict.

The reason collective intentionality is important for understanding the diplomatic construction of the world has to do with the assignment or imposition of functions to objects and beings. For example, a piece of paper may have no value unless it is being *collectively* assigned the function to be traded as a currency. A piece of cloth attached to a wooden pole serves no intrinsic purpose, but it may be *collectively* assigned the function of serving as a national flag. A document signed by a group of people remains just a piece a paper unless it is *collectively* recognised as the function of serving as an international agreement. A person residing in a different country is subject to local prosecution unless she is being collectively recognised as the function of serving as a diplomat. In all the examples above, certain objects or persons (banknotes, flags, international treaties, diplomats) possess or enjoy a specific status (exchanged as money, being waved at international meetings, creating legal obligations or being protected from prosecution) *not* in virtue of their physical characteristics, but because of the collective assignment, imposition or recognition of that status.

Searle calls this type of relations *status-functions* (→ glossary) because 'the status enables the person or object to perform a function which could not be performed without the collective acceptance of that status' (Searle 2008: 32–33). As the examples above cogently illustrate, status-functions create social reality by representing it as existing and this process can be summed up with the following formula: *X counts as Y in C*, which states that an object, person or state of affairs, X, has been assigned a special status, Y, in the context of C. Here are a few examples of status-functions:

- Notes issued by the European Central Bank (X) count as money (Y) in countries that are members to the European Economic and Monetary Union (C).
- A certain amount of CO_2 emission reductions (X) counts as a tradable commodity (Y) within the EU Emissions Trading System (C).
- A document outlining trading conditions (X) counts as a binding international treaty (Y) if properly ratified by the signatory parties (C).
- A person residing in a different country (X) enjoys immunity from local prosecution (Y) if she carries a diplomatic passport (C).

The main reason status-functions are essential for understanding the construction of social reality is because they are vehicles of power in society as they prescribe to agents what they are allowed and what they are forbidden to do in their conduct with each other. According to Searle, all status-functions, without exceptions, carry deontic powers (→ glossary), that is rights, duties, obligations, requirements, permissions and entitlements. These deontic powers can be both of a positive or a negative nature. In the first case, they grant rights to a person to do something she could not otherwise do, for example when a diplomat is empowered to negotiate and conclude an international treaty. In the latter case, deontic powers prescribe obligations to do something one would not otherwise be able to do, for example when a diplomat is not allowed under Article 41.1 of the Vienna Convention on Diplomatic Relations to interfere in the domestic affairs of the host country. Last but not least, these status-functions are not possible without language. Searle is particularly adamant about this: we can imagine a society having language but no money, property, government or marriage, but we cannot imagine a society having money, property, government or marriage but no language (Searle 2010: 109). In short, no language, no status-functions, no deontologies and, by extension, no social reality!

The pattern of relationships constituting 'order as fact' is constantly evolving under the impact of three primary status-functions: security, redistribution and recognition. The protection of 'primary goals of social existence' (Bull 1997: 86), that is security, has been traditionally seen as the key function of international order. It involves existential threats to anything that questions sovereignty, either of military, political, economic, environmental or societal nature. What counts as security depends though on further collective recognition of certain secondary status-functions. For a long period of time, the balance of power was considered, for instance, to be the proper diplomatic instrument for generating security. After WWI, collective security has been reckoned as a better mechanism of ensuring security based on the view that it facilitates a constitutional order in which legal rules, rights, protections and political commitments combine to limit and shape the exercise of military power. More recently, the spread of democratic values and norms has been also valued for its ability to create a set of domestic restraints against using military force for settling international disputes. These methods are not discovered in nature in the same way we might discover oil or gold. They are observer-relative, that is they are always created and imposed by collective intentionality with specific purposes: to grant diplomats the deontic power to engineer alliances against perceived hegemons, to engage in international institutional building or to advocate democratic changes in host countries.

Redistribution, understood as the allocation of economic burdens and benefits to result from taking part in the global economic system, represents the second constitutive status-function of international order. This is so because financial crises have been increasingly recognised as just as crippling for the well-being of international society as security threats (Strange 1986). Without collective recognition of this systemic ordering status, there will hardly be any interest in pursuing economic diplomacy, as actors would lack a shared understanding of what counts as desirable sources of wealth. Similar to security, diplomatic strategies of economic redistribution have been informed by evolving secondary status-functions. Mercantilism played a dominant role in the constitution of the modern world system (Wallerstein 1980) and its more recent version has been largely credited to be the driving force behind the development of East Asian 'tigers' (Johnson 1982). The post-WWII economic order gave rise to a diplomatic method of economic redistribution of liberal inspiration (Ruggie 1982), although with clear hegemonic undertones (Keohane 1980). More recent governance models stress the role of norms of participation, responsibility, accountability and transparency in upholding the rules of economic order by providing credible, sustainable and balanced opportunities for economic growth (Held and Koenig-Archibugi 2005). Economic diplomacy is therefore not a quest for material wealth, but rather the pursuit of deontic powers of assigning, reinforcing or amending values to what counts as wealth within a particular type of international order.

The third primary status-function of international order is recognition, which encompasses the inter-subjective process by which agents are constituted as respected and esteemed members of the society of states (Honneth 1995). Denial of equal treatment and legal protection of one's moral integrity and dignity prompts feelings of humiliation, shame and anger, which has often been a major source of grievance, tension and international conflict (Lebow 2008; Wolf 2011). Confirmation of one's rightful diplomatic standing has been historically based on various secondary status-functions of proper conduct in world politics (see Chapter 2). Being recognised as a legitimate member of the international community entails strong deontic powers, such as the ability to avoid international sanctions, access international financial instruments, accede to international organisations and shape the decision-making of international regimes.

Diplomats resort to three mechanisms to articulate, revise or replace international deontologies: international treaties, diplomatic precedents and soft law. International agreements and covenants are undoubtedly the most commonly used diplomatic instruments for revising, amending or replacing status-functions and deontic powers. The post-WWII agreements establishing the UN Charter, the Bretton Woods system and the International Covenants on Human Rights have provided, for instance, strong and enduring guidelines of diplomatic conduct, despite occasional setbacks: the use of force has been since accepted only for self-defence or collective security (status-function A), commercial and financial relations have had to observe redistributive rules set up by the IMF and the World Bank (status-function B), while claims to status recognition have been increasingly reviewed using domestic implementation of democratic norms and human rights as a normative baseline (status-function C).

The use of diplomatic precedents (→ glossary) represents another important method by which deontological conflicts can be alleviated. The NATO interventions in Kosovo in 1999 and Libya in 2011 have provided, for instance, a major boost to the doctrine of the Responsibility to Protect (R2P) as an emerging diplomatic deontology of international conduct on matters of collective security and status recognition. The resolutions adopted by the UN Security Council during the two crises have asserted and subsequently confirmed not only that governments have an obligation to refrain from using violence against their own people (deontic power A), but most importantly that the international community has a responsibility to protect the civilian population against its own government in situations of grave human rights abuses (deontic power B) (UN Security Council 26 March 1999, 2011). The success of diplomatic precedents in establishing new diplomatic deontologies largely depends on their ability to gather support of key actors. For example, the success of R2P is likely contingent upon its ability to win the support of regional actors, such as the Arab League, the AU or the Union of South American Nations.

Diplomacy may also bring about 'order as fact' by means of 'soft law' (→ glossary) such as conference declarations, executive statements, resolutions, codes of conduct or policy recommendations. Unlike international treaties or diplomatic precedents, soft law instruments tend to trigger weaker constraints on international actors primarily because they lack the binding character of the former or the behavioural pull of the latter. Nevertheless, soft law has the potential to shape the authority of the emerging diplomatic deontologies in three distinct ways: first, they can make the legality of opposing diplomatic positions much harder to sustain (i.e., weaken the deontological authority of competing status-functions); second, they may have a formative impact on the *opinio juris* or state practice that generates new international customary law (i.e., establish new deontic powers); and, third, they may even influence the development and application of binding international treaties (Boyle 2006: 142). The relevance of these three mechanisms is remarkably illustrated, for instance, by the success of the 'soft diplomacy' surrounding the global movement to ban landmines, which had started as a non-governmental initiative in the early 1980s of limited international significance and culminated in 1997 in the signing of an international treaty by over 120 states granting them a whole new set of deontic powers regarding the use, sale and production of landmines (Cameron *et al.* 1998).

Case study: the deontology of climate change diplomacy

Climate change negotiations have generally revolved around three major issues: the type of multilateral instrument necessary to generate a significant reduction of greenhouse gas emissions (GHG) (e.g., binding versus voluntary reduction targets), the level of financial commitment to support adaptation efforts in countries and regions most likely to be affected by climate change, and the design of the institutional framework most capable of generating broad participation, effectiveness and compliance. The framework created by the UNFCCC and its 1997 Kyoto Protocol favours binding GHG reduction targets by an average of 6 per cent below 1990 levels between 2008 and 2012 to be achieved by the use of market-based 'flexible mechanisms' such as the Clean Development Mechanisms (CDM) and Joint Implementation (JI).

The Copenhagen Accord signed in 2009 substituted legally binding reduction targets with voluntary pledges, both for developed and developing countries. Developed countries accepted to individually or jointly implement economy-wide emissions targets, while developing countries agreed to step up their efforts to abate their GHG emissions by undertaking nationally appropriate mitigation actions (NAMA). The

'Durban Platform for Enhanced Action', agreed upon at the 17th Conference of the Parties (COP) of the UNFCCC in December 2011, defined a roadmap for negotiations that would eventually bind major GHG polluters like the US, China and India to mandatorily curb their emissions after 2020.

Figure 9.1 captures the network of climate deontologies to result from concluding an international binding agreement akin to the existing Kyoto Protocol. If climate negotiations decide to settle for voluntary pledges similar to those agreed upon in the Copenhagen Accord, the deontological configuration would remain largely the same with the exception of B and F, and of weaker versions of G and K. The first deontology (A) refers to the deontic powers granted to the CDM Executive Board by the Conference of the Parties serving as the Meeting of the Parties to the Kyoto Protocol (COP/MOP). The Board supervises the Kyoto Protocol's clean development mechanism and is the ultimate point of contact for CDM project participants for the registration of projects (E) and the issuance of certified emission reductions (D) (UNFCCC 2012). National governments have the obligation to submit annual emission inventories and national reports at regular intervals to COP (C) and to accept penalties for non-compliance at the end of the commitment period (B). They could choose to minimise or avoid the penalty by offsetting emission surpluses with assigned amount units purchased from other governments (F). At the same time, national governments impose GHG emission limits on national companies (G), which the latter can meet by improving internal efficiency standards or by purchasing carbon allowances and certified emission reductions from the carbon market (I).

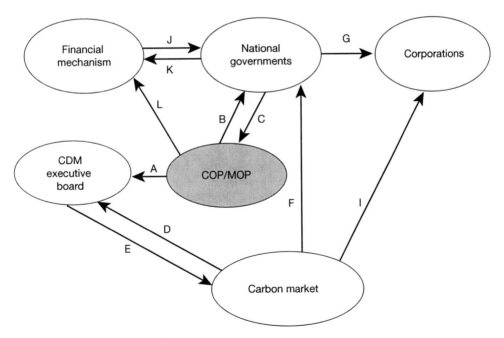

Figure 9.1 Deontologies of climate governance

The financial mechanism includes the Global Environmental Facility and three special funds: the Special Climate Change Fund, the Least Developed Countries Fund
and the Adaptation Fund. It provides adaptation support for the most vulnerable
countries to climate change (J) and it is being funded from contributions made by
developed countries and from carbon trading proceeds (K) under the supervision
of the COP, which decides climate change policies, project priorities and eligibility
criteria for funding (L). The configuration of deontic powers described above (the
power to register and issue certified emission reductions, the authorisation to allocate emission permits, the permission to trade certain types of carbon allowances,
the obligation to meet certain GHG emissions targets, the requirement to contribute
to adaptation funding, etc.) are being defined by three important status-functions of
climate governance, which have been subject to intense negotiations:

1   GHG emission reduction strategies (X) can generate a vital source of economic
    wealth (Y) within the context of a global carbon emissions market (C).
2   Developed countries (X) bear the primary responsibility for reducing GHG emissions
    (Y) because of their larger historical contribution to climate change (C).
3   The international society (X) is on an irreversible path of catastrophic collapse
    (Y) if measures are not taken to significantly cut global GHG emissions, both on
    an interim (e.g., 25–40 per cent by 2020) and long term-basis (e.g., 80–95 per cent
    by 2050) (C).

The important characteristic of these status-functions is that they can exist only in virtue of actors collectively recognising and experiencing them. These institutional facts
are being negotiated with the purpose of generating the deontic powers described
in Figure 9.1. The lack of progress of climate negotiations is explained by the fact
that these new status-functions face an uphill battle against the deontological authority of a few but entrenched diplomatic status-functions: conditions of international
interaction count as security threats if they are perceived to undermine the political
independence of sovereign actors (status-function A); carbon-based resources remain
the main drivers of global wealth production for the foreseeable future (status-function B); and claims about international justice enjoy validity when they rest on a
reasonable degree of fairness (status-function C). For climate change negotiations
to be successful, the deontological authority gap between emerging and established
status-functions must be closed.

The second status-function is particularly controversial as it advances serious revisions of the mechanisms of global economic redistribution and status recognition by
means of the deontic powers B, F, G, J and K (see Figure 9.1). While the first status-
function brings into existence a new major source of wealth ('green' goods, capital
and services), the second unevenly restricts access to traditional instruments of wealth
production (carbon-based factors of production) based on contentious assignments
of international responsibility. This has to be re-negotiated in a manner that combines the historical responsibility of developed states with the requirement for good
governance of developing countries. The fourth climate status-function has yet to
achieve collective recognition as climate change is not yet perceived by the majority
of actors to pose substantial risks to international order, partly because of the unprecedented and future-oriented nature of the risks (third emerging status-function).

The setting of diplomatic precedents by the EU or other regional organisations in framing climate threats as a collective security issue could significantly enhance the deontological authority of this status-function.

Summary

- The diplomatic making of the world involves two layers, 'order as value' and 'order as fact'. The former refers to the entrenched norms, principles and shared understandings that frame diplomatic action. The latter refers to the stable and regular pattern of global activities and institutions to emerge from the application of 'order as value' in practice. 'Order as value' creates the conditions of possibility for 'order as fact', that is for the type of international society to live in.
- From a symbolic interactionist perspective, diplomats shape 'order as value' by the way in which they treat each other. By forging relationships of friendship, rivalry and enmity among states, diplomats help establish 'order as fact' via competing cultures of anarchy, Hobbesian, Lockean and Kantian. The three cultures of anarchy differ by the extent to which they accept war as a legitimate instrument for settling diplomatic differences. The struggle for recognition is assumed to lead to a series of successive grand diplomatic bargains, ending with the establishment of a world-state.
- From a deontological perspective, the diplomatic construction of the world takes place via the assignment of functions to objects and beings. This process is mediated by the notion of collective intentionality, which refers to the beliefs, desires and intentions shared by different people as part of them doing something together. The pattern of relationships constituting 'order as fact' is constantly evolving under the impact of three primary status-functions: security, redistribution and recognition. As makers of international deontologies, diplomats help create and revise 'order as fact' via international treaties, diplomatic precedents and soft law.

Study questions

- What is the difference between 'order as fact' and 'order as value'?
- How do diplomats shape 'order as value' from a symbolic interactionist perspective and what challenges do they face?
- Is Wendt right to argue the struggle for recognition will drive diplomats to seek the formation of a world-state?
- How do diplomats shape 'order as value' from a deontological perspective and what challenges do they face?
- What status-functions are most important for the establishment of 'order as fact' and how do diplomats make and revise them?

Recommended further reading

Bull, Hedley. 1997. *The anarchical society: A study of order in world politics.* 2nd edn. Houndmills, Basingstoke, Hampshire: Macmillan.
This is essential reading for understanding why international relations are viewed in the English School tradition as a complex set of relations among states that form an international society as opposed to an international system.

Hurrell, Andrew. 2007. *On global order: Power, values, and the constitution of international society.* Oxford and New York: Oxford University Press.
Drawing on work in international law, international relations and global governance, this book provides a clear and wide-ranging introduction to the analysis of global political order – how patterns of governance and institutionalisation in world politics have already changed, what the most important challenges are and what the way forward might look like.

Ikenberry, G. John. 2001. *After victory: Institutions, strategic restraint, and the rebuilding of order after major wars.* Princeton: Princeton University Press.
This book asks the question, what do states that win wars do with their new-found power and how do they use it to build order? In examining the post-war settlements in modern history, the author argues that powerful countries do seek to build stable and cooperative relations, but the type of order that emerges hinges on their ability to make commitments and restrain power.

Searle, John R. 2010. *Making the social world: The structure of human civilization.* Oxford and New York: Oxford University Press.
This book does not expliticy address diplomatic issues, but it provides a solid philosophical background to the theory of international deontologies. Searle explains how language creates and maintains the elaborate structures of human social institutions. These institutions serve to create and distribute power relations that are pervasive and often invisible. These power relations motivate human actions in a way that provides the glue that holds human civilisation together.

Wendt, Alexander. 1999. *Social theory of international politics.* Cambridge: Cambridge University Press.
Drawing upon philosophy and social theory, this book develops a theory of the international system as a social construction. The author argues that conflict and cooperation in international politics is best explained by the way in which states view and treat each other as enemies, rivals or friends.

Part V

Discussing normative approaches

10 Remaking the diplomat

Chapter objectives

- To help readers understand supranational and subnational challenges to traditional forms of diplomatic representation.
- To explain the main sources of diplomatic influence (hard, soft and smart power), describe their application in practice and discuss their advantages and shortcomings.
- To explore what methods of diplomatic recruitment and training could facilitate the formation of the twenty-first-century diplomat.

Introduction

Is the current evolution of the international society reshaping the diplomatic method and, if yes, how should diplomacy adapt to the new circumstances? From a supranational perspective, questions keep arising as to whether diplomats should represent only the interests of their governments or whether they should also consider the impact the representation of these interests may have on the international order. The rising influence of subnational governmental authorities in foreign affairs challenges the four-century supremacy of traditional diplomats of the terms of diplomatic representation. Similar questions could be raised about the tools of diplomatic engagement (how should diplomats use power in their work and to what purpose?) or training practices (what are the desired skills, recruitment patterns and knowledge accumulation objectives for the twenty-first-century diplomat?).

In other words, what principles should guide what issues to become subject of diplomatic representation, who is to be recognised as a diplomat, how should diplomats relate to each other and how should they be recruited and trained in order to effectively face these challenges? This chapter will address these questions in three steps. The first section will examine why supranational and subnational challenges are gaining increased diplomatic relevance and what needs to be done to address them. The second section will discuss the main sources of diplomatic influence (hard, soft and smart power), describe their application in practice and discuss their advantages and limitations. The third part will probe how diplomatic training currently takes place and what aspects diplomatic curricula need to take into account in order to prepare diplomats for service in the twenty-first century.

Diplomatic representation

The raison de système

As a result of their unique position at the crossroads between various communities, societies and organisations, diplomats are inclined to see the world differently and with different priorities to those they represent. This has often prompted the question of whether diplomats should represent only the interests of their states or also those of the international society at large. The British Prime Minister, Margaret Thatcher, had a hard time understanding, for instance, why the British ambassador in Bonn, Sir Christopher Mallaby, was supportive of the prospect of German unification in November 1989. She thought he must have 'gone native' (Cameron 2009). Chester Bowles, John Kenneth Galbraith and Daniel P. Moynihan were among the US envoys who carried the stigma of 'going native', while on the Indian side, Naresh Chandra and Nani Palkhivala faced criticism for being too close to the US. All they did was to promote better ties between two sides afflicted with Cold War pathology (Rajghatta 2007).

'Going native' or 'localitis' (i.e., being more sympathetic to the host country than to the sending government) is viewed as a capital 'sin' for the career of any diplomat, because it allegedly impedes her capacity to provide proper diplomatic representation. To prevent this, most diplomatic services operate a four to five year rotation system of diplomatic staff so that the members of the diplomatic mission would not suffer from overexposure to the local political conditions. It remains doubtful though whether the rotation solution prescribed to 'localitis' (→ glossary) is the correct one. The reason for that has to do with the fact that the diplomats' propensity to 'go native' is hardly informed by their desire to substitute the interests of their government with those of the host country. While diplomats may occasionally betray the interests of their country for material, ideological or personal reasons, such situations are actually very rare and they may take place regardless of whether diplomats are being regularly rotated in their posts or not.

The source of 'localitis' is actually a core tension at the heart of the method of diplomatic representation: whether the diplomats should represent *only* the interests of their governments or whether they should also consider the impact the representation of these interests may have on the international or regional stability (see Box 10.1). The interplay of these two opposing sets of considerations places diplomats, especially those of the Great Powers, in front of a difficult dilemma: on the one hand, if they agree for the *raison de système* (→ glossary) to take precedence in guiding their actions then they risk circumscribing the autonomy of their sovereigns and, by implication, their own position. In addition, it requires that the Great Powers identify themselves with a set of common norms, rules and international institutions to the extent that they are willing to bear disproportionate costs that might sometimes go against their interests. On the other hand, if they unrestrainedly pursue diplomatic actions in line with the *raison d'état* doctrine, then they risk undermining the 'fabric' of the system itself by demotivating other diplomats from respecting the shared norms and rules that sustain international order.

Understandably, there is no universal formula for coherently representing the interests of both the state and the international society. Furthermore, the *raison de système* may sometimes provide cover for deeply oppressive international orders such as the colonial system in the nineteenth century (see Box 2.7). The way in

---

Box 10.1 The *raison de système*

The term *raison de système* was coined by Adam Watson who referred to it as 'the use of diplomacy to achieve the ultimate purpose of an international society of independent states' (Watson 1984: 203). Sceptical of the benefits of the doctrine of the *raison d'état* (i.e., the pursuit of state interests free of ethical considerations), Watson pointed out that all members of the international society have not only an interest but also a moral obligation in preserving it and making it work. By disproportionally benefitting from the system, the Great Powers in particular have a moral responsibility 'to ensure that the fabric of the system itself is preserved and its continuity maintained' (Watson 1984: 208).

---

which diplomats learn how to strike a balance between the *raison d'état* and the *raison de système* is from experience, by maintaining a rhetorical consistency between them both and what their principles would like them to do (Sharp 2009: 22). The main virtue to enable diplomats to accomplish this delicate task is prudence (→ glossary: diplomatic prudence) or practical wisdom, that is the capacity to judge what action is appropriate to pursue in a particular context, especially under conditions of high uncertainty of the outcome.

The question then turns to what does it take for a diplomat to exercise prudence when she realises the existence of a potential conflict between the national interests she is mandated to represent and the international order? Building *consensus* with the other members of the international society is one important dimension of diplomatic prudence. As the Nobel Prize Committee pointed out in its 2009 award statement for US President Barack Obama, it is imperative for diplomacy to be 'founded in the concept that those who are to lead the world must do so on the basis of values and attitudes that are shared by the majority of the world's population' (Norwegian Nobel Committee 2009). In other words, consensus is supposed to harmonise diplomatic representations of state and systemic interests by filtering out unnecessary sources of diplomatic tensions and facilitating broader support for transformative initiatives of international order.

What if consensus is not available? Should diplomats refrain from engaging in actions that might be potentially beneficial for both their own state and the international society if they lack the support of other diplomats? Carefully examining the consequences of one's actions and taking *responsibility* for them, especially when they go against the will of the majority of the members of the international society, is another form of cultivating diplomatic prudence. In his famous statement of the 'pottery barn rule', US Secretary of State Colin Powell warned, for instance, President George W. Bush before the US invasion of Iraq: 'You are going to be the proud owner of 25 million people ... You will own all their hopes, aspirations, and problems. You'll own it all' (Woodward 2004: 150). Powell's advice was sensible and insightful: on rare occasions it might be worth 'going alone', but one should be fully aware of the responsibility he bears for the consequences of his actions and be prepared to take corrective measures to address the inevitable distress.

Last but not least, diplomatic prudence also rests on a certain degree of *reasonableness*, that is the ability to reach out to the other side, to stay open to its arguments and to seek a shared solution in support of the international order. Seneca, the famous Roman stoic, argued in his treaties *De Otio* (*On Leisure*) that the purpose of *negotium* (negotiation) is not to benefit oneself but rather to be useful to others: 'It is of course required of a man [sic!] that he should benefit his fellow-men—many if he can, if not, a few; if not a few, those who are nearest; if not these, himself. For when he renders himself useful to others, he engages in *negotium*' (cited in Constantinou 2006: 356). Arguably, few diplomats would enthusiastically follow Seneca's recommendation to its logical end, but the idea of reasonableness as other-perspective taking has practical merits and ought to be recognised as an important element of diplomatic prudence. By encouraging diplomats to see the issue from the perspective of others, reasonableness helps them cut through the fog of misunderstandings and deception, acts as a catalyst for long-term relationship-building and provides a normative anchor for the *raison de système*.

Paradiplomacy

While *raison de système* challenges the substance of state-centric principles of diplomatic representation (what issues to represent?), paradiplomacy questions the type of agency to provide diplomatic representation (who should be authorised to represent?). The concept of 'paradiplomacy' entered the academic debate within the context of the rise of 'new federalism' in the 1970s and 1980s as an expression of the changing political dynamic between central and subnational authorities of federal states in matters of foreign policy (Aguirre 1999: 187). The key feature to distinguish paradiplomacy from traditional forms of diplomatic intercourse is the notion of *non-central* yet *governmental* agency of diplomatic representation. More specifically, paradiplomacy encompasses

> non-central governments' involvement in international relations through the establishment of permanent or *ad hoc* contacts with foreign public or private entities, with the aim to promote socioeconomic or cultural issues, as well as any other foreign dimension of their constitutional competences.
>
> (Cornago 1999: 40)

Typical examples of paradiplomacy (→ glossary) include the cases of the Quebec province in Canada, Catalonia and the Basque Country in Spain, California in the US or of megacities like London, Tokyo, New York, etc. For example, Quebec has been fully participating in all of UNESCO's activities, together with and through Canada's Permanent Delegation, since 2006. The Autonomous Community of the Basque Country in Spain signed an agreement in 1989 with the Aquitaine Region in France involving the exchange of information in various policy areas, promoting the Basque culture and language and the creation of a Common Fund for the financing of Basque projects. In collaboration with a number of Canadian provinces and Mexican states, California has negotiated and established a cap-and-trade programme to reduce greenhouse emissions on a regional level in North America. With London acting as a catalyst, over forty other global cities, including Toronto, Tokyo, New York, São Paolo, Hong Kong and Berlin, have joined forces under the umbrella of the Climate Leadership Group to exercise leadership in reducing emissions and to stimulate both private and governmental action on the issue.

   At the broadest level, we can distinguish between three layers of paradiplomacy. The first layer corresponds to economic issues. In this context, sub-state governments aim at developing an international presence for the purpose of attracting foreign investment, luring international companies to the region and targeting new markets for exports. The prototypical example here is the American, Australian and Canadian states and provinces whose international activity consists essentially of the pursuit of economic interests. The second layer of paradiplomacy involves cooperation (cultural, educational, technical, technological and others). In addition to membership in several transborder associations (for example with the Swiss cantons of Genève, Vaud and Valais), the French region, Rhône-Alpes, has also developed a series of bilateral relations with sub-state entities in various African (such as Mali, Senegal and Tunisia), Asian (such as Vietnam) and Central European countries (such as Poland). The third layer of paradiplomacy involves political considerations. Sub-state governments seek to develop a set of international relations that would affirm the cultural distinctiveness, political autonomy and the national character of the community they represent as is the case for Quebec, Flanders, Catalonia and the Basque Country (Lecours December 2008: 2–3).

Despite its growing significance in global politics, it remains though unclear how paradiplomacy is going to intersect with and possibly affect traditional forms of diplomatic interaction. One possible direction of evolution could involve a growing symbiosis between a variety of state and non-state diplomatic actors, whereby the professional diplomat becomes a facilitator in the development of arena and actor linkages. Hocking calls this 'catalytic' diplomacy (→ glossary) since paradiplomacy builds on, rather than replaces, earlier developments in the diplomatic milieu (Hocking 1996: 452). Such a development would present the advantage of allowing both traditional diplomats and paradiplomatic actors to share critical resources, while maintaining their own identity and goals. At the same time, serious questions of legitimacy might arise about who has or should have the authority to speak on issues involving overlapping jurisdiction. This might explain the general reluctance of state diplomats to cultivate institutional ties with paradiplomatic actors.

For other scholars, the international involvement of non-central governments (NCGs) could be more properly labelled 'postdiplomatic' (Aguirre 1999: 205), because it is a process involving new actors, issues and methods and hence it moves beyond the nation-state and state-centric forms of diplomacy. While the international activity of NCGs parallels that of traditional diplomats to the extent that both seek access to international networks, they nevertheless supply different kinds of public goods and use different methods for acquiring them. What paradiplomacy lacks is the *political* meaning that is constitutive of state-based forms of diplomatic practice, that is the notion that diplomats exist only to serve the territorial-sovereign state and to reproduce the particular type of international society that makes such type of political entity possible. From this perspective, paradiplomacy can be seen as another facet of the process of globalisation, a rather technocratic mode of producing convergence of regulatory norms and enforcing compliance on a transnational basis.

One could also argue that paradiplomacy actually represents a site of political contestation, which serves not only to challenge, but also to reinforce the authority of conventional diplomacy. Undoubtedly, NCGs are engaged in a turf battle with foreign ministries for dividing up jurisdictional competences, but they generally do this from a position that may simultaneously legitimise and undermine the society of states. On the one hand, paradiplomacy serves as an NCG vehicle for diplomatic interventions. In so doing, it gives voice to a number of important political actors, including the staging of new contestations that trespass the boundaries of territorial sovereignty. On the other hand, such forms of pluralisation of diplomacy also serve to legitimise dominant understandings about how the challenges of global governance should be adequately managed, even at the risk of dismantling the organisational achievements (some positive, some negative) of modern states.

Diplomacy and power

The question of power remains a blind spot in diplomatic theory. Sharp points out that diplomacy puts people in touch with power, but rather in a paradoxical manner: diplomats largely live and work in the proximity of power (e.g., political leaders making foreign policy decisions), but they rarely exercise that power directly (Sharp 2009: 58). Neumann is even more critical. Diplomats might have been able to exercise power in the past, but their work nowadays largely involves juggling different bureaucratic scripts, governed by a code of conduct that rewards institutional conformity, protocol compliance and political self-effacement over policy innovation, critical engagement and diplomatic leadership (Neumann 2005). Bjola takes a more optimistic view and argues that diplomats actually have more power than they are generally credited with. They wield the power to make relations! This form of power is less visible because it emerges not prior to actors' interactions but through diplomatic engagement. In other words, diplomats are not exercising power directly one over another, but rather through relations of constitution of enmity/friendship (Bjola 2013).

Whether diplomats have power or not depends on the type of resources that are available to them and the limitations they experience in making use of them. Diplomacy has been traditionally seen by scholars and practitioners alike as a second-order instrument of state power, primarily used to communicate threats and promises in support of first-order policy instruments, especially of military and economic nature. Under the tradition of the doctrine of the *raison d'état*, the main leverage of diplomatic influence has been the *hard power* entailed by the country's particular configuration of material capabilities (e.g., population, territory, natural resources, military forces, economic size or political stability). According to this view, the success of certain diplomatic strategies rests with diplomats' ability to properly recognise and exploit the distribution of capabilities within the system. Morgenthau's four tasks of diplomacy forcefully encapsulate this creed: diplomats must assess the power and objectives of other nations; compare them with their own; determine conditions of compatibility; and then deploy appropriate means (Morgenthau and Thompson 1993: 361–362).

An important application of hard power is coercive diplomacy (→ glossary) or 'forceful persuasion' (George 1991: 4), that is the effort to change the objectionable behaviour of a target state or group through the credible threat of economic sanctions or the use of military force. Coercive diplomacy is supposed to work by demonstrating the superiority of hard power of one party over the other (see Box 10.2). However, in practice, the effectiveness of coercive diplomacy is controversial. Studies of use of coercive diplomacy in the US in the post-Cold War period have shown, for instance, such strategies to have had borderline success in three cases (Haiti 1994, Bosnia 1995 and Libya 2003), outright failure in four situations (Iraq 1991, Kosovo 1999, Afghanistan 2001 and Iraq 2003) and unclear outcomes in four other cases

---

Box 10.2 Determinants of success of coercive diplomacy

- *Credibility of the threat* – the threat should be proportional with the demand, backed up by sufficient resources and the threatening state must have a good reputation of following through.
- *Legitimacy of the demand* – the goal must be perceived as legitimate by the public opinion in the threatening states.
- *Motivation of the parties* – the coercing power must convey that it is more highly motivated to achieve its demands than the adversary is to oppose them.
- *Offer of positive incentives* – the threatened government must be offered sufficient 'carrots' to avoid a humiliating 'loss of face' domestically and internationally.

(George 1991; Sauer 2007)

(China–Taiwan crisis in 1996, Somalia 1992–1993, North Korea 1994 and Iran 2006–present) (Art and Cronin 2003). Most problematically, though, is the question of the legitimacy of resorting to coercive diplomacy. Aside from the fact that the UN Charter explicitly prohibits the threat of the use of force (Article 2.4), there are serious concerns as to whether coercive diplomacy is actually paving the way for war as opposed to preventing it.

On the one hand, supporters of coercive diplomacy point to its success in avoiding a nuclear war between the US and the Soviet Union during the Cuban missile crisis in 1962 or to Libya's decision in 2003 to abandon its programmes for the development of weapons of mass destruction (WMD). According to this line of reasoning, coercive diplomacy can work, even against the hardest authoritarian regimes. Furthermore, coercive diplomacy could be an effective alternative to costly and risky strategies of 'regime change' in countries where governments consistently act in defiance of international law. As the Libyan case suggests, rogue states (→ glossary) only need to know both that the coercer is firm about not accepting too little and also trustworthy about not pushing for too much (Jentleson and Whytock 2005: 82). On the other hand, as military interventions and economic sanctions generally fail to distinguish between bad governments and their people, there is grave risk that coercive diplomacy may lead to long-term diplomatic alienation between the parties, even when the leaders and diplomats responsible for these actions are no longer in office.

Concerns over the effectiveness and legitimacy of the use of hard power have stimulated a growing interest, in the past decade, in the concept of 'soft power' as an alternative instrument of diplomatic engagement. *Soft power* emphasises the 'power of attraction' over that of coercion or inducement, that is the power to seduce others to follow you because of the magnetism exerted by your culture, political values or foreign policies (Nye 2004: 11). Drawing on global surveys measuring public attitudes on five dimensions of soft power (see Box 10.3), a recent global ranking of soft power has found Western countries to enjoy a considerable advantage in this area with the US coming out on top, followed by the UK, France, Germany and Australia. Emerging powers such as China, Brazil and India temporarily lag behind in twentieth, twenty-first and twenty-seventh place, respectively (McClory 2011: 15).

Box 10.3 Sources of soft power

- *Government* – the attractiveness of a state's political institutions and values measured by the degree of individual liberty, political freedom and government effectiveness.
- *Culture* – the ability of a country to promote universal values that other nations can readily identify with measured by the annual number of tourists visiting a country, the global reach of a country's native language and the number of UNESCO World Heritage sites.
- *Foreign policy* – the capacity of a state to maintain its legitimacy and moral authority in its conduct abroad measured by the level of Overseas Development Aid, membership in multilateral organisations and cultural missions abroad.
- *Education* – the ability of a country to attract foreign students, or facilitate exchanges, measured by the number of foreign students in a country, the relative quality of its universities and the output of academic publishing.
- *Business/innovation* – the relative attractiveness of a country's economic model in terms of its openness, capacity for innovation and regulation, corruption and competitiveness.

(McClory 2011: 11–12)

What is less clear, though, is what to make of 'soft power' from the perspective of the diplomats. After all, it is one thing to posit, for instance, that the appeal of American values, the model offered by its political system, the broad presence of its brands overseas and its pop cultural exports help in some vague and very general way to pre-dispose foreign publics towards the US. It is quite another to hold out reliance upon 'soft power' as a means by which an American diplomat can accomplish any specific policy objective (Ford 2012: 93). This is where the notion of public diplomacy comes into play, as an instrument for creating, maximising and rendering soft power into diplomatic influence. The purpose of public diplomacy is to advance the interests and extend the values of those being represented by direct relations with another country's public (Sharp 2005: 106). In practice, this involves three components: daily communications, to explain the context of domestic and foreign policy decisions; strategic communications, to develop a set of simple themes in support of a policy initiative; and relationship-building with key individuals over many years through scholarships, exchanges, training, seminars, conferences and access to media channels (Nye 2008: 102).

As a relatively new but pivotal instrument of foreign policy, public diplomacy places the professional diplomat in front of a crucial dilemma. Should her mission be to promote the policies of her state at any price (e.g., even by twisting the truth as in classical forms of propaganda) or should she aim to genuinely engage the foreign public for the purpose of fostering long-term mutual understanding? The 'tough-minded' school of public diplomacy insists the main purpose should be to maximise influence on the attitudes of foreign audiences. Objectivity is seen as an important tool of persuasion but only to the extent it serves the purpose of the public diplomatic strategy. The 'tender-minded' school argues, in exchange, the main objective of public diplomacy should be the establishment of a climate of mutual understanding. Truth, therefore, is considered essential, much more than a persuasion tactic (Snow 2009: 9). In practice, however, the distinction between the two modes of engaging in public diplomacy is often blurred (see Box 10.4).

Box 10.4 US public diplomacy in the Arab world

In the aftermath of the 2001 attacks, the US government launched Radio Sawa and Alhurra satellite television, designed under a wide-scale public diplomacy plan to improve America's image in the Middle East and win the hearts and minds of the Arab people. The target audience for Radio Sawa and Television Alhurra has been the younger Arab generation, who will be tomorrow's decision-makers. Although the information provided by the two outlets has been highly accurate, its capacity to shape the attitudes of the target audiences has been rather modest. It appears many Arab media users today are intensely aware of the US administration's motives in trying to win Arab hearts and minds and improve its image in the Arab world, and hence they have a tendency not to trust news broadcast on Radio Sawa or Television Alhurra (el-Nawawy 2006: 183–184).

The third potential source of diplomatic influence is *smart power* which brings together hard and soft power via 'the strategic and simultaneous use of coercion and co-option' (Cross 2011: 698). The reasoning behind smart power is that, by combining hard and soft power, the limitations of each could be offset by the strengths of the other. The way to achieve this is by making sure the elements of hard power (military intervention, legal sanctions, economic conditionality) and soft power (aid, public diplomacy, educational exchange, etc.) of a diplomatic strategy reinforce rather than undermine each other. During her tenure as US Secretary of State, Condoleezza Rice pressed, for instance, the department to engage in what she called 'transformational diplomacy'. She expressed her wish to make the State Department 'smarter' by transforming old diplomatic institutions to serve new diplomatic purposes. Rice noted that 'transformational diplomacy is rooted in partnership; not paternalism. In doing things with people, not for them, we seek to use America's diplomatic power to help foreign citizens better their own lives and to build their own nations and to transform their own futures' (cited in Wilson 2008: 117).

For others, smart power is less an issue of catalysing diplomatic transformations in various regions of strategic interest, but rather one of pragmatically building alliances by investing in the production and delivery of global public goods (see Box 10.5). As pointed out by Nye and Armitage in their report on smart power, 'states and non-state actors who improve their ability to draw in allies will gain competitive advantages in today's environment. Those who alienate potential friends will stand at greater risk' (Armitage *et al.* 2007: 10). The upshot of this argument is that, similar to soft power, smart power requires a broader time horizon to yield results but, like hard power, it requires significant material resources to create, deliver and sustain global public goods.

Finally, there is also the view that smart power is less a matter of finding the proper balance between hard and soft power in the abstract, but rather of sorting this balance out in the concrete. One such possible example would be the sharpening of the rapid-reaction skills of diplomats to political events with an emphasis on innovation, agility, adaptability and autonomy. Daryl Copeland draws on these features to introduce the concept of guerrilla diplomacy (→ glossary), a new form of international engagement that has emerged in response to the apparent marginalisation by traditional diplomats of the capacity for dialogue, negotiation and compromise

---

Box 10.5 US smart power as investment in five global public goods

- *Alliances, partnerships, and institutions* – rebuilding the institutional foundation to deal with global challenges;
- *Global development* – developing a unified approach, starting with public health;
- *Public diplomacy* – improving access to international knowledge and learning;
- *Economic integration* – increasing the benefits of trade for all people;
- *Technology and innovation* – addressing climate change and energy insecurity.

(Armitage *et al.* 2007: 5)

---

and the advent of the scientifically and technologically driven age of globalisation. Accordingly, the guerrilla diplomat brings an 'informed, directed, special-forces-style sensibility to bear on the broad objectives of diplomacy, maximizing self-reliance while minimizing the usual investment in plant, infrastructure, and logistical support' (Copeland 2009: 209). In other words, if they want to stay relevant, diplomats must step out of their formal channels of state-to-state interaction and start engaging the populations with whom they desire to build long-lasting relations.

The idea has found support with some top US diplomats, who have suggested the State Department should create and train a new category of personnel, the 'expeditionary diplomat', who would serve 'in the hardest place at a moment's notice' combining local knowledge, cultural sensitivity and technical expertise to facilitate post-conflict reconstruction and stabilisation projects (Seib 2012: 106). The idea of infusing the diplomatic ethos with a more flexible, innovative and culturally sensitive attitude that combines elements of both hard and soft power is definitely welcome, especially in the current globalising diplomatic landscape. Coercive diplomacy is too blunt an instrument for promoting international cooperation, while public diplomacy can be easily abused for propaganda purposes. Diplomacy based on smart power holds out, at least in principle, the promise to avoid such pitfalls by focusing on the production and delivery of critical public goods to foreign publics. The challenge for smart power is to deliver results in real time. One important lesson of the 'Arab spring' is that opportunities for diplomatic re-engagement might arise and disappear at a moment's notice. Seizing such opportunities would be a crucial test for smart-power diplomacy.

Diplomatic recruitment and training

What does it take for a young graduate to become a diplomat? A brief overview of the methods of diplomatic recruitment, promotion and training undertaken by various foreign services provides useful clues about the type of skills sought after in prospective candidates. Unlike the pre-WWI situation when diplomatic recruitment and promotion was reserved to a closed caste of upper-class males, recruitment to the British Foreign and Commonwealth Office (FCO) takes place nowadays by open competition. For the more senior stream – often called the 'fast stream' – candidates are required to have a university degree (second class honours or above) in any discipline. The prospective diplomats need to undergo a selection procedure that consists of a number of stages. The first stage, which is held annually, is a written intelligence and reasoning test. The candidates that passed this first stage proceed to the Civil Service Selection Board which consists of two working days of individual and group exercises, interviews and written tests. At this stage, the examiners are selecting candidates on the basis of their ability to reason and problem-solve rather than on specific knowledge.

For each group of five candidates there are three examiners: a chairman, usually a retired senior civil servant; an 'observer', a younger, middle-ranking civil servant who tests the intellectual ability of the candidates; and a professional psychologist. The final stage involves a forty-five-minute interview with the Final Selection Board in front of five senior members, including one or more academics, business people or even trade unionists. The Final Selection Board takes the decision whether or not to hire a prospective candidate based on all the results of the earlier stages. Once admitted to the Diplomatic Service, promotion boards take decisions concerning career advancement. Promotion boards have access to detailed information based on the annual staff appraisal system which is designed, among other things, to provide information about promotability (Levi 1998). For the most senior jobs, ministers often take the final decision. In addition, the FCO organises and participates in several programmes that promote a greater diversity in the recruitment intake such as 'The Partner University Placement Scheme', or the 'Summer Development Programme'.

Prospective diplomats to the Indian Foreign Service are admitted on the basis of the combined Civil Services Examination. This is a competitive nationwide examination conducted by the Union Public Service Commission and is considered one of the most difficult examinations in the world, with on average about 500,000 candidates and a success rate of about 0.3 per cent of the applicants. The Civil Services Examination is conducted in three stages. The so-called Preliminary examination is a qualifying test that is held annually for applicants to all India Services. It consists of two multiple-choice tests, of which the first one tests the candidate's knowledge of current events and general studies while the second exam tests the candidate's comprehension and reasoning skills. At the second stage, prospective diplomats join the Foreign Service Institute in New Delhi and they receive focused training. The aim of this course is to inculcate in the diplomatic recruit a strong sense of history, knowledge of diplomacy and international relations and a grasp of general economic and political issues (Ministry of Foreign Affairs of India 2012).

The Main examination then consists of nine essays, of which two are qualifying (English and Indian language proficiency) and seven are ranking in nature. The third and final stage is a Personality Test. This is an interview conducted by a board of observers that is aimed at assessing the personal suitability of the candidate for a diplomatic career. The entire examination takes about one and a half years. After this examination, a candidate begins his career abroad as a Third Secretary – a stage at which he is expected to further develop his language proficiency – and is promoted to Second Secretary as soon as he is confirmed in service (Ministry of Foreign Affairs of India 2012). Subsequent promotions are based on seniority and are overseen by the Controlling Authority and departmental Promotion Committees. Indian diplomats can rise through the ranks to the level of First Secretary, Counsellor, Minister and Ambassador/High Commissioner/Permanent Representative. Officers can also be posted to Indian Consulates abroad as Vice-Consuls, Consuls and Consul Generals.

Similar recruitment procedures apply to international organisations as well, such as the UN. One can enter the UN career path in three different ways. For a graduate school student, the typical opportunity is a two-month internship, which is intended to provide a framework by which students from diverse academic backgrounds may be attached to UN offices or departments. It should be noted though that doing such an internship does not automatically lead to a permanent position in the UN system. Recent graduates can enter the UN through a National Recruitment Examination or through the Associate Experts Programme. The latter offers young professionals with limited or no professional experience the opportunity to work for development or regional projects within various UN fields. Finally, a professional with experience can respond to external vacancy announcements (United Nations 2001: 37–39). Junior and senior professionals are recruited through National Competitive Recruitment Examinations (NCRE), which are generally organised as a matter of priority in countries that are inadequately represented among the staff of the Secretariat.

In terms of procedure, the NCRE consists of a written test and an interview. The written examination is subdivided into two parts: the first part is a General Paper in which the candidate's analytical skills, drafting skills and knowledge of international affairs are tested; the second part consists of the Specialized Paper in which the candidate's substantive skills in the occupational group are assessed. Based on the outcome of this written examination, a number of candidates are then invited to an interview by the Board of Examiners. The interview will be conducted in English or French, the two working languages of the Secretariat. The general policy is to recruit from as wide a geographic area as possible, in order to achieve, as closely as possible, equitable representation among member states. The Department of Peacekeeping Operations also maintains a computerised roster of candidatures for civilian assignments to Peacekeeping Operations (United Nations 2001: 43–44).

According to the 2007 Lisbon Treaty, the EU High Representative for Foreign Affairs and Security Policy (e.g., the EU foreign minister) is assisted by the European External Action Service. This service works in cooperation with the diplomatic services of the member states and comprises officials from relevant departments of the General Secretariat of the Council and of the Commission, as well as staff seconded from national diplomatic services of the member states (European Union 2007). A subsequent decision of the Council of the EU stipulated that before 1 July 2013, the EEAS would recruit exclusively officials originating from the General Secretariat of the Council and the Commission, as well as staff coming from the diplomatic services of the member states. After 13 July 2013, all officials and other servants of the EU (particularly the EP) should be able to apply for vacant posts in the EEAS. Staff from member states should represent at least one-third of all EEAS staff by 2013. The Council also decided recruitment to the EEAS should be based on merit while ensuring adequate geographical and gender balance. The staff of the EEAS should comprise a meaningful presence of nationals from all member states (Council of the European Union 2010).

Training for European-level diplomacy has, broadly speaking, followed two streams: first, the European Commission offers a series of skill-driven schemes for a number of Directorates-General involved with external action, as well as for delegation staff; second, the European Diplomatic Programme (EDP) addresses a mixed group of EU offcials and national diplomats not only for vocational reasons, but also for fostering a shared diplomatic culture and a common sense of European purpose in external action (Duke 2011: 98). EDP teaching, which takes place on an annual basis via five modules of two-day meetings, is based on practical learning, with an emphasis on case studies, as well as simulation of and real participation in multilateral negotiations.

The 2012–2013 EDP edition has focused, for instance, on the theme of 'The EU and the Strategic Partnerships'. By approaching the topic from a triple point of view (thematically, geographically and from the EU and members states' perspective), participants are expected to acquire a better and holistic understanding of how the EU is structuring and fostering its relations in various areas with its most prominent counterparts (European Union 2012: 6).

Diplomatic patterns and methods of recruitment and training are likely to face two important challenges in the future. The first one is illustrated by the case of e-diplomacy (→ glossary), that is the use of social media technologies to carry out diplomatic objectives. The US State Department is the world's leading user of e-diplomacy. After starting modestly with a few people in 2002, the e-diplomacy office had developed into a 150-strong unit by 2012, working in twenty-five different e-diplomacy nodes and providing services for more than 900 people at US missions abroad (see Box 10.6). The State Department has been thus the first to recognise the potential of e-diplomacy in creating a revolution in the manner in which diplomats engage in information management, public diplomacy, strategy planning, international negotiations or even crisis management. For example, a single US diplomat can now communicate directly with a million people every day through one of the State Department's 600 social media platforms. This allows US diplomats to convey multiple messages ranging from counterterrorism narratives to the soft promotion of US scientific expertise at very low cost.

Box 10.6 Main objectives of the US e-diplomacy programme

1 *Knowledge management* – to harness departmental and whole-of-government knowledge, so that it is retained, shared and its use optimised in pursuit of national interests abroad.

2 *Public diplomacy* – to maintain contact with audiences as they migrate online and to harness new communications tools to listen to and target important audiences with key messages and to influence major online influencers.

3 *Information management* – to help aggregate the overwhelming flow of information and to use this to better inform policy-making and to help anticipate and respond to emerging social and political movements.

4 *Consular communications and response* – to create direct, personal communications channels with citizens travelling overseas, with manageable communications in crisis situations.

5 *Disaster response* – to harness the power of connective technologies in disaster response situations.

6 *Internet freedom* – to create technologies to keep the internet free and open. This has the related objectives of promoting freedom of speech and democracy as well as undermining authoritarian regimes.

7 *External resources* – to create digital mechanisms to draw on and harness external expertise to advance national goals.

8 *Policy planning* – to allow for effective oversight, coordination and planning of international policy across government, in response to the internationalisation of the bureaucracy.

(Hanson 2012: 4–5)

Unfortunately, the e-diplomacy initiative of the US State Department has attracted few followers thus far, partly because of a lack of understanding of the contributions such a tool can make to diplomatic practice, and partly because of institutional constraints. The process of recruiting, working and training e-diplomats is arguably different to the one for traditional diplomats. It implies the screening of potential applicants for strong IT skills, cultural familiarity with the target audiences and a demonstrable capacity for original thinking. At the same time, e-diplomacy cannot flourish in the bureaucratic framework of conventional foreign ministries. It thrives in a work environment that stimulates informal teamwork, creativity, innovation and out-of-the-box thinking. In short, it requires more the institutional atmosphere of an Apple team of software developers than a group of well-polished and well-seasoned lawyers preparing for international negotiation.

Generalist training is another issue that seems to be slightly inadequate in preparing diplomats for how to cope with future challenges. Most of the diplomatic training is skill-driven. Obviously, vocational training has strong merits in teaching diplomats practical techniques of how to accomplish the general tasks required from them (e.g., preparing a negotiation dossier, chairing a committee, reacting to a diplomatic incident, etc.). The proliferation of issue areas and actors in global politics also puts pressure on diplomats to constantly update their repertoire of skills, especially in areas of cultural adaptability, information integration and analysis or with respect to their ability to show initiative and provide leadership (US Department of State 2012). Arguably, the practice of diplomacy would seriously suffer if diplomats, especially those in the early stages of their career, cannot master the tools of their trade.

The changing global environment requires, however, diplomats to be well-read and up-to-date about the broader intellectual debates informing competing strategic visions of global agenda, the normative and strategic differences underpinning conflicts over international rules, or the legal and institutional instruments mediating linkages between domestic, regional and international forums. This is why skill-oriented training should be also complemented by solid academic tutoring in areas of greater relevance for the conduct of diplomatic relations. Courses addressing the diplomatic management of international crises would allow prospective diplomats to combine theoretical and practical insights of how traditional methods (coercive diplomacy, summits, secret negotiations) and state-of-the-art technologies (e.g., Predator drone strikes, cyber warfare) facilitate or complicate crisis management efforts. Options on international law would assist them in understanding the significance of the *raison de système* in their work or the limitations of paradiplomacy. Theories of international ethics could familiarise aspirant diplomats with the possible implications of their strategies of coercive or public diplomacy.

It is this understanding of the need for recasting the training of aspirant diplomats that seems to drive the recent expansion, both in terms of the number and of the course offerings, of academic centres preparing students for the diplomatic field. Here are a few examples:

- *Diplomatic Academy of Vienna*: teaches postgraduate courses on International Organizations and Multilateral Diplomacy; Multilateral Negotiation; Public Diplomacy; Protocol and Etiquette for the modern Diplomat, as part of the course offerings for the Master of Advanced International Studies.

- *University of Oxford*: teaches postgraduate courses on International Diplomacy; Diplomacy and International Law; Diplomatic Management of International Crises; Climate Change Diplomacy, as part of the course offerings for the MSc in Global Governance and Diplomacy.
- *Paul H. Nitze School of Advanced International Studies, Johns Hopkins University*: teaches postgraduate courses on International Bargaining & Negotiation; International Public Relations and Public Diplomacy; Law of War and War Crimes, as part of the course offerings for the MA and PhD in international relations.
- *The Fletcher School of Law & Diplomacy, Tufts University*: teaches postgraduate courses on Diplomacy: History, Theory, and Practice; United States Public Diplomacy; International Mediation; International Treaty Behavior; The Art and Science of Statecraft; Processes of International Negotiation; The Role of Force in International Politics, as part of the course offerings for the Master of Arts in Law and Diplomacy.
- *Woodrow Wilson School of Public & International Affairs, Princeton University*: teaches postgraduate courses on Diplomacy, Development & Conflict; Negotiation: Theory & Practice; Diplomacy and Security in Northeast Asia; Global Environmental Governance, as part of the Master in Public Affairs.
- *Leiden University and the Netherlands Institute of International Relations 'Clingendael'*: teaches postgraduate courses on Diplomacy Today: Theory and Practice; Diplomacy in Asia; International Negotiations; The Sanctions Practice of the UN Security Council, as part of the course offerings for the MA in International Relations and Diplomacy.
- *The Asia-Pacific College of Diplomacy, Australian National University*: teaches Transnational Diplomacy; Diplomacy, Politics and the United Nations; Contemporary Challenges in Diplomacy: Politics, Economics, Law & Strategy; Negotiation and Conflict Resolution, as part of the course offerings for the Master of Diplomatic Studies.

Summary

- From a supranational perspective, diplomats face a difficult dilemma: whether they should represent only the interests of their governments or whether they should also consider the impact the representation of these interests may have on the international order. The way in which diplomats learn how to strike a balance between the *raison d'état* and the *raison de système* is by exercising prudence or practical wisdom.
- From a subnational perspective, diplomatic representation is challenged by non-central yet governmental forms of diplomatic agency. The relationship between paradiplomacy and conventional diplomacy remains ambiguous. It may encourage the professional diplomat to become a linkage facilitator ('catalytic' diplomacy), it may push diplomacy beyond state-centric forms of representation ('postdiplomacy') or it may unfold a site of political contestation between the traditional and the 'new' diplomats ('contested diplomacy').
- Diplomats have three important sources of power at their disposal. Traditionally, the main leverage of diplomatic influence has been the *hard power* entailed by the country's configuration of material capabilities. *Soft power* emphasises the ability to seduce others to follow you because of the magnetism exerted by

your culture, political values or foreign policies. *Smart power* brings together hard and soft power via the strategic and simultaneous use of coercion and co-option.

- Current methods of diplomatic recruitment, promotion and training fail to fully acknowledge the needs of the twenty-first-century diplomat. The use of social media for diplomatic purposes is generally neglected, while diplomatic training places excessive focus on vocational training at the expense of academic education.

Study questions

- What does the concept of the *raison de système* refer to and what kind of challenge does it pose to how diplomats fulfil their representation function?
- How does paradiplomacy constrain and complement the work of traditional diplomats?
- Are hard and soft power two distinct instruments of diplomatic influence?
- What elements of smart power recommend it as a more suitable instrument of diplomatic action and what are its main limitations?
- To what extent is academic training a prerequisite for preparing young diplomats to cope with the diplomatic challenges of the twenty-first century?

Recommended further reading

Art, Robert J. and Patrick M. Cronin. 2003. *The United States and coercive diplomacy*. Washington, DC: United States Institute of Peace Press.
The book examines eight cases of coercive diplomacy in the post-Cold-War period, from North Korea to Serbia to the Taliban, from warlords to terrorists to regional superpowers.

Copeland, Daryl. 2009. *Guerrilla diplomacy: Rethinking international relations*. Boulder, CO: Lynne Rienner Publishers.
The book makes some strong claims, not always well-substantiated, about providing the tools needed to frame and manage issues ranging from climate change to pandemic disease to asymmetrical conflict and weapons of mass destruction. The essential keystone of the author's approach is the modern diplomat, able to engage with a plethora of new international actors and to mix with the populations with whom she desires to build long-lasting relations.

Nye, Joseph S. 2004. *Soft power: The means to success in world politics*. 1st edn. New York: Public Affairs.
This is a foundational book on the concept of soft power and its practical applications in world politics. Written from a US perspective, the book explains what soft power is made of, how it works and how it could assist the US foreign policy.

Organski, A.F.K. and Jacek Kugler. 1980. *The war ledger*. Chicago, IL: University of Chicago Press.
This book offers an insightful investigation of the role of hard power in world politics. It demonstrates that the power-transition theory, hinging on economic, social and political growth, is more accurate than the balance of power or collective security theory to explain international conflicts. The authors find the differential rate of growth of the two most powerful nations in the system – the dominant nation and the challenger – to be the key precipitating factor of world wars.

Seib, Philip M. 2012. *Real-time diplomacy: Politics and power in the social media era.* 1st edn. New York: Palgrave Macmillan.
This book examines how diplomacy has evolved as media have gradually reduced the time available to policy-makers. It analyses the workings of real-time diplomacy and the opportunities for media-centred diplomacy programmes that bypass governments and directly engage foreign citizens.

11 Remaking states

Chapter objectives

- To draw reader's attention to diplomatic practices of remaking states and peacebuilding (→ glossary).
- To discuss legitimacy of intervention.
- To put purpose of intervention, i.e. peace, under scrutiny.
- To investigate means of establishing peace.

Introduction

A chapter on 'remaking states' seems an odd addition to a book on diplomacy. According to conceived wisdom, diplomacy is about deciding what happens among states and not within states. The UN Charter, for example, is very explicit about safeguarding state sovereignty and the collective security mechanism designed for this purpose. But there is nothing explicit on remaking states. If anything, sovereignty and remaking states seem to contradict one another sharply.

Remaking states, however, has always been part of the state system and it has always had a *strong diplomatic dimension* to it. Take the post-WWII occupation of Germany, for example. France, the Soviet Union, the United Kingdom and the US agreed to carve up Germany into four occupation zones. The Western powers tried to re-build the state along liberal democratic principles in their zones. The Soviet Union attempted to re-build state institutions believed to be capable of transforming the polity into a communist system. Agreeing on the general re-building design, the Western powers decided to merge their three zones in the 1948 London Conference and, therefore, made it possible for the Federal Republic of Germany to be founded in 1949. This was, among other things, a major diplomatic success. It was a major diplomatic success for the three Western powers (and West German actors) to agree on a course of action. The West German Constitution was as much authored by West German political elites as it was authored by the three Western allies. By the same token, the failure of these allies and the Soviet Union to converge on a plan for solving the German Question was a major diplomatic failure. The Democratic Republic of Germany was founded the same year, Germany remained partitioned until the end of the Cold War and severe international crises surrounding the German Question remained on the diplomatic agenda.

Efforts of remaking states rarely ever amount to the kind of sustained and all-encompassing intervention as in Germany's case. The scale and resources used for the making of the German states in the West and East are rather unique. Only a few cases, such as the remaking of Japan, are comparable. Yet the list of cases in which diplomacy became involved in remaking states at a lesser scale is long. To some extent, diplomacy has not had much of a choice. In the post-WWII era, there were many more intra-state wars than inter-state wars, and the latter have been much more destructive than the former. Diplomacy *had to find ways to address these conflicts.* Whether it always acted adequately is another question, however.

Diplomacy has frequently done so under the umbrella of the UN. There was a lot of learning by doing (see Box 11.1). Since the late 1980s, the UN has launched several operations meant to remake states or, using the post-Cold War terminology, to rebuild peace. In Cambodia, the UN assumed quasi-governmental functions for a transition period. In Mozambique and Namibia, too, UN peace support missions had very strong civilian components. At the moment, a number of UN missions with more or less strong peacebuilding mandates are deployed around the world. These include missions in Afghanistan, Congo, Côte d'Ivoire, East Timor, Haiti, Kosovo, Liberia and South Sudan.

This chapter addresses this issue of remaking states by inquiring into the oughts and ought nots of diplomacy in facilitating peacebuilding. The chapter is organised into four sections. First, we take a closer look at the diplomatic dimensions of peacebuilding. Second, we deal with the question of whether peacebuilding is actually a warranted diplomatic endeavour. Third, we discuss the overall purpose of peacebuilding. Fourth, we scrutinise the means for building peace.

Box 11.1 ONUC and learning by doing

In the 1960s, the UN became embroiled in the Congo conflict. The UN Secretariat and member states started reacting to this conflict by applying the recently developed peacekeeping concept. Designed to manage inter-state conflicts by deploying an inter-position force between rivalling parties, the conflict management tool was applied to Congo's intra-state situation. It soon became clear that the concept of an interposition force was not suitable for dealing with internal conflict. Thus, the UN Operation in the Congo (ONUC), authorised by Security Council Resolution 143 (1960), resorted to peace-making efforts because there was no peace to keep, as well as to assuming civilian administrative responsibilities because there was no centralised state authority any more to take care of the basic needs of the population. The operation was very costly for the UN, especially in terms of casualties (including the Secretary-General Dag Hammarskjöld who was killed in a plane crash). At least in hindsight, the operation was not very successful either. Sustainable peace remained elusive in the Congo. Supported financially by Belgium (former colonial power) and the US, Mobuto Sese Seko consolidated his power in the late 1960s and installed his dictatorship that would last until 1997. Given the troubles of the ONUC, it is not surprising that it took decades and an entirely new international environment for the UN to engage in peace missions in intra-state conflicts again. With millions of people dying, the UN – and also the AU and the EU – have tried to re-assert themselves in the Congo in the early 2000s. They have been able to reduce the violence. But they have not been able to put an end to it so far.

The institutionalisation of peacebuilding

Diplomacy sets the parameters of peacebuilding. This includes the very definition of the concept of peacebuilding as well as the institutional infrastructure through which diplomacy comes to decide on concrete peacebuilding missions and their components.

The concept of peacebuilding was introduced to global diplomacy by the UN Secretariat. In his 1992 Agenda for Peace, UN Secretary-General Boutros Boutros-Ghali introduced the term peacebuilding. He defines it as 'post-conflict ... action to identify and support structures which will tend to strengthen and solidify peace in order to avoid relapse into conflict' (Boutros-Ghali 1992: para 21). In his 1995 Supplement for an Agenda for Peace, Boutros-Ghali broadened this definition beyond post-conflict actions. Elaborating on the concept, he links peacebuilding to conflict prevention, management and post-conflict re-construction (Boutros-Ghali 1995: para 47–56). In documents by the Secretary-General, this definition has stayed more or less in place. A few amendments have been made. An influential Decision of the Secretary-General's Policy Committee (September 2010: 5), for example, some-what qualifies that peacebuilding is merely about reducing 'the risk of lapsing or relapsing into conflict', further emphasises the attempt to provide help for self-help with the formulation 'by strengthening national capacities at all levels for conflict management' and stresses that the kind of peace sought after is a 'sustainable' one. Most UN member states have been backing the concept. This applies in particular to member states that define their role in international affairs strongly via their involvement in conflict prevention and peacekeeping (→ glossary) such as Canada.

This does not mean, however, that there is a generally accepted definition of peacebuilding. With different international agencies and states establishing an institutional infrastructure for peacebuilding, more and more definitions of the concept have been developed. In a study systematically dealing with different conceptualisations of peacebuilding, the authors count no less than twenty-four different definitions. They also highlight that this is far from being only an academic issue. It amounts to a major problem if different actors, say the World Bank, the US foreign service and the UN Department of peacekeeping use the same label but interpret it rather differently. These conceptual difficulties *impede coordination efforts* and it is often exactly these efforts that are very important for peacebuilding to succeed (Barnett *et al.* 2007). Peacebuilding is, ultimately, a system of governance. There are many actors involved in it, and these actors are situated on very different levels: international, regional, national and local (Hänggi 2005). Whether these actors succeed in accomplishing anything together has a lot to do with them sharing an understanding of what peacebuilding actually entails (Hänggi 2005).

The coordination problems are well acknowledged by the diplomatic community. In order to overcome them, processes of institutionalisation have accelerated in the last decade. In the mid-2000s, the UN Peacebuilding Commission (UNPBC) has been added to the UN system (see Box 11.2). The PBC is a forum to discuss concrete peacebuilding missions in given countries. It is also a forum for developing a general strategy for peacebuilding (UN Peace Building Support Office 2012). According to Kofi Annan, the UN Secretary under whose watch the PBC was created, the lack of such a strategy amounts to a major problem (Annan 2005). The UN has also established a number of Peacebuilding Offices for coordinating concrete peacebuilding efforts in a number of states, such as the Central African Republic, Guinea-Bissau, Liberia, Sierra Leone and Tajikistan.

Box 11.2 The UN Peacebuilding Commission (UNPBC)

In 2003, UN Secretary-General Kofi Annan created the High Level Panel on Threats, Challenges and Change in order to discuss the main security issues of the twenty-first century. The High Level Panel was composed of sixteen members, including former Prime Ministers such as Gro Harlem Brundtland (Norway) and Foreign Ministers such as Gareth Evans (Australia). It was chaired by Anand Panyarachun, former Prime Minister of Thailand. In 2004, the High Level Panel delivered its final report, entitled *A More Secure World: Our Shared Responsibility*. Among other things, the report laments the absence of an adequate institutional infrastructure for peacebuilding, and suggests forming a Peacebuilding Commission to remedy this problem (UN 2004). In 2005, the Security Council and the General Assembly jointly create the UNPBC. The Commission is an 'inter-governmental advisory body'. It is entrusted with the task of coordinating peacebuilding activities of all actors involved. The key task to be performed is institution-building in the target state (or, in other words, 'remaking' the state). Seven of its members are elected by the Security Council, seven by the General Assembly and another seven by the Economic and Social Council (ECOSOC). Completing its thirty-one members, the top five contributors to the UN budget as well as to military and police personnel to UN missions are also represented. One of the guidelines for electing members is that the Commission is representative of all world regions. The thirty-one members are sovereign states. Interaction with global civil society organisations is fostered by so-called NGO informal briefings, i.e. NGOs are encouraged to share their knowledge and information with the Commission. The PBC has administrative support, most importantly by the PBSO.

To some extent, there is a trend towards institutionalisation of peacebuilding on the regional level as well. The African Unity, for instance, established the Peace and Security Council (AU PSC) in 2004. The AU PSC deals with peace-making (→ glossary), peace-keeping and peacebuilding (Murithi 2007). The EU has created several new institutions that touch upon the issue of peacebuilding. The Political and Security Committee (EU PSC) performs a general steering function in foreign and security policy. It is supported in doing so by more specific institutions, such as the EU Military Committee (EUMC), the EU Military Staff (EUMS) and the Civilian Planning and Conduct Capability (CPCC). The trend towards institutionalisation can also be discerned on the national level. In the US, for example, there is an Office of Conflict Management and Mitigation at the US Agency for International Development and an Office of the Coordinator for Reconstruction and Stabilization at the State Department (Ricigliano 2012: 13). Finally, think-tanks and NGOs have also set up infrastructure to deal with peacebuilding. The Centre on Conflict, Development and Peacebuilding at the Graduate Institute of International and Development Studies, the Geneva Centre for Security Policy, Interpeace and the Quaker UN Office, all based in Geneva, for example, established the Geneva Peacebuilding Platform (GPP).

Peacebuilding remains a hotly debated issue area – among states, among agencies and offices of international organisations (such as the UN's Peacebuilding Support Office (PBSO), the Department of Peacekeeping and the UNDP), among NGOs, among scholars and think-tanks, as well as across all these different kinds of actors. The remainder of this chapter looks at the three key debates: (1) when ought the international community intervene to build peace, (2) to what end and (3) with what means?

The fundamental question: to intervene or not to intervene?

In the peacebuilding literature, there are many authors who strongly endorse external help for a peacebuilding society. They contend that the international community enhances its authority if it engages in peacebuilding activities (Adibe 1998), that such external help is the *sine qua non* of successful war to peace transitions (Regan and Aydin 2006) and that the international legal order, developing a *lex pacificatoria*, increasingly supports external peacebuilding efforts (Bell 2006). There are, however, also a number of critical voices. External peacebuilding efforts are likened to an imperial agenda by the global north to re-mould the global south (Chandler 2006). Another cautioning addresses the nexus of knowledge and hierarchy. In Roger Petersen's view, the West fashions itself the remaker of states without knowing much about these states and their societies: 'Western intervention strategies imply a set of "rational" actions and norms being taught to a lesser people. They also imply a superior knowledge that allows the intervener or occupier to carefully calibrate sticks and carrots in an optimal way' (Petersen 2011: 15). The US-led interventions in Afghanistan and Iraq, which diplomatic and public discourses sometimes squeeze into the category of peacebuilding, fuel these criticisms further.

This is an important debate. Ultimately, it is a debate about whether diplomacy ought to authorise intervention for the sake of building peace and, if so, what kinds of intervention. At first glance, answering these questions seems to be straightforward. It is legally permissible if the government of the target state *agrees* to the external help. Cases of post-conflict and preventive peacebuilding usually take this route. The target state agrees to the intervention, for example with the UN, the African Unity or the EU. Intervention is also legally permissible if the UNSC, determining that there is a threat to peace and security and acting under Chapter 7 (enforcement measures) of the Charter, decides to include peacebuilding efforts in peace-making activities. This latter route is unlikely to be travelled down very frequently because peacebuilding in many ways presupposes an environment in which peace-making is not – or no longer – necessary.

At second glance, however, the permissibility is more complicated. There are at least four reasons for this, ranging from formal-legal to politico-philosophical. First, in rare circumstances, *no internationally recognised government* exists (or this government exists on paper only). Somalia, after Siad Barre's regime had collapsed, amounted to such a case. The UN then based its peacekeeping operation on the agreement among rival factions to let such an operation into the country. This agreement soon collapsed, however, and the UN had to resort to enforcement measures.

Second, once a target state has agreed to peacebuilding and other sets of measures, the intervenors may decide to *adjust the intervention*, for instance by sending more personnel and extending the mandate for intervention. To what extent a deepening and broadening of intervention is legally permissible without explicit consent by the target state is very much a matter of debate in what amounts to a legal grey zone.

Third, the issue of legal permissibility becomes more complicated when external non-governmental actors are factored in. NGOs feature prominently in peacebuilding efforts, especially when it comes to reconciliation and mediation on local levels.

Yet to them, the legal route via the UN applies *at best indirectly*. When the host state agrees to external help for peacebuilding within the framework of the UN, NGOs tend to move swiftly and step up their efforts as well. To some extent, target states can curb and facilitate cooperation with NGOs, for instance through visa policies before international aid workers enter the country and support, or lack thereof, once they are in. Given the number of NGOs in many peacebuilding countries and the weakness of many target states, the latter tend to find these regulatory functions sometimes difficult to perform.

Fourth, there is the politico-philosophical question of *how much external intervention can help a society to build peace*. Some time ago, Michael Walzer contended that military intervention in a state is justified only under extraordinary circumstances, such as genocide. The main reason he gave for this assertion is an interesting one. He argued that nations, in principle, *can win their freedom only themselves* (Walzer 1977). This argument was a philosophical reflection about *ius ad bellum* (just reasons to go to war). More recently, Walzer also reflects upon *ius post bellum* (just reasons to help transition once war is over). Here, he opens the door for intervention considerably wider. In principle, he considers external peacebuilding warranted. But he also adds two qualifiers to his argument. First, peacebuilders ought to intervene in order to help a state complete the transition from war to peace and not in order to pursue a more general regime change and democracy promotion agenda in world politics. This qualifier is directed against George W. Bush's notion of regime change. Second, he hints again at the argument he made earlier about freedom. It is the community of the nation that has to decide upon the basic parameters of how it is to be governed and how to make these parameters last (Walzer 2012). To a considerable extent, this argument overlaps with Petersen's criticism mentioned above. External peacebuilders can only know so much about a domestic conflict situation and how to address it appropriately. In order to prevent them from superimposing a one-size-fits-all model, there has to be a strong domestic input in the peacebuilding process.

UN documents frequently refer to the concept of 'local ownership' in order to clarify the overall principle governing the moral permissibility of external peacebuilding. Yet it is far from clear whether this concept is sufficient. On a conceptual level, it may be better to move away from the 'ownership' metaphor. You can own something by simply buying it. In a metaphorical sense, this could be interpreted as a society's option to sit back and let external actors, with its agreement, build its peace. This option, however, does not exist. What really matters is that the peacebuilding society *authors* the peacebuilding process. The concept of societal authorship emphasises that it is primarily the society itself that actively develops the parameters of the new polity to be established.

On an implementation level, there are also major shortcomings with how the local ownership concept is applied to real cases. Most importantly, the 'local' is, in most cases of actual peacebuilding, reduced to little more than a synonym for the leadership of the two major conflict parties. This is a major problem. Peace cannot be built just from above; it has to be built *from below* as well. Throughout the 2000s, the UN peace missions in the Congo suffered from neglect at local levels. In principle, all social groups with a stake in peacebuilding ought to have a right to author it. This applies to the national level as much as it applies to the village and to urban neighbourhoods. Peacebuilding thus understood is a cluster of different processes, some of which are more appropriately addressed on a national level, some more on a local one and some of which – criss-crossing between them – require authorship across different levels.

The politico-philosophical debates are rather abstract. But where one stands in this debate has major repercussions for every aspect of peacebuilding. Take reconciliation and transitionary justice, for example. Is it possible to facilitate reconciliation and justice from the outside? Is it possible for the international community to devise mechanisms of reconciliation and justice that are applicable to conflicts as different as, say, in the Congo and Kosovo? There are arguments for such mechanisms. In Rwanda, formal courts and local Gacaca Courts have been overwhelmed by the sheer numbers of court proceedings required against alleged participants in the genocide (Sarkin 2001). The International Criminal Tribunal for Rwanda has somewhat helped the situation. There are also arguments against international interference in reconciliation. Indigenous methods may work better for reintegrating certain offenders back into society (Park 2010). Finally, there is a lot of room for a middle path between international mechanisms and indigenous methods. Truth and Reconciliation Commissions may be seen as rooted in international norms but the actual workings of the Commissions vary greatly from transition state to transition state. Furthermore, a division of labour may be found between Truth and Reconciliation Commissions and more locally based indigenous courts (Fiadjoe 2004). Yet however such a middle path may look like, it is important that the society that tries to heal itself is the principal author in how it goes about doing this. There cannot be a universally valid scheme for reconciliation that is applicable anywhere in the world (Crocker 1999).

With diplomacy master-minding and authorising peacebuilding, diplomats have to face even more abstract questions. The next sections deal with the purpose and the means of peacebuilding.

What ought to be the end of peacebuilding?

In a way, the answer to this question is obvious. The purpose of peacebuilding is peace. But it is not that obvious what peace actually is. This, too, is a question with strong philosophical connotations that has major repercussions for how diplomacy ought to approach peacebuilding. What kind of peacebuilding exercises diplomacy ought to support and what kinds it ought to reject has a lot to do with how the peace that is to be built is defined.

Scholarly research on peacebuilding tends to define the 'peace' in peacebuilding as the absence of war, and select clear-cut quantitative indicators for this absence of war. The most frequently used indicator is 1,000 battle-related deaths a year. If the number of casualties in a state is below this threshold, the state is considered at peace. If the number reaches this threshold or exceeds it, scholars equate it with the occurrence of an intra-state war (Sambanis 2004). Some students of peacebuilding consider this threshold too high and rely on a different operational definition of absence of war. The threshold of twenty-five battle-related deaths a year, for instance, is used in the literature as well (Call 2012: 9).

There are, however, major problems with these conceptual and operational definitions. Defining peace conceptually as absence of war, strictly speaking, tells us very little about peace. It tells us what peace is not; but it does not tell us what peace actually is. This problem of the conceptual definitions notwithstanding, the operational definitions suffer from the additional problem that methodologically clear-cut thresholds of battle-deaths are always arbitrary. There is no convincing scholarly justification for why 1,000 battle-deaths should indicate war whereas 999 indicate peace (the same problem applies to the twenty-five battle-deaths threshold).

Peacebuilding practitioners are somewhat more prepared to rethink what the 'peace' in peacebuilding means. As a rule of thumb, different bureaucracies employ their peculiar expertise and experience to try to move the understanding of peace beyond the inter-state analogy. The World Bank and the IMF, for instance, strongly rely on economic indicators in order to determine what constitutes peace in a post-conflict reconstruction effort and what does not. Furthermore, peacebuilders – the many different definitions of peacebuilding used notwithstanding – are moving towards an understanding of the 'peace' in peacebuilding as 'sustainable peace'. Thus, there is some recognition of the problems associated with assuming all too limited time frames for building peace.

What is striking about these definitions, however, is how much out of sync they are with the origins of the peacebuilding concept. The UN traces the concept of peacebuilding back to the scholarly work of Johan Galtung. To Galtung, peace was much more than what it is to today's peacebuilders. Galtung coined the highly influential distinction between negative and positive peace. Negative peace, he submits, is the absence of direct, structural and cultural violence. Direct violence ranges from verbal to physical harm, structural violence is about marginalisation and exploitation, and cultural violence is about ideational resources (taken, for instance, from religion and ideology) to legitimate direct and structural violence. Positive peace is something akin to harmony. There is no direct violence but kindness and even love. There is no structural violence but dialogue and solidarity. Finally, there is no legitimation of violence (cultural violence) but a legitimation of peace (Galtung 1996: 31–33).

Moving away from Galtung's conceptualisations to the extent that the count of battle-related deaths is used as shorthand for peace, narrowing the 'peace' in peacebuilding down to the markers routinely used by a bureaucracy in its everyday work (no matter whether this has something to do with peacebuilding or not), or coining the pleonasm 'sustainable peace' (sustainability is a feature of any meaningful definition of peace) has very little to do with Galtung. Indeed, Galtung's work cautions us against these simplifications. By the same token, however, it is difficult to simply apply his notions of negative or positive peace to peacebuilding. His notion of negative peace has the advantage that it deals with violence more comprehensively. It does not narrow it down to battle-deaths and not even to physical harm. But this still does not solve the problem of negative definitions. Galtung's definition tells us more about violence and, thus, more about what peace is not. But it still does not really tell us what peace is. Galtung tries to accomplish this by outlining his concept of positive peace. But this concept is too demanding for peacebuilding. It would be utopian even to hope – not even to speak of expecting – that peacebuilding efforts lead to the kind of harmony and love that Galtung has in mind when he writes about positive peace.

If Galtung is the one towering scholarly figure in peace and conflict studies, Anatol Rapoport is the other. Rapoport is very good at conceptualising conflict. He contends that three modes of conflict can be distinguished: fights, games and debates. In a fight, the opponent is an enemy to be annihilated. In a game, the opponent is a fellow player to be outwitted. Finally, in a debate, the opponent is a different believer who has to be converted. In many conflicts, all three modes are present, although there are major variations across different conflicts in terms of how prevalent a particular mode is compared to others (Rapoport 1960). Rapoport tells us more about conflict than about peace. But the three modes of conflict are an important starting point for thinking about the 'peace' in peacebuilding.

They point to the following: *peace is when restraint, compromise and dialogue* (→ glossary) *become practices of conflict management.* The key terms used in this definition are conflict management, practices, restraint, compromise and dialogue. Conflict management is not the same as conflict resolution; conflicts may persist but they are managed by means other than war. A practice, as discussed in the previous chapter, is something that has become second nature; actors simply do, without reflecting about what they do and why they do so. A practice of restraint is akin to what Norbert Elias *et al.* (2000) refer to as civilising process; resort to physical violence becomes inconceivable. A practice of compromise is about a reflex of meeting somewhere in the middle when political stances by different social groups are not easily compatible (Bellamy *et al.* 2012). Finally, a practice of dialogue revolves around trying to understand the different stances of each other and even to generate consensus. The latter practice is especially difficult to achieve for a society trying to build peace. Yet some of it is necessary in order to be able to speak of peace. A minimum of consensus has to be produced on the narrative that the nation tells of itself, for example. This includes the past conflict among different social groups.

What ought to be the means to this end?

How to build peace? Diplomats debating about and deciding upon sending peacebuilding missions tend to look at the issue of peacebuilding through a liberal lens. In essence, the concept of peacebuilding assumes that market liberalisation and democratisation are the means to build sustainable peace. Thomas Biersteker provides a good overview of this lens and the means of peacebuilding that become intelligible when looking through it:

> The theoretical underpinnings of the Peacebuilding Commission are profoundly liberal, even if they are not explicitly articulated as such. Support for respect of human rights, the promotion of the rule of law, the construction of representative institutions with periodic elections, the creation of forums for popular participation in politics and encouragement of the emergence of a vigorous and free media are all components of peacebuilding efforts, as well as of the construction of a liberal society.
>
> (Biersteker 2007: 39)

Séverine Autesserre elaborates on what this lens does. It makes it possible to see certain aspects of reality but makes it impossible to see others. Referring to peacebuilding efforts in the Congo, Autesserre contends that the liberal lens

> shaped what international actors considered at all (usually excluding continued local conflict), what they viewed as possible (excluding local conflict resolution), and what they thought was the 'natural' course of action in a given situation (national and international action, in particular the organization of elections).

It authorized and justified specific practices and policies while excluding others, notably grassroots peacebuilding.

(Autesserre 2010: 11)

Most scholars agree that the liberal paradigm – or, more precisely put, the peculiar type of liberal paradigm that has prevailed over the last decade – has its weaknesses. Yet they disagree just how bad these weaknesses are. Some authors reject the existing liberal paradigm entirely. They try to uncover the contradictory assumptions that make up 'peacebuilding discourses' (Heathershaw 2008) and link the means used in liberal peacebuilding to broader hegemonic designs by the West (Chandler 2006). Most scholars, however, shy away from such fundamental criticism. They acknowledge major problems, but argue for adjusting and changing the existing paradigm rather than abolishing it altogether.

Five sets of changes are frequently postulated in the literature. First, starting with Roland Paris' measured critique of the liberal paradigm, several authors make a case for taking *state-building* more seriously. He considers the approach of transforming societies into market economies in order to build peace, in principle, as logically sound but cautions that this process must not be rushed. His argument may be summarised in the formula: institutions first, liberalisation later. The re-building of the state, in this view, is the foundation for peacebuilding (Paris 2004). A number of authors support this view. Without strong state institutions, non-cooperative conflict parties find it easy to derail the peace process, especially during and immediately after free elections (Caplan 2005).

Second, for many observers, it has become a commonplace that *power-sharing* is a key requirement for successful peacebuilding. According to Hartzell and Hoddie, there are several dimensions of power-sharing. Perhaps the most basic dimension is political in nature. Political power-sharing is diametrically opposed to winner-takes-all elections. All former warring parties ought to be represented in the government. But there are other dimensions as well. Economic power-sharing implies that no one party has all the access to economic resources and decision-making processes. Territorial power-sharing is diametrically opposed to a unitary state. Different parties fulfil different governing functions in different parts of the country. Hartzell and Hoddie (2003), for example, endorse provisions of territorial autonomy. Taken together, the authors advocate something that may be labelled a domestic balance of power in which no one party can lay down the law on the others. This theme comes up in a number of studies, no matter whether they deal with peacebuilding processes as a whole (Roeder and Rothchild 2005) or with a particular aspect of it such as restructuring military and police forces (Call 2002).

Third, some authors develop the idea of power-sharing further and advocate a more general *political inclusivity*. Michael Barnett identifies representation, public deliberation and constitutionalism as key factors for successful peacebuilding. Representation is reminiscent of political power-sharing arguments. Elites from different conflict parties ought to be represented in key political decision-making forums. Deliberation goes beyond power-sharing. It emphasises the importance of public deliberation. Such deliberation, criss-crossing elite and civil society levels, is expected to foster a we-feeling across former conflict parties. Finally, constitutionalism is about rules that are difficult to change and makes sure that the institutional foundations on which the newly created inclusive polity rests cannot be abandoned all too easily (Barnett 2006). Charles Call also stresses the importance of inclusivity and links it to what he labels 'legitimacy-focused peacebuilding' (Call 2012: 6). Inclusive institutions last if they are considered legitimate. Peacebuilding, therefore, ought to prioritise efforts to facilitate the creation of institutions that actors consider right. Reflecting upon them, they consider them effective (pragmatic legitimacy), or just (moral legitimacy). Or they take the rightness of these institutions so much for granted that they do not reflect upon them any more at all (cognitive legitimacy).

Fourth, there are more and more calls to include *local* level actors. Perhaps the empirically best supported call has been made by Séverine Autesserre, an NGO activist turned scholar, in a study on the Congo (Autesserre 2010). The prevailing orthodoxy is to talk to and negotiate with the decision-making elites of the primary conflict parties. The number of these parties is usually two. The problem with this orthodoxy is that it glosses over the complexity of conflicts. Conflicts reach much deeper and are much more multi-faceted than could be narrowed down to two opposing elite circles surrounding two opposing leaders. Take South Africa, for example. The transition in this country was not just about reconciling 'black' and 'white', as it was understood in the West. It was, more fundamentally, about re-unifying a country that had been territorially (homelands and townships), politically (e.g., tricameral legislative structure) and, therefore, also economically and socially carved up along racial and ethnic lines. The fate of the transition, therefore, was not only in the hands of the National Party (NP) and Frederic Willem de Klerk on the one hand as well as the ANC and Nelson Mandela on the other. But it was also dependent on, say, relations between the Inkatha Freedom Party (IFP), Gatsha Buthelezi and its local supporters on the one hand as well as the ANC and its local leaders and supporters on the other, especially in the province of Kwazulu-Natal and the townships of the former Transvaal province.

Fifth, peacebuilding measures have to be tailored to a given conflict situation. There cannot be a 'one-size-fits-all' type of peacebuilding. Different situational factors require *different peacebuilding responses* (Richmond and Franks 2009: 205). Take the power-sharing prescription and the cases of Angola and Mozambique, for example. In the early 1990s, Mozambique successfully implemented a peace agreement between the government and a decades-old insurgency movement. To this very day, the country has not lapsed back into war. The Mozambican success has happened although almost none of the power-sharing measures postulated by the literature have been in place. The Frelimo has been very successful at elections, while the Renamo has found itself on the opposition benches in parliament. At the same time, the Angolan peace process collapsed no matter whether the peace agreements to be implemented included power-sharing stipulations (Lusaka Agreement) or not (Bicesse Agreement). The *Uniao Nacional para Independência Total de Angola* (UNITA) went back to war, trying to defeat the *Movimento Popular de Libertaçao de Angola* (MPLA) on the battlefield.

Mapping these five-fold problems of today's peacebuilding on the working definition of peace developed above cautions us that, first, the current repertoire of peacebuilding measures *is more geared towards restraint than to compromise and especially dialogue* and, second, that peacebuilding measures focus more on *fixing immediate problems than working towards more sustainable practices of peace.*

Currently, there is a strong emphasis on measures of restraint. It is well established that the cessation of hostilities has to be verified by military observers and, if the military situation is less stable, requires a peacekeeping operation (at times a very robust one) in order to keep the combatants apart. If cessation and verification are in place, the Security Sector Reform (SSR) as well as the Demobilization, Disarmament and Reintegration process (DDR) of the combatants begins. The international community usually dedicates sufficient resources for the SSR and the 'DD' of the DDR. With the remaining 'R', it tends to be a different matter.

From a perspective that understands peace as practice, this reintegration is of utmost importance. Leading the life of a civilian, being employed as a civilian, having a life of a civilian, being embedded in a civilian community – all of these things are of key importance for former combatants to make the shift from a practice of waging war to a practice of peace (or even waging peace). But they do not come easy. Leaving years – sometimes decades – of fighting behind and starting a civilian life again is something that takes time.

Today's peacebuilding measures put more emphasis on facilitating compromises among parties than, say, two decades ago. To some extent, the literature's demands for power-sharing parallel the lessons-learnt memos of international organisations and foreign services. Mediation efforts, including back-channel diplomacy, are used if the former warring parties find it difficult to arrive at concrete compromises. There are external efforts to shape the Constitutions of transitional societies, including ingraining the rule of law, human rights and minority rights. What still remains to be strengthened though is support in developing a general culture of compromising. Democracy and the rule of law have to take root across a transitional country. This ought to include the capital but it also ought to extend to provincial and local politics. Not everything is about the 'high politics' of the capital; local councils matter, too. Note that the demand for such efforts has implications for diplomacy. It points to new rather than old diplomacy. External state involvement is not enough. In political terms, peacebuilding has to be a network governance encompassing state and non-state actors. The term 'governance' in this context indicates that it is not enough that state and non-state actors are present in facilitating transitions. They have to find ways to steer their many activities into certain directions.

Current peacebuilding measures remain patchy when it comes to dialogue. Peacebuilding remains to be understood primarily as remaking states. But remaking states also entails remaking – in some cases – even making nations that are constituted by a set of shared norms and a narrative that nations tell of themselves. Plurality notwithstanding, there has to be some ideational convergence that makes it possible for a nation to imagine itself as a nation in the first place. Truth and Reconciliation Commissions can play an important role in addressing the past with a view to preparing a common future (see Box 11.3). To establish such commissions has almost become an international norm by now. But we are only beginning to understand what it takes to move from war to a dialogical mode of communication and how this dialogical mode can be fostered from the outside. Robert Ricigliano lists several important measures, including trauma-healing initiatives, community-dialogue programmes, peace camps for youth from divided communities and multi-ethnic media programmes (Ricigliano 2012: 35). Many more could be added. School textbooks, for example, seem to be particularly important.

In the scholarly and practitioners' communities, it is widely acknowledged that a lot remains to be done when it comes to the means of peacebuilding. Dale Walton, for example, calls for a strategy (Walton 2009) and so does Kofi Annan (Annan 2005).

Box 11.3 Reconciliation versus justice?

Reconciliation and justice do not always go hand in hand. On the one hand, a strategy of avoiding speaking about the past or even forgetting it, may, at least in the short term, stabilise a war to peace transition. Perpetrators may be more easily persuaded to lay down their arms and participate in remaking society. Hearing the truth about past crimes may torment a society, leaving it with the belief that any kind of reconciliation is impossible. On the other hand, victims deserve justice. People deserve to know what happened to their loved ones when they disappeared. The newly established system ought not to gloss over the fundamental difference between victim and perpetrator; there ought to be an appropriate form of retribution. Some scholarly arguments solve this dilemma one-sidedly. John Locke, for example, argues against justice and in favour of stability of the polity (Stacey 2004). Yet most contemporary political theorists try to strike a balance. Donald Shriver writes about the need for justice but also for draining 'the memory of its power to continue to poison the present and future' (Shriver 2003: 31). Jean Bethke Elstain makes a similar point with her argument for 'knowing forgetting'. There ought to be remembering but there also ought to be some degree of releasing 'present-day agents from the full burden of the past, in order that they not be weighed down by it utterly' (Elstain 2003).

The former Secretary-General had high hopes for the PBC to develop such a strategy. To some extent, these calls for a strategy are understandable. A strategy, very simply put, is a plan for how to employ what means in a given situation (including the moves of other players) in order to achieve one's goal.

A general peacebuilding strategy, however, is only warranted if we can safely assume that the conflict situations in which peace is to be built are sufficiently similar for the strategy to work. It is doubtful whether this is a safe assumption to make. Conflict situations differ immensely. Such a strategy may amount to yet another attempt to force a 'one-size-fits-all' model of peacebuilding upon a highly heterogeneous set of conflict situations. We need less of a general strategy of peacebuilding than an *adaptive repertoire* out of which domestic and international actors select means of peacebuilding they consider appropriate for the conflict situation to be addressed, adjust these means and add new measures. In short, peacebuilders – domestic and international – ought to make use of the repertoire in order to tailor peacebuilding means to a particular conflict situation.

This, too, is no panacea for resolving problems pertaining to peacebuilding. The media and public opinion in the West often portray peacebuilding as something akin to the routine fixing of a machine. All one needs to do is find the fitting tools from the toolbox and the machine is up and running again. Peacebuilding, of course, is very far from being that simple. There are conflict constellations that make peacebuilding, even if supported by a major international peace mission, simply impossible. Yet we would submit that the diplomatic community can – and has to – improve on the current record. By one account, almost half of war to peace transitions lapse back into war within five years (Collier and Hoeffler 2004). This has to make us think about how the broader diplomatic field – traditional and non-traditional diplomats – can help improve this record. After all, it is diplomacy that put the concept of peacebuilding on the global agenda, and it is diplomacy that applies the concept to concrete situations.

Summary

- The institutionalisation of peacebuilding raises a number of issues with different connotations, ranging from legal to philosophical. We discussed three issues in depth. Under what conditions is it appropriate for external actors to become involved in peacebuilding efforts (*intervention*)? What is the 'peace' in peacebuilding (*purpose*)? What are the appropriate measures for getting closer to this purpose (*means*)?
- Our discussion of the issue of intervention introduced the concept of *societal authorship*. In principle, all social groups with a stake in the peacebuilding process ought to have the right to author the process through which peace is to be built. It is particularly crucial that this authorship applies not only to the top representatives of the major conflict parties but that peacebuilding is also authored from below.
- Diplomacy and the study of diplomacy cannot avoid philosophical questions. The question about what peace is amounts to such a philosophical question. How it is answered – in whatever provisional way possible – has major repercussions for peacebuilding. Our reflections led us to define the 'peace' in peacebuilding as *practising restraint, compromise and dialogue*. Restraint, compromise and dialogue have to become second nature for us to be able to speak of peace. This is a tall order and requires us to rethink the means employed for building peace.
- There can be no general strategy or one-size-fits-all model of peacebuilding. Instead, we argued for an *adaptive repertoire*, from which domestic and diplomatic actors select measures, add measures and adjust measures they consider appropriate to deal with a given conflict situation. These situations vary immensely. The measures have to be tailored to the conflict situation. The selected measures have to be geared towards establishing practices of restraint, compromise and dialogue.

Study questions

- How does diplomacy shape peacebuilding?
- How much external help in peacebuilding is warranted?
- What peace is to be built by peacebuilders?
- How is peace to be built?
- Is there a tension between just and effective peacebuilding? If so, how is it to be resolved?

Recommended further reading

Autesserre, Séverin. 2010. *The trouble with the Congo: Local violence and the failure of international peacebuilding*. Cambridge and New York: Cambridge University Press.
This detailed empirical account advocates for a bottom-up approach to peacebuilding. This contrasts with current practices.

Chandler, David (ed.) 2009. *Statebuilding and intervention: Policies, practices and paradigms.* New York: Routledge.
This edited book identifies current state-building practices and discusses ways to improve on them. Empirical illustrations include cases from Africa, Asia and Europe.

Doyle, Michael W. and Nicholas Sambanis. 2006. *Making war and building peace: United Nations peace operations.* Princeton, NJ: Princeton University Press.
Drawing conclusions from a large analysis of all civil wars since 1945, the authors contend that peacebuilding is, above all, about tailoring the means of peacebuilding to the peculiarities of a conflict situation. When it comes to the aims of peacebuilding, the authors put a strong emphasis on economic factors.

Goetschel, Laurent. 2011. 'Neutrals as brokers of peacebuilding ideas?' *Cooperation and Conflict* no. 46 (3): 312–333.
This article advocates for neutral states to increase their presence in making international order in general and building peace in particular. This view of neutrality as an asset in conflict transformation and resolution echoes the literature on mediation.

United Nations. 2008. *A briefing paper,* prepared by PBSO in close consultation with DGO, DPA, DPKO, OCHA and UNDP. Principal author: Richard Caplan. New York: United Nations.
This document provides a glimpse into UN peacebuilding practices. Note the complex authorship. It is telling about the coordination challenges within the UN system.

12 The peaceful remaking of the world

Chapter objectives

- To identify the main UN instruments of preventive diplomacy and examine the strengths and limitations they face in assisting the peaceful evolution of the international order.
- To discuss the rising importance of international criminal justice as an instrument of diplomatic relations.
- To overview the evolution of the negotiations establishing the International Criminal Court and to explain the ICC role and challenges in fostering international order and peaceful change.

Introduction

Can diplomacy help remake the world for the better? Arguably, the answer to the question much depends on the meaning we attach to the terms 'remake' and 'better'. In Chapter 9, we offered an interpretation for the first term. The diplomatic (re)making of the world involves two layers, 'order as value' and 'order as fact'. What is less clear, however, is what kind of diplomatic processes and instruments can help remake the world for the 'better'? For some, peaceful international orders cannot emerge without diplomats systematically addressing the deep causes of international conflict such as endemic poverty, global health disparities, undemocratic governance or lack of opportunities for human development. For others, these represent legitimate and ambitious goals but hardly feasible given the sheer complexity of the issues and the practical difficulties of mobilising broad coalitions of actors and institutions in support of long-term projects. There is no easy formula to reconcile these two views. Short- and long-term priorities obviously need to be set, but the nature of these priorities remains a subject of intense debate.

In this chapter, we tackle this dilemma in two complementary ways. On the one hand, we adopt a narrow understanding of the normative dimension of the evolution of the world order, which we define in terms of the reduction of international and domestic violence. On the other hand, we discuss a two-pronged approach for reaching this objective. In the short term, diplomats ought to work to negatively alter the actors' structure of incentives for resorting to violence. In the long term, diplomats ought to engage in actions that address structural causes of conflict (poverty, ethnic tensions, institutional deficiencies, environmental degradation, etc.), while also undermining the legitimacy of the idea of using force for settling disputes.

To this end, we focus on two important mechanisms by which diplomats can help reduce the use of violence both internationally and domestically: preventive diplomacy and international criminal justice. The former is supposed to assist the peaceful evolution of the international order by anticipating threats to international peace and security and eliminating them before they take place, both in the short and the long term. International criminal justice is supposed to facilitate peaceful change by acting much deeper. By imposing criminal responsibility directly upon individuals, regardless of the national law, international criminal justice does not merely aim to deter actors from resorting to violence in the short term, but it also aspires them to undermine the legal and moral legitimacy of the method of using force for settling disputes in the long term.

Preventive diplomacy

From a historical perspective, the notion of preventive diplomacy (→ glossary) is not as modern as one might think. Machiavelli took great care, for instance, to advise young diplomats to gather information not only about matters in the course of negotiations or about those that are concluded and done, but also about matters yet to be done. He considered the latter to be the most difficult to address as 'to conjecture the issue correctly ... you have nothing to depend upon except surmises aided by your own judgement' (Machiavelli 2001: 42). Cardinal Richelieu was even more adamant about the need for engaging in continuous negotiations for its own sake:

> I dare say emphatically that it is absolutely necessary to the well-being of the state to negotiate ceaselessly, either openly or secretly, and in all places, even in those from which no present fruits are reaped and still more in those from which no future prospects as yet seem likely.
>
> (Richelieu 1961: 95)

If that is the case, then what exactly would preventive diplomacy imply, how could it be successfully deployed and what limitations would it most likely face? As the UN remains the main international decision-making body for addressing issues of collective security, we will address these questions largely from its perspective.

From a political perspective, UN Secretary-General Dag Hammarskjöld was the first to articulate the concept of preventive diplomacy as an extension of the ability of the UN Secretary-General (UNSG) to act neutrally (see Box 12.1). Other UNSGs such as U Thant and Kurt Waldheim further developed the notion of 'good offices' (→ glossary), Javier Perez de Cuéllar built capacity for early warning (→ glossary: early warning systems) through the Office for Research and the Collection of Information (ORCI), whereas Boutros Boutros-Ghali integrated the ORCI into the Department of Political Affairs and drafted the ground-breaking report on the *Agenda for Peace: Preventive Diplomacy, Peacemaking and Peacekeeping*. Following on these steps, Kofi Annan pushed ahead with a bold agenda for the prevention of armed conflict, while Ban Ki-moon has used his authority to repeatedly call attention to the link between climate change and conflict prevention (Ramcharan 2008: 31–58).

Box 12.1 Origins of the concept of preventive diplomacy

What I should like to call active preventive diplomacy ... may be conducted by the UN through the Secretary-General or in other forms, in many situations where no government or group of governments and no regional organization would be able to act in the same way. That such interventions are possible for the UN is explained by ... the acceptance of an independent political and diplomatic activity on the part of the Secretary-General as the 'neutral' representative of the Organization.

(Hammarskjöld and Falkman 2005: 137–138)

These initiatives suggest a gradual evolution of the concept of preventive diplomacy from a classical diplomatic act of provision of 'good offices' (e.g., neutral mediation by the UNSG), to a more complex and proactive form of diplomatic engagement, which involves issues pertaining to the management of conflict and post-conflict situations. The definition currently used by the UN for preventive diplomacy supports this understanding: 'diplomatic action taken, at the earliest possible stage, to prevent disputes from arising between parties, to prevent existing disputes from escalating into conflicts and to limit the spread of the latter when they occur' (UN Secretary-General 2011: 2). This move invites two questions: is there legal support for the extension of the concept of preventive diplomacy and, if yes, what kind of institutional framework is necessary to sustain it?

From an international legal perspective, the International Court of Justice (ICJ) acknowledged in its advisory opinion concerning the 1962 *Certain Expenses of the United Nations Case* that peacekeeping operations fall under the purview of Chapter VII of the Charter (McCorquodale and Dixon 2003: 566). Pursuant to Articles 10 and 11 of the Charter, the General Assembly enjoys broad authority to consider conflict prevention in all its aspects, develops recommendations as appropriate and calls the attention of the Security Council to situations that are likely to endanger international peace and security. The effectiveness of the UNGA's actions in the area of preventive diplomacy is nevertheless constrained by the fact that its resolutions have a non-binding character. This may be compensated by the fact that, according to Article 34 of the Charter, the Security Council has the responsibility to 'investigate any dispute, or any situation which might lead to international friction or give rise to a dispute, in order to determine whether the continuance of the dispute or situation is likely to endanger the maintenance of international peace and security'. In the same vein, Article 99 gives the UN Secretary-General the power to 'bring to the attention of the Security Council any matter which in his opinion may threaten the maintenance of international peace and security' (UN 1945), a role that has been taken up by succeeding UNSGs with different degrees of success.

From a bureaucratic perspective, the UN framework on preventive diplomacy currently encompasses three important components, which confirms the ongoing broadening of the mandate of the concept: crisis management, peacekeeping operations and post-conflict reconstruction (see examples in Box 12.2). The first component is coordinated by the UN Department of Affairs and includes good offices provided by the UNSG, mediation efforts undertaken by special envoys appointed

---

Box 12.2 UN cases of preventive diplomacy

- In Sudan, preventive diplomacy ensured the successful holding of the January 2011 independence referendum for Southern Sudan. The Security Council was actively engaged, including through its statements and visits to the country. The Secretary-General appointed a high-level panel that also encouraged actions and agreements to permit the smooth holding of the referendum.
- In Guinea, from 2009–2010 the UN Office for West Africa (UNOWA) worked to keep on track a political transition from a military coup to the country's first democratic elections since independence.
- In Sierra Leone, the UN Integrated Peacebuilding Office (UNIPSIL) helped prevent the potential escalation of violence following tensions between the governing and opposition parties in 2009.
- In Iraq, the UN political mission has facilitated peaceful dialogue over Kirkuk and other disputed internal territories, and assisted in smoothing the path to elections in 2009 and 2010.
- In Kenya, following the outbreak of post-electoral violence in 2008, the UN quietly provided strong support to the AU-led mediation efforts that succeeded in stopping the violence and resolving the political–electoral conflict through negotiations.
- In Kyrgyzstan, the UN Centre for Preventive Diplomacy for Central Asia (UNRCCA) worked closely with key governments and the OSCE to encourage an end to the 2010 inter-ethnic violence and a return to constitutional order. The office is also encouraging agreements on the peaceful sharing of water resources in the region.
- In the Democratic Republic of the Congo, the timely dispatch of an envoy of the Secretary-General in the autumn of 2008 helped to quell unrest and ease tensions between Rwanda and the DRC that might have deteriorated into renewed regional war.

(UN Department of Political Affairs 2012)

---

by the UNSG, conflict de-escalation initiatives sponsored by regional offices in West Africa, Central Africa and Central Asia, and crisis management strategies prepared by resident political missions.

Working on the basis of the consent of the parties involved, peacekeeping operations deliver security, political and early peacebuilding support. They are led by the UN Department of Peacekeeping Operations (DPKO) and, as of 2012, they include sixteen missions served by 120,988 personnel from 115 countries at the approved budget of US$7.84 billion from 1 July 2011 to 30 June 2012 (UN Department of Peacekeeping Operations 2012). Recognising that around half of civil wars are due to post-conflict relapse, the Security Council and the General Assembly established the UNPBC in 2005 (see more details in Chapter 11). As of October 2012, Burundi, Central African Republic, Guinea, Guinea-Bissau, Liberia and Sierra Leone are on the agenda of the Commission. The UN Secretary-General also launched a Peacebuilding Fund in 2006 to support activities, actions, programmes and organisations that seek to build a lasting peace in countries emerging from conflict (UN Peace Building Commission 2005).

Aside from the perennial funding problem that has been plaguing the UN system from its inception, preventive diplomacy faces a few other important challenges.

First, the quality and level of coordination of the various early warning units within the UN require further improvement (see Box 12.3). At the moment, the Secretariat has no officers dedicated solely to collecting, analysing and integrating all the UN early warning reporting. Second, closer and more operational cooperation is needed between the UN and those regional and sub-regional organisations that have already developed strong capacity in the fields of conflict early warning, prevention, peace-making, peacekeeping and peacebuilding (e.g., EU, OSCE, AU, OAS) (UN Security Council 2010). Finally, the sustainability of results may require the broadening of preventive diplomacy engagements from the circle of decision-makers to senior officials to the civil society at large (track-two diplomacy).

The financial and organisational difficulties mentioned above should not obscure though some important conceptual tensions inherent in the UN approach to preventive diplomacy. First of all, it is not evident whether the expansion of the mandate of preventive diplomacy from 'good offices' and mediation to peacekeeping and peacebuilding is really warranted. On the one hand, successful management of

---

Box 12.3 UN early warning systems

- The UN Department of Political Affairs (UNDPA) produces analytical reports and briefing notes warning of incipient crises to the Under Secretary-General for Political Affairs, who chairs the ExComm on Peace and Security.
- Created in 2001, the UNDP's Bureau of Crisis Prevention and Recovery has a mandate 'to help countries prevent and recover from armed conflicts and natural disasters'.
- DPKO maintains a twenty-four-hour Situation Centre that serves as a continuous link between UN Headquarters, field missions, troop-contributing countries and relevant NGOs. The Situation Centre has two early warning components, the Operations Room and the Research and Liaison Unit.
- The Office for the Coordination of Humanitarian Affairs (OCHA) maintains an Early Warning and Contingency Planning Section within its Coordination and Response Division, which advises the Under-Secretary for Humanitarian Affairs and Emergency Relief Coordinator and senior management of potential emergency scenarios and preparedness actions.
- The WFP pioneered the inter-agency Humanitarian Early Warning website (HEWS-Web), which was based on the WFP's already-extant Global Early Warning system. HEWS-Web reports on sources of natural disasters – including storms, flooding and volcanic and seismic activity – based on data from external partners.
- The Office of the High Commissioner for Human Rights (OHCHR) monitors and publicly reports on human rights situations in specific countries. When a special rapporteur or working group notices human rights violations portending conflict, they can sound the alarm through mechanisms including regular reports to the Human Rights Council and the General Assembly.
- The Office of the Special Adviser of the Secretary-General on the Prevention of Genocide was created in 2004 to act as a mechanism of early warning to the Secretary-General and the Security Council about potential situations that could result in genocide.
- The Global Pulse initiative was launched by the UN Secretary-General in the aftermath of the 2008 financial crisis with the aim to create a decision support network that would enable rapid and effective action to protect poor and vulnerable populations in times of compound global crises.

(Zenko and Friedman 2011: 32)

international crises largely depends on active mediation efforts of a neutral party, with strong negotiation skills and with good credibility in the eyes of the conflicting factions. By contrast, peacekeeping and peacebuilding involve actions requiring a different repertoire of skills ranging from proficiency in military tactics, humanitarian assistance and post-conflict reconstruction, which generally fall outside the traditional realm of diplomatic competences. In addition, diplomacy is shaped by a set of norms and rules of conduct (e.g., recognition, openness, dialogue, constructive ambiguity) that may sit uneasily with certain strategies of peacekeeping and peacebuilding. Put differently, diplomats may find themselves overwhelmed and ill-prepared for shifting gears from the practice of negotiating agreements to that of implementing and sustaining them by means of peacekeeping and peacebuilding.

On the other hand, one may argue the expansion of preventive diplomacy to the full spectrum of conflict prevention measures reflects the changing nature of diplomacy within the context of emerging security issues such as terrorism, organised crime, fragile states, environmental threats, etc. This explains the growing appeal of the idea of training 'guerrilla' or 'expeditionary' diplomats to complement the work of traditional diplomats (see details in Chapter 10). One important finding of the UN experience in mediating conflicts is that building sustainable peace requires strong leadership not only in negotiating but also in implementing agreements. The role of the mediator does not end once an agreement is reached as the terms of the settlement are being constantly re-negotiated by the parties during the implementation phase. If the arising issues are left unattended, the entire peace process may collapse as it happened, for instance, with the failure of the Arusha Accord that led to 800,000 deaths in Rwanda in 1994.

Second, the objectives of preventive strategies are not always clearly stated and they often get mixed up in practice with negative results. Broadly speaking, preventive measures take aim at correcting direct and structural sources of conflict (→ glossary: direct and structural prevention). Direct prevention has a short-term agenda and aims to reduce or eliminate the immediate causes of violence between parties (e.g., ceasefire, peacekeeping, disarmament). Structural prevention has a longer-term perspective and aims to provide a more comprehensive solution to the deep-seated causes of the conflict (e.g., democratisation, economic development, transitional justice, ethnic integration, arms control, etc.) (Wallensteen 2002: 213–214). In principle, UN-sponsored mediation efforts are supposed to address direct sources of conflict, peacebuilding takes care of structural ones, while peacekeeping falls somewhere in between. In practice the situation is a bit more complicated as the life-stage of the conflict is critically important for when and how to engage in preventive actions (see Figure 12.1).

Ideally, direct prevention should take place at the first signs of violence between the aggrieved parties. In the case of Kosovo, for instance, ethnic tension and armed unrest began to escalate in 1993 following systemic discrimination and acts of police violence against ethnic Albanians by Serbian authorities. One could argue though the six-nation 'Contact Group' (US, Russia, Britain, France, Germany and Italy) formed in 1994 for negotiating peace in the Balkans decided much too late to engage in preventive diplomacy and that might explain its subsequent ineffectiveness. As the revocation of Kosovo's autonomy by the Serbian President, Slobodan Milošević, in 1989 provided the catalyst for conflict, the question arises as to whether measures of structural prevention (economic assistance, democratisation programmes, etc.)

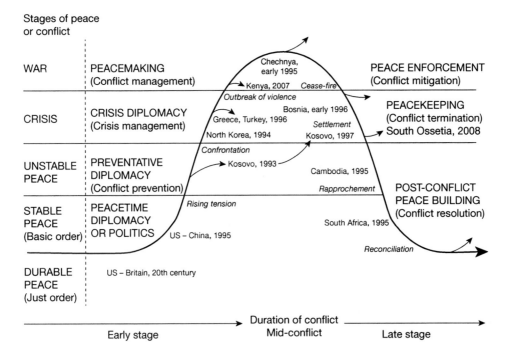

Stages of peace
or conflict

| WAR | PEACEMAKING (Conflict management) | | PEACE ENFORCEMENT (Conflict mitigation) |

Chechnya, early 1995

Kenya, 2007   *Cease-fire*

Outbreak of violence

| CRISIS | CRISIS DIPLOMACY (Crisis management) | | PEACEKEEPING (Conflict termination) |

Bosnia, early 1996

Greece, Turkey, 1996

Settlement

North Korea, 1994

South Ossetia, 2008

Kosovo, 1997

Confrontation

| UNSTABLE PEACE | PREVENTATIVE DIPLOMACY (Conflict prevention) | | |

Kosovo, 1993

Cambodia, 1995

Rapprochement

POST-CONFLICT PEACE BUILDING (Conflict resolution)

| STABLE PEACE (Basic order) | PEACETIME DIPLOMACY OR POLITICS | *Rising tension* | |

South Africa, 1995

US – China, 1995

Reconciliation

| DURABLE PEACE (Just order) | US – Britain, 20th century | | |

Duration of conflict

Early stage   Mid-conflict   Late stage

Figure 12.1 Life-history of conflicts and phases of diplomatic engagement

Source: Lund (2008: 290)

would not have been more appropriate and feasible to apply in 1990 to prevent the conflict from turning violent a few years later.

By contrast, the 2008 conflict in South Ossetia challenged the time sequence between direct and structural prevention from the other end. By the time it violently reignited in the summer of 2008, the Georgian–Ossetian conflict had been lying relatively dormant for sixteen years with the help of a joint force of peacekeepers, generous economic assistance and technical support from the EU, the US, the World Bank and the UNDP. These efforts proved insufficient though to convince the Georgian government led by President Mikheil Saakashvili to continue to comply with the terms of the 1992 ceasefire and to avoid reuniting the country by force. The main lesson to draw from this case is probably that confidence in structural prevention should not stifle international vigilance about re-engaging in direct prevention when the conditions on the ground significantly shift. Although different strategies may be necessary at distinct phases, there is a growing consensus among practitioners that an integrated approach in which both types of prevention, direct and structural, work in tandem is the most effective course of action for successful preventive diplomacy in any given conflict-affected area.

Third, aside from the scope and objectives of preventive diplomacy, there is also the thorny question of who should be authorised to conduct it. The UN is the obvious player, not only because of its long-standing experience in conflict prevention, but also because it enjoys strong international legitimacy due to its symbolic association with what is often referred to as the international community. At the same time, the UN has a propensity for engaging in 'conflict resolution from above', such as elite-based negotiations, which have been found problematic on account of the fact they have often resulted in unfortunate outcomes, including giving public legitimacy to individuals who are criminals responsible for grave human rights abuses (Aggestam 2003: 15). In addition, due to its constant financial strain, the UN has limited institutional capacity to fully engage in conflict prevention, hence the pressure it regularly faces to prioritise operation prevention (e.g., crisis management and peacekeeping) over structural and long-term engagement.

Non-governmental organisations (NGOs) have emerged after the end of the Cold War as credible partners of both states and the UN in assisting conflict resolution efforts (see Box 12.4). NGOs are able to fulfil a variety of conflict management roles by serving as early warning monitors of impending conflict, channels of communication, mediators or facilitators of official or unofficial negotiations, or promoters of the process of reconciliation through grassroots engagements (Ahmed and Potter 2006). Despite this, the relationship between NGOs and international organisations and states remains improvised and unstable. Each side remains distrustful and uncomfortable about working together, partly because they differ in their understandings

---

Box 12.4 Examples of NGO conflict prevention initiatives

- Founded in Rome, Italy, in 1968, the Community of Sant'Egidio is a religious organisation that has been involved in peace processes in Mozambique, Algeria, Guatemala, Albania, Kosovo, Burundi, Togo, Casamance and, most recently, the Democratic Republic of the Congo, Sudan, Northern Uganda and Ivory Coast. The community offers direct connections to non-state actors, especially violent ones, which find themselves without proper connectivity to the international system.
- The Carter Center established by former US President Jimmy Carter in 1982 employs a full-time staff dedicated to programmes including human rights, democracy, conflict resolution and health. Aside from its key role in monitoring elections worldwide, the Carter Center is well reputed for its ability to create direct frameworks of political dialogue among belligerent parties such as in Korea (1993), Yugoslavia (1994), Burundi (1991), Haiti (1994), Uganda (2002), Sudan (1990) and Liberia (1992).
- The Center for Humanitarian Dialogue was established in 1999 as a Swiss foundation intended to explore new concepts of humanitarian dialogue. It brings to the table senior-level diplomats and leaders of armed groups to resolve their differences peacefully, while discreetly managing these processes. Since 1999, the Center has been involved in peacebuilding activities, including mediation, in Asia, Africa, Latin America, the Balkans and the Middle East, and developed humanitarian ceasefire agreements in Darfur and 'cessation of hostility' agreements in Aceh.
- The Crisis Management Initiative (CMI) was founded in 2002 by former President of Finland, Martti Ahtisaari, as an organisation that works to strengthen the capacity of the international community in crisis management and conflict resolution by using traditional settings and innovative strategies of engagement. The most prominent activity of mediation undertaken by CMI was in Aceh where President Ahtisaari offered the effective formula of 'self-government' as a way to frame the parameters of a solution amenable to all parties.

(Bartoli 2008)

of diplomacy and conflict resolution and partly because they speak to different constituencies. There are, for example, many governments who evaluate information emanating from NGOs as inaccurate and unbalanced because NGOs are considered to have their own agendas, which do not conform to the views held by many governments (Aggestam 2003: 19).

International criminal justice

Preventive diplomacy is supposed to assist the peaceful evolution of the international order by anticipating threats to international peace and security and eliminating them before they take place. International criminal justice (ICrJ) (→ glossary) is supposed to facilitate peaceful change by acting much deeper. The purpose of ICrJ is not merely to dispute the effectiveness of the use of force, but also its legitimacy. In other words, actors are encouraged to forgo the use of force not only because it does not 'pay off', but also because it lacks the moral authority to serve as a legitimate instrument for settling international disputes, except for a few and very limited circumstances identified in Chapter VII of the UN Charter (see also Chapter 3). Arguably, ICrJ faces a more difficult challenge than preventive diplomacy in facilitating peaceful change largely because states are notoriously jealous of their sovereignty and, hence, they are very suspicious of any attempt to seriously weaken their legal instruments of protection against external interference.

Recent research suggests, though, that international law is not epiphenomenal to states' interests and their willingness to restrain their resort to military force, but it actually plays a central role in peaceful dispute resolution. For example, the strength of the legal claim has been found to be the decisive factor in determining whether parties will seek to resolve their dispute peacefully or by force. Disputes that are marked by an asymmetry in the strength of the parties' legal claims are more likely, for instance, to be resolved than disputes where neither side can marshal a compelling legal case for the contested territory (Huth *et al.* 2011: 433). These are, of course, encouraging findings, but they raise the further question of how to boost the authority of legal norms in a way that it maximises their impact on international actors' behaviour with respect to the use of force.

The solution to be discussed in this section is international criminal justice which, broadly speaking, refers to the doctrines by which international law imposes criminal responsibility directly upon individuals, regardless of the national law (Broomhall 2003: 10). The institution at the centre of ICrJ is the International Criminal Court (ICC), the first permanent, treaty-based, criminal court with international jurisdiction, to help end impunity for the perpetrators of the most serious crimes of concern to the international community (ICC 2002). The ICC is an instructive case to examine from a diplomatic perspective for two important reasons. First, the long and convoluted negotiation process preceding the establishment of the ICC offers an excellent opportunity for understanding why diplomats may succeed in forging strong international legal norms, despite occasional setbacks and states' resistance. Second, the evaluation of the ICC's performance thus far sheds light on why ICrJ still remains a work in progress and what kind of challenges may lie ahead for diplomats to transform the ICC into a solid instrument of international order and peaceful change.

How can we make sense of the establishment of the ICC? The creation of the Court illustrates very well how diplomats, putting to use existing international law, may come to converge on new international law. Benjamin Schiff captures this process with a very apt metaphor. He contends that it was a 'river of justice' that led to the creation of the ICC (Schiff 2008). The streams feeding the river are evolving sets of established international law. From the mid-nineteenth to the early twentieth century, there was the growing codification of *ius in bello*. During the negotiations for the 1864 Geneva Convention, judicial panels were proposed to overlook compliance but the proposal did not make it into the Convention. Before WWII, two more Geneva Conventions followed (1906 and 1929) as well as the two Hague Conventions (1899 and 1907). The 1928 Kellogg-Briand Pact focused on *ius ad bellum* and outlawed war 'as an instrument of national policy'. During the same time period, the institutionalisation of permanent international courts began. The Permanent Court of Arbitration (1899) and the Permanent Court of International Justice (1922) were created as facilitators for the peaceful resolution of inter-state disputes.

International responses to a shocking event constituted another stream. WWI allies took a stance during the Armenian Genocide. On 24 May 1915, they sent the following message via the then still neutral US to the Ottoman government:

> In view of those new crimes of Turkey against humanity and civilization, the Allied governments announce publicly to the Sublime-Porte that they will hold personally responsible [for] these crimes all members of the Ottoman government and those of their agents who are implicated [involved] in such massacres.
> (quoted in Schiff 2008: 20)

The formulation 'hold personally responsible' is of key importance. It is not that any of these threats ever materialised. The 1923 Treaty of Lausanne extended amnesties to those who could have been held responsible. But an idea had entered diplomatic discourse that would not go away.

At a League of Nations conference in 1933, the Polish prosecutor Rafael Lemkin proposed the definition of the international 'crime of barbarity'. In a later book, written during WWII, Lemkin coined a neologism: genocide. At the same time, NGOs moved into the same direction. In the mid-1920s, the European Inter-Parliamentary Union and the International Association of Penal Law made proposals for the Permanent Court of Justice to extend its jurisdiction over states and individuals to the crime of aggression. In 1937, it seemed that these initiatives would pay off. The League of Nations adopted a treaty for the creation of an international criminal court. But with too many states refusing to ratify it, the treaty never entered into force.

Germany's and Japan's horrific war crimes, and especially the Holocaust, pushed the question of individual responsibility onto the agenda. German and Japanese perpetrators were tried at the Nuremberg Trials and Tokyo Trials, respectively. It is especially the Nuremberg Trials that set an important precedent in international law. The Trials dealt with four categories of crimes: participation in crimes against peace; planning, initiating and waging wars of aggression; war crimes; and crimes against humanity. These four categories were defined in an agreement among the US, the Soviet Union, Great Britain and France, reached at the London Conference in 1945. On the one hand, the four powers applied existing law, such as the Kellogg-Briand Pact as well as the Geneva and Hague Conventions. On the other hand, they developed the legal understanding of international crimes further by including the category of crimes against humanity. This time, holding someone accountable for genocide was not just an empty threat as it had still been in the Ottoman case. This time, the offenders really were held responsible and there was a legal category in place that enabled a Court to do so.

As Schiff shows, these streams of law swell further in the post-WWII era (see Box 12.5). Much of this happened under the umbrella of the UN. The Convention on the Prevention and Punishment of the Crime of Genocide and the Universal Declaration of Human Rights were giant steps towards protecting innocent people and holding perpetrators accountable. The ILC, a body of legal experts assisting the General Assembly to progressively develop and codify international law, submitted a draft statute for an international criminal court to the General Assembly in 1954. Yet the initiative stalled amid the tensions of the Cold War. From the 1970s onwards, civil society movements – especially in the West – pressured for a more peaceful world. Organisations such as Amnesty International became voices to be taken seriously. These voices have vigorously advocated for legal instruments such as the Convention against Genocide and the Universal Declaration of Human Rights to be implemented, and have provided important information on states' records in doing so.

With the end of the Cold War came a different opportunity structure for creating an international criminal court. The Security Council – much more cooperative in the 1990s than in the decades before – authorised the creation of the International Criminal Tribunal for the former Yugoslavia and the International Criminal Tribunal

---

Box 12.5 The negotiation process of Rome Statute establishing the International Criminal Court (ICC)

- 1948: the UNGA adopts the Convention on the Prevention and Punishment of the Crime of Genocide.
- 1948–1989: Initiatives for establishing an International Criminal Court abandoned within the context of the Cold War.
- 1989: proposal resurrected by Trinidad and Tobago.
- 1994: at the request of the UN General Assembly, the ILC prepares a preliminary draft.
- 1996–1998: six sessions held at the UN HQ by the Preparatory Committee (established by the UNGA) to prepare a consolidated draft.
- 1997: the UNGA decides to convene the UN Conference of Plenipotentiaries on the establishment of an ICC.
- 17 June–17 July 1998: 160 countries participate in the negotiations and 200 NGOs closely monitor these discussions; 120 nations vote in favour of the adoption of the Rome Statute of the ICC, with seven nations voting against the treaty (including the US, Israel, China, Iraq and Qatar) and twenty-one states abstaining.
- 11 April 2002: the sixtieth ratification necessary to trigger the entry into force of the Rome Statute was deposited by several states in conjunction.
- 1 July 2002: the treaty enters into force.

for Rwanda. The creation of these *ad hoc* tribunals, the first ones since Nuremberg and Tokyo, originally expected to be more of a gesture towards international justice than substantial progress, generated momentum for a permanent international criminal court. The ILC, directed by the Cambridge-based legal scholar James Crawford, prepared a draft ICC statute. Sometimes referred to as the 'father of international criminal law', Mahmoud Cherif Bassiouni – also a legal scholar – involved NGOs and discussed with them how to develop this draft further in a meeting in Siracusa, Italy. It then took four more years, from 1994 to 1998, for the diplomats of states to agree on a statute. They did so in a final round of negotiations in Rome in 1998.

Let us zoom in on one single diplomat at these negotiations: Philippe Kirsch. The Canadian diplomat with extensive multilateral experience was the chairman of this final round of negotiations. He used the prerogatives of the chairman very effectively. He encouraged the input from NGOs, which pushed for a strong ICC (i.e., a court with an independent prosecutor and the ability to initiate investigations without Security Council approval). He crafted a package deal out of proposals of like-minded states in favour of establishing a meaningful ICC and defended this deal with all procedural powers at his disposal; in a controversial move, for instance, he refused to send potentially contentious parts of the package to the Drafting Committee, in order to keep the whole package intact. He was very prudent in choosing the right point in time to fight off hostile amendments from the Indian and American delegations; in what is a rather unusual move given UN practices, he put the amendments to the vote, which were defeated by 'enormous majorities' (Washburn 1999: 372).

All of these moves proved crucial for the adoption of the Rome Statute. But these moves alone – and Kirsch alone – could not have accomplished anything. The dynamics among the delegations played into the hands of Kirsch. The Like-Minded Group (LMG) was a group of states advocating together for the ICC. Another approximately twenty states closely cooperated with the LMG. There was also close cooperation between these states and the NGO Coalition for an International Criminal Court (→ glossary). Taken together, they formed a key negotiating bloc. This bloc was supported by the UN Secretariat, especially the Secretary-General, who argued that the ICC would be an important institution for upholding the UN Charter. The US, by contrast, was a rather isolated player in this arena, finding it very difficult to shape the negotiation process. In other words, for all of Kirsch's prudence, there is something that made a great majority move in the same direction. And this something is the evolution of the law on which the Rome Statute is built. On 17 July 1998, 120 states adopted the Rome Statute. After being ratified by sixty states, it came into force on 1 July 2002. Since then, 121 states have become parties to the Statute of the Court, a fact that speaks well of its worldwide support, especially in South America, Europe and partially in Africa and Asia.

Three important lessons can be derived from the long and tortuous process of negotiation of the ICC. First, historical events are decisive in creating opportunities for change that can lead to the creation of robust norms of international law (i.e., Schiff's 'rivers of justice'). The role of diplomats under the circumstances is informed by two contrasting conditions: on the one hand, they are best placed to seize opportunities opened up by international crises and to build diplomatic momentum behind initiatives to strengthen international law; on the other hand, as state representatives, they are less likely to enthusiastically pursue and negotiate agreements that would significantly constrain state actions. This tension leads to the second lesson: non-state actors play a key role in keeping ICrJ issues on the international agenda and in facilitating coalitions among state and non-state actors that can deliver results. Without the efforts of Lemkin, IAPL, Bassiouni and the CICC, the ICC would have likely remained in the project phase to this very day. Third, diplomatic work is not concluded with the signing of the agreement. As illustrated by the situation of the thirty-two states that signed the Rome Statute but have not ratified it yet (including Israel, Sudan and the US of America which have 'unsigned' the treaty), the future of the ICC much depends on its ability to maintain diplomatic consensus regarding its relevance for upholding international peace and ensuring peaceful change.

What did negotiators of the Rome Statute agree upon? First of all, they approved the scope of the ICC's jurisdiction, which includes four categories of crimes: genocide, crimes against humanity, war crimes and aggression (the Court will not be able to exercise its jurisdiction over this crime until after 1 January 2017). Second, the negotiators decided the composition and organisation of the ICC. The eighteen judges working at the ICC are split into three Judicial Divisions, i.e. the Pre-Trial, Trial and Appeals Divisions. The President and two Vice-Presidents are recruited from among the judges. Including administrative staff, the Court has over 700 employees. Third, and critically important, the Rome Statute introduced the Office of the Prosecutor (OTP) (→ glossary), which is headed by an independent Prosecutor and assisted by the Deputy Prosecutor. The main duty of the Prosecutor is 'to establish the truth, extend the investigation to cover all facts and evidence relevant to an assessment of whether there is criminal responsibility under [the] Statute, and, in doing so, [to] investigate incriminating and exonerating circumstances equally' (Article 54.1a, UN 2012).

It is difficult to overestimate the novelty and significance of this permanent criminal court. The usefulness of the ICC is not only retroactive by virtue of its capacity to provide justice to victims. The ICC has also a preventive character by instituting a credible threat of prosecution aimed to deter many would-be perpetrators of gross human rights abuses. To be sure, the ICC is anything but a guarantee that all perpetrators of horrific international crimes will be put behind bars. Some crucial states, including China, Russia and the US, stand outside of the Rome Statute and, thus, in principle, put their citizens outside of the regime as well. The Security Council (and with it the Permanent Five) has the right of referral, which seems to amount to a *de facto* veto against Court proceedings in particular cases. Finally, the complementarity rule stipulated in Article 17(a) give states some discretion in avoiding the ICC jurisdiction as long as they show ability and willingness to carry out the investigation or prosecution on its own.

Nonetheless, the Rome Statute is a landmark in the evolution of international law. It clearly recognises that it is not states that ultimately do the acting in global politics but human beings. These human beings sometimes commit terrible wrongs. The Court is 'determined to put an end to impunity for the perpetrators of these crimes and thus to contribute to the prevention of such crimes', as the Preamble of the Rome Statute puts it. This applies to the above-listed categories of crimes, no matter whether they were perpetrated in an intra-state or an inter-state situation. Indeed, all the situations listed above deal with the former rather than the latter. Some time ago, Friedrich Kratochwil pointed out correctly that sovereignty, in its Westphalian variant, includes a government's 'right to do wrong' within one's boundaries (Kratochwil 1995). The creation of the ICC shows that this absolute understanding of sovereignty is a thing of the past. Our understanding of sovereignty has moved towards 'sovereignty as responsibility' (→ glossary) long before the Rome Statute was ratified.

At the same time, the future of the ICC remains uncertain in the face of a serious diplomatic challenge: how to maintain support among its members and prevent further defections. As pointed out above, the thirty-two states that signed the Rome Statute in 1998 have not ratified it yet, while three of them (Israel, Sudan and the US) have even 'unsigned' the treaty. As most other international organisations, the ICC does not possess any instruments of hard power to ensure compliance with its objectives, procedures and decisions. The best the ICC can do is to rely on the 'soft power' generated by its ability to deliver justice in an effective, impartial, consistent manner. Therefore, the future of the ICC is contingent on diplomatic efforts to enhance the legitimacy of the Court in the eyes of its members, both in the short and in the long term. As a first priority, the ICC needs to address concerns over the perceived investigation bias. Thus far, fourteen cases, distributed over seven situations, have been brought before the ICC. All cases and situations deal though with events taking place on the African continent, i.e. in Uganda, Democratic Republic of the Congo, Sudan, Central African Republic, Kenya, Libya and Côte d'Ivoire. The best known of these situations is probably the one concerning Sudan. In response to the policies of the Sudanese President Al Bashir during the Darfur Crisis, Chamber I of the Pre-Trial Division has issued an arrest warrant against him. Al Bashir is the first sitting head of state charged with genocide by the ICC.

The fact that Africans have featured prominently on the ICC's lists has not gone unnoticed, especially among African leaders. Rwandan President Paul Kagame once said the ICC was 'put in place only for African countries', while AU Commission chief Jean Ping complained about Africa being made 'an example to the world' (Jacinto 15 March 2012). Under the leadership of the current Prosecutor, Fatou Bensouda, a Gambian lawyer who previously held the position of Deputy Prosecutor between 2004 and 2012, the ICC has expanded its scope of scrutiny to non-African states as well. In addition to Guinea, Nigeria and Mali, the OTP is currently conducting preliminary examination of cases in Afghanistan, Georgia, Colombia, Honduras and Korea. Successful prosecution of non-African cases could boost the legitimacy of the Court in the short term, but more sweeping measures arguably need to be taken in the long term in order to solidify the reputation of the Court as an indispensable legal instrument of international order. Greater cooperation and mutual understanding between the ICC and its member states could be fostered in three ways.

From a *communication* perspective, a well-designed programme of first- and second-track public diplomacy is much needed to explain the Court's mission and procedure, especially in countries located in conflict-ridden regions. Victims of violence in Uganda perceive, for instance, the ICC to be 'so far away that the people do not know the procedures and they do not mean anything to the communities'. As a result, they fear the 'ICC does not cement relationships among the communities in the region [and ...] does not help national reconciliation' (OHCHR 2007: 63–64). Current ICC outreach programmes such as the joint seminars organised by the ICC and the AU and the information campaigns organised in situation-related countries, are a step in the right direction, but they are mostly uni-directional (e.g., they explain what the ICC does and why). Second-track initiatives at the community level that address concerns over the impact of the Court's decisions on the reconciliation process are much needed in order to close the expectation gap between the mission of the Court and the justice concerns of the communities affected by the crimes.

From a *representation* perspective, the Court would benefit from extending its presence through field or liaison offices in regions and areas of concern. A network of offices would undoubtedly serve the ICC by assisting it in gathering information about potential cases, conducting investigations and in engaging in first- or second-track initiatives of public diplomacy. Cognizant of this, the ICC has already established four field offices in Congo, Chad, Uganda and Central African Republic and one Liaison Office to the UN. However, the existing field offices are severely underfunded and operate under a narrow mandate of outreach programmes. More is clearly needed to increase the ICC profile in countries and regions of interest. One solution could be the negotiation of Cooperation Agreements between the ICC and key supporting countries and regional organisations (e.g., Canada, EU, Japan, Australia, Brazil, the AU) for the purpose of facilitating diplomatic logistic support. The 2005 EU–ICC Co-operation and Assistance Agreement provides a good template for such collaboration. According to Article 14, the EU agrees to provide the Court, upon its request, with 'such facilities and services as may be required, including, where appropriate, support at the field level' (Council of the EU 2005).

Finally, from a *negotiation* perspective, the ICC ought to take steps to encourage at least the passive if not the full collaboration of key countries that currently stand outside its framework such as the US, China and Russia. One way of doing this is by member states agreeing to extend the Court's jurisdiction over terrorist acts through, for instance, an amendment to the Statute that would encode terrorism as a crime against humanity (systematic attack against the civilian population). As Steven C. Roach points out, the ICC's complementary role in the struggle against terrorism would operate on two levels. The ICC could either pursue judicial proceedings against the perpetrators of crimes against humanity, or it could actively adjudicate cases involving the treatment of suspected terrorists being detained in controversial facilities such as that at Guantanamo Bay (Roach 2009: 234). As countries that have both faced strong international criticism over their methods of dealing with perpetrators of terrorist acts, the US and Russia might welcome ICC involvement and agree to negotiate separate agreements of cooperation, at least for situations involving low-priority suspects. American and Russian collaboration would also make it difficult for China to openly oppose ICC investigations, even though it would not directly benefit from the extension of its jurisdiction.

Summary

- Diplomats help remake the world for the better if they reduce or eliminate the use of force as a means for resolving international disputes. Preventive diplomacy has emerged in the post-Cold-War period as a proactive application of the principle of collective security. It aims to prevent disputes from escalating into conflicts and to limit the spread of conflicts when they occur via three components: mediation and 'good offices' initiatives, peacekeeping operations and post-conflict reconstruction.

- International criminal justice refers to the doctrines by which international law imposes criminal responsibility directly upon individuals, regardless of the national law. On the one hand, ICrJ makes clear that certain types of crimes (against peace, war crimes, crimes against humanity or genocide) are international crimes and hence they may be prosecuted before both national and international courts. On the other hand, the relationship between national and international courts is complicated, not only by conditions over how the jurisdiction between the two systems of courts is to be exercised, but also by the political role of the UN Security Council in potentially limiting recourse to courts in certain situations.

- Measures to enhance the legitimacy of the ICC include: successful prosecution of non-African cases in order to address growing concerns over the perceived ICC investigation bias; a well-designed programme of first- and second-track public diplomacy to better explain the Court's mission and procedure, especially in countries located in conflict-ridden regions; the extension of the presence of the Court through field or liaison offices in regions and areas of concern; and proactive steps to encourage at least the passive, if not the full, collaboration of key countries that currently stand outside its framework such as the US, China and Russia.

Study questions

- Is it possible for diplomats to remake the world for the better? If yes, what would that involve?
- Should diplomats be involved not only in conducting mediation and 'good offices' but also in peacekeeping and peacebuilding?
- What tensions exist between direct and structural prevention and how should diplomats deal with them?
- What is the relationship between international criminal justice and diplomacy?
- What diplomatic measures are necessary for increasing the effectiveness and legitimacy of the International Criminal Court?

Recommended further reading

Bercovitch Jacob, Viktor Aleksandrovich Kremeniuk and I. William Zartma (eds). 2008. *The Sage handbook of conflict resolution.* Thousand Oaks, CA: Sage Publications.
This book brings together various conceptual, methodological and substantive elements of conflict resolution into one volume of over thirty-five specially commissioned chapters.

Cassese, Antonio. 2009. *The Oxford companion to international criminal justice.* Oxford and New York: Oxford University Press.
This book provides a thorough overview of the emerging field of international criminal justice. The first part offers a comprehensive survey of issues and debates surrounding international humanitarian law, international criminal law and their enforcement. The second part contains over 400 case summaries on different trials from international and domestic courts dealing with war crimes, crimes against humanity, genocide, torture and terrorism.

Hampson, Fen Osler and David Malone (eds). 2002. *From reaction to conflict prevention: Opportunities for the UN system.* Boulder, CO: Lynne Rienner Publishers.
In this book the authors consider the causes and dynamics of war, the tools that are being developed to predict the outbreak of conflict, and what is being done to enhance conflict prevention within the UN system.

Schiff, Benjamin N. 2008. *Building the international criminal court.* Cambridge and New York: Cambridge University Press.
The book analyses the International Criminal Court, melding historical perspective, international relations theories and observers' insights to explain the Court's origins, creation, innovations, dynamics and operational challenges. The author also examines how the Court seeks to combine divergent legal traditions in an entirely new international legal mechanism.

UN Department of Political Affairs. 2012. *Preventive diplomacy report: Delivering results* (accessed 20 March 2012). Available at http://www.un.org/wcm/content/site/undpa/main/issues/preventive_diplomacy /main_preventive.
In this report, UN Secretary-General Ban Ki-moon describes the growing importance of preventive diplomacy for the UN and its partners, underscoring its potential to save lives and protect development gains at a low cost to the international community.

Part VI
Conclusion

13 Towards inclusive diplomacy

Studying diplomacy as communication

This book is titled *Understanding International Diplomacy*. What is there actually to understand about diplomacy? In a nutshell, our answer to this question is communication. Or, more precisely put, a peculiar kind of communication: diplomacy is institutionalised communication. It is communication among internationally recognised representatives of internationally recognised entities. The communication is about the public good, it involves the production of decisions, relations and global norms, and it is not confined by the boundaries of the state. This conclusion summarises how we propose to study diplomacy as communication, discusses how our proposal differs from other textbooks and monographs on diplomacy, juxtaposes diplomacy with its conceptual nemesis, anti-diplomacy, and introduces the concept of inclusive diplomacy as a possible framework for addressing the challenges that lie ahead for doing and studying diplomacy.

Communication constituting diplomacy and shaping world politics has evolved over time. To mention just the most important landmark developments, the emergence of sovereign statehood provided an impetus for establishing resident embassies that represent these sovereign states abroad. Trying to cope with disaster and learning the lessons of history has transformed diplomacy at several critical junctures. Perhaps most importantly, lessons learnt from WWI singled out secretive practices as causes of war, and embraced the belief in institution-building, above all collective security mechanisms, as a vehicle for leaving an age of major wars behind. More recently, ever-increasing flows of globalisation have stretched the perimeters of diplomacy. We are witnessing a double-multiplication: one of issue areas and one of actors.

The double-multiplication increases the complexity of diplomacy. Indicating this complexity, we frequently use the term 'diplomatic field' when we address the global age of diplomacy. Navigating this field for the purpose of doing research is not an easy thing to do. We provide a simple map for helping us do so. The map consists of two major building blocks: context and tasks. The context consists of international public law as well as the repertoire of ideas that practitioners take so much for granted and which largely inform how diplomats think about issues in global politics and what to do about them. We refer to this repertoire as deeper backgrounds. The context helps actors orient themselves in the diplomatic field and perform their tasks. All their tasks revolve around communication. We distinguish four clusters of tasks, i.e. messaging, negotiating, mediating and talking. Each of these clusters can be specified further. Talk, for example, is about cheap talk, rhetorical strategies, persuasive attempts and dialogue. Performing these tasks, in turn, does something to the context. Some performances simply reproduce it as is. Others push and shove it in different directions.

The map provides us with clues for what basic units for analysis to look out for when studying diplomacy. The diplomat is embedded in context. This context shapes the agency of the diplomat (performance of tasks) and these, in turn, re-shape the context. But all of this is still at a rather high level of abstraction. Explaining diplomatic outcomes requires more zooming in. We discuss explanations for three degrees of complexity: decisions, relations and world. When diplomats perform their tasks, they make decisions. But how do they make their decisions? We provided the reader with an overview of ongoing debates in the social sciences about what makes agents tick. Four logics of action feature prominently in these debates: consequences, appropriateness, argumentation and practice. Discussing empirical cases revolving around questions whether to continue diplomacy or go to war, we highlighted the strengths and weaknesses of these logics, and made a case for creative eclecticism.

There are few terms that are as closely associated with diplomacy as relations. It matters whether relations between states are good or bad, whether they are close or distanced, amicable or hostile, and so on. To a very considerable extent, diplomacy communicates these relations into being. We put three different schools of thought under scrutiny that – explicitly or implicitly – deal with the diplomatic making of relations: Realism, Liberalism and Constructivism. To put it very simply, for a (Classical) Realist the art of making relations revolves around standing apart and balancing; for a Liberal it is about cooperation and even integration; and for a Constructivist it is about generating community. We empirically illustrated the strengths and weaknesses of these frameworks by discussing the evolution of the relations between North Korea and the US, the coordination of the EU Foreign Policy and the dramatic worsening of relations between Eritrea and Ethiopia.

Diplomats not only take decisions and make relations, but they also shape the world we live in. They do this at two levels. At the deeper level, diplomats help engineer, legitimate and reproduce organising principles of global politics, that is shared understandings about who has the right to create global order, by what means and how responsibilities for upholding global order should be distributed among the stakeholders ('order as value'). At the policy level, they apply these principles to build a stable and regular pattern of global activities and institutions ('order as fact'). By forging relationships of friendship, rivalry and enmity among states, diplomats establish 'order as fact' via competing cultures of anarchy. By establishing international deontologies ('order as value'), diplomats define, in turn, what objectives (security, redistribution or recognition) are important for them to pursue in a particular historical context and what strategies are most appropriate to use to that end.

It would be misleading to think that diplomacy is only about shaping international affairs. It is also, although to a lesser degree, about shaping domestic affairs. Since the end of the Cold War, the re-shaping of political systems in a number of states has preoccupied diplomats, especially at the UN. We are witnessing a new age of interventionism. External intervention is often aimed at remaking states: turning authoritarian systems into democratic ones and replacing war with peace. This raises thorny normative questions. When is intervention warranted? What ought to be the end of such interventions? What ought to be the means used to attain this end?

Discussing these questions, we developed three concepts: societal authorship; peace as restraint, compromise and dialogue; and adaptive repertoire. Taken together, these concepts emphasise that diplomacy ought to reach far – our definition of peace is ambitious – and, at the same time, refrain from superimposing one-size-fits-all recipes onto a highly diverse universe of cases.

As the international order evolves, so does the role of the diplomat. These transformations have invited debates about the principles of guiding what issues become subject of diplomatic representation, who is to be recognised as a diplomat, how diplomats are to relate with each other and how they should be recruited and trained in order to effectively face these challenges. The answers we have discussed are not free from controversy. Diplomats have to balance how to represent the interests of their governments while also considering the impact the representation of these interests may have on the international order. The relationship between paradiplomacy and conventional diplomacy remains ambiguous. They may grow together ('catalytic' diplomacy), follow different tracks ('postdiplomacy') or stay in conflict with each other ('contested diplomacy'). 'Smart power' is likely to emerge as an important tool of diplomatic influence by bringing together hard and soft power via the strategic and simultaneous use of coercion and co-option. The success of the twenty-first-century diplomat therefore much depends on the way in which diplomatic recruitment, promotion and training would manage to adapt to these new circumstances.

Last but not least, diplomats also play an important role in the peaceful remaking of the world. Diplomats have now two important instruments at their disposal by which they can reduce the use of violence, both internationally and domestically: preventive diplomacy and international criminal justice. The former is supposed to assist the peaceful evolution of the international order by addressing the direct and structural incentives for resorting to violence. By imposing criminal responsibility directly upon individuals, the latter aims not only to deter actors from resorting to violence in the short term, but also to undermine the legal and moral legitimacy of the method of using force for settling disputes in the long term. Both approaches remain though controversial. On the one hand, the extension of preventive diplomacy from 'good offices' to peacekeeping and peacebuilding might involve a fundamental revision of diplomatic tasks, which few practitioners might agree with. On the other hand, the relationship between diplomacy and international criminal justice remains inchoate, not least due to the difficulties experienced by the International Criminal Court in accomplishing its mission and in maintaining the support of its members.

Adding to our understanding

The purpose of this book was not only to take stock of the literature on diplomacy. It was also to discuss how to apply sets of literature to the study of diplomacy that are usually applied to political and social phenomena other than diplomacy. In other words, we took a detailed look at the existing tools for how to study diplomacy as well as added new tools to the toolbox. We took these new tools from inside and outside of political science and international relations, reaching into adjacent disciplines such as communications, economics, law, ethics, psychology and sociology.

This helped us address a number of issues that otherwise remain marginalised or entirely neglected. Three are particularly noteworthy. First, diplomats do much more than negotiating and mediating. There is no question about it that these are key tasks of the diplomat. But there are other key tasks as well. We dealt with them under the headings of *messaging* and *talk*. Messaging – especially the kind with lots of room for interpretation for the messenger and the receiver of the message – can have major constitutive effects. Diplomatic talk is anything but inconsequential either. Cheap talk and rhetorical strategies, for example, have major consequences for the outcomes of negotiations. More generally, different forms of talk also have system-relevant consequences. They contribute to reproducing orders, ranging from a narrowly confined issue area such as nuclear non-proliferation to the *raison de système* more broadly.

Second, it is not enough to discuss diplomatic tasks (as important as they are), but we also have to pay attention to diplomatic contexts in general, and to *deeper backgrounds* in particular. The context constitutes diplomacy and diplomats. It provides orientation for diplomats about how to make up their minds and how to act. Part of the context consists of law, especially public international law (and, here, diplomatic law) or, more recently, international criminal law. This part of the context is very much out in the open. Diplomats are experts in law. This applies to as foundational a legal text as the UN Charter as much as it applies to the nitty-gritty details of the rules of procedure of a particular committee, or to how to deal with suspected war criminals. Another part of the context, much more easily overlooked but as important, is the deeper background in which diplomats are embedded. Diplomats take many ideas for granted. Without doing so, they would be unable to act. Seemingly self-evident ideas serve as their compass for navigating the diplomatic stage. International deontologies (status-functions and deontic powers) shape, for instance, the broader context in which diplomats learn about how to address fundamental questions of international security, redistribution or status recognition.

Third, studying diplomacy is not just about how things are, but also about how they *ought to be*. Diplomacy is full of important normative questions. What political issues to put on the diplomatic agenda, where to put them, how to deal with them – all of these are political decisions with strong normative dimensions, no matter whether these are acknowledged or not. Some normative decisions pertain to a narrowly confined issue, for instance developing the institution of Additional Protocols in the nuclear non-proliferation regime. Others are very broad in nature. How diplomats ensure peaceful transformations of the international order is, for example, an absolute key question for diplomacy. Similarly, who has the right to be recognised as a diplomat in an increasingly globalised world or what forms of power are appropriate for diplomatic intercourse are questions that fundamentally challenge how diplomacy is supposed to be practised in the twenty-first century. Scholars and practitioners alike tend to dismiss addressing these broad normative questions all too easily as being purely 'philosophical' and, thus, outside of the realm of diplomacy. We would submit that it is precisely these philosophical questions that we have to address in a much more nuanced manner because they constitute the foundations of our international order.

Anti-diplomacy

For a book examining the instruments, institutions and processes that make diplomacy work, it may appear odd to conclude it with a discussion about its conceptual nemesis, anti-diplomacy. We do this for two reasons. On the one hand, when diplomats act they do it against a wall of public expectations, both domestic and international, about what objectives *not* to pursue and how they are *not* supposed to perform their tasks. A brief examination of these issues helps shed light on the risks the diplomats may take in breaching these expectations and the methods they may employ to avoid such outcomes. On the other hand, the juxtaposition of conventional diplomatic methods with their opposites is also instructive for providing a framework for assessing the quality of diplomatic endeavours. While diplomatic methods vary in scope and effectiveness, sometimes a certain type of 'anti-diplomatic' behaviour may help 'shake things up' and provide a much needed 'jolt' to stalled negotiations or bland methods of diplomatic communication.

As we pointed out in Chapter 1, our definition of diplomacy encompasses four components: institutionalised communication, double recognition, focus on delivering public goods and productive capacity (i.e., making decisions, relations and global norms). In line with this understanding of diplomacy, we define anti-diplomacy as the set of practices, instruments and processes that significantly challenge diplomatic competences for communication, legitimate representation, public good management and international cooperation. But what does this mean concretely? From a communication perspective, anti-diplomacy implies the erosion of the dialogical quality of diplomatic intercourse. As discussed in Chapter 6, the most important resource diplomats have is the power of the word, whether that is expressed through messaging, negotiation, mediation or talk. This power can be taken away from diplomats when communication turns from dialogue to monologue. Diplomats may still engage each other communicatively, but they talk past each other, failing to take notice of each other's arguments, or even refusing to acknowledge the right of the other side to speak. The abrasive and antagonistic talk between the US and its European allies at the height of the Iraq crisis in 2003 is a clear example of anti-diplomatic communication (Bjola 2010: 200–202).

From a representation perspective, anti-diplomacy is about pursuing strategies aimed at subverting or even delegitimising the right to sovereignty of political communities that meet the Montevideo conditions of statehood (see Box 1.1) *and* the collective recognition of the majority of other states. The key function of diplomatic representation is not to make two actors like each other or even work together, but to provide an institutional channel by which they can raise concerns about each other's policies and so that they can address them before they become unruly. When such recognition is subverted or declined, exactly the opposite happens. The estranged relationship between the two political communities only continues to aggravate, paving the way for a possible violent resolution of the dispute. The use of Iranian consulates for the distribution of arms to political allies in the Lebanon and Muslim republics of the former Soviet Union (Sharp 2009: 31) or the refusal by the Iranian government to even acknowledge the right of existence of Israel are examples of anti-diplomatic behaviour.

From a public good perspective, anti-diplomacy implies a consistent effort to exploit diplomatic institutional channels and resources for private ends in a manner that critically undermines diplomats' capacity to provide public goods. As discussed in Chapter 4, diplomacy has changed significantly in the past century and it continues to evolve. It now has to cope not only with matters of war and peace, but also with serious issues of economic and financial governance, development, environment, global health and migration. These are core global public goods that require sustained and concerted action at different diplomatic levels: bilateral, regional or multilateral. When diplomatic instruments are being hijacked in pursuit of private ends, either at the individual or corporate level, the provision of goods that are beneficial for the international order to reproduce itself is being left out. In extreme situations, the validity of international treaties might even come into question – as per Article 50 of the 1969 Vienna Convention on the Law of Treaties – if diplomats are found to be involved in acts of corruption.

Finally, from the prospective of the ability of diplomats to be productive in making decisions, relations or global norms, anti-diplomacy goes beyond the quantitative dimension of the process (whether diplomats are effective in concluding treaties) and also refers to its qualitative aspect (whether the decisions, relations or norms produced by diplomats assist or not political communities to live peacefully together despite their differences). Obviously, the boundary between diplomacy and anti-diplomacy is more difficult to prescribe in this case as diplomatic outcomes that may look beneficial today, may have major negative consequences tomorrow. The Responsibility to Protect (R2P), for instance, is viewed today as a potentially useful diplomatic instrument for deterring governments from abusing their own citizens. At the same time, without proper institutional restraints, it may also lead to catastrophic military interventions. The qualitative difference may well rest with how diplomats employ or not diplomatic prudence in their production of decisions, relations or norms. As pointed out in Chapter 10, systemic violations of principles of consensus-building, responsibility-taking and reasonableness are more likely than not to lead to bad outcomes.

At the same time, diplomacy has been often criticised for its laborious, slow-paced and formalistic method of addressing pressing issues of international politics. For example, the 1970 pledge of developed countries to allocate 0.7 per cent of their gross national product to Official Development Assistance has remained work in progress to the present day. Similarly, after twenty years of diplomatic talks, international negotiations on climate change are actually moving backwards despite the growing intensity of the climate crisis. In such conditions, a certain type of anti-diplomatic behaviour may actually be productive, by infusing energy in the process and motivating actors to take action. Celebrities have been particularly skilful in engaging in such anti-diplomatic behaviour through their advocacy campaigns. The series of super-concerts organised by singers Bob Geldof and Bono in the past twenty-five years as well as their unconventional public statements have been instrumental in mobilising international support for addressing debt cancellation and the deeper structural causes of poverty in Africa.

A glimpse into the future: inclusive diplomacy?

In their influential introduction to Comparative Politics, Mark Lichbach and Alan Zuckerman define the scope of Comparative Politics very comprehensively. They state that '[n]o political phenomenon is foreign to it' (Lichbach and Zuckerman 1999), and proceed to provide a whole paragraph of examples. These include civil war in Afghanistan, EU decision-making, the nexus of religion and politics, democratisation, colonialism, ethnic conflict, and so on. In contrast to Comparative Politics, of course, the study of diplomacy is not about politics contained by state borders. It is about the politics that happens across these borders (although this may have repercussions for domestic politics as well). Furthermore, the unlimited scope that Lichbach and Zuckerman postulate cannot be fully applied to the study of diplomacy. By the same token, however, it is striking that all the research areas mentioned above require a deep understanding of diplomacy. The forces of globalisation push issue areas into the realm of diplomacy that were previously squarely within the realm of domestic politics. Diplomacy has become much more than exchanges of foreign services, primarily on matters of war and peace as well as economics. Diplomacy plays a crucial role in global governance.

The diplomatic field, populated by traditional and non-traditional diplomats, is situated at the core of the steering mechanisms that are supposed to channel the forces of globalisation in warranted directions. Whether it is war, terrorism, global economic crises, alarming poverty rates, disaster relief or shocking health statistics, it depends on diplomacy whether solutions can be found to these problems or not. Diplomacy has changed crucially over the last decades. Many more issue areas have been added to the diplomatic agenda. Many more actors have entered the diplomatic field. These actors are more and more connected to actors from other fields. The Global Compact, for example, links diplomacy and international business. War to peace transitions requires diplomacy to link up to local levels of conflict management and transformation. International criminal justice forces leaders to be held accountable not only by their own people but also by the international community. Private actors (individuals, NGOs, corporations, social movements) have become increasingly vocal in asserting themselves as legitimate participants in international negotiations, crisis management and multilateral conventions.

Sometimes these deep transformations are seen as the end of diplomacy. Evidence given for this claim usually includes the pressures on foreign ministries to compete with the many new actors, including experts from other ministries (such as economics, finance and environment). We would submit that these transformations signal the end of a particular diplomatic area. Most likely than not, diplomats will increasingly have to function as facilitators and social entrepreneurs between domestic and civil society groups, to establish and manage global policy networks, and to skilfully manage the tensions to arise from the growing tendency of international interference in domestic affairs (Hocking *et al.* 2012: 6). In other words, our global age requires a different kind of diplomacy. It requires an *inclusive diplomacy* that takes its part in steering global politics carefully and thoughtfully (see Box 13.1). This is not the end of diplomacy. But it is the beginning of a new diplomatic age. We hope that our book contributes to our understanding of the perils and opportunities of this new diplomatic age.

Box 13.1 Inclusive diplomacy

- Innovative use of diplomatic networks for maximising input of legitimate state and non-state stakeholders.
- Facilitation of people-directed diplomacy as a counterpoint to elite-based interactions.
- Careful balancing of state interests and their impact on the international order.
- Qualified recognition of sovereignty subject to proper treatment by governments of their citizens.
- Consistent compliance with the provisions of international public law, especially diplomatic and international criminal law.
- Legitimate exercise of diplomatic power.
- Constructive involvement in the supply, management and distribution of global public goods.
- Scrupulous exercise of diplomatic prudence when revising, updating and adopting new principles of diplomatic conduct.

Glossary

Accreditation   In line with the 1961 Vienna Convention on Diplomatic Relations, a would-be ambassador of a sending state has to present his or her letters of credence to the host state's head of state. The signature of the latter constitutes the status of the former as ambassador in the host state. Outside the context of the state-centric Vienna Convention, accreditation processes do not only apply to state-to-state relations. NGOs, for example, seek accreditation with international organisations to attend major conferences.

Actor   Actor is a metaphor taken from drama that is widely used in social sciences to describe an individual or an anthropomorphised social or political entity (for the sake of simplification, the entity is assumed to have the faculties of a human being) that is taking part in interaction. Additionally, for many authors, the term actor also indicates that the individual or entity has the capacity to leave a mark in political encounters. The agency-structure debate links the term closely to structure (see below under structure).

Anticipatory self-defence   The customary norm of anticipatory self-defence emerged in the aftermath of the *Caroline* incident in 1837 when a British force from Canada entered US territory at night, seized the Caroline steamer and set it on fire because it was used for supplying reinforcements to armed insurgents against the British rule in Canada. According to the US Secretary of State at the time, Daniel Webster, the use of force in anticipatory self-defence must meet both criteria of imminence and proportionality. The state taking pre-emptive action would need to demonstrate that the threat of an armed attack by another state is imminent and the response is proportional to the threat (Shewmaker 1983).

Back-channel diplomacy   When it proves difficult for conflict parties to find an agreement, negotiators and mediators sometimes resort to back-channel diplomacy. This form of diplomacy is geared towards opening up new communication channels between the conflict parties. These channels have two crucial features: (1) they are shielded from the public; (2) they are shielded from possible spoilers.

Balance of power   With Realists (see below under Realism) putting a strong emphasis on this concept, the balance of power is one of the key concepts in international relations. Depending on how Realists use the term, it is also of major salience for the study of diplomacy. Waltz (1979) claims that the balance of power is a nomothetic law. Comparable to an apple falling from the tree (law of gravity), states always balance. Diplomacy has no room in this conceptualisation. For Morgenthau (1985), by contrast, the balance of power is something that occurs rather rarely and, if it does, it is due to the art of diplomacy. To some extent, current debates about off-shore balancing in the US echo Morgenthau's more diplomacy-focused conceptualisation of the balance of power.

Catalytic diplomacy One possible way of improving coordination between paradiplomacy and conventional diplomacy could be catalytic diplomacy, whereby the professional diplomat becomes a facilitator in the development of arena and actor linkages. Such symbiosis could allow both traditional diplomats and paradiplomatic actors to share critical resources, while maintaining their own identity and goals.

Coalition for an International Criminal Court Created in 1995, this NGO is composed of around 2,500 civil society organisations in 150 countries coordinated to strengthen international cooperation with the ICC, ensuring that the Court is fair, effective and independent, and advancing stronger national laws that deliver justice to victims of war crimes, genocide and crimes against humanity. The Coalition was crucial in establishing the Rome Statute and the nascent phases of the ICC and strives to increase the number of state parties in the ICC.

Coercive diplomacy As an application of a state's hard power, this type of diplomacy refers to the effort to change the objectionable behaviour of a target state or group through the credible threat of economic sanctions or the use of military force. The effectiveness of coercive diplomacy and the legitimacy of its use are both controversial, as its success rate in post-Cold-War international relations is debatable and its use is prohibited by the UN Charter.

Cold War The Cold War was the major defining feature of the post-WWII order that ended in the late 1980s. The metaphor is, for the most part, adequate when it comes to interactions between the Cold War's superpowers, i.e., the US and the Soviet Union. There were, with minor exceptions during the Korean War (and these were kept secret for a long time), no direct military clashes between them. The term is not appropriate, however, when it comes to the Third World. The US and the Soviet Union, often helped by their allies in NATO and the Warsaw Pact, respectively, fought wars by proxy in order to install or back a regime of their liking.

Collective intentionality The set of beliefs, desires and intentions shared by individuals as part of a group committed to working together, such as a group of diplomats working together to avoid a dangerous diplomatic escalation leading to a military conflict. Collective intentionality, based on 'a sense of doing [wanting, believing, etc.]' something together, as Searle explains, is important because it enables 'order as value' by collectively assigning and accepting status-functions.

Concert of Europe Established in the aftermath of the 1814 settlement of the Napoleonic Wars, this form of summit diplomacy held regular face-to-face consultation between Great Britain, Austria, Prussia, Russia and France with the purpose of maintaining peace, containing revolution and restoring the system of law in Europe. This congress system encouraged self-restraint among its members by making visible the balance of power to those who constituted it, and helped prevent a direct conflict between the Great Powers until the Crimean War in 1856.

Constructivism   A set of approaches in international relations that understands the world actors inhabit as socially constructed by these actors. Constructivist scholarship deals with context (especially what we label deeper background, i.e., taken for granted ideas), the processes through which actors come to act politically while putting this context to use and the mechanisms through which actors, acting politically, come to make and remake context. On an ontological scale from material to ideational, Constructivism leans (at times heavily) towards the ideational (see below under ontology).

Context   Actors are enabled to do what they do by the contexts in which they are embedded. These contexts constitute them as actors with a particular authority in the first place, provide them with clues for what moves to make and, more generally, provide orientation in the world. In diplomacy, two overlapping kinds of context are of major importance: law (especially international public law) and deeper backgrounds (e.g., identity-constituting norms).

Continuous negotiation   Cardinal Richelieu introduced the principle of diplomacy of 'continuous negotiation', which called for diplomats to maintain sustained engagement through negotiation and dialogue with their counterparts, even in conditions of political tension and war. This concept led to the establishment of the first foreign ministry by France in 1626, the *Ministère des Affaires Etrangères.*

Culture of anarchy   Given the lack of a central authority and the atmosphere of distrust induced by the security dilemma within the international system, diplomats actively make, shape and reproduce distinct cultures of anarchy, which consist of disparate dynamics of diplomatic conduct and patterns of state interaction, ranging from antagonism based on self-help to cooperation based on collective security. The Hobbesian, Lockean and Kantian cultures of anarchy are three such competing examples (Wendt 1999).

Deliberative legitimacy   Diplomats seeking to build to the strongest case possible, in favour or against, the legitimacy of use of force can ensure the persuasiveness of their arguments by meeting conditions of deliberative legitimacy. In short, facts supporting their case must be truthful and complete, all affected parties are allowed to participate in the debate with equal rights to present or challenge a validity claim and participants must show genuine interest in using argumentative reasoning for reaching an understanding on the decision to use force.

Democratic war   A complementary term for 'democratic peace', this concept refers to cases of democracies resorting to the use of force. Democratic war can refer to cases of the use of force for individual or collective self-defence, humanitarian intervention, individual action authorised by the UN Security Council and collective action authorised by the Security Council and carried out under UN command. This concept is particularly relevant in analysing post-World-War-II state conduct in light of the increase in number of democratic states and the set-up of the UN legal framework.

Deontic powers   The rights, duties, obligations, requirements, permissions or entitlements that come with particular status-functions. Ranging from positive to negative natures, deontic powers can grant rights or privileges to a person to do something otherwise prohibited, for example a diplomat that is empowered to negotiate and conclude on behalf of states, and can also prescribe particular obligations and duties to a person, for example diplomats that are not allowed to interfere in the host country's domestic affairs. Deontic powers can be held by individuals just as they can be held by states and governing bodies.

Dialogue   Diplomatic discourse is full of references to dialogue. This usually signals the preference for leaving communication channels open with a view to influence the other side and make it change its mind in certain ways (e.g., critical dialogue between the EU and Iraq). In scholarly discourse, dialogue means something different. Through communicating with one another, two (or more) parties seek to improve their understanding of one another; they try to step into each other's shoes. The scholarly definition of dialogue is a much more demanding form of communication than the practitioners' one.

Diplomatic precedents   The use of a states', or a group of states', previous behaviour is one mechanism available to diplomats who seek to articulate, revise or replace international deontologies. For example, diplomats seeking to boost the doctrine of Responsibility to Protect as an emerging diplomatic deontology of international conduct on matters of collective security and status recognition can harness the behavioural pull of diplomatic precedents such as the NATO interventions in Kosovo in 1999 and in Libya in 2011.

Diplomatic prudence   The capacity to judge what action is appropriate to pursue in a particular context, especially under conditions of high uncertainty. The willingness to build consensus with other members of the international society, to take responsibility for one's actions and to demonstrate a minimum degree of reasonableness in collaborating with the other side and remaining open to their arguments are all important dimensions of this capacity.

Direct and structural prevention   Preventive measures aim at correcting both direct and structural sources of conflict. Accordingly, direct prevention has a short-term agenda and aims to reduce or eliminate the immediate causes of violence between parties, e.g. ceasefire, peacekeeping and disarmament. Structural prevention has a longer-term perspective and aims to provide a more comprehensive solution to the underlying causes of the conflict, e.g. democratisation, economic development, transitional justice, ethnic integration and arms control. Theoretically, direct prevention is conducted through UN-sponsored mediation efforts, while structural prevention is done through peacebuilding efforts.

Early warning systems   Early warning systems aim at integrating information and data that portend imminent socio-political crises or natural disasters from various sources, such as UN bodies, NGOs, states and other sources, in order to enable rapid and effective reaction. Examples of early warning systems within the UN include the twenty-four-hour Situation Centre at DPKO, which serves as a continuous link between UN Headquarters, field missions, troop-contributing countries and relevant NGOs. The main challenge for the effectiveness of early warning systems is the deficiency of operational coordination between the various early warning units within the UN.

E-diplomacy   Used especially by the US State Department, e-diplomacy is the innovative use of the wide variety of social media technologies to carry out diplomatic objectives. The main objectives of the US e-diplomacy programme are knowledge management, public diplomacy, information management, consular communications and response, disaster response and promoting internet freedom. The wide use of e-diplomacy is constrained mainly by the bureaucratic framework of conventional foreign ministries and the need for rethinking recruitments for those conducting a state's e-diplomacy.

Emotions   Although emotions were considered very important by Jeremy Bentham (1970 [1789]), who, in many ways, paved the way for today's Rationalist approaches, rational choice frameworks leave no room for them. A rational decision, in the latter view, is one that is made without any interference from emotions. Political psychology approaches this issue very differently. There are more and more authors contending that human beings cannot make the world intelligible to themselves and figure out what to do without putting emotions to use for doing so.

Episteme   This concept is originally coined by Michel Foucault (1970 [1966]) who likened it to a lens through which to look at the world. The lens enables actors to make the world intelligible to themselves but channels this making intelligible into certain directions rather than others. The Idea of Europe, for example, is such a lens. The formula of 'integration breeds peace and standing apart breeds war' is the prism through which pro-European decision-makers have looked at intra-European relations in the last half century. This predisposed them to an integration scheme that has softened the boundaries among European nations. The *episteme* is part of the deeper layer.

Fourteen Points   On 8 January 1918, US President Woodrow Wilson delivered his 'Fourteen Points' speech to the US Congress in which he outlined, among other imperatives, the need for accountability and transparency in diplomacy (Point 1), the importance of self-determination for peoples as an extension of individual rights at the state level (Point 5) and the need for a general framework of collective security between states based on mutual trust and cooperation (Point 14). These liberal guiding principles of diplomatic conduct remain valid in state conduct today.

Games   Game theory uses the term game as a metaphor for the kind of strategic interaction (see below under strategy) through which actors are assumed to make decisions. Similar to a chess game, actors are portrayed as being selfish and concerned with outwitting one another. In more technical language, they play in order to maximise their expected utility. Very well-known games are the prisoners' dilemma and the chicken game. Game theory is criticised by rival perspectives (for instance psychological approaches) for assuming superhuman computational capacities.

General Assembly (GA)   The Charter places the GA at the core of the UN system. At least on paper, it is the key forum for debate and policy-making. All UN members have a seat in the GA. The GA meets from September to December each year. Additionally, *ad hoc* sessions are scheduled depending on need. The GA deliberates on the full range of issue areas in which the UN becomes involved. This includes international security. With the 1950 Uniting for Peace Resolution (Resolution 377 (V)), the GA even authorised itself to make recommendations about collective security measures in cases where the veto of a permanent member of the Security Council (see below) blocks action to be taken by the Security Council. Yet, in practice, it is the Security Council that has stayed firmly in charge when it comes to determining whether a threat to the peace has occurred and, if so, what action should be taken.

Globalisation   A catchword since the 1990s. Given that globalisation is such a broad and deep-reaching phenomenon, it is difficult to define. Scholars tend to look at two different dimensions of the phenomenon: the material side, especially more and more rapid and frequent economic transactions (e.g., finance) and ongoing technological revolutions (in particular telecommunications), and the ideational side of coming to imagine communities beyond the nation-state. Globalisation pressures have a lot to do with the multiplicities of global diplomacy. Globalisation pushes items on the global agenda that used to be (at least primarily) on the domestic political agenda.

Good offices   Usually used by the leaders of international or regional organisations, good offices generally refers to the diplomatic functions provided by state leaders or heads of international organisations, premised on their credibility, prestige and the weight of the international community they represent. This classical diplomatic act of providing good offices, such as holding conversations between conflicting parties or launching a fully fledged neutral mediation by the UN Secretary-General, is one means of preventing disputes from escalating into conflict and of limiting the spread of conflicts. Its use, as part of preventive diplomacy, is now evolving into more complex and proactive forms of diplomatic engagement.

Governance   Governing without a central authority that can put down the law. In global politics, there is no equivalence to a government or a parliament in domestic politics. Even in highly integrated regional polities such as the EU, there is no clear equivalent. Instead, multiple actors, communicating with one another on various levels, have to converge on common courses of action in order to steer the polity into certain directions. For the salience of diplomacy, governance is a two-edged sword. On the one hand, diplomacy becomes even more important because more and more communication occurs among state-representatives and other diplomatic actors. On the other hand, traditional diplomats (foreign services) become sidelined when communication addresses the many technical aspects of problem-solving in our globalising age (e.g., trade, finance, environment, etc.).

Guerrilla diplomacy   Conducted by 'guerrilla' or 'expeditionary' diplomats, this new form of international engagement refers to the diplomatic process of facilitating post-conflict reconstruction and stabilisation projects. For a diplomat to stay relevant, in this age of scientifically and technologically driven globalisation, they must step out of their traditional channels of state-to-state interaction and start engaging the populations with whom they build relations, through a 'special-forces-style sensibility' (Copeland 2009) combined with local knowledge and technical expertise fit for the, typically volatile, region.

Habitus   A concept that is used by a number of scholars but has become most closely associated with the work of the French social theorist Pierre Bourdieu (1977; 1998). He conceptualises the habitus as background knowledge that provides actors with orientation when doing things. This knowledge is so much taken for granted that the actors putting it to use do not reflect upon it. Actors, in other words, have reasons upon which to act. But these reasons remain underneath the radar screen of explicit communicative encounters.

Humanitarian intervention   The interference into the domestic affairs of a state by using (the threat of) military force that is aimed at improving the humanitarian situation of the population in this state. The defining feature of humanitarian intervention, therefore, is the humanitarian intention of the intervenor (states or international organisations).

ICC Office of the Prosecutor   Headed by an independent Prosecutor and assisted by the Deputy Prosecutor, this office was created by the Rome Statute and has three functional divisions: Investigations Division, Prosecution Division and Jurisdiction, Complementarity and Cooperation Division. The Prosecutor's main duty is 'to establish the truth', conduct investigations to cover all relevant facts and evidence, and to assess whether there is criminal responsibility under the Statute, thereby investigating incriminating and exonerating circumstances equally.

Identity   Interacting with significant others, every actor – individual or collective – comes to define and redefine his or her identity. Identity is often conceptualised as narrative. Thus, it is the story that an actor tells of itself. History features very prominently. But there are other components as well, such as an *episteme* (see above) and identity-constituting norms (see below under 'norms').

International Court of Justice (ICJ)   The main judicial organ of the UN. The Court decides about contentious issues and provides legal opinions. It rules about contentious issues after states have agreed to submit a dispute to the Court and to abide by its ruling. According to the UN Charter, the UN has the authority to enforce its ruling if parties end up not complying with it. In practice, however, the UN Security Council (and the five veto powers) has proven highly reluctant to engage in such enforcement measures. The Court provides legal opinions at the request of UN bodies and agencies. Although these are only opinions, they can be rather influential. The ICJ does command a significant amount of respect in the diplomatic community.

International Criminal Justice (ICrJ)   This field of legal practice encompasses the doctrines by which international law imposes criminal responsibility directly upon individuals, regardless of national law, for certain types of crimes, mainly crimes against humanity, war crimes and genocide. The practice is complicated by not only how the jurisdiction between national and international courts will be determined but also the political role played by the UN Security Council in determining recourse to courts in certain situations. Further, states are notoriously protective of their sovereignty and are thus suspicious of attempts to weaken their legal instruments of protection against external interfere.

International organisations   An institution featuring formal decision-making procedures, formal membership and a permanent secretariat. In order for an institution to qualify as an international organisation, it has to have at least three members. Thus, an international organisation is always a multilateral arrangement.

Jus fetiale (ius fetiale)   A feature of Roman conduct of foreign relations carried over to Greek diplomacy, any declaration of war had to follow the proper procedure, as determined by *jus fetiale*, or fetial law. The college of *Fetiales*, a religious body composed of priests whose duties also included overseeing international treaties, informed the enemy of Rome's grievances and, barring any other event occurring during a fixed period, a declaration would be made at the border of the enemy's territory and a javelin would be thrown across the border.

League of Nations Established at the Paris Peace Conference following the end of World War I, this multilateral institutional framework was created to facilitate the peaceful resolution of disputes by disallowing member states recourse to war until they had exhausted procedures for arbitration and conciliation provided by the League. The League was a precursor to the UN in efforts of institutionalising collective security among states.

Liberalism A set of approaches in international relations that share a focus on the individual and its political efficacy. It is assumed that individuals pursue their interests and that some of these interests are shared. Individuals can develop cooperation out of these shared interests. Compared to Realism, this is a more optimistic view of world politics. Liberalism believes in human progress, whereas Realists insist that power politics – and with it conflict and war – always haunt world politics.

Lifeworld A conceptualisation of the context in which actors are embedded. The lifeworld enables actors to make sense of the world in certain ways but not others (Habermas 1984). A shared lifeworld is of crucial importance for Habermasian and Habermas-inspired approaches because this is seen as the prerequisite for actors to be able to communicate meaningfully with one another. A shared lifeworld, in this reading, is the *sine qua non* for reaching agreements. The concept of lifeworld has been employed by several philosophers and social theorists. Yet it is the social theorist Jürgen Habermas with whom the concept is associated the most.

Lingua franca It was required for the permanent resident ambassador to be a good linguist and fluent in Latin, the *lingua franca* of the time, meaning the language that was systematically used for communication between individuals who do not share their mother tongue. The actual language of the *lingua franca* used by diplomats has changed over the centuries and is a function of agreement between the interlocutors of the era, having evolved from Latin to French to English.

Localitis Also known as 'going native', localitis occurs when a diplomat becomes more sympathetic to the host country than to their sending government. The four to five year rotation system of diplomatic staff aims to mitigate this grave risk, since localitis is deemed to impede the diplomat's capacity to provide proper diplomatic representation.

Logics of action How do actors come to act a certain way and not another one? On a rather abstract level, logics of action seek to provide broad frames for answering this question. Four logics of action are frequently discussed in the social sciences: the logic of consequences holds that actors carefully calculate the consequences of the courses of action available to them (e.g., game theory). The logic of appropriateness assumes that actors follow identity-constituting norms when they embark on a certain course of action. The logic of argumentation revolves around persuasion (an argument outperforms another argument). The logic of practice is about following the common sense that is ingrained in the *habitus* (see above).

Monroe doctrine US President James Monroe articulated this doctrine on 2 December 1823, to US Congress, laying an ideological cornerstone of US foreign policy. President Monroe demanded the European powers respect the Western Hemisphere as the US' sphere of interest and not to interfere in affairs of the region. Monroe also noted that the US would not interfere with existing European colonies or in internal affairs of European countries.

Mutually assured destruction (MAD)   A military doctrine that bases deterrence on the distribution of nuclear military capabilities between states. State A and B have the capabilities to annihilate one another in an exchange of nuclear weapons, no matter whether state A or state B attacks first. A and B have a full second strike capability. MAD has been a highly influential military doctrine during the Cold War (see above).

New diplomacy   Diplomatic conduct post-WWI was inspired from three liberal principles espoused by President Woodrow Wilson: public accountability, self-determination and collective security. As new diplomacy assumed that these elements, crucial to conducting domestic affairs in a liberal democracy, could be translated to the conduct of a state's foreign relations, its proponents sought to introduce more honesty, cooperation and deterrence of the use of force in international relations. For the opposite, i.e., old diplomacy, see below.

Norms   Norms define the oughts and ought nots of conduct in a collective of actors. For any collective, norms amount to shared expectations about what to do and not to do. Norms are part of the context in which actors are situated. Norms, as any component of the context, change and evolve over time. The territorial integrity norm, for example, is something that only found its firm entry into diplomatic relations in the twentieth century. By now, international diplomacy has moved even further towards a territorial status quo norm. There is not only a norm that recognised state borders must not be violated, but there is also more and more evidence for a norm according to which territorial status quos have to be recognised (even if only provisionally).

Nuncius   The main form of diplomatic representation in Europe during the early Middle Ages, a nuncius was an agent whose main function was to provide a channel of communication between rulers and to explore opportunities for concluding treaties and alliances. Sending a nuncius was chosen over a written letter, on certain occasions, for his actual wording and responses to his interlocutor. While benefitting from immunity from harm, the nuncius spoke on behalf of the principal but was not given full powers (*plena potestas*) to enter into private contracts and to negotiate agreements on behalf of their leaders.

Nuremberg trials   A series of military tribunals were held in the city of Nuremberg, Germany, between 1945 and 1946 to prosecute prominent members of the leadership of Nazi Germany. The Trials dealt with four categories of crimes: participation in crimes against peace; planning, initiative and waging wars of aggression; war crimes; and crimes against humanity. The legacy of these trials was fundamental in setting an important precedent for the field of international criminal justice, having established that certain types of crimes are international crimes and so can be prosecuted before both national and international courts.

Old diplomacy Diplomatic conduct among European powers during the eighteenth and nineteenth centuries can be understood on the basis of five premises: (1) the five major European powers were central to politics; (2) a global hierarchy existed between the Great Powers and the Small Powers due to wider range of interests, responsibilities and resources; (3) the Great Powers were responsible for maintaining peace; (4) a professional diplomatic service was required; and (5) continuous and confidential negotiation was crucial for diplomacy. When 'old diplomacy' was blamed for failing to restrain the Great Powers from warfare, the pre-eminence of this type of diplomatic conduct was fundamentally undermined. For the opposite, i.e., new diplomacy, see above.

Ontology There are two key ontological debates in the social sciences: (a) the agency-structure debate interrogates to what extent an actor is autonomous in his or her actions (see below under structure); (b) the material-ideational debate inquires into the salience of material and ideational forces as well as how the ideational and material hang together. A Constructivist answer to this question privileges the ideational: ideas attach meaning to the world (including its material dimensions). A typical Rationalist answer privileges the material: ideas are epiphenomenal. This means that material factors are the actual causes of human action; actors merely use ideas to justify what they do.

'Order as fact' As one layer of the diplomatic making of the world, 'order as fact' refers to the stable and regular pattern of relationships of global activities and institutions which ensure the stability and predictability of actors' behaviour in global politics. This pattern of relationships is constantly evolving under the impact of three primary status-functions: security, redistribution and recognition. 'Order as fact' must be analysed with 'order as value', the normative framework that makes 'order as fact' possible in the first place.

'Order as value' A second, deeper layer of the diplomatic making of the world, 'order as value' refers to the set of norms, principles and shared understandings that frame diplomatic action. As the normative dimension of world-making, these sets of values create the conditions of possibility for 'order as fact'. Symbolic interactionism, defended by Alexander Wendt, and deontological theory, expounded by John R. Searle, provide different explanations of how 'order as value' is shaped. The former theory underlines the importance of relationships between diplomats while the latter focuses on the role of collective intentionality in shaping this normative dimension.

Pacifism An uncompromising belief in non-violence. Thus, pacifists are opposed to military solutions to conflicts and wars. Violence, according to this belief, only breeds further violence. Pacifism can be seen as a *ius ad bellum* statement: resorting to war is never just.

Paradiplomacy This concept refers to the diplomatic involvement of *non-central* yet *governmental* bodies in international relations. Paradiplomacy is conducted through the establishment of permanent or *ad hoc* contacts with foreign public or private entities, with the aim to promote socioeconomic, cultural and any foreign issues of their constitutional competences (Cornago 1999: 40). Examples include agreements between regions of different states and multilateralism between global cities.

Paradigm   A prism through which to look at the world. The term was coined by Thomas Kuhn (1964) in his work on scientific revolutions. Scholars, he maintains, see the world through certain lenses. This enables them to see certain things but makes it impossible for them to see others.

Peacebuilding   The term peacebuilding originates with the peace researcher Johan Galtung. He used this term in order to postulate a bottom-up process of institutionalising a comprehensive and sustainable peace in a society. The term forcefully entered diplomatic discourse with UN Secretary-General Boutros Boutros-Ghali's 1992 *Agenda for Peace*. Being attached to outside intervention, the concept puts less emphasis on bottom-up processes but on outside facilitation of re-building societies after war (and, at times, also to prevent them from escalating into war in the first place). Peacebuilding efforts require consent by the parties concerned.

Peacekeeping   Although peacekeeping is not mentioned anywhere in the Charter, it may very well be the most widely known means of UN conflict management. Originally designed as an interposition force to stabilise a ceasefire between states or state-like entities, peacekeeping operations have become much more comprehensive over time. Since the 1990s, most operations have been multifunctional in nature. They have military, civilian and police components. The civilian components oftentimes blend into peacebuilding efforts. Peacekeeping, too, requires consent by the parties concerned.

Peacemaking   While peacekeeping and peacebuilding are about stabilising situations in which parties have stopped fighting one another on the battlefield, peacemaking is designed to bring war to an end. Peacemaking does not wait for consent by the parties concerned. It forges an agreement between the parties. In cases where diplomacy fails to forge such an agreement, the peacemaker may resort to enforcement measures. Within the Charter system, it is, in principle, only the Security Council that can authorise such measures.

Perceptions   Political psychology suggests that human beings do not have privileged access to the objective reality. Instead, making sense of the world is a subjective endeavour. Different people, therefore, make sense of the world differently; they perceive it (and particular aspects of it) differently. Where there is perception, there is also misperception (Jervis 1976).

Power   One of the most important concepts for making sense of world politics. It is also one of the most contested ones. Traditionally, power has been understood as power *over* someone. This view, being forcefully formulated by the German sociologist Max Weber, assumes that power is something that has to be exercised. Over time, the scholarly understanding of power has broadened. Power is now often understood as power *to* do something. Power, in this reading, is not something that has to be necessarily exercised in order for it to leave its mark in political encounters.

Preventive diplomacy   According to the UN, this refers to 'diplomatic action taken, at the earliest possible stage, to prevent disputes from arising between parties, to prevent existing disputes from escalating into conflicts and to limit the spread of the latter when they occur' (UN 2011). Diplomatic preventive measures, whose use has emerged in the post-Cold-War period as a proactive means of collective security, can dissuade state and non-state actors of the use of force as an effective instrument for dispute settlement. The UN used preventive diplomacy in Sudan to ensure a successful independence referendum in January 2011 through active engagement by the UN Security Council and the appointment of a high-level panel by the Secretary-General.

Proxenos As one of three types of diplomatic representation in the Ancient Greek system, the *proxenos* would reside in his own state while acting for another state, out of a general sympathy for the political system or culture of that other state. To facilitate inter-state negotiations, the *proxenos* was expected to protect their nationals residing in the receiving-state, while performing duties ranging from providing hospitality and assistance to visitors from the relevant state to contributing to public policy-making.

Public diplomacy Aims at influencing the publics in host states. Thus, it departs from the traditional state-to-state communication of diplomacy. The influencing can be directed at a particular public in a particular state. It can also be directed more generally at publics around the world. As the means to create, maximise and render soft power into diplomatic influence, diplomats use various tools of public diplomacy to advance the interests and extend the values of their state to another country's public. As Joseph Nye (2008) explains, this type of diplomacy includes daily communication, strategic communication and relationship-building with key individuals through scholarships, exchanges, training, seminars, conferences and access to media channels.

Raison d'état According to this doctrine of international conduct, literally meaning 'reason of state', a ruler or government will conduct its foreign policy with state interests as the ultimate objective, and with disregard for ethical considerations. This doctrine was specifically influential in the establishment of the Westphalian concept of sovereign state. The norms, rules and principles of the international system legitimated by this doctrine thus gave rise to eighteenth-century dynastic absolutism and recourse to war. The diplomatic pursuit of the doctrine of *raison d'état* is known as Realpolitik. States assure their survival through the accumulation and rational use of power, defined primarily in military terms. Realpolitik helps ensure the survival of the state through a foreign policy that skilfully balances or cuts favours with the dominant power(s).

Raison de système Coined by Adam Watson, this doctrine refers to 'the use of diplomacy to achieve the ultimate purpose of an international society of independent states' (Watson 1984: 203). In contrast to the doctrine of *raison d'état*, members of the international society have an inherent interest in preserving the system and thus subsume national interests to broader systemic considerations. Looking to the EU as one such example, the diplomats' jobs is to balance their national interests with the inherent interest of preserving the system.

Rationality Rationality is, very simply put, about figuring out what to do. How human beings figure out what to do is highly contested among scholars. On the one hand, there are demanding assumptions about the computational capacities of human beings (rational choice). On the other hand, there is an array of approaches that is more sceptical about these computational capacities. They pay more attention to emotions, routines, common sense, trial and error methods, etc.

Realism   Realism may very well be the most influential school of thought in international relations. Different Realist strands share the following assumptions in common: the actors on the global stage are states (statism); there is no common power in international politics (anarchy); because there is no common power, states have to safeguard their security by themselves (self-help); and the only kind of tenuous peace possible is the balance of power. These shared assumptions notwithstanding, there are important differences among Realist strands. Classical Realism, for example, puts strong emphasis on diplomacy. Neo-classical Realism echoes this emphasis to some extent. Neorealism, by contrast, leaves very little room for diplomacy or indeed any kind of agency and focuses on structural forces (distribution of military capabilities) instead.

Resident ambassador   A major innovation in diplomatic representation at the end of the fifteenth century which soon became common practice in Western Europe, the office of resident ambassador was established mainly to gather information on domestic political conditions in the host state and to report back relevant developments to their home state. Thus, the resident ambassador was required to build close relationships with those who held power, form good channels of communication between the two governments and advise the sending government on the best course of action.

Responsibility to protect (R2P)   Provocatively put, state sovereignty tends to amount to a government's privilege to do whatever it wants to do within the borders of a state. The R2P principle qualifies this privilege. According to the principle, sovereignty is not an absolute privilege but a responsibility. If the government fails to exercise this responsibility, the principle of external non-interference no longer applies. Failing to exercise this responsibility means, in the context of R2P, a government's targeting of its own population (genocide, war crimes, ethnic cleansing and crimes against humanity) and, more generally, a government's inability to protect its population.

Rogue states   A country that consistently acts in defiance of international law, stability and cooperation, and that seeks to undermine the international system, can be considered a rogue state. While this term has no standing in international law, it has been used in state rhetoric to define 'outlaw' states. More specifically, coercive diplomacy can be effective with rogue states when the coercer is firm about not accepting too little and is trustworthy about not pushing for too much.

Security community   The members of a security community are states. Within a transnational region, peaceful change is a deeply taken for granted norm among these states. Dealing with conflict by violent means, therefore, becomes unthinkable. Security communities vary in terms of how tightly coupled the states constituting the security community are with one another (Adler and Barnett 1998). The transatlantic security community (NATO), for instance, is less tightly coupled than the European security community (EU).

Security Council   The UN Charter puts the Security Council in charge of maintaining international peace and security. The Security Council has three principal sets of means available for doing so: Chapter 6 measures (peaceful settlement of disputes); Chapter 7 measures (enforcement); and, located in between the two (but closer to Chapter 6), peacekeeping. The Security Council has five permanent and ten non-permanent members. Reflecting the outcome of WWII, the five permanent members are China, France, Russia, the United Kingdom and the US. Each of the five permanent members has the power to veto decisions on substantive matters (but not on procedural ones). Since the end of the Cold War, the veto has been used more sparingly. But it is still being used. In a recent case, China and Russia vetoed a resolution on Syria in July 2012. The resolution would have threatened enforcement measures in case of non-compliance.

Soft law Diplomats use soft law instruments, which include conference declarations, executive statements, resolutions, codes of conduct and policy recommendations, to articulate, revise or replace international deontologies. Soft law can shape the authority of these emerging deontologies in three ways: (1) by making the legality of opposing diplomatic positions much harder to sustain; (2) by having a formative impact on the *opinio juris* or state practice that generates new international customary law; and (3) by influencing the development and application of binding international treaties.

Sovereignty The right to exercise supreme authority over a piece of territory. The 1648 Peace of Westphalia codified many aspects of what we refer to as state authority today. Our current state system is the contingent outcome of a historical process. In the Europe of the Middle Ages, for instance, there was no exclusive authority over a piece of territory. Instead, there was a system of overlapping authority, in which the Pope, the Holy Roman Emperor and local princes featured prominently.

Sovereignty as responsibility While the traditional Westphalian variant of sovereignty is rather absolute in allowing a government to 'do wrong' within its own boundaries, the development of international criminal justice, and particularly the creation of the ICC, reflect a changing notion of sovereignty. Sovereignty is now increasingly linked to a state's responsibility in upholding international law, particularly the protection from and prosecution of certain international crimes.

Status-functions Certain functions are performed by objects or persons only by virtue of the collective acceptance of that object or individual's particular status. Referred to as status-functions, they are essential for understanding how social reality is constructed because they prescribe to agents what they are allowed and forbidden to do in their conduct with each other. The process of assigning status-functions is summed up by the formula: X counts as Y in C, which states that an object, person or state of affairs, X, has been assigned a special status, Y, in the context of C.

Strategy To put it simply, strategy is a plan for action. Different theoretical frameworks conceptualise the term differently. Literature on grand strategy tends to equate strategy with linking interests to means in the issue area of peace and war. In game theory, strategy is a key concept; actors are assumed to behave strategically, i.e., they seek to outwit other players in order to maximise their benefits. In rhetorical studies, there is the concept of rhetorical strategies. Here, the concept is closely associated with communicative moves. These range from efforts to persuade others by a convincing argument to attempts to vilify and outcast them.

Structure To what extent an actor (individual or an anthropomorphised political entity) has political efficacy depends on the structure in which this actor is embedded. The structure is what makes an actor in the first place; it places an actor into the driver's seat of decision-making or banishes him/her onto the backbench.

Structure also enables the actor to make sense of the world and to do something in this world. How much structure matters and, with it, how much autonomy actors have in world politics, is contested among scholars (see under ontology). It is also contested how largely material as opposed to ideational factors feature in constituting structure. Realists, for example, put a lot of emphasis on material factors (military capabilities) whereas Constructivists foreground ideational forces (e.g., identity and its constituting norms).

Struggle for recognition Responsible for defining, negotiating and applying the foundational principles of recognition in international politics, diplomats are the key players in the struggle for recognition, or the inter-subjective process by which agents are constituted as respected and esteemed members of the society of states. According to Wendt, political entities establish international orders that progressively satisfy individuals' desire for recognition, which encompasses needs for physical security and equal and respectful treatment by others.

Track-two diplomacy Track-one diplomacy is state-to-state diplomacy with states being represented by their governments, foreign ministries and/or other ministries. Track-two diplomacy is only loosely linked to governments. It can involve a host of actors such as parliamentarians, private citizens, activists, scholars, religious communities and so on. The advantage of track-two diplomacy is that it does not require the many formalities and routine posturing of official diplomacy. Opening up the second track, therefore, can provide a stabilising element in troubled relations among states and help to improve these relations. The literature points, for instance, to the importance of track-two diplomacy to help manage and reduce tensions between the Soviet Union and the US during the Cold War.

UN veto system Within the UN Security Council, the five permanent members each hold the right to veto decisions considered by the Council, as per Article 27 of the UN Charter. This feature, which provides major powers strong incentives to remain engaged in the system, was specifically designed to address a key weakness of the League of Nations framework, or the alienation or exclusion of a major power from the decision-making body responsible for setting and implementing rules of international conduct. See also the entry 'security council' above.

***Uti possidetis* (*uti possidetis iuris*)** The norm of *uti possidetis* found its most important application during the decolonisation processes in the nineteenth century (Latin America) and the twentieth century (Africa, Asia). Newly independent states recognised former colonial borders as state borders. This meant, especially in the African case, the recognition of highly arbitrary boundaries. Yet the rationale behind this recognition is probably rather compelling. Not recognising colonial borders would open Pandora's box; there would be a plethora of territorial claims and potential for war. *Uti possidetis* is still applied in world politics when states disintegrate. When Yugoslavia disintegrated, for instance, the former boundaries between the Yugoslav republics became state borders of the newly independent states. The case of Yugoslavia also illustrates that there have always been exceptions to the rule of *uti possidetis*. The recognition of Kosovo as a sovereign state by many states in the international community is such an exception. During Yugoslav times, Kosovo was part of the Yugoslav republic of Serbia (albeit an autonomous region until Slobodan Milošević did away with this status in the late 1980s).

References

Adibe, Clement E. 1998. 'Accepting external authority in peace-maintenance'. *Global Governance* no. 4: 107–122.

Adler, Emanuel and Michael Barnett (eds). 1998. *Security communities.* Cambridge: Cambridge University Press.

Adler, Emanuel and Peter M. Haas. 1992. 'Conclusion: Epistemic communities, world order, and the creation of a reflective research program'. *International Organization* no. 46 (1): 367–390.

Adler, Emanuel and Vincent Pouliot. 2011. 'International practices'. *International Theory* no. 3 (1): 1–36.

Aggestam, Karin. 2003. 'Conflict prevention: Old wine in new bottles?' *International Peacekeeping* no. 10 (1): 12–23.

Aguirre, Iñaki. 1999. 'Making sense of paradiplomacy? An intertextual enquiry about a concept in search of a definition'. *Regional & Federal Studies* no. 9 (1): 185–209.

Ahmed, Shamima and David M. Potter. 2006. *NGOs in international politics.* Bloomfield, CT: Kumarian Press.

Al Jazeera. 19 February 2010. *Talk to Al Jezeera – President Isaias Afwerki* (accessed 17 July 2012). Available from www.youtube.com.

Allison, Graham T. 1969. 'Conceptual models and the Cuban missile crisis'. *The American Political Science Review* no. 63 (3): 689–718.

American Law Institute, the. 1987. Restatement of the Law Third, Foreign Relations Law of the United States. In *Part I, Chapter 1, Restatement of the Foreign Relations Law of the U.S., § 101.* Philadelphia: American Law Institute.

Annan, Kofi. 2005. '"In larger freedom": Decision time at the UN'. *Foreign Affairs* (May/June 2005): 63–74.

Armitage, Richard L. Jr., Joseph S. Nye and Craig Cohen. 2007. *A smarter, more secure America.* Centre for Startegic & International Studies (accessed 2 April 2012). Available from http://csis.org/publication/smarter-more-secure-america.

Art, Robert J. and Patrick M. Cronin. 2003. *The United States and coercive diplomacy.* Washington, DC: United States Institute of Peace Press.

Asghedom, T. 1999. 'Behind the Ethiopian authorities' wars of aggression against Eritrea', *Eritrea Profile,* Asmara, 27 February.

Autesserre, Séverine. 2010. *The trouble with the Congo: Local violence and the failure of international peacebuilding.* Cambridge and New York: Cambridge University Press.

Ballis, William Belcher. 1973. *The legal position of war: Changes in its practice and theory from Plato to Vattel.* New York: Garland Pub.

Bank for International Settlements. 2010. *Triennial Central Bank Survey: Foreign exchange and derivatives market activity in April 2010, preliminary results* (accessed 17 July 2012). Available from http://www.bis.org/publ/rpfx10.htm.

Barker, J. Craig. 2006. *The protection of diplomatic personnel.* Aldershot: Ashgate.

Barnett, Michael. 2006. 'Building a republican peace: Stabilizing states after war'. *International Security* no. 30 (4): 87–112.

Barnett, Michael and Martha Finnemore. 1999. 'The politics, power, and pathologies of international organizations'. *International Organization* no. 53 (4): 699–732.

Barnett, Michael, Hunjoon Kim, Madalene O'Donnell and Laura Sitea. 2007. 'Peacebuilding: What is in a name'. *Global Governance* no. 13: 35–58.

Bartoli, Andrea. 2008. 'NGOs and conflict resolution'. In *The sage handbook of conflict resolution*, edited by J. Bercovitch, V. A. Kremenyuk and I. W. Zartman. Thousand Oaks, CA: SAGE Publications.

Beardsley, K. 2008. 'Agreement without peace? International mediation and time inconsistency problems'. *American Journal of Political Science* no. 52 (4): 723–740.

Beaumont, Peter, Martin Bright and Ed Vullyami. 2003. 'Revealed: US dirty tricks to win vote on Iraq war'. *The Guardian*, 2 March 2003.

Bell, Christine. 2006. 'Peace agreements: Their nature and legal status'. *The American Journal of International Law* no. 100: 373–412.

Bellamy, Richard, Markus Kornprobst and Christine Reh. 2012. 'Introduction: Meeting in the middle'. *Government and Opposition* no. 47 (3): 275–295.

Bentham, Jeremy. 1970 [1789]. *An introduction to the principles of morals and legislation*, edited by J.H. Burns and H.L.A. Hart. New York: Methuen.

——. 1974 [1789]. 'Principles of international law'. In *Peace projects of the eighteenth century*, edited by M.C. Jacobs, New York: Garland.

Bercovitch, J. and Ayse Kadayifci. 2002. 'Exploring the relevance and contribution of mediation to peace-building'. *Peace and Conflict Studies* no. 9 (2): 21–41.

Bercovitch, J. and A.S. Kadayifci-Orellana. 2009. 'Religion and mediation: The role of faith-based actors in international conflict resolution'. *International Negotiation* no. 14 (1): 175–204.

Berger, Peter L. and Thomas Luckmann. 1966. *The social construction of reality: A treatise in the sociology of knowledge*. Garden City, NY: Doubleday.

Berridge, Geoff. 2004. 'Introduction'. In *Diplomatic classics: Selected texts from Commynes to Vattel*, edited by Geoff Berridge, pp. ix, 199. Basingstoke: Palgrave Macmillan.

Betts, Alexander. 2010. 'Survival migration: A new protection framework'. *Global Governance* no. 16 (3): 361–382.

Bianchi, A. 1999. 'Immunity versus human rights: The Pinochet case'. *European Journal of International Law* no. 10 (2): 237.

Biersteker, Thomas J. 2007. Prospects for the UN Peacebuilding Commission. Paper read at Disarmament Forum 2. Geneva: United Nations Institute for Disarmament Research. Available from http://graduateinstitute.ch/webdav/site/admininst/shared/iheid/800/biersteker/UNPBC_Disarmament_Forumpdf-art2630%5B1%5D.pdf (accessed 22 February 2013).

Bjola, Corneliu. 2005. 'Legitimating the use of force in international politics: A communicative action perspective'. *European Journal of International Relations* no. 11 (2): 266–303.

——. 2008. 'Legitimacy and the use of force: Bridging the analytical–normative divide'. *Review of International Studies* no. 34 (4): 627–644.

——. 2009. *Legitimising the use of force in international politics: Kosovo, Iraq and the ethics of intervention*. London and New York: Routledge.

——. 2010. 'The power of the public sphere: (Anti)-diplomacy and crisis management within security communities'. In *Arguing global governance: Agency, lifeworld and shared reasoning*, edited by Corneliu Bjola and Markus Kornprobst, pp. 194–209. Milton Park, Abingdon, Oxon and New York: Routledge.

——. 2013. 'Enmity and friendship in world politics: A diplomatic approach'. *The Hague Journal of Diplomacy* no. 8 (2): 1–20.

Bjola, Corneliu and Markus Kornprobst. 2007. 'Security communities and the habitus of restraint: Germany and the United States on Iraq'. *Review of International Studies* no. 33 (2): 285–305.

——. 2011. 'Introduction: The argumentative deontology of global governance'. In *Arguing global governance*, edited by Corneliu Bjola and Markus Kornprobst, pp. 1–16. London and New York: Routledge.

Boisbouvier, Christophe. 16 February 2010. *50 years later, Françafrique is alive and well.* Radio France Internationale (accessed 27 July 2012). Available from http://www.english.rfi.fr/africa/20100216-50-years-later-francafrique-alive-and-well.

Bourdieu, Pierre. 1977. *Outline of a theory of practice, Cambridge studies in social and cultural anthropology.* Cambridge: Cambridge University Press.

——. 1988. *Homo academicus.* Cambridge: Polity Press.

——. 1990. *The logic of practice.* Stanford, CA: Stanford University Press.

——. 1998. *Practical reason: On the theory of action.* Cambridge: Polity Press.

Boutros-Ghali, B. 1992. *An agenda for peace,* report of the Secretary-General pursuant to the statement adopted by the Summit Meeting of the Security Council on 31 January 1992. In *A/47/277 – S/24111, 17 June 1992.* New York: United Nations Publications.

——. 1995. Supplement to *An agenda for peace,* position paper of the Secretary-General on the occasion of the 50th anniversary of the United Nations. In *A/50/60 – S/1995/13 January 1995.* New York: United Nations Publications.

Boutros-Ghali, B. and United Nations. 1992. *An agenda for peace: Preventive diplomacy, peacemaking and peace-keeping,* Article 37. New York: United Nations Publications.

Boyd, Carl. 1980. *The extraordinary envoy: General Hiroshi Ōshima and diplomacy in the Third Reich, 1934– 1939.* Washington, DC: University Press of America.

Boyle, Alan. 2006. 'Soft law in international law-making'. In *International law,* edited by Malcolm D. Evans, pp. 141–158. Oxford and New York: Oxford University Press.

Bozorgmehr, Najmeh. 21 June 2011. Iranian deputy foreign minister dismissed. *Financial Times,* (accessed 14 March 2012). Available from http://www.ft.com/cms/s/0/0add71fa-9c05-11e0-bef9-00144feabdc0.html#axzz1qDOH0X6M.

Broadbridge, Anne F. 2008. *Kingship and ideology in the Islamic and Mongol worlds.* Cambridge and New York: Cambridge University Press.

Broomhall, Bruce. 2003. *International justice and the International Criminal Court: Between sovereignty and the rule of law.* Oxford and New York: Oxford University Press.

Brown, Jonathan. 1988. 'Diplomatic immunity: State practice under the Vienna Convention on Diplomatic Relations'. *International & Comparative Law Quarterly* no. 37 (1): 53–88.

Brownlie, Ian. 2003. *Principles of public international law.* 6th edn. Oxford and New York: Oxford University Press.

Bryce, Trevor. 1997. *The anarchical society: A study of order in world politics.* 2nd edn. Houndmills, Basingstoke, Hampshire: Macmillan.

——. 1999. *The kingdom of the Hittites.* Oxford: Oxford University Press.

Bull, Hedley. 1995. *The anarchical society: A study of order in world politics.* New York: Columbia University Press, p. 158.

Call, Charles T. 2002. 'War transitions and the new Civilian Security in Latin America'. *Comparative Politics* no. 35 (1): 1–20.

——. 2012. *Why peace fails: The causes and prevention of civil war recurrence.* Washington, DC: Georgetown University Press.

de Callières. 2004. 'The art of negotiating with sovereign princes'. In *Diplomatic classics: selected texts from Commynes to Vattel,* edited by Geoff Berridge, p. 148. Basingstoke: Palgrave Macmillan.

Cameron, Fraser. 2009. 'We do not want unification': Margaret Thatcher's irrational hatred of a united Germany. *Atlantic Times* (accessed 15 September 2012). Available from http://www.atlantic-times.com/archive_detail.php?recordID=1934.

Cameron, Maxwell A., Robert J. Lawson and Brian W. Tomlin. 1998. *To walk without fear: The global movement to ban landmines.* Toronto and New York: Oxford University Press.

Campbell, Brian. 2001. 'Diplomacy in the Roman World (c. 500BC–AD235)'. *Diplomacy and Statecraft* no. 12 (1): 1–22.

Caplan, Richard. 2005. *International governance of war-torn territories: Rule and reconstruction.* Oxford: Oxford University Press.

Carnevale, P.J. and D.W. Choi. 2000. 'Culture in the mediation of international disputes'. *International Journal of Psychology* no. 35 (2): 105–110.

Carr, D.L. and E.S. Norman. 2008. 'Global civil society? The Johannesburg world summit on sustainable development'. *Geoforum* no. 39 (1): 358–371.

Carr, Edward Hallett. 2001. *The twenty years' crisis, 1919–1939: An introduction to the study of international relations.* Houndmills, Basingstoke, Hampshire and New York: Palgrave.

Carter, Charles H. 2004. 'The ambassadors of early modern Europe: Patterns of diplomatic representation in the early seventeenth century'. In *Diplomacy*, edited by Christer Jönsson and Richard Langhorne. London and Thousand Oaks, CA: Sage Publications.

Chandler, David. 2006. *Empire in denial: The politics of state-building.* London and Ann Arbor, MI: Pluto Press.

Chataway, C.J. 1998. 'Track II diplomacy: From a track I perspective'. *Negotiation Journal* no. 14 (3): 269–287.

Chatterjee, Charles. 2007. *International law and diplomacy.* London and New York: Routledge.

Chowdhury, Arjun and Ronald. R. Krebs. 2010. 'Talking about terror: Counterterrorist campaigns and the logic of representation'. *European Journal of International Relations* no. 16 (1): 125–150.

Cohen, R. 2001. 'Resolving conflict across languages'. *Negotiation Journal* no. 17 (1): 17–34.

Collier, Paul and Anke Hoeffler. 2004. 'The challenge of reducing the global incidence of civil war'. *Copenhagen Consensus Challenge Paper*, March 2004.

Commission on Global Governance. 1995. *Our global neighbourhood: The report of the Commission on Global Governance.* Oxford: Oxford University Press.

Conrad, Geoffrey W. and Arthur Andrew Demarest. 1984. *Religion and empire: The dynamics of Aztec and Inca expansionism.* Cambridge and New York: Cambridge University Press.

Constantinou, Costas M. 1996. *On the way to diplomacy.* Minneapolis: University of Minnesota Press.

——. 2006. 'On homo-diplomacy'. *Space and Culture* no. 9 (4): 351–364.

Cooper, Andrew Fenton. 2008. *Celebrity diplomacy.* Boulder, CO: Paradigm Publishers.

Copeland, Daryl. 2009. *Guerrilla diplomacy: Rethinking international relations.* Boulder, CO: Lynne Rienner Publishers.

Cornago, Noé. 1999. 'Diplomacy and paradiplomacy in the redefinition of international security: Dimensions of conflict and co-operation'. *Regional & Federal Studies* no. 9 (1): 40–57.

Council of the European Union. 2005. *Agreement between the International Criminal Court and the European Union on cooperation and assistance* (accessed 18 October 2012). Available from http://register.consilium.eu.int/pdf/en/05/st14/st14298.en05.pdf.

——. 2010. *Council Decision 2010/427/EU establishing the organisation and functioning of the European External Action Service* 26 July 2010 (accessed 21 March 2012). Available from http://www.europarl.europa.eu/oeil/popups/summary.do?id=1119304&t=f&l=en.

Craig, Gordon Alexander. 1994. 'The German Foreign Office from Neurath to Ribbentrop'. In *The Diplomats, 1919–1939*, edited by Gordon Alexander Craig and Felix Gilbert, pp. 406–436. Princeton, NJ: Princeton University Press.

Craig, Gordon Alexander and Alexander L. George. 1983. *Force and statecraft: Diplomatic problems of our time.* New York: Oxford University Press.

Crawford, James. 1979. *The creation of states in international law.* New York: Clarendon Press and Oxford: Oxford University Press.

——. 2006. *The creation of states in international law.* 2nd edn. Oxford: Oxford University Press.

Crawford, Neta. 2002. *Argument and change in world politics: Ethics, decolonization, and humanitarian intervention.* Cambridge: Cambridge University Press.

Crocker, David A. 1999. 'Reckoning with past wrongs: A normative framework'. *Ethics & International Affairs* no. 13 (1): 43–64.

Cross, M.K.D. 2011. 'Europe, a smart power?' *International Politics* no. 48 (6): 691–706.

Dahli, H. 2000. 'Ethiopia's obsession with the Red Sea', *Eritrea Profile*, Asmara, 20 July.

Darwin, John. 2001. 'Diplomacy and decolonization'. In *International diplomacy and colonial retreat*, edited by Kent Fedorowich and Martin Thomas, pp. 5–24. London and Portland, OR: Frank Cass Publishers.

de Callières, François. 1750. *De La Maniére De Negocier Avec Les Souverains: De l'utilité des Négotiations, du choix des Ambassadeurs & des Envoyés, & des qualités nécessaires pour réussir dans ses emplois. [On the Art of Diplomacy.]* Paris: Nourse.

De Certeau, Michel. 1984. *The practice of everyday life.* Berkeley: University of California Press

———. 1988. *The practice of everyday life.* Berkeley: University of California Press.

de Saint-Pierre, Abbé Charles Irenée Castel. 1986 [1712]. *Project pour rendre la paix perpétuelle en Europe.* Paris: Fayard.

Deitelhoff, Nicole. 2009. 'The discursive process of legalization: Charting islands of persuasion in the ICC case'. *International Organization* no. 63 (1): 33–65.

Denza, Eileen. 2008. *Diplomatic law: Commentary on the Vienna Convention on Diplomatic Relations.* 3rd edn. Oxford: Oxford University Press.

Der Derian, James. 1987. *On diplomacy: A genealogy of Western estrangement.* Oxford: Blackwell.

Deshingkar, Giri. 2004. 'Strategic thinking in ancient India and China: Kautilya and Sunzi'. In *Diplomacy,* edited by Christer Jönsson and Richard Langhorne. London and Thousand Oaks, CA: Sage Publications.

Detienne, Marcel and Jean-Pierre Vernant. 1974. *Les ruses de l'intelligence : la mètis des Grecs.* Paris: Flammarion.

Diamond, Louise and John W. McDonald. 1996. *Multi-track diplomacy: A systems approach to peace.* 3rd edn. *Kumarian Press books for a world that works.* West Hartford, CT: Kumarian Press.

Dicken, Peter. 2007. *Global shift: Mapping the changing contours of the world economy.* 5th edn. London: Sage Publications.

Duke, Simon. 2011. 'Diplomatic Training and the Challenges Facing the EEAS'. *The Hague Journal of Diplomacy* no. 7 (1): 95–114.

Dumont, Jean-Christophe, Gilles Spielvogel and Sarah Widmaier. 2010. 'International migrants in developed, emerging and developing countries: An extended profile'. *OECD Social, Employment and Migration Working Papers* no. 114: 57.

Dyson, Stephen B. 2006. 'Personality and foreign policy: Tony Blair's Iraq decisions'. *Foreign Policy Analysis* no. 2 (3): 289–306.

———. 2007. 'Alliances, domestic politics, and leader psychology: Why did Britain stay out of Vietnam and go into Iraq?' *Political Psychology* no. 28 (6): 647–666.

Elias, Norbert, Eric Dunning, Johan Goudsblom and Stephen Mennell. 2000. *The civilizing process: Sociogenetic and psychogenetic investigations.* Rev. edn. Oxford and Malden, MA: Blackwell.

el-Nawawy, Mohammed. 2006. 'US public diplomacy in the Arab world,' *Global Media and Communication* no. 2 (2): 183–203.

Elstain, Jean Bethke. 2003. 'Politics and forgiveness'. In *Burying the past: Making peace and doing justice after civil conflict,* edited by Nigel Biggar, pp. 45–64. Washington, DC: Georgetown University Press.

Encyclopædia Britannica. 2011. Berlin West Africa Conference 2011 (accessed Dec 14 2011). Available from http://www.britannica.com/EBchecked/topic/62214/Berlin-West-Africa-Conference.

Esty, Daniel C. 2008. 'Climate change and global environmental governance'. *Global Governance* no. 14 (1): 111–118.

EU Commission. 1992. *Europe and the Challenge of Enlargement,* 24 June. Prepared for the European Council, Lisbon, 26–27 June 1992. Brussels: Bulletin of the European Communities, Supplement 3/92.

European Council. 1992. *Conclusions of the Presidency.* Lisbon, 26 and 27 July 1992.

EU High Representative. 8 July 2010. *Declaration by the High Representative on political accountability* (accessed 21 March 2012). Available from http://tepsa.be/DECLARATION%20BY%20 THE%20HIGH%20REPRESENTATIVE.pdf.

European Union. 1950. *The Schuman Declaration* 9 May 1950 (accessed 17 July 2012). Available from http://europa.eu/about-eu/basic-information/symbols/europe-day/schuman-declaration/index_en.htm.

———. 2007. *Treaty of Lisbon amending the Treaty on European Union and the Treaty establishing the European Community signed at Lisbon,* Official Journal of the European Union, C 306, (accessed 4 October 2012). Available from http://eur-lex.europa.eu/LexUriServ/LexUriServ.do?uri=OJ:C:2007:306 :FULL:EN:PDF.

——. 2012. *The European Diplomatic Programme: 13th Edition* (accessed 4 Oct 2012). Available from http://eeas.europa.eu/delegations/edp/programmes/13th_edp_brochure_en.pdf.

Fabry, Mikulas. 2010. *Recognizing states: International society and the establishment of new states since 1776*. New York: Oxford University Press.

Fiadjoe, Albert. 2004. *Alternative dispute resolution: A developing world perspective*. London: Cavendish.

Fichtner, Paula Sutter. 1976. 'Dynastic marriage in 16th-century Habsburg diplomacy and statecraft – interdisciplinary approach'. *American Historical Review* no. 81 (2): 243–265.

Finnemore, Martha and Kathryn Sikkink. 1998. 'International norm dynamics and political change'. *International Organization* no. 52 (4): 887–917.

Florini, Ann. 1996. 'The evolution of international norms'. *International Studies Quarterly* no. 40 (3): 363–389.

Fogel, Joshua A. 2009. *Articulating the Sinosphere: Sino-Japanese relations in space and time*. Cambridge, MA: Harvard University Press.

Ford, Christopher A. 2012. 'Soft on "Soft Power"'. *SAIS Review* no. 32 (1): 89–111.

Foucault, Michel. 1970 [1966]. *The order of things: An archeology of the human sciences*. New York: Random House.

Freeman, Charles W. 1997. *The diplomat's dictionary*. Rev. edn. Washington, DC: United States Institute of Peace Press.

Gadamer, Hans-Georg. 1960. *Wahrheit und Methode: Grundzüge einer philosophischen Hermeneutik*. Tübingen: Mohr.

Galtung, Johan. 1996. *Peace by peaceful means: Peace and conflict, development and civilization*. London: Sage Publications.

George, Alexander L. 1991. *Forceful persuasion: Coercive diplomacy as an alternative to war*. Washington, DC: United States Institute of Peace Press.

Gigerenzer, G. and P.M. Todd. 1999. 'Fast and frugal heuristics: The adaptive toolbox'. In *Simple heuristics that make us smart*, edited by G. Gigerenzer, P.M. Todd and the ABC Research Group, pp. 3–36. Oxford: Oxford University Press.

Gilkes, Patrick, Martin Plaut and Royal Institute of International Affairs. 1999. *War in the Horn: The conflict between Eritrea and Ethiopia, discussion paper*. London: Royal Institute of International Affairs.

Goldman, Alvin L., Jacques Rojot and MyiLibrary. 2003. *Negotiation theory and practice*. Hague and New York: Kluwer Law International.

Graham, Sarah Ellen and John Robert Kelley. 2009. 'US engagement in East Asia: A case for "Track Two" diplomacy'. *Orbis* no. 53 (1): 80–98.

Greenpeace. 2006. *Infos zur Ausstellung: Semipalatinsk* (accessed 17 July 2012). Available from http://www.greenpeace.de/themen/atomkraft/atomunfaelle/artikel/infos_zur_ausstellung_semipalatinsk.

Greig, Michael J. 2001. 'Moments of opportunity'. *Journal of Conflict Resolution* no. 45 (6): 691–718.

Greig, Michael J. and P.F. Diehl. 2006. 'Softening up: Making conflicts more amenable to diplomacy'. *International Interactions* no. 32 (4): 355–384.

Gstöhl, Sieglinde. 2007. 'Governance through government networks: The G8 and international organizations'. *Review of International Organizations* no. 2: 1–37.

Guymer, Laurence. 2010. 'The wedding planners: Henry Bulwer and the Spanish Marriages, 1841–1846'. *Diplomacy and Statecraft* no. 21 (4): 549–573.

Haas, Ernst. 1958. *The uniting of Europe: Political, economic, and social forces*. Stanford, CA: Stanford University Press.

Habermas, Jürgen. 1984. *The theory of communicative action*. Vol. 1. Boston: Beacon Press.

Hall, Rodney Bruce. 1999. *National collective identity: Social constructs and international systems*. New York: Columbia University Press.

Hamilton, Keith and Richard Langhorne. 1995. *The practice of diplomacy: Its evolution, theory, and administration*. London and New York: Routledge.

Hammarskjöld, Dag. 1961. *The international civil servant in law and in fact: A lecture delivered to Congregation on 30 May 1961*. Oxford: Clarendon Press.

Hammarskjöld, Dag and Kaj Falkman. 2005. *To speak for the world: speeches and statements*. Stockholm: Atlantis.

Hänggi, Heiner. 2005. 'Approaching peacebuilding from a security governance perspective'. In *Security governance in post-conflict peacebuilding*, edited by Alan Bryden and Heiner Hänggi, pp. 3–19. Münster: Lit Verlag.

Hanson, Fergus. 2012. *Revolution @State: The Spread of Ediplomacy*. Lowy Institute for International Policy, March 2012 (accessed 2 October 2012). Available from http://www.brookings.edu/~/media/research/files/reports/2012/3/ ediplomacy%20hanson/03_ediplomacy_hanson.pdf.

Hartzell, Caroline and Matthew Hoddie. 2003. 'Institutionalizing peace: Power sharing and post-civil war conflict management'. *American Journal of Political Science* no. 47 (2): 318–332.

Heathershaw, John. 2008. 'Unpacking the liberal peace: The dividing and merging of peacebuilding discourses'. *Millennium-Journal of International Studies* no. 36 (3): 597–621.

Held, David and Mathias Koenig-Archibugi. 2005. *Global governance and public accountability*. Malden, MA: Blackwell.

Hocking, Brian. 1996. 'The woods and the trees: Catalytic diplomacy and Canada's trials as a "forestry superpower"'. *Environmental Politics* no. 5 (3): 448–475.

Hocking, Brian, Jan Melissen, Shaun Riordan and Paul Sharp. 2012. *Futures for diplomacy: Integrative diplomacy for the 21st century*. Netherlands Institute of International Relations 'Clingendael' (accessed 22 October 2012). Available from http://www.clingendael.nl/publications/2012/20121017_research_melissen.pdf.

Homeira, Moshirzadeh. 2011. 'Intercivilizational dialogue and global governance'. In *Arguing global governance*, edited by Corneliu Bjola and Markus Kornprobst, pp. 117–140. London and New York: Routledge.

Honneth, Axel. 1995. *The struggle for recognition: The moral grammar of social conflicts*. Cambridge: Polity Press.

Hopf, Ted. 2002. *Social construction of international politics: Identities and foreign policies, Moscow, 1955 and 1999*. Ithaca, NY and London: Cornell University Press.

Hurrell, Andrew. 2007. *On global order: Power, values, and the constitution of international society*. Oxford and New York: Oxford University Press.

Huth, P.K., S.E. Croco and B.J. Appel. 2011. 'Does international law promote the peaceful settlement of international disputes? Evidence from the study of territorial conflicts since 1945'. *American Political Science Review* no. 105 (2): 415–436.

ICC. 2002. *About the court* (accessed 15 October 2012). Available from http://www.icc-cpi.int/en_menus/icc/about%20the%20court/Pages/about%20the%20court.aspx.

International Conference of American States. 1933. *Convention on the Rights and Duties of States (Montevideo Convention)*. The Avalon Project, Yale Law School (accessed 20 July 2011). Available from http://avalon.law.yale.edu/20th_century/intam03.asp#art1.

International Labour Organization (ILO). 2008. *ILO action against trafficking in human beings*. Geneva: ILO.

International Organization for Migration. 2005. 'World migration 2005: Costs and benefits of international migration'. In *IOM World Migration Report Series*, Geneva: IOM.

Irwin, G.W. 1975. 'Precolonial African diplomacy: The example of Asante'. *International Journal of African Historical Studies* no. 8 (1): 81–96.

Jabri, Vivienne. 1996. *Discourses on violence: Conflict analysis reconsidered*. Manchester: Manchester University Press.

Jacinto, Leela. 15 March 2012. *From Lubanga to Kony, is the ICC only after Africans? France24* (accessed 18 October 2012). Available from http://www.france24.com/en/20120315-lubanga-kony-icc-africans-international-justice-hague-syria-congo.

Janis, Irving Lester. 1972. *Victims of groupthink: A psychological study of foreign-policy decisions and fiascoes*. Boston: Houghton Mifflin.

Jentleson, B.W. and C.A. Whytock. 2005. 'Who "won" Libya? The force-diplomacy debate and its implications for theory and policy'. *International Security* no. 30 (3): 47–86.

Jervis, Robert. 1976. *Perception and misperception in international politics.* Princeton, NJ: Princeton University Press.

Johnson, Chalmers. 1982. *MITI and the Japanese miracle: The growth of industrial policy, 1925–1975.* Stanford, CA: Stanford University Press.

Johnston, Ian. 2001. 'Treating international institutions as social environments'. *International Studies Quarterly* no. 45 (4): 487–515.

Johnstone, Ian. 2003. 'Security council deliberations: The power of the better argument'. *European Journal of International Law* no. 14 (3): 437–480.

Jones, Stephen. 2009. *The Islamic Republic of Iran: An introduction* (accessed 21 March 2012). Available from www.parliament.uk/briefing-papers/rp09-92.pdf.

Jönsson, Christer and Maria Strömvik. 2005. 'Negotiations in networks'. In *European Union negotiations: Processes, networks and institutions,* edited by Ole Elgström and Christer Jönsson, pp. 13–28. London: Routledge.

Kagan, Robert. 2003. *Of paradise and power: America and Europe in the new world order.* New York: Knopf.

Kahneman, D. and A. Tversky. 1979. 'Prospect theory: An analysis of decision under risk', *Econometrica* no. 47(2): 263–292.

Kant, Immanuel. 2004. *Critique of practical reason.* Mineola, NY: Dover Publications.

Kaplan, Robert D. 2000. 'Was democracy just a moment?' In *Globalization and the challenges of a new century: A reader,* edited by Patrick O'Meara, Howard D. Mehlinger and Matthew Krain, pp. 196–214. Bloomington, IN: Indiana University Press.

Kennan, George F. 1946. *The Long Telegram,* 22 February. Available online at: http://www.gwu.edu/~nsarchiv/coldwar/documents/episode-1/kennan.htm (accessed 7 March 2013).

Kennedy-Pipe, Caroline and Rhiannon Vickers. 2007. '"Blowback" for Britain?: Blair, Bush, and the war in Iraq'. *Review of International Studies* no. 33 (2): 205–221.

Keohane, Robert O. 1980. 'The theory of hegemonic stability and changes in international economic regimes'. In *Change in the international system,* edited by O. Holsti, R. Siverson and A. George. Boulder, CO: Westview.

Kerr, Paul. 2004. *More U.S. claims on Iraq WMD rebutted.* Arms Control Association (accessed 27 July 2012). Available from http://www.armscontrol.org/act/2004_10/Iraq_WMD.

Kirchner, Emil Joseph and James Sperling. 2007. *EU security governance.* Manchester: Manchester University Press.

Kissinger, Henry A. 1957. *A world restored: Metternich, Castlereagh and the problems of peace, 1812–22.* Boston, MA: Houghton Mifflin.

——. 1994. *Diplomacy.* New York: Simon & Schuster.

Kleiboer, Marieke. 2002. 'Great power mediation: Using leverage to make peace'. In *Studies in international mediation,* edited by Jacob Bercovitch, pp. 127–140. Basingstoke: Palgrave Macmillan in association with the Program on Negotiation, Harvard Law School.

Kleiner, Jürgen. 2010. *Diplomatic practice: Between tradition and innovation.* Singapore and Hackensack, NJ: World Scientific.

Kornprobst, Markus. 2002. 'The management of border disputes in African regional sub-systems: Comparing West Africa and the Horn of Africa'. *The Journal of Modern African Studies* no. 40 (3): 369–393.

——. 2008. *Irredentism in European politics: Argumentation, compromise and norms.* Cambridge and New York: Cambridge University Press.

——. 2009. 'International relations as rhetorical discipline: Toward (re-)newing horizons'. *International Studies Review* no. 11 (1): 87–108.

——. 2012. 'How rhetorical strategies reproduce compromise agreements: The case of the nuclear non-proliferation regime'. *Government and Opposition* no. 47 (3): 342–367.

Kornprobst, Markus and Raluca Soreanu. 3–6 September 2009. 'Habitus and metis in diplomatic encounters: North Korea, the United States and nuclear non-proliferation'. Workshop on Unclenching Fists at the University of Hamburg, 3–5 June 2010.

Koser, Khalid. 2010. 'Introduction: International migration and global governance'. *Global Governance* no. 16 (3): 301–315.

Krasner, Stephen D. 1983. 'Structural causes and regime consequences: Regimes as intervening variables'. In *International regimes*, edited by Stephen D. Krasner, pp. x, 372. Ithaca, NY: Cornell University Press.

Kratochwil, Friedrich V. 1989. *Rules, norms, and decisions on the conditions of practical and legal reasoning in international relations and domestic affairs, Cambridge studies in international relations*. Cambridge: Cambridge University Press.

——. 1995. 'Sovereignty as dominium: Is there a right of humanitarian intervention?' In *Beyond Westphalia: State sovereignty and international intervention*, edited by Gene M. Lyons and Michael Mastanduno. Baltimore, MD: Johns Hopkins University Press: pp. 21–42.

Kuhn, Thomas S. 1964. *The structure of scientific revolutions*. Chicago, IL: University of Chicago Press.

Kydd, A.H. 2006. 'When can mediators build trust?' *American Political Science Review* no. 100 (3): 449–462.

Layne, Christopher. 2009. 'America's Middle East grand strategy after Iraq: The moment for offshore balancing has arrived'. *Review of International Studies* no. 35 (1): 5–25.

League of Nations. 1924. *The Covenant of the League of Nations Yale Law School – The Avalon Project* (accessed 9 February 2012). Available from http://avalon.law.yale.edu/20th_century/leagcov.asp.

Lebow, Richard Ned. 2008. *A cultural theory of international relations*. Cambridge and New York: Cambridge University Press.

Lecours, André. December 2008. *Political issues of paradiplomacy: Lessons from the developed world*. Netherlands Institute of International Relations 'Clingendael' (accessed 24 September 2012). Available from http://www.clingendael.nl/publications/2008/20081217_cdsp_diplomacy_paper_paradiplomacy.pdf.

Leguey-Feilleux, Jean-Robert. 2009. *The dynamics of diplomacy*. Boulder, CO: Lynne Rienner Publishers.

Leitenberg, Milton. 2006. *Deaths in wars and conflicts in the 20th century*. Occasional Paper Series, no. 29. Ithaca, NY: Cornell University, Peace Studies Program.

Levy, Jack S. 2000. 'Framing effects, loss aversion, and international conflict: Perspectives from prospect theory'. In *Handbook of War Studies II*, pp.93–222, edited by Manus Midlarsky. Michigan: Michigan University Press.

Lichbach, Mark I. and Alan S. Zuckerman. 1999. 'Research traditions and theory in comparative politics: An introduction'. In *Comparative politics: Rationality, culture, and structure*, pp. 3–16. Cambridge: Cambridge University Press.

Low, Maurice A. 1918. 'The vice of secret diplomacy'. *The North American Review* no. 207 (747): 209–220.

Lund, Michael S. 2008. 'Conflict prevention: Theory in pursuit of policy and practice'. In *The Sage handbook of conflict resolution*, edited by Jacob Bercovitch, Viktor Aleksandrovich Kremenyuk and I. William Zartman, pp. 287–321. Thousand Oaks, CA: Sage Publications.

Lynch, Marc. 2000. 'The dialogue of civilisations and international public spheres'. *Millennium* no. 29 (2): 307–330.

Machiavelli, Niccolò. 2001. 'Advice to Raffaello Girolami'. In *Diplomatic theory from Machiavelli to Kissinger*, edited by Geoff Berridge, H.M.A. Keens-Soper and Thomas G. Otte, pp. 39–46. Houndsmill, Basingstoke, Hampshire and New York: Palgrave.

March, James G. and Johan P. Olsen. 1989. *Rediscovering institutions: The organizational basis of politics*. New York: Free Press.

——. 2004. 'The logic of appropriateness'. *ARENA Working Papers* no. 4 (9): 28.

Marquardt, James J. 2011. *Transparency and American primacy in world politics*. Farnham, Surrey and Burlington, VT: Ashgate.

Marshall, Peter. 1997. *Positive diplomacy*. Basingstoke: Macmillan.

Martin, Lisa L. and Beth A. Simmons. 1998. 'Theories and empirical studies of international institutions'. *International Organization* no. 52 (4): 729–757.

Mattingly, Garrett. 1955. *Renaissance diplomacy*. London: Cape.

———. 2004. 'The first resident embassies: Medieval Italian origins of modern diplomacy'. In *Diplomacy*, edited by C. Jönsson and R. Langhorne. London and Thousand Oaks: Sage Publications.

McClory, Jonathan. 2011. *The new persuaders II: A 2011 global ranking of soft power*. Institute for Government (accessed 4 October 2012). Available from http://www.instituteforgovernment. org.uk/sites/default/files/publications/The%20New%20PersuadersII_0.pdf.

McCormick, James M. 2005. *American foreign policy and process*. 4th edn. Belmont, CA: Thomson/ Wadsworth.

McCorquodale, Robert and Martin Dixon. 2003. *Cases and materials on international law*. 4th edn. Oxford and New York: Oxford University Press.

McDougal, Myres Smith and Florentino P. Feliciano. 1994. *The international law of war: Transnational coercion and world public order. The New Haven studies in international law and world public order*. New Haven, CT: New Haven Press.

Mead, George Herbert. 1934. *Mind, self & society from the standpoint of a social behaviorist*. Chicago, IL: The University of Chicago Press.

Mead, George Herbert and Charles W. Morris. 1962. *Mind, self, and society: From the standpoint of a social behaviorist*. Chicago, IL: University of Chicago Press.

Mears, Natalie. 2001. 'Love-making and diplomacy: Elizabeth I and the Anjou marriage negotiations, c.1578–1582'. *History* no. 86 (284): 442–466.

Meerts, Paul and Peter Beeuwkes. 2008. 'The Utrecht negotiations in perspective: The hope of happiness for the world'. *International Negotiation* no. 13: 157–177.

Mercer, Jonathan. 2010. 'Emotional beliefs'. *International Organization* no. 64 (1): 1–31.

Ministry of Foreign Affairs of India. 2012. Indian Foreign Service (accessed 15 March 2012). Available from http://www.mea.gov.in/mystart.php?id=5002.

Mitchell, Christopher R. 1981. *The structure of international conflict*. London: Macmillan Press.

Mitrany, David. 1966 [1943]. *A working peace system*. Chicago, IL: Quadrangle Books.

Mitzen, Jennifer. 2005. 'Reading Habermas in anarchy: Multilateral diplomacy and global public spheres'. *American Political Science Review* no. 99 (3): 401–417.

———. 2011. 'Governing together: Global governance as collective intention'. In *Arguing global governance*, edited by Corneliu Bjola and Markus Kornprobst, pp. 52–66. London and New York: Routledge.

Moravcsik, Andrew. 1999. *The choice for Europe: Social purpose and state power from Messina to Maastricht*. London: UCL Press.

———. 2004. 'Striking a new transatlantic bargain'. *Foreign Affairs* no. 82 (4): 74–89.

Morgenthau, Hans J. and Kenneth W. Thompson. 1985. *Politics among nations: The struggle for power and peace*. 6th edn. New York: Knopf.

———. 1993. *Politics among nations: The struggle for power and peace*. New York: Knopf.

Mosley, D.J. 1971. 'Diplomacy and disunion in Ancient Greece'. *Phoenix* no. 25 (4): 319–330.

Munn-Rankin, Joan M. 2004. 'Diplomacy in Western Asia in the early second millennium B.C.'. In *Diplomacy*, edited by Christer Jönsson and Richard Langhorne. London and Thousand Oaks, CA: Sage Publications.

Murithi, D.T. 2007. 'The responsibility to protect, as enshrined in article 4 of the Constitutive Act of the African Union'. *African Security Studies* no. 16 (3): 14–24.

Murray, Eustace Clare Grenville. 1855. *Embassies and foreign courts*. London and New York: Routledge.

National Geographic. n.d. *Deforestation* (accessed 17 July 2012). Available from http://environment. nationalgeographic.com/environment/global-warming/deforestation-overview.

Neumann, Iver. B. 2002. 'Returning practice to the linguistic turn: The case of diplomacy'. *Millennium-Journal of International Studies* no. 31 (3): 627–651.

———. 2005. 'To be a diplomat'. *International Studies Perspectives* no. 6: 72–93.

Nicolson, Harold. 1988. *The evolution of diplomatic method, Cassell history*. London: Cassell.

Norwegian Nobel Committee. 2009. *The Nobel Peace Prize 2009 – Press Release* (accessed 25 September 2012). Available from http://www.nobelprize.org/nobel_prizes/peace/laureates/2009/press. html.

Nye, Joseph S. 2004. *Soft power: The means to success in world politics*. 1st edn. New York: Public Affairs.

——. 2008. 'Public diplomacy and soft power'. *Annals of the American Academy of Political and Social Science* no. 616: 94–109.

Ogburn, D. 2008. 'Dynamic display, propaganda, and the reinforcement of provincial power in the Inca Empire'. *Archeological Papers of the American Anthropological Association* no. 14 (1): 225–239.

OHCHR. 2007. *Making peace our own: Victims' perceptions of accountability, reconciliation and transitional justice in Northern Uganda* (accessed 18 October 2012). Geneva: UNHCR. Available from http://www.unhcr.org/refworld/country,,OHCHR,,UGA,456d621e2,46cc4a690,0.html/

Onuf, Nicholas Greenwood. 1989. *World of our making: Rules and rule in social theory and international relations. Studies in international relations.* Columbia, SC: University of South Carolina Press.

Owen, Lord David. 2006. 'Hubris and nemesis in heads of government'. *Journal of the Royal Society of Medicine* no. 99 (11): 548–551.

Panebianco, Stefania. 2006. 'The constraints on EU Action as a "norm exporter" in the Mediterranean'. In *The European Union's roles in international politics: Concepts and analysis*, edited by Ole Elgström and Michael Smith, pp. 136–154. London: Routledge.

Paris, Roland. 2004. *At war's end: Building peace after civil conflict.* Cambridge and New York: Cambridge University Press.

Park, Augustine S.J. 2010. 'Community-based restorative transitional justice in Sierra Leone'. *Contemporary Justice Review* no. 13 (1): 95–119.

Petersen, Roger Dale. 2011. *Western intervention in the Balkans: The strategic use of emotion in conflict. Cambridge studies in comparative politics.* Cambridge and New York: Cambridge University Press.

Phillipson, Coleman. 2001. *The international law and custom of ancient Greece and Rome.* Vol. 2. Buffalo, N.Y.: W.S. Hein.

Porter, Tony. 2009. 'Why international institutions matter in the global credit crisis'. *Global Governance* no. 15 (1): 3–8.

Pouliot, Vincent. 2008. 'The logic of practicality: A theory of practice of security communities'. *International Organization* no. 62 (2): 257–288.

Prendergast, John. 7 September 2001. 'U.S. leadership in resolving African conflict: The case of Ethiopia-Eritrea'. In *Special Report.* Washington, DC: United States Institute of Peace.

Price, Richard. 1998. 'Reversing the gun sights: Transnational civil society targets land mines'. *International Organization* no. 52 (3): 613–644.

Public Broadcasting Service (PBS). 2009. *German declaration of war on the Soviet Union* (accessed 17 July 2012). Available from http://www.pbs.org/behindcloseddoors/pdfs/NaziInvasionDeclaration.pdf.

——. n.d. *Stalin ignores warnings about Nazis* (accessed 17 July 2012). Available from http://www.pbs.org/behindcloseddoors/episode-1/ep1_stalin_ignores_warnings.html.

Putnam, Linda L. and Martin Carcasson. 1997. 'Communication and the Oslo negotiation: Contacts, patterns, and modes'. *International Negotiation* no. 2 (2): 251–278.

Putnam, Robert D. 1988. 'Diplomacy and domestic politics: The logic of two-level games'. *International Organization* no. 42 (3): 427–460.

Queller, Donald E. 2004. 'Medieval diplomacy'. In *Diplomacy*, edited by Christer Jönsson and Richard Langhorne. London and Thousand Oaks. CA: Sage Publications.

Rajghatta, Chidanand. 2007. *Localitis charge singes Indian envoy* (accessed 15 September 2012). Available from http://articles.timesofindia.indiatimes.com/2007-08-23/us/27994596_1_diplomats-ronen-sen-envoy.

Ramcharan, Bertrand G. 2008. *Preventive diplomacy at the UN.* Bloomington, IN: Indiana University Press.

Rapoport, Anatol. 1960. *Fights, games, and debates.* Ann Arbor, MI: University of Michigan Press.

Regan, Patrick M. and Aysegul Aydin. 2006. 'Diplomacy and other forms of intervention in civil wars'. *Journal of Conflict Resolution* no. 50 (5): 736–756.

RIA Novosti. 21 March 2011. *Putin über 'mittelalterliche' Libyen-Resolution des UN-Sicheitsrates entrüstet* (accessed 27 July 2012). Available from http://de.rian.ru/world/20110321/258628006.html.

Richelieu, Armand Jean du Plessis. 1961. *Political testament: The significant chapters and supporting selections.* Madison, WI: University of Wisconsin Press.

Richmond, Oliver P. and Jason Franks. 2009. *Liberal peace transitions: Between statebuilding and peacebuilding.* Edinburgh: Edinburgh University Press.

Ricigliano, Rob. 2012. *Making peace last: A toolbox for sustainable peacebuilding.* Boulder, CO: Paradigm Publishers.

Ripsman, N.M. and J.S. Levy. 2008. 'Wishful thinking or buying time? The logic of British appeasement in the 1930s'. *International Security* no. 33 (2): 148–181.

Risse, Thomas. 1999. 'International norms and domestic change: Arguing and communicative behavior in the human rights area'. *Politics & Society* no. 27 (4): 529–559.

——. 2000. '"Let's Argue!": Communicative action in world politics'. *International Organization* no. 54 (1): 1–39.

Ristuccia, Cristiano Andrea. 2000. 'The 1935 Sanctions against Italy: Would coal and oil have made a difference?,' *European Review of Economic History* no. 4 (1): 85–110.

Roach, Steven C. 2009. *Governance, order, and the International Criminal Court: Between realpolitik and a cosmopolitan court.* Oxford: Oxford University Press.

Roeder, Philip G. and Donald S. Rothchild. 2005. *Sustainable peace: Power and democracy after civil wars.* Ithaca, NY: Cornell University Press.

Roosen, William J. 1973. 'The true ambassador: Occupational and personal characteristics of French ambassadors under Louis XIV'. *European Studies Review* no. 3 (2): 121–139.

Rosenau, James N. 2002. 'Governance in a new global order'. In *Governing globalization: Power, authority and global governance*, edited by David Held and Anthony McGrew, pp. 70–86. Cambridge: Polity.

Rostow, Walt W. 1960. *The stages of economic growth: A non-communist manifesto.* Cambridge: Cambridge University Press.

Ruggie, J.G. 1982. 'International regimes, transactions, and change: Embedded liberalism in the post-war economic order'. *International Organization* no. 36 (2): 379–415.

——. 1993. 'Territoriality and beyond: Problematizing modernity in international relations', *International Organization* 46/1, pp. 139–174.

Rung, E. 2008. 'War, peace and diplomacy in Graeco-Persian relations from the sixth to the fourth century BC'. In *War and peace in ancient and medieval history*, edited by Philip De Souza and John France. Cambridge and New York: Cambridge University Press.

Russell, Joycelyne Gledhill. 1969. *The Field of Cloth of Gold: Men and manners in 1520.* London: Routledge & K. Paul.

Salacuse, J.W. 1998. 'Ten ways that culture affects negotiating style: Some survey results'. *Negotiation Journal* no. 14 (3): 221–240.

Sambanis, Nicholas. 2004. 'What is civil war? Conceptual and empirical complexities of an operational definition'. *Journal of Conflict Resolution* no. 48 (6): 814–858.

Sarkin, Jeremy. 2001. 'The tension between justice and reconciliation in Rwanda: Politics, human rights, due process and the role of the Gacaca Courts in dealing with the genocide'. *Journal of African law* no. 45 (2): 143–172.

Satow, Ernest Mason. 1917. *A guide to diplomatic practice: Contributions to international law and diplomacy*, edited by L. Oppenheim. London: Longman.

——. 1979. *Satow's guide to diplomatic practice.* 5th edn. London and New York: Longman.

Sauer, T. 2007. 'Coercive diplomacy by the EU: The Iranian nuclear weapons crisis'. *Third World Quarterly* no. 28 (3): 613–633.

Savun, B. 2008. 'Information, bias, and mediation success'. *International Studies Quarterly* no. 52 (1): 25–47.

Schiff, Benjamin N. 2008. *Building the international criminal court.* Cambridge and New York: Cambridge University Press.

Schimmelfennig, Frank. 2003. *The EU, NATO and the integration of Europe: Rules and rhetoric.* Cambridge: Cambridge University Press.

Schmitter, Philippe, C. 2004. 'Neo-neofunctionalism'. In *European integration theory*, edited by Antje Wiener and Thomas Diez, pp. 45–74. Oxford: Oxford University Press.

Schweller, Randall L. 2006. *Unanswered threats: Political constraints on the balance of power.* Princeton: Princeton University Press.

Seabury, Paul. 1954. *The Wilhelmstrasse: A study of German diplomats under the Nazi regime.* Berkeley, CA: University of California Press.

Searle, John R. 1995. *The construction of social reality.* New York: Free Press.

———. 1998. *Mind, language, and society: Philosophy in the real world.* 1st edn. *MasterMinds.* New York: Basic Books.

———. 2005. 'What is an institution?' *Journal of Institutional Economics* no. 1 (1):1–22.

———. 2008. *Philosophy in a new century: Selected essays.* Cambridge and New York: Cambridge University Press.

———. 2010. *Making the social world: The structure of human civilization.* Oxford and New York: Oxford University Press.

Seckinelgin, Hakan. 2005. 'A global disease and its governance: HIV/AIDS in sub-Saharan Africa and the agency of NGOs'. *Global Governance* no. 11: 351–368.

Sedelmeier, Ulrich. 2006. 'The EU's role as a promoter of human rights and democracy: Enlargement policy practice and role formation'. In *The European Union's roles in international politics: Concepts and analysis,* edited by Ole Elgström and Michael Smith, pp. 118–135. London: Routledge.

Seib, Philip M. 2012. *Real-time diplomacy: Politics and power in the social media era.* 1st edn. New York: Palgrave Macmillan.

Sharp, Paul. 2005. 'Revolutionary states, outlaw regimes and the techniques of public diplomacy'. In *The new public diplomacy: Soft power in international relations,* edited by Jan Melissen. Basingstoke and New York: Palgrave Macmillan.

———. 2009. *Diplomatic theory of international relations.* Cambridge: Cambridge University Press.

Sharp, Paul and British International Studies Association. 2009. *Diplomatic theory of international relations. Cambridge studies in international relations.* Cambridge: Cambridge University Press.

Shepard, Jonathan. 2004. 'Information, disinformation and delay in byzantine diplomacy'. In *Diplomacy,* edited by Christer Jönsson and Richard Langhorne. London and Thousand Oaks, CA: Sage Publications.

Shewmaker, K.E. (ed.) 1983. *The Papers of Daniel Webster: Diplomatic papers, Vol 1 1841–1843.* Hanover, NH: University Press of New England.

Shriver, Donald W. 2003. 'Where and when in political life is justice served by forgiveness?' In *Burying the past: Making peace and doing justice after civil conflict,* edited by Nigel Biggar, pp. 25–43. Washington, DC: Georgetown University Press.

Simon, H.A. 1957. *Models of man: Social and rational,* New York: Wiley.

———. 1982. *Models of bounded rationality,* Vols. 1 and 2. Cambridge, MA: MIT Press.

Siracusa, Joseph M. 2010. *Diplomacy: A very short introduction. Very short introductions.* Oxford: Oxford University Press.

Smith, Robert Sydney. 1989. *Warfare and diplomacy in pre-colonial West Africa.* 2nd edn. Madison, WI: University of Wisconsin Press.

Snow, Nancy. 2009. 'Rethinking public diplomacy'. In *Routledge handbook of public diplomacy,* edited by Nancy Snow and Philip M. Taylor, pp. 3–11. New York: Routledge.

Somers, Margaret R. 1994. 'The narrative constitution of identity: A relational and network approach'. *Theory and society* no. 23 (5): 605–649.

St Clair, Asunción Lera. 2006. 'World Bank as a transnational expertised institution', *Global Governance* no. 12: 77–95.

Stacey, Simon. 2004. 'A Lockean approach to transitional justice'. *Review of Politics* no. 66 (1): 55–81.

Steele, Brent J. 2007. 'Making words matter: The Asian tsunami, Darfur, and "reflexive discourse" in international politics'. *International Studies Quarterly* no. 51 (4): 901–925.

Strange, Susan. 1986. *Casino capitalism.* Oxford and New York: Blackwell.

Tekle, A. 2000. 'Old Ethiopian foreign policy tactic is repeating itself', *Eritrea Profile,* Asmara, 29 September.

Thomas, Caroline and Martin Weber. 2004. 'The politics of global health governance: Whatever happened to health for all by the year 2000?' *Global Governance* no. 10: 187–205.

Thompson, John A. 2010. 'Wilsonianism: The dynamics of a conflicted concept'. *International Affairs* no. 86 (1): 27–48.

Thompson, Leigh L. 2009. *The mind and heart of the negotiator.* 4th edn. Upper Saddle River, NJ and Harlow: Pearson Education.

Thompson, William R. 1999. 'Why rivalries matter and what great power rivalries tell us about world politics'. In *Great power rivalries,* edited by William R. Thompson, pp. 3–28. Columbia, SC: University of South Carolina Press.

Touval, Saadia and I. William Zartman. 1985. *International mediation in theory and practice. SAIS papers in international affairs.* Boulder, CO and Washington, DC: Westview Press.

UN Department of Peacekeeping Operations. 2012. *Peacekeeping Fact Sheet* (accessed 20 March 2012). Available from http://www.un.org/en/peacekeeping/resources/statistics/factsheet.shtml.

UN Department of Political Affairs. 2012. *Preventive Diplomacy Report: Q&A* 2012 (accessed 20 March 2012). Available from http://www.un.org/wcm/content/site/undpa/main/issues/preventive_diplomacy/qa_preventive.

UN General Assembly. 24 October 1970. *Declaration of principles of international law concerning friendly relations and co-operation among states in accordance with the Charter of the United Nations* (accessed 9 January 2012). Available from http://www.unhcr.org/refworld/topic,459d17822,459d17a82,3dda1f104,0.html.

——. 9 December 1994. *Measures to eliminate international terrorism, annex to UN General Assembly resolution 49/60, A/RES/60/49* (accessed 17 July 2012). Available from http://www.un.org/documents/ga/res/49/a49r060.htm.

——. 1 May 1996. *Resolution adopted by the General Assembly, A/RES/50/225* (accessed 17 July 2012). Available from http://unpan1.un.org/intradoc/groups/public/documents/un/unpan014746.pdf.

——. 2000. *United Nations Millennium Declaration, A/Res/55/2* (accessed 17 July 2012). Available from http://www.un.org/millennium/declaration/ares552e.htm.

——. 24 October 2005. *Resolution adopted by the General Assembly 60/1. 2005 World Summit Outcome. A/RES/60/1.* Available from http://unpan1.un.org/intradoc/groups/public/documents/un/unpan021752.pdf.

UN Office on Drugs and Crime (UNODC). 2011. Promoting health, security and justice: Cutting the threads of drugs, crime and terrorism, 2010 Report. Vienna: UNODC.

UN Peacebuilding Commission. 2005. *Mandate of the Peacebuilding Commission* (accessed 20 March 2012). Available from http://www.un.org/en/peacebuilding/mandate.shtml.

UN Peacebuilding Support Office. September 2010. *UN peacebuilding: An orientation* (accessed 17 July 2012). Available from http://www.un.org/en/peacebuilding/pbso/pdf/peacebuilding_orientation.pdf.

UN Secretary-General. 2011. *Preventive diplomacy: Delivering results* (accessed 11 October 2012). Available from http://www.un.org/wcm/webdav/site/undpa/shared/undpa/pdf/SG%20Report%20on%20Preventive%20Diplomacy.pdf.

UN Security Council. 1994. S/RES/912. *Resolution 912 (1994) adopted by the Security Council at its 3368th meeting, on 21 April 1994* (accessed 17 July 2012). Available from http://www.unhcr.org/refworld/docid/3b00f15f2b.html.

——. 1999. *Security Council rejects demand for cessation of the use of force against Federal Republic of Yugoslavia* 26 March 1999 (accessed 2 June 2011). Available from http://www.un.org/News/Press/docs/1999/19990326.sc6659.html.

——. 2010. *Statement by the President of the Security Council* (accessed 20 March 2012). Available from http://www.securitycouncilreport.org/atf/cf/%7B65BFCF9B-6D27-4E9C-8CD3-CF6E4FF96FF9%7D/RO%20SPRST%202010%201.pdf.

——. 2011. 'Security Council approves "no-fly zone" over Libya, authorizing "all necessary measures" to protect civilians, by vote of 10 in favour with 5 abstentions' no. 2011 (2 June).

UNEP. 2011. *Rules for the participation of non-governmental organizations (NGOs) in the intergovernmental negotiating committee (INC) for a legally binding instrument on mercury* (accessed 17 July 2012). Available from http://www.unep.org/hazardoussubstances/Portals/9/Mercury/Documents/INC3/Rules%20for%20the%20participation%20of%20NGOs%20in%20the%20INC_.pdf.

UNFCCC. 2012. EB Meetings 2012 (accessed 17 August 2012). Available from http://cdm.unfccc. int/EB/index.html.

Union of Concerned Scientists. 22 April 2011. *Chernobyl cancer death toll estimate more than six times higher than the 4,000 frequently cited, according to a new UCS analysis* (accessed 17 July 2012). Available from http://www.ucsusa.org/news/press_release/chernobyl-cancer-death-toll-0536.html.

United Nations. 1945. *Charter of the United Nations* (accessed 12 January 2011). Available from http:// www.un.org/aboutun/charter.

——. 2001. *A Guide to a Career with the United Nations* (accessed 15 March 2012). Available from http:// esa.un.org/techcoop/associateexperts/APPLICANTS/Guide_to_employment/unpan000153. pdf.

——. 2004. *A more secure world: Our shared responsibility* (accessed 17 July 2012). Available from http:// www.un.org/secureworld/report2.pdf.

——. 2011. *Report of the Secretary-General, preventive diplomacy: Delivering results.* New York: United Nations.

——. 2012. *Rome Statute of the International Criminal Court* (accessed 17 October 2012). Available from http://treaties.un.org/Pages/ViewDetails.aspx?src=TREATY&mtdsg_no=XVIII-10&chapter= 18&lang=en.

United States General Accounting Office. 1 October 1996. 'Nuclear nonproliferation: Implications of the U.S./North Korean agreement on nuclear issues'. In *GAO Report to the Chairman, Committee on Energy and Natural Resources, U.S Senate.* Washington: United States General Accounting Office. Available from http://www.gao.gov/archive/1997/rc97008.pdf.

United States Holocaust Memorial Museum. 2012. Czechoslovakia, 11 May 2012 (accessed 15 August 2012). Available from http://www.ushmm.org/wlc/en/article.php?ModuleId=10005688.

US Department of State. 2005. *Protocol for the modern diplomat,* edited by Foreign Service Institute. Washington, DC: Transition Center.

——. 2012. *Foreign Service Officer Qualifications: 13 Dimensions* (accessed 31 October 2012). Available from http://careers.state.gov/uploads/7e/3b/7e3b2a09abdf83eb5afc24af5586c896/3.0.0_ FSO_13_dimensions.pdf.

US Senate Committee on Foreign Relations. 2011. *Rules of the Committee on Foreign Relations* (accessed 15 March 2012). Available from http://www.foreign.senate.gov/about/jurisdiction.

——. n.d. *Overview* (accessed 17 July 2012). Available from http://diplomacy.state.gov/ discoverdiplomacy/explorer/places/170312.htm.

US State Department. 2010. Nuclear Security Summit 2010 (accessed 17 March 2012). Available from http://www.state.gov/t/isn/nuclearsecuritysummit/2010/index.htm.

Van Wicquefort, Abraham. 1682. L'ambassadeur et ses fonctions. *[The ambassador and his functions.]* La Haye, M.G. Veneur.

Vasquez, John A. 2009. *The war puzzle revisited. Cambridge studies in international relations.* Cambridge: Cambridge University Press.

Vattel. 2004. 'The law of nations'. In *Diplomatic classics: Selected texts from Commynes to Vattel,* edited by Geoff Berridge, p. 189. Basingstoke: Palgrave Macmillan.

Vucetic, Srdjan. 2011. *The Anglosphere: A genealogy of a racialized identity in international relations.* Stanford, CA: Stanford University Press.

Wæver, Ole. 1996. 'European security identities'. *Journal of Common Market Studies* no. 34 (1): 103–132.

Wallensteen, Peter. 2002. 'Reassessing recent conflicts: Direct vs. structural prevention'. In *From reaction to conflict prevention: Opportunities for the UN system,* edited by Fen Osler Hampson and David Malone, pp. 213–228. Boulder, CO: Lynne Rienner Publishers.

Wallerstein, Immanuel Maurice. 1980. *Mercantilism and the consolidation of the European world-economy, 1600–1750. The modern world-system.* New York: Academic Press.

Walton, Dale C. 2009. 'The case for strategic traditionalism: War, national interest and liberal peacebuilding'. *International Peacekeeping* no. 16 (5): 717–734.

Waltz, Kenneth N. 1979. *Theory of international politics.* Long Grove, IL: Waveland.

Walzer, Michael. 1977. *Just and unjust wars: A moral argument with historical illustrations.* New York: Basic Books.

——. 2012. 'The aftermath of war: Reflections on jus post bellum'. In *Ethics beyond war's end*, edited by Eric Patterson, pp. 35–46. Washington, DC: Georgetown University Press.

Wan, M. 2010. 'Review: Articulating the Sinosphere: Sino-Japanese relations in space and time'. *The Journal of Japanese Studies* no. 36 (1): 153–158.

Washburn, John. 1999. 'The negotiation of the Rome Statute for the International Criminal Court and international lawmaking in the 21st century'. *Pace International Law Review* no. 11/2 (Fall 1999): 361–377.

Washington, George. 1924. *Washington's Farewell Address 1796*. Yale Law School: The Avalon Project (accessed 8 March 2012). Available from http://avalon.law.yale.edu/18th_century/washing.asp.

Watson, Adam. 1982. *Diplomacy: The dialogue between states*. London: Eyre Methuen.

——. 1984. *Diplomacy: The dialogue between states*. London: Eyre Methuen.

Wendt, Alexander. 1999. *Social theory of international politics*. Cambridge: Cambridge University Press.

——. 2003. 'Why a world state is inevitable'. *European Journal of International Relations* no. 9 (4): 491–542.

Wicquefort. 2004. 'The embassador and his functions'. In *Diplomatic classics: Selected texts from Commynes to Vattel*, edited by Geoff Berridge, p. 133. Basingstoke: Palgrave Macmillan.

Wight, Martin, Hedley Bull and Carsten Holbraad. 1978. *Power politics*. New York: Holmes & Meier.

Wilson, E.J. 2008. 'Hard power, soft power, smart power'. *Annals of the American Academy of Political and Social Science* no. 616: 110–124.

Wilson, Woodrow. 22 January 1917. *Address to the Senate of the United States: 'A World League for Peace'*, (accessed Jan 9 2012). Available from http://www.presidency.ucsb.edu/ws/?pid=65396.

——. 22 January 1918. *Address to a joint session of Congress on the conditions of peace* (accessed 8 January 2012). Available from http://www.presidency.ucsb.edu/ws/?pid=65405.

Wiseman, Geoffrey R. 2005. 'Pax Americana: Bumping into diplomatic culture'. *International Studies Perspectives* no. 6 (4): 409–430.

Wolf, Reinhard. 2011. 'Respect and disrespect in international politics: The significance of status recognition'. *International Theory* no. 3 (1): 105–142.

Woodward, Bob. 2004. *Plan of attack*. New York: Simon & Schuster.

World Health Organization. 2011. *World Health Statistics 2011*. Geneva: WHO.

World Resources Institute. 17 February 2009. *Aggregate contributions of major GHG emitting countries: 2005* (accessed 17 July 2012). Available from http://www.wri.org/chart/aggregate-contributions-major-ghg-emitting-countries-2005.

World Trade Organization. 2011. *International Trade Statistics 2011* (accessed 17 July 2012). Available from http://www.wto.org/english/res_e/statis_e/its2011_e/its11_toc_e.htm.

X. 1947. 'The sources of Soviet conduct'. *Foreign Affairs* 25 no. 4: 566–582.

Yale Law School. 27 September 1940. *Three-power pact between Germany, Italy, and Japan* (accessed 15 August 2012). Available from http://avalon.law.yale.edu/wwii/triparti.asp.

Zenko, Micah and Rebecca R. Friedman. 2011. 'UN Early Warning for Preventing Conflict.' *International Peacekeeping* no. 18 (1): 21–37.

Zhang, Juyan. 2006. 'Public diplomacy as symbolic interactions: A case study of Asian tsunami relief campaigns'. *Public Relations Review* no. 32 (1): 26–32.

Zonova, Tatiana V. 2007. 'Diplomatic cultures: Comparing Russia and the West in terms of a "modern model of diplomacy"'. *The Hague Journal of Diplomacy* no. 2: 1–23.

Index